PlayStation

secrets · strategies · solutions

Paragon Publishing Ltd

Paragon Publishing Ltd
Paragon House
St Peter's Road
Bournemouth
Dorset BH1 2JS
United Kingdom

Tel: +44 (0) 1202 299900
Fax: +44 (0) 1202 299955
Email: books@paragon.co.uk
Web: http://paragon.co.uk

PlayStation Secrets, Strategies, Solutions Volume 3
© 1997 RDT Ltd
© 1997 Paragon Publishing Ltd

British Library Cataloguing-in-Publication Data
A catalogue for this book is available from the British Library

ISBN 1 873650 15 9

Written by: Ryan Butt, Phil King, Paul Morgan
Designed by: Mark Wynne, Steve Gotobed
Printed and bound in the UK by: Stephens and George Magazines
Published by: Paragon Publishing Ltd, Bournemouth

Other superb titles in the Secrets, Strategies, Solutions series
For availability or to order, call 01202 200200 (international dial +44 1202 200200), fax 01202 299955,
point your browser to **http://paragon.co.uk/specials** or email **books@paragon.co.uk**

PlayStation Secret, Strategies, Solutions Volume 1 • RRP £14.95 • ISBN 1 873650 05 1
PlayStation Secret, Strategies, Solutions Volume 2 • RRP £14.95 • ISBN 1 873650 06 X
A-Z of PlayStation Secrets, Strategies, Solutions • RRP £9.95 • ISBN 1 873650 19 1
Final Fantasy VII Secrets, Strategies, Solutions • RRP £9.95 • ISBN 1 873650 12 4
Tomb Raider II Secrets, Strategies, Solutions • RRP £9.95 • ISBN 1 873650 13 2
Nintendo 64 Secrets, Strategies, Solutions • RRP £14.95 • ISBN 1 873650 08 6
Goldeneye Secrets, Strategies, Solutions • RRP £9.95 • ISBN 1 873650 11 6
Lylat Wars Secrets, Strategies, Solutions • RRP £9.95 • ISBN 1 873650 14 0
Super Mario 64 Secrets, Strategies, Solutions • RRP £9.95 • ISBN 1 873650 07 8
PC Games Secrets, Strategies, Solutions • RRP £9.95 • ISBN 1 873650 18 3

Check out NetGamer, Europe's only guide dedicated to multiplayer PC gaming. Point your browser to **http://netgamer.net** to experience the future.

Visit **http://whatsonline.co.uk** to discover the very best of the Internet.

PlayStation

secrets · strategies · solutions

ryan butt · phil king · paul morgan

the authors/contents

continued

About the Authors

Ryan Butt

Currently the editor of Play, the dedicated hints and tips magazine for the Sony PlayStation, Ryan Butt is a 23-year-old whizzkid who has already worked for a host of magazines, including Console XS, Super Gamer, SegaPro, Games World, Ultimate Player, Saturn+ and PowerStation. In the process he's played games on every console devised and written comprehensive playing guides for countless top titles. A complete Street Fighter nut, Ryan has beaten every game in the series, discovering all their secrets along the way. When he's not got a joypad in his hand, he likes playing football, going clubbing, watching B movies and listening to indie music.

Phil King

The Kingster has been playing video games since the early Eighties and has been writing about them in a host of magazines for over eight years, including CRASH and ZAPP! 64, and more recently SegaPro, Games World, PC Power and PowerStation (of which he is the editor). After playing and tipping literally hundreds of games on every system going, he's still crazy about the hobby and is constantly finding sneaky tricks to beat everyone at his favourite soccer sims. When not glued to the screen, single guy Phil enjoys listening to indie/alternative music (including Beck, The Cocteau Twins and Nine Inch Nails) and composing his own electronic 'masterpieces'. He still hopes to appear on Top of the Pops one day... with a couple of fruity dancing girls!

Paul Morgan

Like many seasoned games players, Paul 'PC' Morgan's passion for video games was sparked with the introduction of the rubber-keyed Sinclair Spectrum in the early Eighties. Since then he has played every console and computer system available. He has written authoritatively for a number of magazines, including Saturn+, 3DO Magazine, X•Gen, CD-ROM Games and Ultimate Player, and currently writes for PowerStation. Paul's hobbies include football, squash, and most other forms of sport. He's heavily into music – which includes New Jack Swing, Rap, G-Funk and Techno – yet still manages to find time for a drink or two at the local pub.

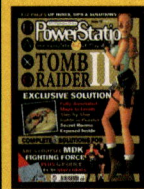

Contents

Publisher:	Psygnosis
Price:	£44.99
Format:	UK

start

Formula 1 '97

After the **incredible success of the original** *Formula 1*, those 'Bizarre Creation' experts at Psygnosis **have scored another scorching victory**. **And so have we** with this **exclusive** *F1 '97* **guide**, packed with **expert racing tips** and **glorious annotated maps** for **all 18 tracks**...

1 player	Memory	2 player	Split-screen

Formula 1 '97

Danka Arrows Yamaha

Engine: Yamaha V10
Tyres: Bridgestone
Starts: 294
Wins: 0   Poles: 1
Constructors: 0
First Grand Prix: 1978 – Brazil
Principal: Tom Walkinshaw

Damon Hill
Nationality: GB
Number: 1
Age: 36
Birth Date: 17/9/60
First Grand Prix: 1992

Pedro Diniz
Nationality: Brazil
Number: 2
Age: 27
Birth Date: 22/5/70
First Grand Prix: 1995

Scuderia Ferrari Marlboro

Engine: Ferrari V10
Tyres: Goodyear
Starts: 576
Wins: 109   Poles: 118
Constructors: 8
First Grand Prix: 1950 – Monaco
Principal: Jean Todt

Michael Schumacher
Nationality: Germany
Number: 5
Age: 28
Birth Date: 3/1/69
First Grand Prix: 1991

Eddie Irvine
Nationality: GB
Number: 6
Age: 31
Birth Date: 10/11/65
First Grand Prix: 1993

West McLaren Mercedes

Engine: Mercedes-Benz V10
Tyres: Goodyear
Starts: 449
Wins: 105   Poles: 79
Constructors: 7
First Grand Prix: 1966 – Monaco
Principal: Ron Dennis

Mika Hakkinen
Nationality: Finland
Number: 9
Age: 28
Birth Date: 28/9/68
First Grand Prix: 1991

David Coulthard
Nationality: GB
Number: 10
Age: 26
Birth Date: 27/3/71
First Grand Prix: 1994

Rothmans Williams Renault

Engine: Renault V10
Tyres: Goodyear
Starts: 305
Wins: 99   Poles: 97
Constructors: 8
First Grand Prix: 1978 – Argentina
Principal: Frank Williams

Jacques Villeneuve
Nationality: Canada
Number: 3
Age: 26
Birth Date: 9/4/71
First Grand Prix: 1996

Heinz-Harald Frentzen
Nationality: Germany
Number: 4
Age: 30
Birth Date: 18/5/67
First Grand Prix: 1994

Mild Seven Benetton Renault

Engine: Renault V10
Tyres: Goodyear
Starts: 240
Wins: 26   Poles: 13
Constructors: 1
First Grand Prix: 1981 – Italy
Principal: Flavio Briatore

Jean Alesi
Nationality: France
Number: 7
Age: 33
Birth Date: 11/6/64
First Grand Prix: 1989

Gerhard Berger
Nationality: Austria
Number: 8
Age: 38
Birth Date: 27/8/59
First Grand Prix: 1984

B&H Total Jordan Peugeot

Engine: Peugeot V10
Tyres: Goodyear
Starts: 103
Wins: 0   Poles: 1
Constructors: 0
First Grand Prix: 1991 – USA
Principal: Eddie Jordan

Ralf Schumacher
Nationality: Germany
Number: 11
Age: 22
Birth Date: 30/6/75
First Grand Prix: 1997

Giancarlo Fisichella
Nationality: Italy
Number: 12
Age: 24
Birth Date: 14/1/73
First Grand Prix: 1996

GENERAL TIPS

Slipstreaming
Overtaking your opponents is a must in motor racing. Now, although some prefer 'slamming the rear' or 'nudging your opponent off the track' techniques, these are not – to say the least – good sporting manoeuvres. Not all Formula 1 cars have the same engine power. So to compensate for this on the long straights, the slipstream effect can often enable the car behind to overtake. This works due to the reduced air flow behind the leading car. And once you're in the reduced drag, you can dart out from behind, and with that extra speed boost, you should be able to overtake. Just watch out when you approach the bends – if you're too close to the car in front, you'll probably end up in the back of him; and that's the end of your race!

On Your Marks...
It's important to get a good start. After all, you spent a hard enough time fighting for your grid position, so the last thing you want is to lose a couple of places. Timing is everything. So, just as the final red light comes on, press down hard on the throttle and don't let go. This way you'll achieve minimum wheel spinning, and maintain your position, if not gain one or two.

Tyre Compounds
Some like it hard, some like it soft, the choice is up to you. If you choose a hard tyre compound, you'll run slightly faster but won't have quite so much grip as with soft tyres.

F1 '97

continued

Tyre Wear
If the damage/wear to your tyres is too great, the handling of the car will be affected. Try not to brake too hard for great lengths of time. Also, wheel spinning is not advised. If your tyres are worn too quickly, you may find yourself having to take unscheduled pit stops which will cost you time, and undoubtedly race positions.

Downforce
This determines the grip that your F1 car has. Less downforce on the car means more speed, but less grip. If the downforce is high, your car has considerably more grip available, but you sacrifice speed as a result.
It all depends on personal preference and the current location. If the course has many tight bends, and few straights, a higher downforce would be preferable. However, if the track is a fast one with long straights, sweeping bends, and only a few tight corners, a lower downforce will provide you with faster lap times.

Car Damage
One of the main causes of early retirement, or at best, a low finishing position. The slightest bump can cause damage to the tyres, or front/back wing.

Using The Whole Track
On many bends throughout *Formula 1 '97*, going slightly up on the kerbs can prove time-saving; as long as you avoid the grass, of course. Even just a couple of extra inches can help to keep the throttle high around tight corners, thus reducing your lap times by a fraction.

Prost Ligier Gitanes

Engine: Mugen-Honda V10
Tyres: Bridgestone
Starts: 332
Wins: 9   **Poles:** 9
Constructors: 0
First Grand Prix: 1977 – Sweden
Principal: Alain Prost

Olivier Panis
Nationality: France
Number: 14
Age: 31
Birth Date: 2/9/66
First Grand Prix: 1994

Shinji Nakano
Nationality: Japan
Number: 15
Age: 26
Birth Date: 1/4/71
First Grand Prix: 1997

Red Bull Sauber Petronas

Engine: Ferrari V10
Tyres: Goodyear
Starts: 71
Wins: 0   **Poles:** 0
Constructors: 0
First Grand Prix: 1993 – South Africa
Principal: Peter Sauber

Johnny Herbert
Nationality: GB
Number: 16
Age: 33
Birth Date: 27/6/64
First Grand Prix: 1989

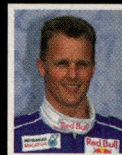

Nicola Larini
Nationality: Italy
Number: 17
Age: 33
Birth Date: 19/3/64
First Grand Prix: 1987

Tyrrell Ford

Engine: Ford V8
Tyres: Bridgestone
Starts: 391
Wins: 23   **Poles:** 14
Constructors: 1
First Grand Prix: 1970 – Canada
Principal: Ken Tyrrell

Jos Verstappen
Nationality: Holland
Number: 18
Age: 25
Birth Date: 4/3/72
First Grand Prix: 1994

Mika Salo
Nationality: Finland
Number: 19
Age: 30
Birth Date: 30/11/66
First Grand Prix: 1994

Minardi Hart

Engine: Hart V10
Tyres: Bridgestone
Starts: 194
Wins: 0   **Poles:** 0
Constructors: 0
First Grand Prix: 1985 – Brazil
Principal: Giancarlo Minardi

Ukyo Katayama
Nationality: Japan
Number: 20
Age: 34
Birth Date: 29/5/63
First Grand Prix: 1992

Jarno Trulli
Nationality: Italy
Number: 21
Age: 23
Birth Date: 13/7/74
First Grand Prix: 1997

Weather Conditions

Dry
Obviously the best conditions in which to race. When the track is dry, the tyre compound used is slicks. These rely on the temperature of the tyres being incredibly hot, which provides grip, but they tend to wear out fast if mistreated. Don't use wet tyres in the dry or they'll overheat and wear out very quickly – so if the track dries out, get into the pits and change them.

Wet
This is when the fun begins, and the skills of a driver are tested to the max. Each lap tends to be on average 5 to 10 seconds slower than if raced in the dry. So, when racing in the wet, don't push the car too hard or you'll probably end up spinning off. The wets/monsoon tyres have treads in them (not unlike road cars) to quickly disperse the water from the track and avoid aquaplaning. Don't use slicks in the wet or you'll skid all over the place!

Stewart Ford

Engine: Ford V10
Tyres: Bridgestone
Starts: 6
Wins: 0   **Poles:** 0
Constructors: 0
First Grand Prix: 1997 – Australia
Principal: Paul Stewart

Rubens Barrichello
Nationality: Brazil
Number: 22
Age: 25
Birth Date: 23/5/72
First Grand Prix: 1993

Jan Magnussen
Nationality: Denmark
Number: 23
Age: 24
Birth Date: 4/7/73
First Grand Prix: 1995

Formula 1 '97

Australian Grand Prix

Albert Park *Melbourne*

F1 Active Years: 1996
F1 Championships: 1
Location: Melbourne city centre
Race Distance: 191.052 miles, 307.516 km
No of Laps: 58 laps
Lap Distance: 3.294 miles, 5.302 km

There's always a group of protesters somewhere causing trouble – no doubt there are protesters protesting about the protesters! And this year they were out in force, covering the track with oil. Melbourne plays host to one of the few street circuits remaining in Formula 1, hence those damn protesters!

ARCADE MODE
SHORT-CUTS

01

02

The key to winning any and all arcade tracks is simple: take short cuts whenever possible; if there's unused road, use it. If you can slide across the grass, do so.

03
JONES STAND
As you exit the bend, keep the throttle pressed firmly down. This is a good stretch to overtake on.
| GEAR | 3 | MPH | 124 |

04
WHITFORD STAND
As you exit the bend, you should reach speeds in excess of 165 mph. Another good overtaking spot.
| GEAR | 2 | MPH | 108 |

05
LAUDA STAND
Don't worry too much about going up on the kerb. You may have to sometimes to keep on the track.
| GEAR | 3 | MPH | 96 |

06
CLARK STAND
A tricky right turn, leading up to a fast left. Keep to the racing line, apply the brake, then accelerate.
| GEAR | 1 | MPH | 81 |

07
FITTIPALDI STAND
As the road bends to the left, keep the throttle pressed firmly down. Another good overtaking point.
| GEAR | 2 | MPH | 118 |

08
WAITE STAND
As you approach the bend, release the throttle a little, before once again roaring off down a straight.
| GEAR | 4 | MPH | 140 |

09
HILL STAND
As you fly down the straight, you'll soon come to a tight right. Slow down and take it at about 60 mph.
| GEAR | 8 | MPH | 181 |

START

02
BRABHAM STAND
After passing the Fangio Stand, slap on the accelerator. You may need to adjust the speed gradually.
| GEAR | 2 | MPH | 83 |

01
FANGIO STAND
This is one of the many tight bends on the Melbourne circuit. As you approach the turn, brake hard.
| GEAR | 6 | MPH | 144 |

12
SENNA STAND
You're into the home straight, the clock is ticking, put the pedal to the metal and grab that grid position.
| GEAR | 3 | MPH | 126 |

11
PROST STAND
After exiting a tight left, you'll come to the final bend (right) before entering the start/finish straight.
| GEAR | 1 | MPH | 79 |

10
STEWART STAND
After one tight right you begin to accelerate away, before shortly approaching a 70 mph corner.
| GEAR | 2 | MPH | 105 |

F1 '97

continued

Brazilian Grand Prix

Autodromo José Carlos Pace *Interlagos*

F1 Active Years: 1973–77, 79–80, 90 to present
F1 Championships: 14
Location: Sao Paulo suburb
Race Distance: 190.777 miles, 307.075 km
No of Laps: 71 laps
Lap Distance: 2.687 miles, 4.325 km

As well as their famous passion for football, the Brazilians also love their motor racing. The track, a favourite of most racing drivers – both real and the likes of us – is a fast and bumpy track to test your nerve.

ARCADE MODE
SHORT-CUTS

Your car may take off from time to time, but keeping control of it is not a problem. Sliding along the grass is usually the best way to take some corners. By doing so, you keep your top speed, not to mention shaving off a few extra seconds from those lap times. Now that can't be bad eh!

01 CURVA 1
After screaming down the start/finish straight, you need to slow down just as the track bends.
GEAR 2 | MPH 95

05 JUNCAO
A real test of your car's grip, and your nerve, as you fling your car round this fast right bend.
GEAR 6 | MPH 168

07 CURVA DO PINHEIRINHO
Apply a short burst of speed as you approach this tight left-hander, then brake and stick to the inside.
GEAR 2 | MPH 62

06 CURVA DO LORANJA
A somewhat slower bend than the next one. Keep in first gear, then accelerate out of this slow right.
GEAR 1 | MPH 58

02 'S' DO SENNA
After a slow first left, slam the throttle down out of this quick right, and keep to the racing line.
GEAR 2 | MPH 100

03 CURVA DO SOL
A nice fast left bend, keep the speed increasing. The upcoming straight is perfect for overtaking.
GEAR 4 | MPH 141

12 ARQUIBANCADAS
Now you're really moving. This long straight is by far the best point on the track for overtaking.
GEAR 6 | MPH 166

04 SUBIDA/DESCIDA DO LAGO
If you stick tight to the inside you'll be OK. But, if you find yourself nearing the grass, apply the brake.
GEAR 3 | MPH 123

09 MERGULHO
After a very tight right, keep the pedal pressed firmly down as you glide around this fast left-hander.
GEAR 3 | MPH 126

10 CURVA 4/JUNCAO
After braking into the tight left, keep the accelerator down as the track begins to straighten up.
GEAR 2 | MPH 84

08 CURVA DO COTOVELO
Get into first gear for this tight right. Keep tapping the accelerator as you turn into/out of the bend.
GEAR 1 | MPH 59

11 SUBIDA
You'll be reaching top speeds as you approach the finish line. Better watch out for those pits.
GEAR 3 | MPH 128

START

Formula 1 '97

San Marino Grand Prix

Autodromo Enzo e Dino Ferrari *Imola*

F1 Active Years: 1980 to present
F1 Championships: 17 (Italian GP 1980, San Marino GP from 1981)
Location: 20 miles southwest of Bologna
Race Distance: 191.52 miles, 308.385 km
No of Laps: 63 laps
Lap Distance: 3.04 miles, 4.895 km

Imola will always be remembered for that fatal day when Ayrton Senna and Roland Ratzenberger died in 1994. The following season, changes were made to help prevent such accidents from ever happening again. But although the 1995 safety modifications reduced the overall speed of the circuit, the new layout offers a few new challenges.

03 — TOSA
A fairly easy right. As you exit the bend, apply more of the throttle and head down the straight.

GEAR	4	MPH	132

04 — PIRATELLA
A tight left coming up. Let go of the throttle, apply the brake, then glide round before using the throttle.

GEAR	1	MPH	70

05 — ACQUE MINERALE
This right may be third gear, but the imminent right requires nothing more than second, 68 mph.

GEAR	3	MPH	123

06 — VARIANTE ALTA
Stick close to the first kerb as you enter. Lay off the throttle a little as you pass the second kerb.

GEAR	6	MPH	148

07 — RIVAZZA
The upcoming left is no different than the one you've just exited. Power the throttle as you exit.

GEAR	1	MPH	83

01 — TAMBURELLO
The first corners are a lovely start to this course. Brake just before entering, then floor it out.

GEAR	2	MPH	96

02 — VILLENEUVE
Like the previous section, only this time, you'll be fast approaching a very tight right-hander.

GEAR	5	MPH	163

08 — VARIANTE MARLBORO/BASSA
The final chicane before the finishing straight. If taken well, you should get the chance to overtake.

GEAR	1	MPH	54

START

ARCADE MODE
SHORT-CUTS

Fling your car across the gravel in order to gain positions and decrease your lap times. However, the gravel does start to slow you down, so don't try and cut across too much.

F1'97

continued

Monaco Grand Prix

Monte Carlo
F1 Active Years: 1955 to present
F1 Championships: 43
Location: Downtown Monte Carlo
Race Distance: 163.176 miles, 262.626 km
No of Laps: 78 laps
Lap Distance: 2.092 miles, 3.367 km

The Monaco Grand Prix is always the highlight of the Formula 1 season. Set within beautiful harbourside surroundings, this fantastic street circuit provides the drivers with the toughest overtaking challenges on any F1 circuit. So it's not surprising that this course is usually won using superior pit-stop strategies.

Supposedly the toughest track in arcade mode – nonsense. Just power-slide around the corners to save precious seconds, and use the kerbs whenever possible, as in pic 02.

13 VIRAGE ANTHONY NOGHES
The final bend before the start/finish straight. Take it nice and easy through, then floor it.
GEAR 1 MPH 44

12 VIRAGE LA RASCASSE
One of the slowest corners on this magnificent track. So don't even try to rip round it, otherwise, oomf!
GEAR 1 MPH 41

10 VIRAGE DU BUREAU DE TABAC
A fairly fast bend, taken at 100 mph (give or take a few mph). Then accelerate out of the bend.
GEAR 2 MPH 97

09 CHICANE/NOUVELLE CHICANE
Braking early is of the utmost importance. Otherwise, you'll slam head-on into the barriers.
GEAR 1 MPH 55

11 VIRAGES PISCINE
After a quick left, you only have a couple of seconds before you reach a tight right. Slow to 80 mph.
GEAR 2 MPH 114

01 VIRAGE DE SAINTE DEVOTE
The first bend sums up this track superbly. A tight right, in which you need to brake very early to make it.
GEAR 2 MPH 44

03 VIRAGE MASSENET
A long winding left bend. Unfortunately you'll have to keep taping the throttle as you go round.
GEAR 2 MPH 108

02 MONTEE DU BEAU RIVAGE
Forget about the brake on this part of the track, just scream up this section, sticking to the racing line.
GEAR 4 MPH 141

05 VIRAGE MIRABEAU
Take the corner nice and slow. Be careful not to skid, as it won't do your tyres the least bit of good.
GEAR 1 MPH 33

07 VIRAGE DU PORTIER
Yet another slow turn on this street circuit. Apply the throttle as you exit the bend and enter the tunnel.
GEAR 1 MPH 49

START

04 VIRAGE CASINO
A good fast flowing winding right. Just don't try to overtake, otherwise you'll end up in the barriers.
GEAR 2 MPH 113

06 VIRAGE DE LA GARE/LOEWS
Keep at a steady 40–50 mph. Try not to oversteer, and keep off the throttle for long periods.
GEAR 1 MPH 43

08 TUNNEL
The tunnel is a spectacular point for overtaking, as long as you can keep control of your car, that is!
GEAR 3 MPH 124

Spanish Grand Prix

Circuito de Catalunya at Montmelo
Barcelona

F1 F1 Active Years: 1991 to present
F1 Championships: 6
Location: 22 Miles North of Barcelona
Race Distance: 190.515 miles, 307.255 km
No of Laps: 65 laps
Lap Distance: 2.931 miles, 4.727 km

This track was especially designed for Formula 1. Apart from the notorious tight first corner – which makes for exciting starts – there are gorgeous long straights to really put your foot down on. Definitely one of the more enjoyable tracks in the Grand Prix season.

01 CURVONE ELF
After bombing down the start/finish straight, the brakes will soon be called into action.

| GEAR | 4 | MPH | 110 |

02 REVOLT RENAULT
A nice, fast sweeping right-hander is always welcome. Just stick to the racing line to gain max speed.

| GEAR | 4 | MPH | 148 |

04 REVOLT SEAT
Keep releasing the throttle from time to time; just to avoid running onto the grass.

| GEAR | 1 | MPH | 82 |

03 REVOLT REPSOL
As you approach the right corner ahead, apply the brake when you near the outside of the track.

| GEAR | 2 | MPH | 103 |

06 REVOLT CAMPSA
This sweeping right only requires braking when you reach the tightest point, otherwise floor it.

| GEAR | 3 | MPH | 121 |

START

ARCADE MODE
SHORT-CUTS

Barcelona is a great track for short-cuts, because you can miss out some pretty big chunks of the track, thus saving bags of time, not to mention gaining positions at a rapid rate.

05 REVOLT WURTH
After a couple of slowish bends, the course begins to open up. Stick to the inside, then switch.

| GEAR | 1 | MPH | 72 |

08 REVOLT LA CAIXA
After a brilliant straight, it's inevitable that another slow corner will turn up.

| GEAR | 1 | MPH | 68 |

07 NISSAN
Power your way down this lightning part of the track. One of several great overtaking points.

| GEAR | 5 | MPH | 155 |

09 BANC DE SABADELL
As you exit the bend, move to the outside of the track to set yourself up for the forthcoming slower right.

| GEAR | 2 | MPH | 99 |

F1'97

continued

Canadian Grand Prix

Circuit Gilles Villeneuve *Montreal*

F1 Active Years: 1978 to present
F1 Championships: 18
Location: East of Montreal city centre
Race Distance: 189.543 miles, 305.049 km
No of Laps: 69 laps
Lap Distance: 2.747 miles, 4.421 km

Named after the great Gilles Villeneuve, the Montreal Grand Prix is a cross between a street circuit and a permanent racetrack. One of the better tracks for overtaking, the Circuit Gilles Villeneuve includes high-speed straights, as well as a few blind corners.

ARCADE MODE
SHORT-CUTS

The short-cut-tastic-fun continues on this mega-fast track. As in pic 01, you can really cut up the tracks. Some may call it cheating... nonsense, it's all about winning. Approach the grass, tap the brake, then slam the throttle down to power-slide. Simple!

START

01 ISLAND HAIRPIN
As you approach the hairpin at great speed, get ready to slow down, then turn sharply inside.
GEAR 2 | MPH 121

03 CASINO CORNER
Just zoom down this section of the track. This is also the best opportunity for overtaking others.
GEAR 6 | MPH 178

02 PITS HAIRPIN
The slowest corner on the track. Brake quick, turn sharply, then exit like your backside's on fire.
GEAR 1 | MPH 38

Camera Views

Front Wing
This produces the full speed effect. A favourite of all *Ridge Racer* fans and speed freaks.

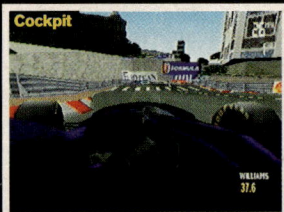

Cockpit
Arrh yeah! Now this is racing; full on, blood-pumping cockpit action. Can be a bit too much...

Airbox
This view is for the experts, the ones that master every single bend and corner of the track.

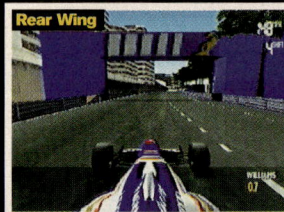

Rear Wing
Just a little higher than the airbox, giving you a slightly better view of the track. Still pretty tough though.

Chase 1
Superbly low on the ground and positioned just behind the car, this provides you with a feel of real speed – but not the taste!

Chase 2
Better than the previous view, mainly because it's further behind the car and just a little higher. One of the best in the game.

Tail
The best view there is, it has everything: a clear sight of the track ahead and a good feeling of speed. What else could you possibly want?

Sky
A more distant view than the Tail Camera, revealing more of the road ahead. The perfect perspective for beginners learning the track.

French Grand Prix

Circuit de Nevers *Magny-Cours*

F1 Active Years: 1991 to present
F1 Championships: 6
Location: Central France, 7 miles south of Nevers
Race Distance: 190.08 miles, 306 km
No of Laps: 72 laps
Lap Distance: 2.64 miles, 4.25 km

Magny-Cours can thank local boy, the late President Mitterand for the Circuit de Nevers. It was his backing that ensured development from a club track to the wonderful Grand Prix venue it is today. With tight hairpins and some pretty merciless slow turns, this exhausting circuit is a real challenge.

ARCADE MODE
SHORT-CUTS

With the numerous chicanes and hairpins throughout Magny-Cours, there are many short-cut opportunities to increase your race position, in order to reach first place.

09 CHATEAUX D'EAU — Keep to the inside of the track. As the track straightens up, move over to the outside. **GEAR 2 MPH 91**

05 ESSE — Keep that throttle pressed firmly down as you power past an easy right and onto a long straight. **GEAR 2 MPH 107**

08 IMOLA — A fast right, then left before reaching Chateaux d'Eau. No need for the brake as this point. **GEAR 2 MPH 124**

10 CHICANE — After a nice fast straight, release the accelerator and tap the brake before taking this tight left. **GEAR 2 MPH 90**

11 LYCEE — A slow right corner, leading into the start/finish straight. This is the best time for overtaking others. **GEAR 1 MPH 59**

01 GRANDE COURBE — This section of track is a quick left, before having to slow down for the upcoming long left bend. **GEAR 4 MPH 150**

04 ADELAIDE — The tightest hairpin on the track. Switch down to first gear and tap the throttle in short bursts. **GEAR 1 MPH 51**

02 ESTORIL — A fast sweeping right-hander. Be careful though: the track tightens up as you come to the end of it. **GEAR 3 MPH 125**

06 NURBURGRING — Keep the accelerator pressed firmly down as your car comes screaming out of this fast left. **GEAR 3 MPH 129**

03 GOLF — After coming out of a sweeping right, the road opens up, enabling you to overtake your rivals. **GEAR 5 MPH 158**

07 180 — Simply known as 180. This slow left-hander sweeps left, then right at great speed once exited. **GEAR 1 MPH 68**

START

F1 '97

continued

British Grand Prix

Silverstone

F1 Active Years: 1950–54, 55–60 (alt. with Aintree), 63–85 (alt. with Brands Hatch), 87 to present
F1 Championships: 30
Location: 3 miles south of Towcester, Northamptonshire
Race Distance: 195.2 miles, 314.15 km
No of Laps: 61 laps
Lap Distance: 3.2 miles, 5.15 km

Set in a converted airfield, Silverstone has been host to the British Grand Prix since the 1950s, although alternating with a couple of other locations at times. Silverstone is still the heart of British racing. Many changes have taken place, and the most recent ones have meet with approval from most drivers.

ARCADE MODE
SHORT-CUTS

With Silverstone being a pretty open area – plenty of grass, in other words – there are countless points at which you'll be able to cut across. Remember, when attempting a short-cut, slide across the grass if you can. However, if you must cut across like in pic 01, then that's OK.

01 COPSE CORNER
Start how you mean to go on, and in this case it's damn fast. Keep to the inside whilst whizzing round.
| GEAR | 5 | MPH | 145 |

02 MAGGOTTS CURVE
A sweeping right to be taken a high speed. Keep the accelerator down for this part of the track.
| GEAR | 6 | MPH | 174 |

03 BECKETTS CORNER
A medium speed corner. Unlike the previous bend, you're going to need to release the throttle a little.
| GEAR | 2 | MPH | 105 |

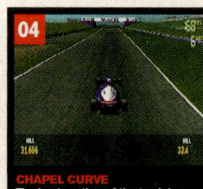

04 CHAPEL CURVE
The best section of the track in which to overtake the opposition. Just stay away from the grass!
| GEAR | 6 | MPH | 168 |

05 HANGAR STRAIGHT
The tyres are really warming up now. With speed in access of 170 mph, concentration is a must.
| GEAR | 6 | MPH | 178 |

14 LUFFIELD
As you begin to accelerate away from the previous bend, the finishing straight is in sight ahead.
| GEAR | 2 | MPH | 119 |

06 STOWE CORNER
With the brake only needed a little, you can soon slap the throttle back down to the floor.
| GEAR | 2 | MPH | 117 |

START

07 VALE
Yet another good opportunity to overtake any cars that may still be in front of you.
| GEAR | 5 | MPH | 153 |

13 BROOKLANDS
This bend may start off tight, but it begins to open up. Slowly increase your speed as you charge through.
| GEAR | 2 | MPH | 90 |

11 BRIDGE
You'll need to brake once you have passed the bridge, as a tight right awaits you.
| GEAR | 3 | MPH | 134 |

12 PRIORY
Stay close to the kerb for this sweeping left. Then switch to the outside for another tight left.
| GEAR | 1 | MPH | 85 |

10 FARM STRAIGHT
After a slow left, whack the throttle down and thrust the car up the straight, overtaking any stragglers.
| GEAR | 2 | MPH | 106 |

09 ABBEY CURVE
After a fast straight, you'll need to brake for this slower left. As you exit the turn, put the throttle down.
| GEAR | 1 | MPH | 80 |

08 CLUB CORNER
Stick to the inside of the corner, then slowly start to accelerate out as you enter the upcoming straight.
| GEAR | 1 | MPH | 86 |

German Grand Prix

Hockenheimring *Hockenheim*

F1 Active Years: 1970, 77–84, 86 to present
F1 Championships: 20
Location: 16 miles South West of Heidelberg
Race Distance: 190.755 miles, 307.035 km
No of Laps: 45 laps
Lap Distance: 4.239 miles, 6.823 km

The fastest course in Formula 1. Hockenheim, although originally a test track for Mercedes, has proven to be every F1 player's favourite: due to the maximum speeds you can thrash out of your race car. But with the added chicanes, it proves a much greater test to the driver.

ARCADE MODE
SHORT-CUTS

The chicanes prove a brilliant opportunity to gain a few places. Just go flat out over the corners, thus saving bags of time. Power-slide around the last section of the track.

03

OSTKURVE
The second chicane needs to be taken a little slower than the previous. Once out of it, floor it.
| GEAR | 1 | MPH | 78 |

04

SCHIKANE 2/SENNAKURVE
A fast right, leading into an equally quick left. This next straight provides a great overtaking chance.
| GEAR | 3 | MPH | 116 |

05

ONKOKURVE/AGIPKURVE
After a lightning fast straight, your brakes are once again called into action for this 90 degree corner.
| GEAR | 3 | MPH | 114 |

06

SACHSKURVE
A pretty tight hairpin. However, if you follow the racing line you should do just fine.
| GEAR | 1 | MPH | 74 |

07

ELFKURVE/FIAMMKURVE
The penultimate corner before the start/finish straight. Keep a good steady speed of around 85 mph.
| GEAR | 1 | MPH | 83 |

START

General Tips
Overtaking

If you've seen the Grand Prix coverage on television, you'll notice that drivers try to outbrake each other when approaching particular bends. It's quite easy to do in Formula 1: just brake a little later than your opponent, er, and that's it! You should shoot far enough ahead to keep in front of your opponent – but leave it too late and you'll end up off the track!

02

SCHIKANE 1/JIM CLARKKURVE
The first tricky chicane on this long track. Brake and turn hard into it, then put the throttle down.
| GEAR | 3 | MPH | 122 |

01

NORDKURVE
The first bend in the German Grand Prix. Only release the throttle as you near the end of the bend.
| GEAR | 5 | MPH | 143 |

08

SUDKURVE/OPELKURVE
If you're quick out of this sweeping right, you may have an overtaking opportunity.
| GEAR | 2 | MPH | 116 |

F1 '97

continued

Hungarian Grand Prix

Hungaroring
F1 Active Years: 1986 to present
F1 Championships: 11
Location: 12 miles east of Budapest
Race Distance: 189.805 miles, 305.536 km
No of Laps: 77 laps
Lap Distance: 2.465 miles, 3.968 km

Although it lies within beautiful surroundings, the course is far from lovely. It's very narrow and tight, therefore limiting your overtaking possibilities. This race is won not only in qualifying, but by the pit-stop strategies as well. The only safe overtaking opportunity is during the start/finish straight.

There are only a few short-cuts available on this scenic course. So it should only take you a lap or two to work out which corners to power-slide round, and which bends to cut across.

CURVE 5
After a short spurt of speed, this tight right-hander will prove a real test for your tyres.
GEAR 1 MPH 92

CURVE 6
After accelerating out of the previous right, you'll need to brake once again for this chicane.
GEAR 1 MPH 60

CURVE 7
As you start speeding out of curve 6, continue accelerating round curve 7.
GEAR 2 MPH 114

CURVE 8
A sweeping right is always a great spectacle to watch, especially if you can gather more speed.
GEAR 2 MPH 101

CURVE 4
As you reach the top of the hill, brake quickly, then continue round, throttling out as you straighten up.
GEAR 4 MPH 129

CURVE 9
This fast left is barely noticeable as you go flat out, fighting to gain ground upon the car in front.
GEAR 4 MPH 141

CURVE 3
After the previous tight corners, this sweeping right is very much welcome. Go through it flat out.
GEAR 3 MPH 131

CURVE 13
An identical corner to curve 1. Thus the speed and braking required is almost exactly the same.
GEAR 2 MPH 101

START

CURVE 1
A fairly easy corner to ease you into the twisty nature of the track. Brake a little before exiting it.
GEAR 2 MPH 96

CURVE 2
A sharper corner than the last. You can either brake, or glide round the bend without touching the throttle.
GEAR 1 MPH 83

CURVE 12
This second-to-last curve is almost identical to curve 2. Well, perhaps a little tighter!
GEAR 1 MPH 81

CURVE 10
As the curve straightens out you're able to increase you speed, and hopefully shave a few seconds off.
GEAR 4 MPH 126

CURVE 11
By keeping close to the kerb on this first curve, you're better lined up to handle the next one.
GEAR 2 MPH 87

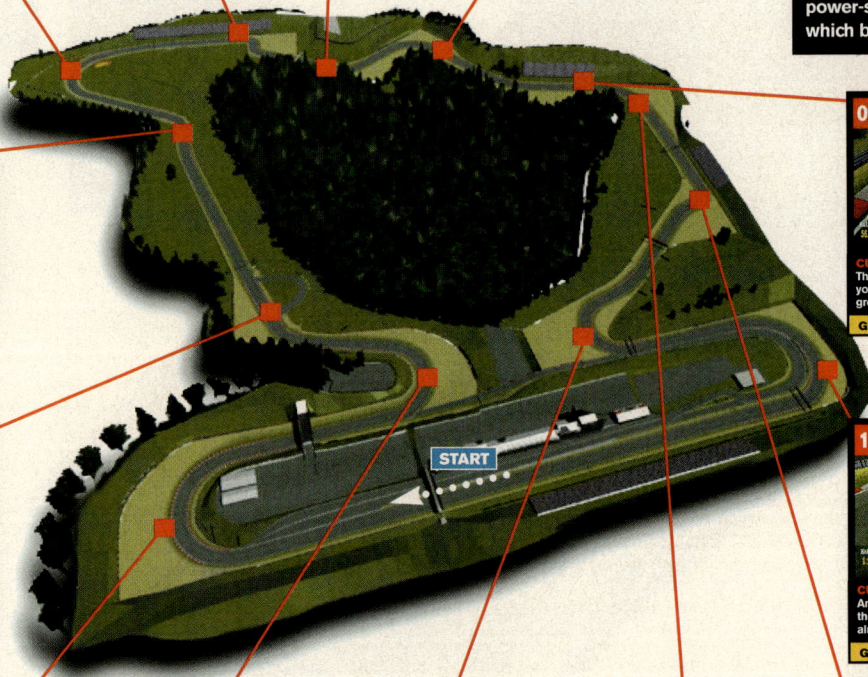

Belgian Grand Prix

Spa-Francorchamps

F1 Active Years: 1950–70, 83, 85 to present
F1 Championships: 31
Location: Ardennes
Race Distance: 190.476 miles, 306.592 km
No of Laps: 44 laps
Lap Distance: 4.329 miles, 6.968 km

Just by looking at the circuit you can understand why it is one of the most demanding tracks in *Formula 1*. Not only this, it contains the most challenging corner, which is a big enough test for even the most experienced games player – until now, that is!

ARCADE MODE
SHORT-CUTS

Spa is another F1 track which provides little in the way of short-cuts. However, the few it does offer prove their worth. As in pic 01, you can cut across the grass and onto used track.

---

01 LA SOURCE
The first and most deadly bend on Spa is this first-gear, 40 mph right hairpin. Start braking now!

GEAR	6	MPH	150

02 L'EAU ROUGE
After a devilish hairpin, you find yourself speeding down a straight, gaining speed every second.

GEAR	4	MPH	147

03 LE RAIDILLON
A sweeping right up the hill, before darting to the left in an equally quick bend.

GEAR	6	MPH	171

04 KEMMEL
The best section of track in which to overtake. You can reach speeds in excess of 200 mph down here.

GEAR	6	MPH	164

05 LES COMBES
After shifting down a few gears, and braking bloody fast, you zoom passed Les Combes into Malmedy.

GEAR	2	MPH	88

06 MALMEDY
A sweeping right-hander leading into a short straight. Accelerate out of this and down towards Rivage.

GEAR	2	MPH	98

07 RIVAGE
A fairly fast 180° sweeping right heading downhill, and almost straight into a 90° swine of a turn.

GEAR		MPH	93

08 LE POUHON
This particular corner can be taken at a fairly fast pace. Just stick to the racing line and off the grass.

GEAR	4	MPH	140

09 LES FAGNES
Third gear should provide ample acceleration past here and into the next left.

GEAR	3	MPH	122

10 LIEGE/STAVELOT
One final third-gear turn before the last section. But instead of braking, try just releasing the throttle.

GEAR	3	MPH	137

11 BLANCHIMONT
Yeah! Now this is more like it, reaching high speeds and bombing past any and all opponents.

GEAR	6	MPH	173

12 BUS STOP/CLUBHOUSE
Brake hard some distance before the chicane. Then turn sharply to the left, then right; across the kerb.

GEAR	1	MPH	61

START

F1 '97

Italian Grand Prix

Monza
F1 Active Years: 1950–79, 81 to present
F1 Championships: 46
Location: 9 miles northeast of Milan
Race Distance: 190.005 miles, 305.81 km
No of Laps: 53 laps
Lap Distance: 3.585 miles, 5.770 km

The fanatical Ferrari fans (the *tifosi*) certainly make every race at Monza one to remember. And with the passion of the crowd mixed with the speed of the circuit, the atmosphere is second to none. There may be a few chicanes amongst the long straights, but they just add to the excitement.

ARCADE MODE
SHORT-CUTS

The short-cut bonanza continues with a bucketful of chances to catch up your opponents. There is basically no need to slow down – just charge over the grass and slide the corners.

03
VARIANTE DELLA ROGGIA
The adrenaline's rushing through your veins, storm out of the chicane and down the next straight.
| GEAR | 1 | MPH | 66 |

04
CURVE DI LESMO
After a fast right, speed down the straight – just remember there's another right up ahead.
| GEAR | 4 | MPH | 139 |

05
CURVA DEL SERRAGLIO
One of the many great opportunities to overtake on this superbly fast and exciting track.
| GEAR | 6 | MPH | 167 |

06
VARIANTE ASCARI
After carefully negotiating your way through Curva Del Vialone, step on the gas down this next straight.
| GEAR | 2 | MPH | 116 |

07
RETTIFILO CENTRALE
As you scream down the straight, move to the left side of the track, in readiness for the upcoming bend.
| GEAR | 6 | MPH | 181 |

09
RETTIFILO TRIBUNE
As you approach the start/finish line, you'll be at the limit of your car, and the best overtaking point.
| GEAR | 6 | MPH | 166 |

08
CURVA PARABOLICA
The final bend before your approach to the finishing straight. Take it easy, and stay on the inside.
| GEAR | 2 | MPH | 91 |

Murray's
Comedy Quotes

1. "And Damon Hill is coming into the pit lane, yes it's Damon Hill coming into the Williams pit, and Damon Hill in the pit, no it's Michael Schumacher!"

2. [During a F1 race, describing how the leader can see the driver following him] "…Mansell can see him in his earphone…"

3. Murray: "What's that? There's a BODY on the track!!!"
James: "Um, I think that that is a piece of BODYWORK, from someone's car."

4. Murray: "There's a fiery glow coming from the back of the Ferrari."
James: "No Murray, that's his rear safety light."

5. "…Cruel luck for Alesi, second on the grid. That's the first time he had started from the front row in a Grand Prix, having done so in Canada earlier this year…"

6. "…and there's no damage to the car… except to the car itself."

7. "Ukyo Katayama is undoubtedly the best Formula 1 driver that Grand Prix racing has ever produced."

8. "We're watching the Finnish driver who is third, but he won't for very much llllong… oh yeah, he might be actually."

9. "And an enormous gap building before Mika Hakkinen goes through in third position… when I say enormous it's 1.5 seconds."

10. Murray: "And there are flames coming from the back of Prost's car as he enters the swimming pool."
James: "Well, that should put them out then."

START

02
CURVA GRANDE
A great sweeping right leading towards the first chicane on this beautiful historic course.
| GEAR | 5 | MPH | 154 |

01
VARIANTE GOODYEAR
The first chicane shouldn't provide you with any problems. In fact, you could probably take it faster.
| GEAR | 2 | MPH | 98 |

Formula 1 '97

Austrian Grand Prix

A-1 Ring Österreichring

F1 active years: 1970–87, 97 to present
F1 Championships: 18
Location: Zeltweg, 70 km northwest of Graz, 200 km southeast of Salzburg
Race distance: 189.57 miles, 306.649 km
No of Laps: 71 laps
Lap Distance: 2.67 miles, 4.319 km

The Österreichring makes a welcome return to the F1 schedule for the first time in a decade. Set upon the Styrian mountains, it's arguably the most scenic circuit in Formula 1. The long straights provide ample overtaking opportunities.

ARCADE MODE
SHORT-CUTS

This scenic beauty provides you with ample opportunities to cut across various sections of the track; in order to gain higher places and clock quicker laps. Power-sliding and grass-crossing points will come thick and fast. And with the numerous long straights scattered around the track, 1st place is almost assured.

03

SEBRING-AUSPUFFKURVE
This corner can often catch you out if you try speeding round it too fast. Take it slow, and safely.

GEAR	2	MPH	83

04

VALVOLINE-GERADE
This is one of the few fast straights on the track, so make the most of it. Get ready for the upcoming right.

GEAR	5	MPH	156

05

BOSCH/KRAINER-KURVE
The track ahead may not seem tight, but it needs to be taken extremely cautiously.

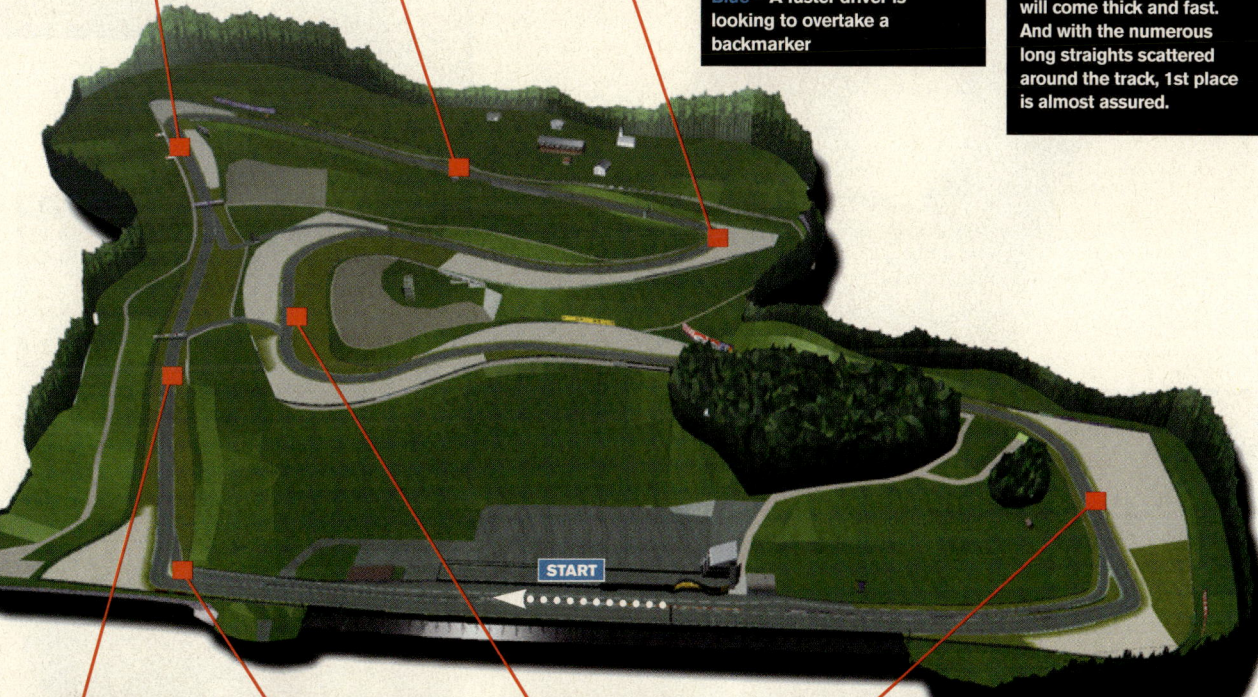

GEAR	1	MPH	70

START

02

FLATSCHACH
With a tight bend at both ends of this straight, you'd better make the most of it.

GEAR	4	MPH	147

01

VOEST-HUGEL
After thrashing your car down the start/finish straight, start braking at this point to avoid overrunning.

GEAR	6	MPH	146

06

PANORAMA-KURVE
After accelerating from the previous hairpin, pick up a little speed before braking for this left.

GEAR	2	MPH	110

07

JOCHEN-RINDT-KURVE
As you approach the final bends, accelerate past this curve, then brake for the final tight right.

GEAR	2	MPH	114

F1 '97

continued

Luxembourg Grand Prix

Nürburgring
F1 Active Years: 1951,54–58,61–69,71–76, 84–85, 95 to present
F1 Championships: 26
Location: 37 miles west of Koblenz
Race Distance: 201.001 miles, 323.476 km
No of Laps: 71 laps
Lap Distance: 2.831 miles, 4.556 km

Eh? Since when has the Nürburgring been in Luxembourg? This famous track formerly hosted the German Grand Prix. Due to its previous size, some 17.5 miles, and Niki Lauda's horrific accident in '76, the circuit had to undergo major changes before being accepted once again into the Grand Prix season.

ARCADE MODE
SHORT-CUTS

The Luxembourg arcade provides the driver with every short-cut you could dream of (well, almost) as you fling your rather expensive car over kerbs, grass, gravel, and basically everything else on the ground.

09 VEEDOL-SCHIKANE
After safely steering around the chicane, accelerate round the curve and towards the final bend.
| GEAR | 1 | MPH | 55 |

10 ROMER/COCA-COLA KURVE
The final bend. Keep at a steady speed until you exit, then scream down the finishing straight.
| GEAR | 1 | MPH | 92 |

01 CASTROL-S
Taking the first bend well is essential, as you need a good line to turn into the following left.
| GEAR | 1 | MPH | 76 |

02 VALVOLINE-KURVE
As you speed through Sachs-passage, you'll need to brake a little for this sweeping left.
| GEAR | 2 | MPH | 111 |

03 FORD-KURVE
As you exit the fast right-hander (Ford-kurve), start powering down to Dunlop-kurve.
| GEAR | 1 | MPH | 95 |

08 HATZENBACH/ITT-BOGEN
The second of two quick sweeping corners. Although overtaking is possible, it's not advised.
| GEAR | 4 | MPH | 149 |

START

07 BIT-KURVE
You can keep the throttle down a little harder for this corner. Remember, stick to the racing line.
| GEAR | 3 | MPH | 119 |

06 RTL-KURVE
After that gorgeously fast section of the course, the brake is once again called into use for this bend.
| GEAR | 2 | MPH | 92 |

05 SHELL-KURVE
This is the fastest part of the track, where the driving is fast, and the overtaking is spectacular.
| GEAR | 5 | MPH | 163 |

04 DUNLOP-KEHRE
This tight hairpin warrants first gear, and no more than 80 mph on your speedometer.
| GEAR | 1 | MPH | 85 |

Formula 1 '97

Japanese Grand Prix

Suzuka
F1 Active Years: **1987 to present**
F1 Championships: **10**
Location: **50 miles southwest of Nagoya**
Race Distance: **189.488 miles, 304.928 km**
No of Laps: **52 laps**
Lap Distance: **3.644 miles, 5.864 km**

With its unique figure-of-eight layout, Suzuka attracts fans from all over the world. Featuring a couple of fast straights, the Japanese Grand Prix is much-loved by the Formula 1 drivers and games players alike.

ARCADE MODE
SHORT-CUTS

Suzuka is one of the many tracks in arcade mode that provides you with countless short-cuts. In 01 you can powerslide across the grass at the Hairpin, whereas in 02 you can cut across the chicane at Cassio Triangle.

07 SPOON CURVE
This sweeping right gradually tightens up towards the exit of the curve, so you'll need to brake a bit.
GEAR 2 | MPH 112

06 HAIRPIN
After braking hard in the entrance to this point, start accelerating as you begin to exit the hairpin.
GEAR 1 | MPH 51

09 '130 R'
With the pit entrance to your right, start braking early so that you don't overrun the chicane.
GEAR 5 | MPH 127

08 CROSSING/UNDERPASS
The second of two great overtaking stretches along this twisty track. It's also very fast.
GEAR 6 | MPH 169

10 CHICANE/CASSIO TRIANGLE
This tricky final part of the course requires a real test of your brakes. So turn sharply right, then left.
GEAR 1 | MPH 43

04 DUNLOP CURVE
Although you won't be able to go flat out around this long left, you'll still reach some pretty fast speeds.
GEAR 3 | MPH 118

05 DEGNER CURVE
You could probably get away without having to brake at this point, just release the accelerator.
GEAR 1 | MPH 76

03 S CURVES
You must stick to the racing line during these S Curves, otherwise you'll end up in the dirt.
GEAR 3 | MPH 113

02 SECOND CURVE
This bend will need to be taken at a slower pace than the previous curve, as it's just a little tighter.
GEAR 1 | MPH 92

01 FIRST CURVE
A simple name for a simple bend. To obtain the maximum speed round it, stick to the inside.
GEAR 2 | MPH 90

START

F1 '97

Portuguese Grand Prix

Autodromo Do Estoril
Race Distance: 189.63 miles, 305.2 km
No of Laps: 70 laps
Lap Distance: 2.709 miles, 4.360 km

Estoril was removed from the F1 calendar due to unfinished work on the safety modifications. But seeing as Psygnosis had already digitised it, it seemed a waste not to include it!

ARCADE MODE
SHORT-CUTS

There aren't quite as many short-cuts at Estoril as you might hope. But not to worry: by power-sliding around the various bends you can gain positions almost as quickly. Just apply the brake a little, turn, and slam that throttle down as hard as you can. Then you'll slip-slide away!

09 ESSES
After a tight left-hander, accelerate down the short straight and into the sweeping right.
GEAR 2 | MPH 101

10 PARABOLICA
The final sweeping right before entering the start/finish straight. As you exit the bend, throttle it!
GEAR 2 | MPH 102

06 PARABOLICA INTENX
Identical to the VIP curve at point 5. Like the previous, don't use your brake, just release the accelerator.
GEAR 1 | MPH 76

08 CURVE DO TANQUE
Probably the slowest corner of any Formula 1 circuit. Brake hard, turn sharply, then ease yourself up.
GEAR 1 | MPH 26

07 CURVA 7
Although it may not look tight on the map, when you come across it, you'd do well to take it a bit slower.
GEAR 1 | MPH 80

04 CURVA 3
After coming off a sweeping right, head to the inside of the track and slow down for this tight right.
GEAR 1 | MPH 79

START

05 VIP
As you glide round the VIP in 2nd gear, thrust the throttle down as you exit for the upcoming straight.
GEAR 2 | MPH 84

03 CURVA 2
This long right can be taken at speeds up to 144 mph. But your tyres must be in good condition.
GEAR 3 | MPH 126

01 PADDOCK
The start/finish straight is the best point on the track at which to overtake your opposition.
GEAR 6 | MPH 183

02 CURVA 1
The first curve must be taken at the optimum approach in order to get the highest speed out of it.
GEAR 2 | MPH 99

Formula 1 '97

European Grand Prix

Jerez
F1 Active Years: 1986–1990, 1994
F1 Championships: 6
Location: Northeast of Jerez de la Frontera, 22 miles northeast of Cadiz
Race Distance: 180.849 miles, 291.042 km
No of Laps: 69 laps
Lap Distance: 2.621 miles, 4.218 km

Under the guise of the European Grand Prix, Jerez was added mid-season to replace the Portuguese Grand Prix at Estoril. It hosted the Spanish Grand Prix until 1990. As well as a nice long straight for overtaking, there are plenty of winding bends.

ARCADE MODE
SHORT-CUTS

A superb course for short-cuts. But for some reason you will always be pushed for time. Cut across the gravel at any opportunity, and power-slide around the corners to better lap times.

07
CURVA PELUQUI
The exit to this seemingly long right-hander. As you accelerate out of the curve, follow the racing line.
| GEAR | 2 | MPH | 120 |

08
CURVA AYRTON SENNA
No braking required here. Just keep the pedal pressed firmly to the floor.
| GEAR | 3 | MPH | 137 |

09
CURVA FERRARI
As your speed increases, you find yourself rapidly closing on a tight 60–70 mph left-hander.
| GEAR | 6 | MPH | 163 |

01
CURVA EXPO 92
The first bend can spell trouble if taken too fast. It suddenly starts to sharpen up as you exit it.
| GEAR | 2 | MPH | 73 |

06
CURVA ANGEL NIETO
This long winding right links into the Curva Peluqui. You'll need a constant speed to stay on track.
| GEAR | 3 | MPH | 122 |

02
CURVA MICHELIN
This hell of the turn is a test for any driver. You may find yourself having to change down into first gear.
| GEAR | 2 | MPH | 90 |

START

04
CURVA DRY SAC
After a fantastic long straight, you'll need to brake early in order not to end up on the grass.
| GEAR | 1 | MPH | 54 |

05
CURVA DUCADOS
This brilliant sweeping right will need a short dab on the brakes as you reach the next blue/white kerb.
| GEAR | 2 | MPH | 109 |

03
CURVA SITO PONS
The fast sweeping bends just keep on coming as you find yourself accelerating through Sito Pons.
| GEAR | 4 | MPH | 138 |

F1 '97

Argentinian Grand Prix

Autodromo Oscar Alfredo Gálvez
Buenos Aires

F1 Active Years: 1954–60, 72–81, 95 to present
F1 Championships: 18
Location: Southern suburbs of Buenos Aires
Race Distance: 193.464 miles, 311.4 km
No of Laps: 72 laps
Lap Distance: 2.687 miles, 4.325 km

Argentina had the honour of holding the first ever Grand Prix outside of Europe, back in 1954. This twisty circuit was built as a showcase for their 1950s champion, the legendary Juan Manuel Fangio. As you can probably guess, this is a real brake tester.

05

CURVA DEL OMBU
Be careful on this part of the course. The corners are tight, so quick turns & thinking are required.

| GEAR | 1 | MPH | 75 |

Grass, Sand Or Gravel Traps

If you pay regular visits onto the grass, or the sand/gravel traps, you may find this little bit of advice will be helpful. Revving your engine and skidding like a madman is not a good way to get back on the road. Short, quick taps of the throttle is the best technique so your car stays under control.

02

CURVA DE ASCARI
Like a bat out of hell, you fly round the track. A good place for overtaking, if you have the balls!

| GEAR | 6 | MPH | 172 |

04

VIBORITA
Keep the throttle down through this part of the track. Try and stick to the racing line like glue.

| GEAR | 2 | MPH | 112 |

START

ARCADE MODE
SHORT-CUTS

The best technique when it comes to cornering is to power-slide around. Tap the brake into a turn, then immediately re-engage the accelerator to slide (obviously whilst steering).

01

CURVA DE LA CONFITERIA
A fairly slow left corner. Keep to the inside, then accelerate out of the bend and move to the outside.

| GEAR | 2 | MPH | 88 |

03

ENTRATA A LOS MIXTOS
This tight right corner demands you be in first gear. Stay close to the inside, then accelerate out.

| GEAR | 1 | MPH | 68 |

06

SENNA 'S'
No slowing down for this bend, just floor it and don't look back. Take the next right in first gear, 40 mph.

| GEAR | 2 | MPH | 100 |

Formula 1 '97

In order to reveal the hidden track in each stage you must win every race in that difficulty stage.

You're flying down the straight, your opposition is just to your left, why not smash into him?

Another corner, another powerslide. Just fling the car round the bend; it's not your car after all.

This first extra track keeps up the right blend of tight and twisty turns, mixed with a few long straights.

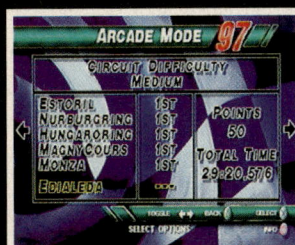

In order to reveal the hidden track in each stage you must win every race in that difficulty stage.

The race has started, you're at the back of the grid. Why not plough through a few of those cars ahead?

What, you're still in last place! Don't worry about those kerbs, just charge over them.

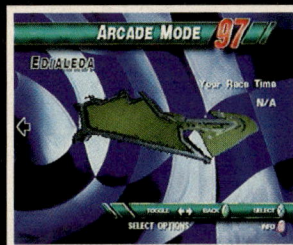

This second extra track is set in Adelaide – Australia for all those who failed Geography!

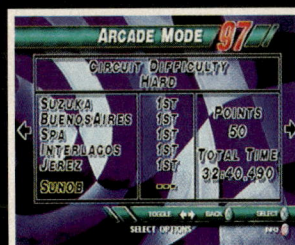

In order to reveal the hidden track in each stage you must win every race in that difficulty stage.

As you power down the hill, you will see yourself in the large screen. Smile...

Keep the power-sliding up, but watch out for that Psygnosis sign. No mistakes now.

The hidden track from the first Formula 1 makes a welcome appearance in the sequel.

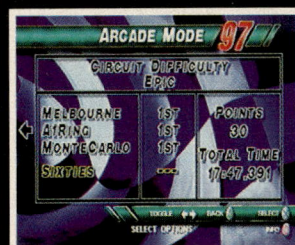

To reveal the Epic difficulty mode you must earn 100 points or more in easy, medium & hard stages.

Yep! That's right folks. Stirling Moss makes a remarkable return into F1, in his Championship car!

Unfortunately this is the closest you can get to a cockpit view. Is that Damon's dad at the wheel?

You'd better believe it! By winning the Epic difficulty you'll reveal a hidden Sixties race at Silverstone.

EXTRA TRACKS IN ARCADE MODE PLUS BONUS 60s MODE

F1 '97

NEW CHEATS

To activate the cheat/s, simply select 'Grand Prix' from the main menu. Then choose 'Select Driver'. Now edit that driver's name and enter the following names for the desired effect:

Virtual Reality Style Graphics
VIRTUALLY   VIRTUAL

If you can't spot the difference straight away, then you're obviously trapped in your own strange reality (but then again, who isn't, it would appear in these troubled days?). This cheat changes the majority of graphics into those similar to the classic *Virtua Racing*. Controls remain the same, but the graphics do make a dramatic change.

Background Music And New Sound Effects
SWAP SHOP

Although there's nothing new to be seen with this cheat, the sound is dramatically revamped. For instance, there's a bizarre hip-hop beat instead of music, plus the odd guitar riff taking the place of tyre screeches, and some unidentified form of noise sounding a collision. Unfortunately there's little other reward from this cheat.

Overinflated Tyres
LITTLE WEELZ

If you've ever fancied your hand at racing monster trucks, then now's your chance. When racing with this cheat, you'll immediately notice the huge tyres attached to your racing car. However, bigger wheels don't mean more grip in this case – in fact, there's no change, except that you can't see!.

'Wipeout 2097' Mode
PI MAN

This cheat had the potential to be utterly fantastic. But although it's still pretty cool, it's not a significant difference to normal racing. The controls are almost identical, and your car is the only one on the track with a power trail. If only you had weapons too! Oh well, back to ramming I suppose.

Helicopter Viewpoint
ZOOM LENSE

The idea of a helicopter viewpoint is fairly smart, it could prove an essential tool for learning every corner on the track – if you haven't already! The only downside is that you can't see what's coming up – and that's a bloody huge problem. Still, it's only a cheat after all!

Murray & Martin Sprite Commentators
BOX CHATTER

Now I've seen it all. Although not accurate portraits of our dynamic duo, Murray Walker and Martin Brundle, these sprite representations certainly do the job. When Murray talks, the bold sprite on the left starts talking. But if Martin starts to say something profound, = the sprite with the dodgy hair on the right begins to open his mouth in unison. Whatever next?

Frogs Instead Of Raindrops
CATS DOGS

One of the weirder cheats to appear in F1 '97. As well as the rain bucketing down

from above, you've also got hundreds of frogs failing from the skies. Unfortunately, there's no splat marks on the track!

Round 16 In Championship
OEAN ALESI (200 Points, 2nd Place)
NEAN ALESI (0 Points, Last Place)
PEAN ALESI (200 Points, 3rd Place)
QEAN ALESI (200 Points, 4th Place)

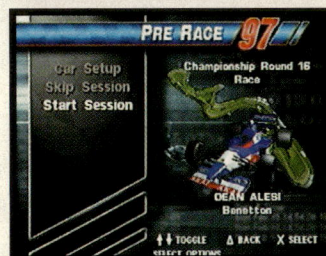

Each cheat takes you directly to track 16 in the Grand Prix F1 Championship. Simply adjust Alesi's name, change the race type to Championship, and start.

FOUR EXTRA TRACKS
BILLY BONUS

Although all four tracks are accessible by winning on Grand Prix mode, how many of you are actually going to bother spending all that time doing it! That's what I thought. The fourth hidden track is a little different than most. It's staged at Silverstone, but in the 1960s; with the black & white view, dodgy reception lines down the screen, and authentic '60s cars. Awesome stuff!

fighting force

Publisher:	Eidos
Price:	£44.99
Format:	UK

Fighting Force

UNIVERSAL MOVES

All these moves perform the same action for all the characters.

✕	Jab
✕ ✕	One-two punches
✕ ✕ ✕	Double punch, power punch
✕	Use a weapon you're holding
◼	Kick
◼ ◼	Double kick
◼	Kick floored opponent
●	Jump
▲	Back-fist
▲ ▲	Double back-fist, punch (character will turn around to throw the punch)
R1 + ✕	Sliding attack
R1 + ◼	Flying attack
▲	When close, grab bad guy

PERV FACTOR

Fighting Force stars a couple of right ravers. Mace sports a red PVC jacket with black bra and trousers, while Alana opts for skin-tight black crop-top and hot pants. What a lovely pair!

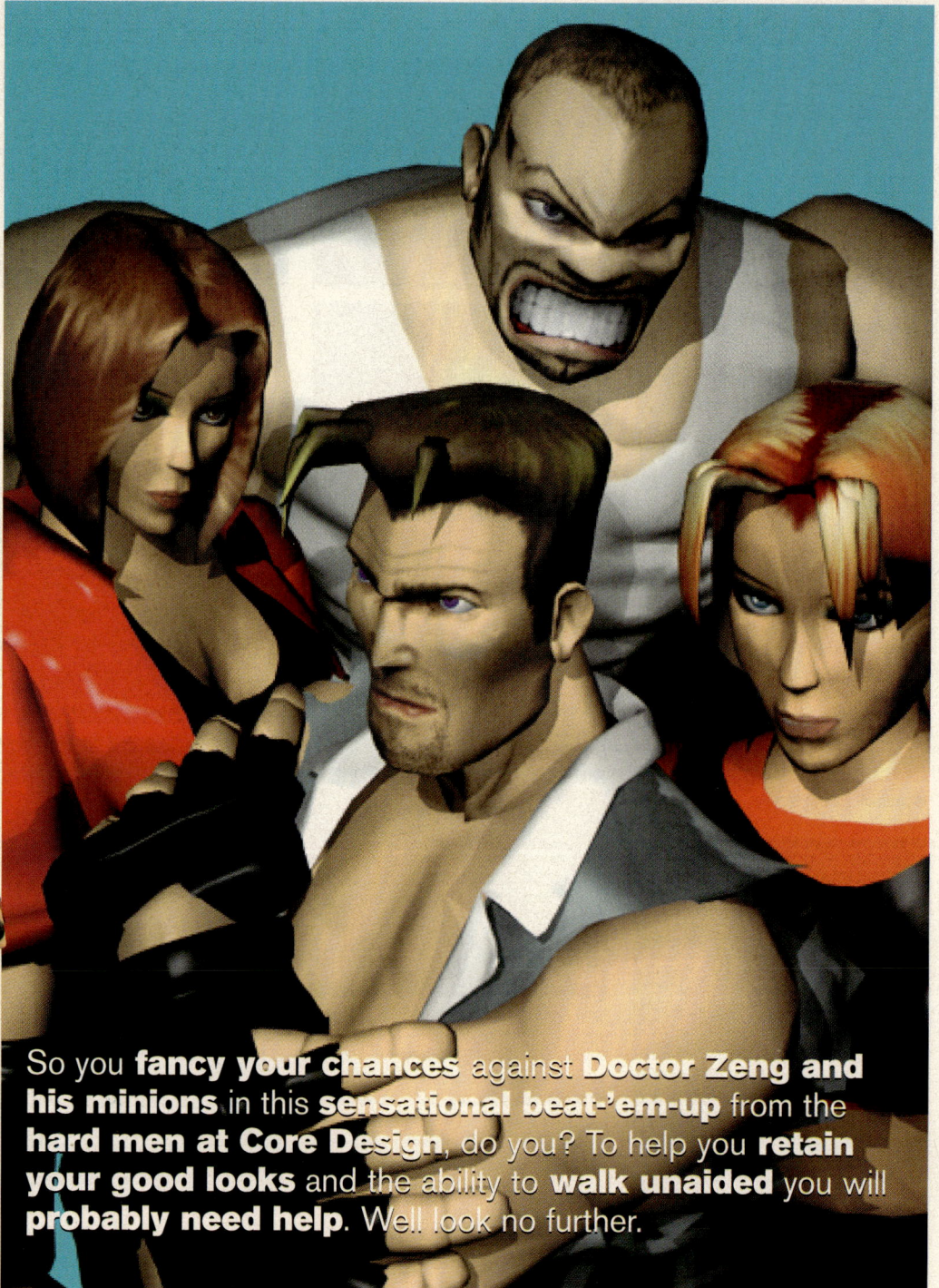

So you **fancy your chances** against **Doctor Zeng and his minions** in this **sensational beat-'em-up** from the **hard men at Core Design**, do you? To help you **retain your good looks** and the ability to **walk unaided** you will **probably need help**. Well look no further.

Mace Daniels

Age: 21 **Height:** 5'7 **Hair :** Brunette **Eyes:** Green **IQ:** 200

Best thing to say when she decks someone: *"Do you want your teeth back mate?"*

Special Moves
● + ✕ 360° leg sweep (depletes energy bar)

▲ + ✕ Jump and leg smash

Grappling Moves
▲ Leg squeeze throw

● Flip throw

■ Knee to face

✕ Face slap combo

Mace is a fast character with rapid kicks and punches at her disposal. Unfortunately she is very poor at taking hits, so stay on the move at all times.

Mace Special

Mace Useful

Mace Special
Mace's special is the spinning sweep. Not only does it clear surrounding enemies but you also crouch when you are performing the move so you cannot be shot.

Mace Useful
If you pick up a weapon such as a knife or iron bar, then grab your opponent and perform the face slap combo, she will use the weapon instead of her bare hands to inflict more damage.

Ben (Smasher) Jackson

Age: 29 **Height:** 6'4 **Hair:** Brown **Eyes:** Hazel **IQ:** 106

Best thing to say when he decks someone: *"Give my regards to Elvis when you see him."*

Special Moves
● + ✕ 360° shockwave

▲ Body slam

● Knee to face

Grappling Moves
● Slam

✕ Headlock smash

■ Super uppercut

▲ Pick up opponent

(then press ■ for a piledriver, or ✕ to throw him to the ground)

Smasher is the slowest and largest of the four characters. He can take and dish out a lot more damage than most people, but his low speed lets him down.

Smasher Special

Smasher Useful

Smasher Special
Smasher delivers a massive shockwave that sends the bad guys tumbling to the floor. This move has a large range so take care not to hit your own team-mate in two-player mode.

Smasher Useful
Pick up your opponent by holding forward and tapping △. While the poor fool is being held in the air his mates will not attack.

Hawk Manson

Age: 26 **Height:** 6'2 **Hair:** Blonde **Eyes:** Blue **IQ:** 187

Best thing to say when he decks someone: *"Anyone else for physiotherapy?"*

Special Moves
● + ✕ 360-degree spin kick

■ Kick while jumping

▲ Jump and stomp

Grappling Moves
● Shoulder throw

✕ Punch

✕ ✕ Punch then headbutt

■ Knee in the stomach

▲ Headbutt

▲ + ⇨ Backflip throw

Hawk has the fastest kicks in the game, enabling you to attack bad guys from a distance. Unfortunately he has slow punches which leave him wide open for countermoves.

Hawk Special

Hawk Useful

Hawk Special
Hawk's special move is not that good. To improve its range, run at your opponents before you use it.

Hawk Useful
Hawk's backflip throw is good for getting him out of tight situations, as when you perform it Hawk will backflip away from his attackers.

Alana

Age: 17 **Height:** 5'5 **Hair:** Blonde **Eyes:** Blue **IQ:** 240

Best thing to say when she decks someone: *"Mess with the best and you die like the rest."*

Special Moves
● + ✕ Spinning bird kick

▲ Jump spin stamp

●, ■ Flip kick

Grappling Moves
● Back flip kick

✕ Knee crush kick

■ Knee in the face

▲ Kick flip

Apart from being an obvious blonde babe, Alana is probably the best character in the game. Her powerful high-speed attacks and dazzling special moves take most enemies to the cleaners with ease.

Alana Special

Alana Useful

Alana Special
Alana rolls forward when she delivers her special move, giving it range as well as power.

Alana Useful
Her best move is the running kick as it gives 360° coverage, enabling her to cut a swathe through the bad guys.

fighting force

continued

Car Park

Reception

Lift

Corridor

ROUTE ONE: Park 1 & Park 2, leading to The Subway

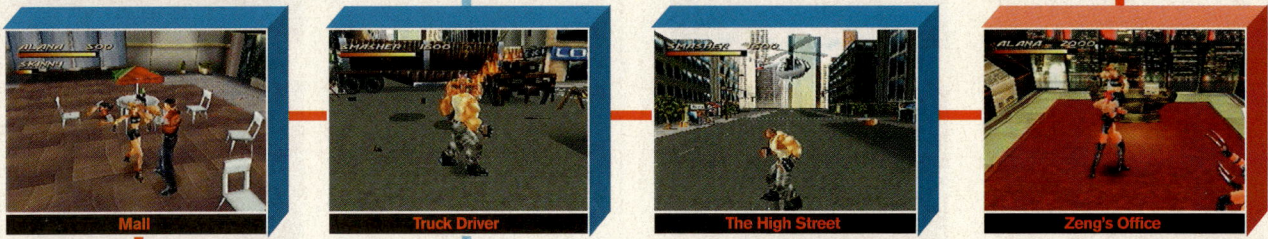

Mall

Truck Driver

The High Street

Zeng's Office

ROUTE TWO: The Bridge & The Bronx, leading to The Subway

Subway/Subway Boss

Train

Naval Base/Naval Base 2

Naval Boss

The Entire Game Route
There are several routes you can take to complete the game, some easier than others. Here's a handy route map, showing you how the levels connect.

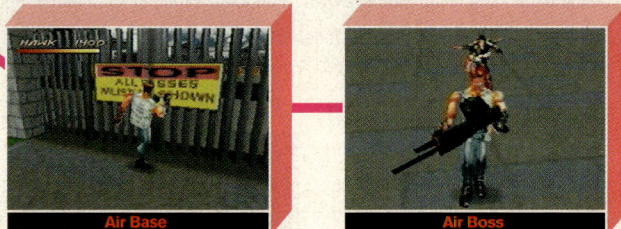

Air Base

Air Boss

Doctor Zeng

After the Subway Boss, you get a choice of train: one to the Naval Base, the other to the Air Base. Whichever you choose, the intermediate train stage is identical.

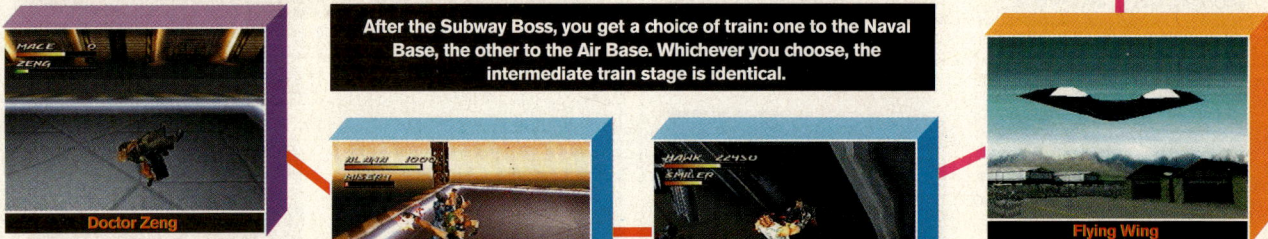

Island Lift

Island Lab

Flying Wing

Doctor Zeng

To ensure the evil Doctor Zeng is fed through plastic tubes for the next three years, follow the top tips in our play guide.

Hovercraft

Fighting Force

WALKTHROUGH

Level 1: The Car Park

You are dropped into the hot spot by helicopter with nothing more than your bare hands to rely on. Luckily there's an abundance of weapons concealed about this level, with which to dismember the bad guys.

The first mob of gangsters are upon you before your feet touch the ground. Mash them and head towards the parked police car. Smash this into dust and a rocket launcher will fall out of the boot – you can also help yourself to the tyres which come in handy as projectiles. Down the second and third waves of gangsters and use the rocket launcher on the door – stand well back from it before you fire to avoid being caught in the blast. Two more groups of mobsters will run from the gates towards you: use the remaining rockets to make short work of these fools before heading across the fallen gates and into the main car park.

To the right of the car park are some crates. Run over to these and destroy them to stock up on health. There is also a small crate amongst them that can be thrown. Your explosive entrance does not go unnoticed for long, as you will discover when reinforcements arrive in a black van. You can rip off the barriers at the sides of the car park to assist you in kicking the cack out of these poorly armed minions. When you have finished this group, head towards the limo and scrap it, and a shotgun will fall out of the boot for you to use on the next group of reinforcements that are pouring out of the lobby. Ambush the next wave with running attacks as they appear and you should have no trouble completing this stage.

Level 2: Reception

There's not much room to manoeuvre on this level, but there are loads of weapons to break heads with. As soon as you enter reception you are confronted by an array of bad guys. Slide-attack your way through them and go right: there's a bin standing next to a mesh screen. Pick up the bin and hurl it at the gangsters to buy some time to destroy the screen. Once the screen is down you can get break the crates behind it and tool yourself up with a couple of guns and some grenades. If you get low on energy, knock down the other mesh screen, as the crates behind it contain some health packs.

When you have hospitalised the first few waves of men, more enter through the doors at the side. Some of these have guns so stay on the move. If you are hard pressed, wreck the cola machine to the left of the entrance: it supplies you with teeth-destroying beverages and a few iron bars into the bargain.

Once all the bad guys in this area have been disposed of, break open the two security doors opposite where you came in. These lead to the lift, but before you can enter it you must deal with another gang of tuxedoed hard men. There is another cola machine to your left when you enter this section which you can scavenge for weapons and energy. The bin next to the cola machine can be thrown at oncoming bad guys, but don't use it against the men with guns or they will pick you off. Dispense with the two waves of reinforcements that come out of the lifts to finish the stage.

Level 3: The Lift

This time you are fighting in a really confined space. Use the slide attack to clear bad guys from your path if you become surrounded. As the lift starts moving, head for the fire box: hit it a few times and the axe will fly out. Pick it up and attack the bad guys as they rush

General Hints

Double Tap

Double-tap the pad to swiftly turn and face that direction. This move comes in very handy when you are dealing with multiple opponents.

Cola Machine

Smash any vending machines or confectionery stands you find as not only do they provide you with weapons and energy-replenishing food, they give you a chance to avenge yourself for being overcharged at railway stations.

Run And Slide

The most useful move in the game is the slide kick. Guaranteed to clear gun-toting thugs from your path and give you much-needed breathing space.

Go For Weapons

If you are outnumbered (which is most of the time) always go for the armed bad guys first. Use a sliding or flying kick to knock them to the floor, then scoop up their weapons and use them to even the odds.

Stay On The Move

Use hit-and-run tactics to avoid getting caught in a mob of fists. Run in, slide kick, attack one bad guy, then retreat. This will buy you some time if you are running low on energy.

Bad Guy Shield

If you are fighting in a confined space, like the lift, back into a corner so the bad guys can't get behind you. By doing this the person you are fighting against will shield you from any projectile attacks. Clever or what?

Crates Space

When you pick up a heavy object such as a crate or barrel be sure there is enough space between you and the bad guys as they have a habit of running in and decking you before you can throw anything successfully.

Change Direction

When you are in the middle of a two- or three-hit attack and you floor your opponent, you can turn and face the other bad guys and use the remaining strikes on them. This works particularly well when you are armed with a pipe or iron bar, as they have a good attacking range.

fighting force

continued

foolhardily into the lift. The axe turns you from Hawk Manson into Shirley Manson as bad guy blood splatters the walls.

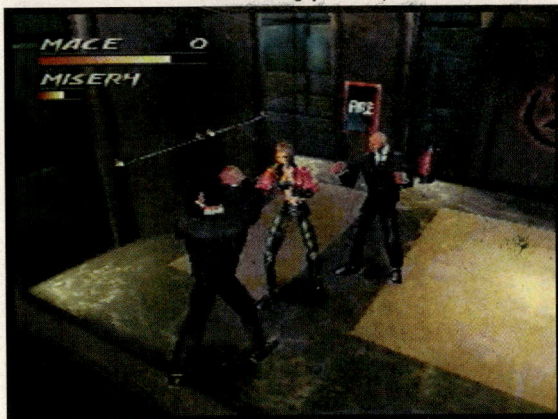

Looks like time to engage your power move as thugs close in on you from all sides.

When you have finished maiming the initial group of bad guys, more will smash their way in through the roof. Rip off the safety rails at the sides of the lift and bludgeon these interlopers to the floor. If you run out of rails you can pick up the baseball bats and planks of wood the bad guys obligingly drop and put them to good use. The next few waves of gangsters are tricky as some drop through the roof while their mates enter via the lift doors in an effort to surround you. Use of the sliding attack and your special move is a must if you hope to survive.

Smash the VDU monitor with a flying kick and pick it up to throw at the two massive blokes that turn up on the final floor. If they give you any hassle, grab the fire extinguisher and wrap it round their heads.

Level 4: The Corridor

This level is fairly straightforward. The best method to defeat all the gangsters is to slide-attack the guys with guns and use their dropped weapons to kill the others. If you need more weapons, smash up the bins to the right of the corridor. There are not many guards on this level so it

The best way to deal with the unfashionable baseball-cap-wearing guards is with their own firearms.

shouldn't take much to complete. The only really tough enemies are the two massive Big Ron lookalikes that bust their way in through the security doors, but a couple of slide attacks will soon put these two down.

Level 5: Zeng's Office

Doctor Zeng makes a guest appearance just before he laughs heartily and legs it to his chopper, leaving you to contend

with his Vixen bodyguards. Looking like an Eighties dance troupe, these nubile young ladies attack in packs of three and are constantly being reinforced. You will have to defeat 13 of them to complete this stage. To do this you should use your running attacks and stay on the move – if you get into a fist fight you will come off worse. So don't just lay into them, no matter how tempting! Thankfully, after this stage you can save your game.

Level 6: High Street

A tough biker gang join the battle against the good guys. To complete this level you will have to kick some serious leather-clad backside. You start off standing next to some crates as the first group attack: chuck these before the bad guys get too close. If you miss, be prepared to dodge as the bikers usually chuck them back. Stay on the move and watch out for the bikers on Hawgs that try to ram you. To deal with these bozos, stand near the kerb and wait until they drive towards you before dodging out of the way: they will crash, enabling you to pick up iron bars and tyres from the wreckage with which to inflict more carnage.

When you have dealt with the first group, walk on down the road. An armoured car will cause a taxi to crash and several gangsters will jump from the back. Most of these dudes are armed with switchblades and bottles. Naturally you must take this glassware for yourself and perform some unnecessary surgery. If you run out of weapons, head to the kerb and pick up the crates lying there. Don't bother trying to wreck the taxi or the van as they are indestructible.

Once you have finished with the crew of the armoured car, some jaffa in a helicopter turns up and tries to put a few holes in you with an automatic weapon. Keep running and turning and he will eventually run out of ammo and leave. Continue down the road and the last group of bikers will arrive to have a go. Get as many weapons as you can to fight these fools off, but watch out for reinforcements coming out of the shop doors to outflank you.

Level 7: Truck Driver

Somebody must have nicked his Yorkie because this guy's really annoyed. After ploughing through a row of parked cars he jackknifes his rig and comes storming out ready for a ruck. The police 'bravely' cordon off the area, leaving you to deal with this meatball of a man. Stay away from him at all costs as his fists inflict serious damage. Keep running around the arena and pick up wreckage to hurl at him. If you can get your hands on the fire axe you're in business: hack away at him Jack Nicholson style and kick him when he's down. He won't sustain too much of this abuse before expiring.

Whilst he is being carted away in the back of an ambulance, you are given a choice of route. You can go to the Bronx (A8), the park (B8), or the mall (C8/9) by walking in the appropriate direction.

Level A8: Bridge To The Bronx

To get to the mean streets of the Bronx you must first cross a barricaded bridge laden with assorted punks. If you want to increase your destruction bonus you can smash up the barriers at the start before getting on with the job in hand.

Grab a paving slab and walk up the street: four punks will drop from the bridge to bar your path. The punks come at you in a group, so the paving slab should take out a few of them before you wade in with your fists. Scrap the car near you to get the gun and walk up the street. Some charming young ladies will step from the shadows and attempt to give you a makeover, 'switchblade' style. Use the gun to drop them before they get too close and pick up the blades to replace your empty gun.

As you approach the school bus it erupts in a ball of fire. A gang of punks emerge from the wreckage: floor the one with the rocket launcher first, then use it

on the rest of the gang. When you have dealt with these minions, run behind the bus and smash up the crate to gain a health pack. Another bunch of punks advance down the street to have a go, use the launcher to rapidly dispose of these poorly dressed individuals. Run to the abandoned car when you are out of ammo and smash it up to get the shotgun. Fire at the last gang until your shells run out, then leg it back down the road and pick up some paving slabs to finish them off before continuing on to finish the level.

Level A9: The Bridge Part Two, The Bronx

As you enter the Bronx you are almost immediately surrounded by thugs. Down the guy with the baseball bat and use his weapon to clear some fighting space. When the first wave have died violently, head right towards the crates and smash them up to get some health. You can also equip yourself with a box to throw at the next gang of punks.

Take care as you approach the bridge, as dynamite is dropped when you go beneath it. Don't waste time trying to smash up the car or you will be hit by the dynamite – there's only an iron bar in the boot anyway. Instead run quickly under the bridge and head towards the end of the street . To the left is a crate containing health and some chuckable paving slabs. Use the latter to deal with the final gang and finish this deadly section at long last.

Level B8: The Park

There is not much to the park level, it's just a wide open space with a few weapons and health kits dotted around. Only choose the park route if you have a fast character, as there is a lot of space for you to exploit. The medikits on the first section are located in the drinking fountains to the left of the park. You can

equip yourself with huge rocks from the garden to lob at your adversaries – look out for the winos as they have the same idea and are better shots with the blocks of concrete than you are.

There is a biker that decides to make an appearance near the end of the section, but you can lure him into the benches and knock him off his bike with ease. The parts of his machine make excellent GBH-inflicting devices, as do the litter bins scattered about the park. All you need to do to complete this level is to slide-attack the bad guys constantly whilst picking up their weapons to supplement your attacks.

Level 9: Park Part Two

Packing crates prove invaluable for improving race relations.

Much the same as the previous level but with a few more motorbikes and a wider fighting arena to contend with. The health kits are in the fountains to the top-left of the screen, in case you need them.

Level C8/9: The Mall

Some guys just don't know how to take a hint. Use the bottles provided to ruin his good looks.

When the going gets tough, the tough go shopping. Well, it seems that every tough guy in town has gone down to Kwiksave today and you have to fight them all for the last pack of No Frills crisps. The first gang of angry shoppers are soon upon you so keep your mind on the action. Kick the tables to knock the bottles off and use them to carve up some bad guys. If you get low on energy, demolish the hot-dog stand and gorge yourself back to health. If you are in a Jackie Chan mood, lure the bad guys towards you and kick the chairs at them – they have a habit of rebounding

fighting force

continued

off bad guy shin so stand well back when you have sent one flying.

In the next section there are more bad guys on the lookout for bargains. Beat them to the floor whilst smashing the shop fronts to pick up destruction points. The final battle of this section takes place in a car showroom. You can wreck the car and the surrounding speakers to get more destruction points, but don't forget to deal with the bad guys beforehand as most of them are packing heat.

Level 10: The Subway

The three alternate routes converge here. Barriers block your entry to the subway station: you can either demolish the token machine and buy your way in or demolish the barriers to get in for free. Once you have got through this minor obstacle the real action begins. Suitcases and hat boxes go flying as a couple of street gangs attempt to drive you off their turf. Naturally you must join in this highly amusing activity and cause your opponents severe harm in the process. If you get low on energy and weapons there's a trusty cola machine in the bottom-right corner of the platform, asking to be written off.

Once you have dealt with the first few waves of thugs, reinforcement gangsters will start arriving by train . Run past these and head towards the far end of the platform where there are cones aplenty to hurl at the oncoming hordes. If you start taking a beating there are some crates in the top-left corner of the screen that can be smashed up to get medipacks.

Level 11: Exo The Subway Boss

This bandit packs a meaty punch so don't go hand to hand with him unless you have to. The best way to deal with this metal-limbed freak is to attack him at a distance with the luggage that is strewn about the platform. Put a lot of distance between you and him before you pick anything up or the words 'dead' and 'meat' will be applicable. After you have bounced seven or so boxes off his riveted skull you can finally board the train to your next destination You can head for either the naval base (D13) or the military base

Level 12: The Train

It's wall to wall with bad guys from the off on this level. Use your special move to clear some space as they close in. Then, while they're wondering what's hit them, leg it down to the end of the carriage and get some luggage to use before they recover.

In the second car you are attacked from in front and behind so stay on the move. If you manage to get some space, smash the first box in the car as it contains a shotgun which will shorten the odds dramatically. If you are getting a pasting, smash the end two boxes in the car to get a couple of medipacks.

More bad guys pour in as you enter the third carriage. To deal with this lot do a few running attacks down the corridor as it is so narrow the poor fools cannot get out of the way. When you have floored them, quickly grab some boxes to throw and you should finish them off in no time.

Do a running attack as you head into the final car, to clear a path towards the end box which contains a much-needed medikit. When you have got this, turn around and do another running attack back down the corridor to the first box which contains some dynamite. Chuck the dynamite towards your opponents and floor them with a running attack. By the time they can stand up, the dynamite will have gone off, leaving them toasted.

(E13/14) by getting on the relevant train, after which you will be given a chance to save your progress. Note that the intermediate train stage (level 12) is identical, whichever route you choose.

Level D13/14: Air Base

Two soldiers are guarding the gate to the base: use a running attack to knock them to the ground where they can be disposed of easily. Knock the gate off its hinges and enter the main fighting arena. On the far side opposite the gate are three crates and two barrels. The crates contain a health pack, a gun, and some hand grenades. Quickly run to the crates and grab a barrel: a group of squaddies should be hot on your heels so it'll come in handy.

When these tough guys have been defeated smash up the crates and take a hand grenade. A truck will come roaring through the gates, so chuck the grenade towards it as is slows down. Reinforcements should be climbing out of the truck just as the grenade is going off, which is unfortunate for them.

Once this truckload of troops are dealt with, a chopper will fly in more men so go and get another hand grenade and chuck it at the chopper when it lands. Having made short work of the helicopter crew, a group of squaddies will run from the hangar to avenge their comrades. Run over and pick up the barrel (collecting the medikit if you need it) and chuck it at them when they arrive.

Snatch up another hand grenade when you have defeated the squaddies and run to where the chopper first landed – it's just about to make a return visit. Use the hand grenade as you did before and finish off the remainder of the chopper crew to complete the stage.

Level D15: The Rocket Pack Soldier
This airborne adversary has powerful attacks that will leave you a bit charred. If you stand still for too long he hits you with his afterburners which take off a massive chunk of energy. The best way to defeat him is to run left as you enter the arena and smash open the first box you come to. To buy yourself enough time for this, do a running high-kick and deck the jet-packer.

In the crates are three grenades: grab one, run over to the black crates, and lob it at them – they should be destroyed, revealing a gun and a health pack. Go

back to the remaining grenades and pick another one up. This time head to the three wooden crates at the other end of the field and blow them up to find a high powered gun and a rocket launcher. When you have done this, get the final grenade and chuck it at the remaining crates to release a health pack and a gun.

Now you have all this fire power it's time to use it. Pick up the gun and unload it on the jet-packer. Then proceed over to the high-powered rifle and start dispensing death with it – there are plenty of rounds in the chamber, but make every one count. Use the rocket launcher next, but stay out of the blast radius when you fire it, to stay healthy. Finally, grab the last pistol and unload it. If the jet-packer is still alive, chuck the gun at him, Police Squad style, and use a couple of running drop kicks to win this mighty scrap.

Level D16: Flying Wing
No sooner has the jet-packer been carted off on a stretcher than you are beamed aboard the flying wing. The loading bay you start in is devoid of opponents so you have ample time to rip off the iron safety railings before you enter the cockpit.

It's 'bad guy in a can' time as troops join in the melee from every side. To boost your score, smash up the stacks of computer equipment and the pilot's chair. If you need weapons, walk to either side of the cockpit and help yourself to some more safety railings. Keep running around and use the sliding attack liberally to defeat the mob of soldiers – if you remain stationary for too long they will close you down and uniformly beat the hell out of you.

Once the last of these Tom Cruise wannabes has had his flying career ended permanently, you can safely crash the flying wing into Doctor Zeng's secret base.

Level E13: Naval Base
As you walk into the naval base you are confronted by a forklift truck: stay out of the way of its forks and attack the cab at every opportunity. It cannot take more than a few hits before exploding in a ball of fire. When the truck is wasted, a nice bunch of sailors arrive to help you aboard their ship – in a body bag, that is. Don't bother smashing the crates unless you're after points, as they contain nothing.

This guy's not going to offer you a lift. So it's time to fork out some more extreme violence. Crate stuff.

Level E14: The Naval Base Part Two
No sea shanties or flared trousers to watch out for on this level, just plenty of bad guys looking for a kicking. On this stage you are attacked by a constantly reinforced group of thugs. Stay on the run to avoid being surrounded, while rushing in with a few good attacks when you have the chance. There are plenty of oil drums lying around waiting to be thrown, and quite a few barriers begging to be ripped off and used to inflict severe brain damage. If you get low on health, smash the two boxes at the bottom-right of the area or the two boxes top-left for health packs. Practically everything at the side of the arena can be destroyed, so use any spare time you have to beef up your destruction bonus.

Level E15: Vulkan
This guy's one tough hombre. Clad in a powerful armoured exoskeleton and equipped with a machine gun and rocket pack, he seems impossible to defeat at first. Get too close and he fries you with electricity; run too far away and he guns you down. To smash this metal mutha into junk you will need to grab one of the oil barrels and chuck it at him when he lands. When you have hit him with three barrels, this mechanical muchacho will trouble you no more.

Of all the bars in all the wolrd you had to get hit over the head with this one.

Level E16: Hovercraft
Quickly run to the crate and destroy it before the hovercraft crew surround you. Pick up the shotgun and kick some butt. When the crew have been gunned down,

fighting force

continued

smash up the two flare-gun racks in the middle of the craft and tool yourself up with them. A helicopter will fly some soldiers in for you to deal with. Use the pistols to even the odds before using your unarmed combat skills to dispense with them.

Where is captain Birdseye and his tasty fish fingers when you need him?

The next wave of troops are dropped in by hoverbikes. If you get low on energy, smash the air ducts at the back of the hovercraft to reveal some medipacks. When you have taken out the helmeted flyboys, the helicopter will land more thugs on the hovercraft deck. Dust these and another two waves of helmeted minions to complete the level.

Level 17: The Lab

The previous route branches converge here. Plenty of powerfisted thugs guard the lab. If you give them space to hit you, their gloves will take off a wedge of energy. They are backed up by protective-suited minions which block your flying attacks and get in a few punches if you are not ready for them. At the bottom-left of the screen are two crates: one of them contains a health pack while the other one has a stick of TNT concealed within. Collect the health and use the TNT to blast a path through the bad guys. Smash the crate at the far end to reveal a hand grenade and use it to finish off the last of

Dental work can be expensive, what with all those dentists going private nowadays, so don't stay still for long.

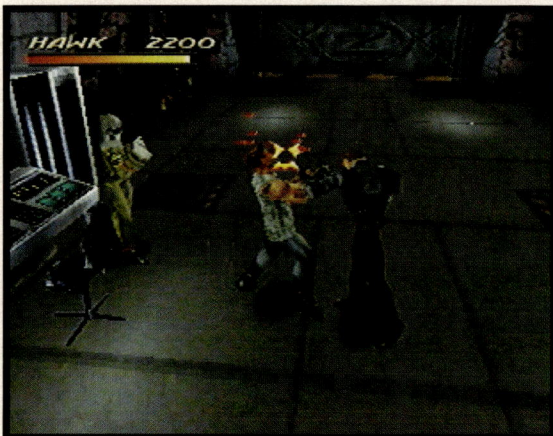

the lab guards before heading through the blast doors to the next section.

Smash the crates and get the health before running up to the cryovats. Quickly batter the creatures in the vats before the fluid drains away and they

become aggressive. The creatures regain health if you leave them for too long so be sure to give them a good working over to avoid having to fight them on full energy again. More powerfisted guards enter the lab when the creatures from the cryovat have been wasted: chin these guys and more men flood in, accompanied by some cryovat creatures. Take out the human guards before you tackle the creatures or you will get overwhelmed by enemies. Run to the lift doors and destroy the crates there to get some medipacks – you will definitely need them for the next tricky level!

Level 18: The Tower Lift

There are no health kits or weapons on this level, so you've got your work cut out. The first wave of troops begin on the platform so stay on the move and pick them off one by one to conserve energy. The next two waves are flown in by jet bikes. The easy way to deal with these guards is to isolate one and deck him, then run away if his mates get too close, before running back in to do more damage. Repeat this to deal with the rest

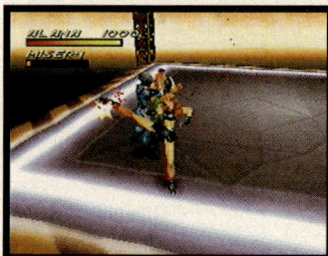

of the guards. The next wave of troops climb onto the platform: defeat these, and another wave of airborne guards that are dropped in by jet bikes, to complete the level.

Level 19: Doctor Zeng

After wading through Doctor Zeng's formidable guards, you are finally faced with the demented genius himself. Pack that ego in a box and consider the ahrm you're doing, you might say, and thankfully he is not as tough as the previous bosses. The easiest way to defeat him is to attack with quick punches then, when he blocks quickly, use a throw and put him through the floor. You need to have at least half energy remaining to defeat him, as he is bound to get in the odd uppercut whilst you are throwing him. When you have finally made him spit teeth, you can relax and watch his base collapse in ruins.

Game Over

With that slaphead Doctor Zeng out of the way, you can sell your story to a reputable tabloid. Looks like he should break out in time for the sequel though.

Publisher:	BMG Interactive
Price:	£44.99
Format:	UK

SPIDER

Spider

No **incy wincy spider**, this **eight-legged menace** is **armed to the fangs** with **lethal weapons:** from **flames** to **homing missiles**, **poison** to **electricity**. There's no **stepping on this spider** without **retribution**. And **who better** to guide you through each **creepy-crawly level** than the **bug busters?**

CHEATS

Recharge Weapons & Energy

For a complete recharge of both weapons and energy, simply pause the game and enter the following code:
△, X, X, X, O, X, □, △, X, △, O.

Shrink

Just pause the game and press:
△, □, O, △.

PASSWORDS

Laboratory
Lab Floor
1FMLC939GPR8F3BF7KT1
Sinks
CHMLC939GPR8F3LWGTS3
Lab Top 86MLC939GPR8F3VFQ5S4
Seventies Room
FW1MC939GPR8F3BF7KT1

Factory
Boxes FW1MC939GPR8F36DTTS3

Conveyors BSRMC939GPR8F3VTKKT1
Machine Room
WDRQC939GPR8F3LM8S95
Tubes 8WV5L939GPR8F36DTTS3
Mechanical Arm Boss
8WV5L939GPR8F3G1QJB4

City
Down The Street
9WV5L939GPR8F3LRT6S4
Side Of Building
6SXXS939GPR8F3LRT6S4
Park W9PNT839GPR8F3B9LVS3
Under The Street
N7KB3Y19GPR8F3V95HR5
Along The Street
N7KB3Y19GPR8F3GGK4T3

Museum
Display Cases
P7KB3Y19GPR8F3BPFGC3
Volcano G7KB3Y11GPR8F3BPFGC3
Dinosaur Bones
H7KB3Y1QFPR8F3QXSDS4
Model City J7KB3Y1GWPR8F31766D1
Temple K7KB3Y1B15S8F3QXSDS4
Museum Boss
K7KB3Y1B15S8F3BTQBB4

Sewer
Wells V7KB3Y1B15S8F3QS7QC1
Along The Sewer
W7KB3Y1VBVP8F3LC1M95
Food Carton
X7KB3Y1VLN7BF31CH1C3
Up The Well
Y7KB3Y1VV16QF3QS7QC1
Ryan's World

Q7KB3Y1LDRTQD3VKCDT1

Evil Lab
Circuit Boards
Q7KB3Y1LDRTQD3LCQSR3
Lab Top R7KB3Y118H56T1WTY4R4
Hard Drives
S7KB3Y118H56T1TCQSR3
Brian's Folly
T7KB3Y118H56T1FNY4R4
On The Ceiling
T7KB3Y118H56T1TC4LD1
Kip's Bonus
68KB3Y118H56T151P6C4
Brain Boss 68KB3Y118H56T1TMVM35

BASIC TACTICS

• **At the beginning** your only form of defence is a simple slash. However, you should refrain from using it. If you can jump/crawl past an enemy without engaging them in combat, do so. This is important when confronted by enemies that appear whilst screen rotates.

• **Most creatures will follow** one of two patterns: they either walk in one direction around a crate, or pace back and forth along a straight surface. Anticipating their movement is easy, so if you can get by without using any weapons, do so.

• **The accumulation of DNA** icons leads to the reward of one life every time you reach one hundred; although there's little urgency to collect them as you have unlimited continues with the game already.

murder death kill

Publisher:	Interplay
Price:	£44.99
Format:	UK

start

1 player   Memory   Dual Analogue

With the world in danger, a new breed of **hero is born**. And as **Kurt dons a shiny metallic outfit** and battles the **forces of evil**, the **gun-toting specialists** bring you **the exclusive solution** to this **dark**, massive and humorous **shoot-'em-up extravaganza**.

PICK UPS

Health:

Sweet
It may not be much, but this 1% is still hard to refuse.

Apple
The most common health boost throughout the game. This juicy apple gives you an extra 10% of health.

Turkey
A hunk of meat! This Christmas meal will give you a much-needed 50% of health.

Shake
This green concoction gives you a massive 100% health boost. A tasty and most welcomed treat. However, this health shake is very rare. So use it only when you're near death.

World's Most Cowardly Power-Up
Now we've seen it all. A pick-up with legs that gets scared and runs away if approached!

Normal:

Bones Air-Strike
Your partner in crime (a white dog!) takes out the enemies with a barrage of fire-power.

Dummy Decoy
You'll find these life-saving decoys on most levels. By flinging one of these out, your enemies will turn their attentions onto this blow-up doll (ahem), leaving you to open fire on them without any resistance whilst they're distracted.

Earthworm Jim
One of the more amusing pick-ups. But only to be used when you have an enemy in your sights. By moving over one, a large cow falls from the sky and squishes an enemy.

Gunta Snack
Self-explanatory really. This sea-lion-like food feeds the enormous Gunta.

Hand Grenade
Used for destroying/damaging most things that move in the game. Just don't stand too close to the explosion, otherwise you'll feel the effects too.

Super Chain Gun
A weapon even Arnie would be envious off. This powerful pick-up increases the strength of your chain gun by more than 100%. The only downside is its limited 200 bullets.

Thumper
If you want to give your opponents a bumpy ride, this hammer will certainly do the job. It damages anything near it by vibrating the ground.

Tornado
When the tornado is tossed out, it then begins creating a massive wind, drawing helpless enemies to their doom.

World's Most Interesting Bomb
Truly a fascinating weapon. This bomb catches the attention of all the enemies nearby. As they crowd round to stare at this remarkable weapon, they're helpless to do anything about the imminent explosion.

World's Smallest Nuclear Bomb
Not since the editor's underpants has something contained such a powerful explosive device. This particular lethal weapon is used for removing atomic locks which prevent you from leaving through the Arena doors.

Sniper:

Homing Bullets
These only come into effect when in Sniper Mode. They're a more accurate bullet than the standard issue to use, due to their homing capabilities.

Homing Sniper Grenade
Like the homing bullets, these grenades can home in on their target, providing you with a more accurate shot. But even more important, they can follow moving targets for up to five seconds.

Mortar
Another weapon used exclusively for Sniper Mode. This bomb-like weapon is fired high into the air, then, if judged correctly, falls down and blows the targeted enemy sky high. This particular brand of homicidal device also comes in the usual homing style destructive issue.

Sniper Grenade
The standard sniper grenade is a very effective weapon, especially if the head-shot technique is executed (see walkthrough World 1, Arena 2). Just remember, you only receive a certain amount of bullets, so don't miss your target.

murder death kill

continued

Arena 1

From the starting ledge, enter Sniper Mode and zoom in on the two Sentry Guns at the end of the arena. Destroy both of them and then exit Sniper Mode. Use the chain gun to kill the Flying Guard as it moves towards you, then float down into the arena.

Take out the first set of Guards with the chain gun, then position yourself in the centre of the arena and use Sniper Mode to zoom in on the two Doorstops that are holding the large door shut in the distance. Shoot both of these off and the door will crash down and destroy the Sentry. Stay in Sniper Mode and head-

On your approach to wee bony Scotland, collect the pick-ups if possible.

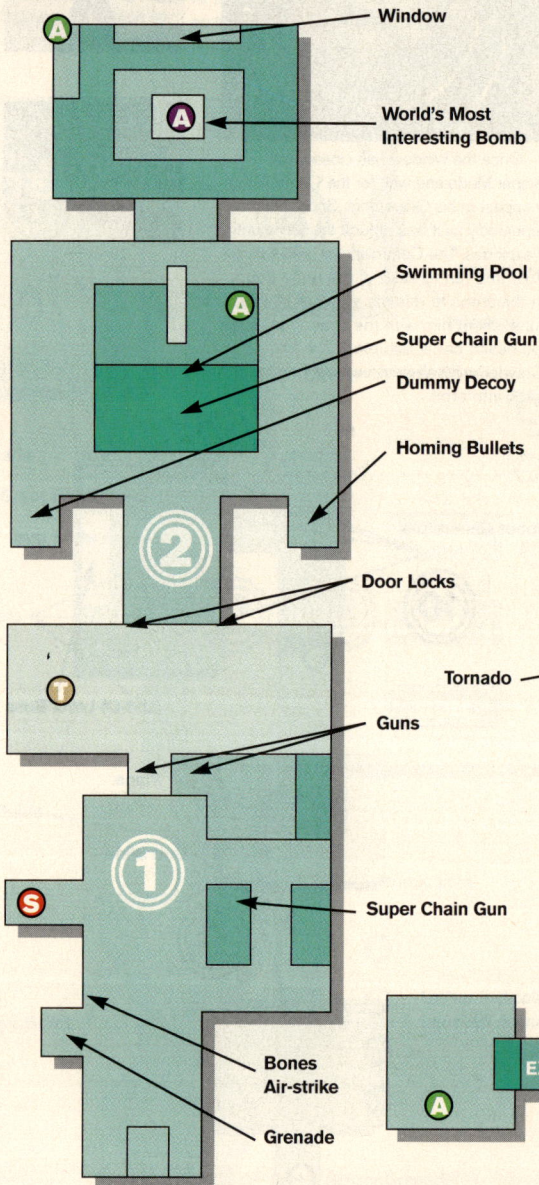

shoot the two Suicide Guards who come running out towards you.

Next, find the ramp on the right-hand side of the room and follow it up. Then jump across to the upper platform. Kill the Leaping Guard which is standing there, then climb onto the sloping platform on your left. Follow this up and jump over to the platform with the Super Chain Gun pick-up. Collect this and then jump and float across to the other side of the arena to collect the Bones Air-Strike pick-up. Drop back down to the arena floor and exit the level by the open doorway, killing any surviving Guards in the arena.

Arena 2

Stand in the entrance to this arena and

use sniper mode to kill both of the Sentry Guns. Exit sniper mode and use your chain gun to destroy the guards to the left and right of the entrance. Run into the two alcoves behind the guards and collect the two pick-ups; Homing Sniper bullets and a Dummy Decoy. Drop down into the drained pool and collect the Super Chain Gun. Climb back out of the pool and kill all of the Guards who have dropped into the arena. Once these have been destroyed, walk behind the diving board to find the pool annex. Kill all of the guards in here and collect the Apple health power-up. Wait for the two Flying Drones and the Sky Sled riding Guard to break into the room through the window, and then kill the two drones. Throw the

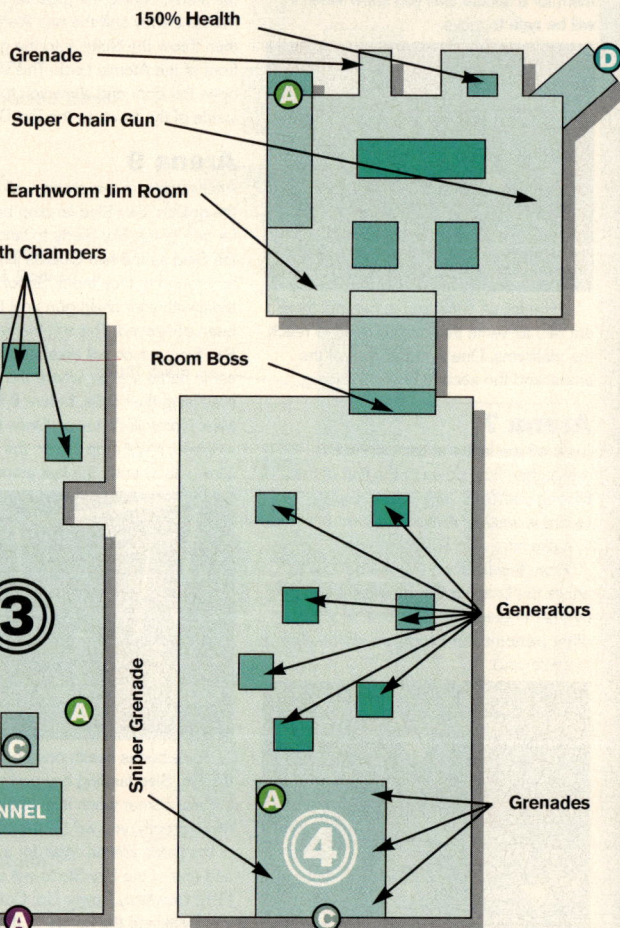

Window

World's Most Interesting Bomb

Swimming Pool

Super Chain Gun

Dummy Decoy

Homing Bullets

Door Locks

Guns

Super Chain Gun

Bones Air-strike

Grenade

150% Health

Grenade

Super Chain Gun

Earthworm Jim Room

Growth Chambers

Tornado

Room Boss

Sniper Grenade

Generators

Grenades

EXPLODING TUNNEL

Dummy Decoy back towards the pool area to distract the Guard on the Sky Sled and then enter Sniper Mode (making sure you're in a position to shoot his head. Zoom in on his face and perform a head shot to cause the Sky Sled to drop to the floor. Exit sniper mode and jump on to the Sled to collect the Worlds Most Interesting Bomb from the top of the room. Drop down the shaft to exit the arena.

Arena 3

Kill both of the Sentry Guns at the start of this arena, then enter the glass tunnel. Use a Homing Sniper bullet to head-shoot the Guard at the end of the tunnel and to break it open. Float down into the room and make your way to the room at the rear of the arena. Collect the Twister pick-up and then use your chain gun to shoot each of the three Guard Containers until they break. When the last one is destroyed, the pipe leading back in the main room will turn green and shatter. Come back out and jump on to the platform in the centre of the arena.

Arena 4

Collect all of the pick-ups in this tiny room and then shoot repeatedly at the wall with your chain until the room breaks and reveals the arena outside. Use your grenades to blow up the seven Guard Generators in this room, at the same time taking out any Guards. If the room gets crowded, use the Twister pick-up to destroy the Guards.

Finally, kill the Sentry at the exit to unlock the door which leads to the arena.

Arena 5

Walk to the edge of the platform which looks down into this arena, then use Sniper Mode to shoot the two Sentry Guns in each corner of the room.

Next, jump onto the Blue Triangular

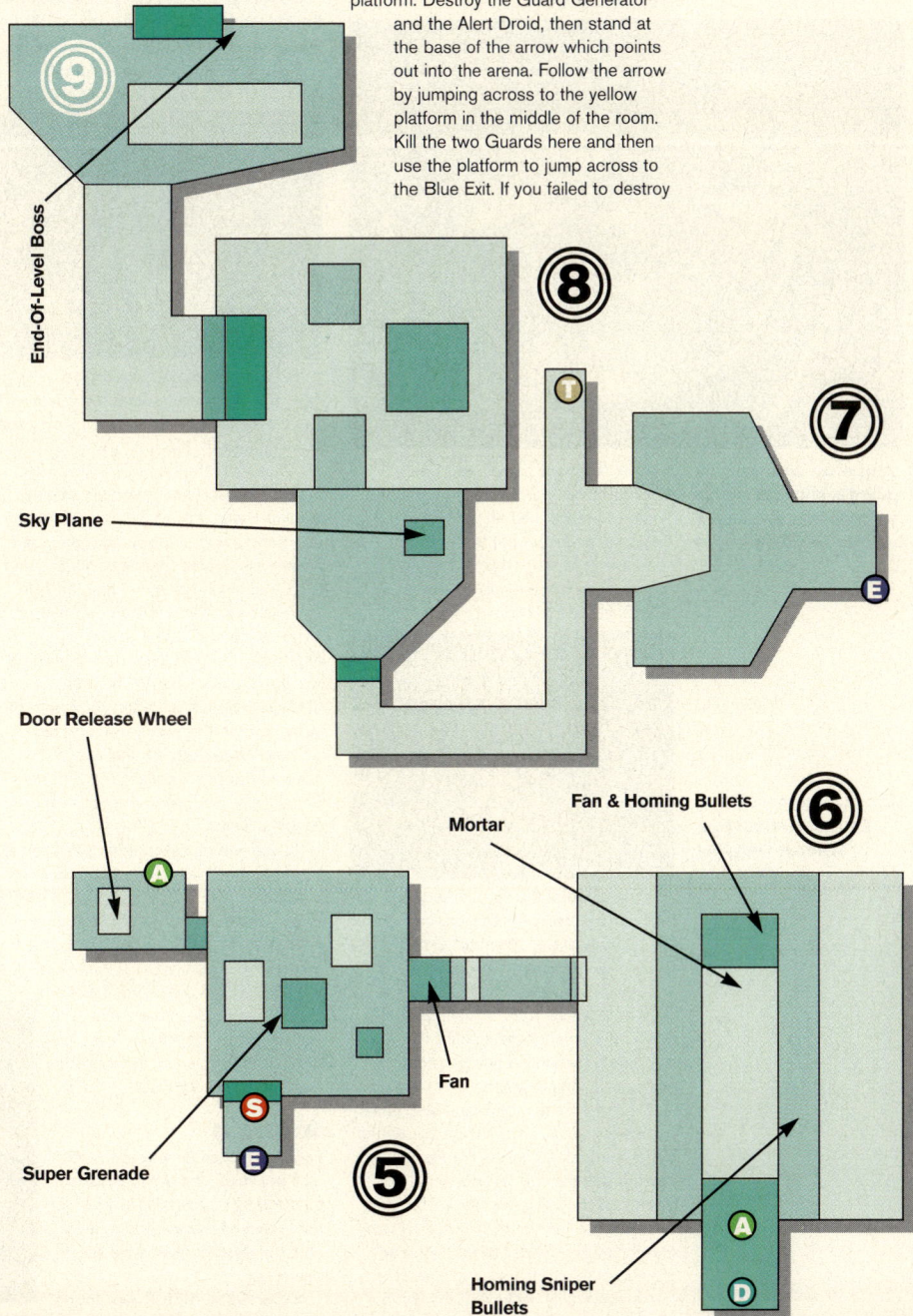

platform to your right, and enter Sniper Mode again. Target the Blue Exit in the top right of the arena and wait for the Floating Sentry to appear. Now shoot him until he's destroyed – a good tip here is to use Sniper Grenades.

Drop down to the floor and collect the Most Cowardly power-up. Watch out for the Leaping Guards in this room. Try to jump in to the Blue Cave on the left-hand side of the room and then pick them off from here. Once they have been killed,

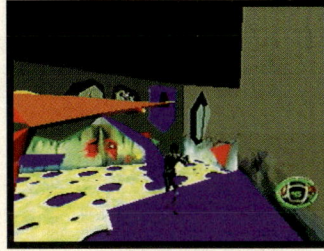

It's Rainbow time, but hey, where's Geoffrey & Bungle?. Oh look, there they are, hiding behind the blue window.

jump up to the left red cave and follow the red passageway up to the green platform. Destroy the Guard Generator and the Alert Droid, then stand at the base of the arrow which points out into the arena. Follow the arrow by jumping across to the yellow platform in the middle of the room. Kill the two Guards here and then use the platform to jump across to the Blue Exit. If you failed to destroy

⑨

End-Of-Level Boss

⑧

①

⑦

Sky Plane

E

Door Release Wheel

Fan & Homing Bullets

Mortar

⑥

A

Fan

S

E

⑤

Super Grenade

A

D

Homing Sniper Bullets

murder death kill

continued

the Floating Sentry at the start of this arena, watch out for it when you jump into the exit!

Arena 6

Stand at the top of the slop that leads down into this arena and use Sniper Mode to zoom in and destroy the two Sentry Guards at the far end of the arena. Next, target the rotating Gun Pod and zoom in closer. Fire one shot at it to get its attention, the quickly shoot through its open front section to head-shoot the operator.

Above: An unsuspecting guard is about to get his just desserts as a sniper bullet is aimed directly at his forehead.

Walk down the slope and kill all of the Guards that jump down into the trench. When you reach the end of the trench, jump into the air-current to be lifted to the upper levels of the arena. At the top, quickly move forward and kill all the Guards at the top of the air-shaft.

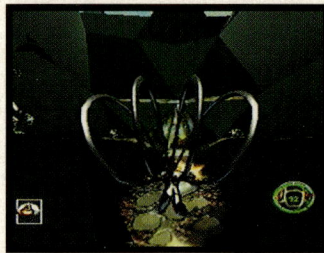

Right: Using your Ribbon Chutes, take out your enemies with your chain gun.

Now, stand at the rear of the arena, so that you are facing the Sentry and the Two Guards at the other end. Enter Sniper Mode and zoom in on the Sentry. If you have a Sniper Grenade, use this to perform a one-hit head shot. If not, just use normal sniper bullets until it has been destroyed. Remember you can strafe while still in Sniper Mode.

Once the Sentry has been killed, take out the two guards and then move up the trench's edge and collect the Apple power-up at the end. As you move to collect it, four Flying Drones will fly down the length of the trench, followed by two Guards on Sky Sleds. When they reach the end of the trench, they will pause and turn around to fly back up. Zoom in on

them when stationary and use the head-shot technique to leave a Sky Sled floating in the air. Run back down to it and jump on. This will then fly you over to collect the Thumper and the Health power-up. Jump off the sled when it has stopped moving and exit through the door in the top left of the arena.

Arena 7

After floating up the air-shaft, stand in front of the glass window and select the Thumper from your inventory. Shoot the glass with your chain gun and then throw the Thumper down into the arena. This will kill and damage some of the Guards in the arena. Now jump down and finish the rest off with your chain gun.

Note: If you did not collect the Thumper from the previous arena, you will have to kill the guards with just your chain gun and sniper gun.

Once all of the enemies in this arena have been destroyed, jump up onto the block in the middle of the floor. Once on top, turn around until you can see a dark hole in a wall, above another block. Jump across to this block then enter the hole.

Inside you will find a three-pointed object at the bottom of a slope, and a health power-up. Collect the power-up and then shoot repeatedly at the object to make it spin. Leave the room and the large door in the arena will now have opened. Walk through the newly opened door and collect the Sweet power-ups, but watch out for a lone Suicide Guard.

At the end of the corridor, you'll find a large room with a strange Alien Structure guarded by two Leaping Guards. Kill both of the Guards and then shoot at the front left side of the structure with your chain gun so that it sprays red fragments. Once this section has collapsed, destroy the opposite side in the same way. When both sections have been destroyed, shoot the exposed inside to reveal the Exit.

Arena 8

Follow the passageway to the left until you reach the arena entrance, guarded by an Alert Droid. The right-hand passageway is a dead end, but does contain a Health power-up.

Destroy the Alert Droid, then

wait for the Guard on a Sky Sled to fly into the room. Use your chain gun to kill him and then jump onto the grounded Sled. This will then take off and fly around the arena. As you move, turn on the spot and use your chain gun to kill

the Flying Drones as they attack you. The Sky Sled will eventually crash through the far wall and you will enter the last arena.

Arena 9

Enter the arena and collect the Turkey Health power-up hidden on the right-hand side of the room. Then stand in front of the large wheel on the rear wall of the room. A wave of the Alien Dogs will roll out from the holes under the wheel and attack you. At the same time, the Mine Controller will start to rotate the wheel. Kill all of the Alien Dogs with your chain gun and then wait for the wheel to stop spinning. When it does, enter Sniper Mode and zoom in on the one of the four Red Domes that appear on the rim of the wheel. Shoot it off and then exit Sniper Mode. The remaining Domes will then shoot once before disappearing as the wheel starts to spin again. Repeat this process for the rest of the Domes: when they've all been destroyed, the Mine Controller will fall out of his room and explode. Well done! It's time to move on...

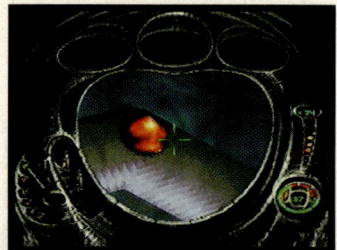

WORLD FOUR

Arena 1

After landing, jump off and float down into the chasm with your Ribbon Chutes. As you float down, turn around so that you're facing the opposite direction. As you near the bottom, position yourself so that you are directly over the Ice Sheet and drop down onto it. The Ice will break and allow you to continue floating down into the next room. If you turned to face the right direction, you should now be in a direct line of sight with the large Sentry. Shoot at him with your chain gun to destroy him.

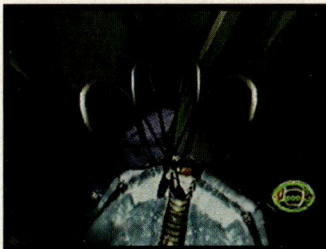

There is also a Super Chain Gun pick-up on the platform to your right, protected by a Guard. You can kill this Guard and collect the Super Chain Gun to help kill the Sentry faster. Once he has been destroyed, kill the rest of the Guards in the room and then climb up to the platform where the Sentry was floating. Here you will find a Snowboard: walk onto it and it'll launch you down the ramp, through the glass door.

Arena 2

Steer left and right to navigate the tunnel – holding ⇩ will make you brake. Shoot the Guards and Stop Boards in this arena as you approach them, and be careful to avoid the large rocks.

Arena 3

Once you have landed in this arena, shoot the Guard standing next to the Console, then fire a couple of shots at the Console to summon a Ship. Stand back as the Ship lands, and kill the two Guards as they leap out. Once they have been destroyed, walk into the Ship to enter Bombing Mode. The Ship will now fly you around the arena, before returning you to the start area.

As you are flown around, use the fire button and the on-screen target to drop bombs on to the arenas Guards and Gun Towers. This will make your journey

through the arena easier.

Once back on the ground, destroy the small hut next to you and collect the Dummy Decoy pick-up from inside. Now run into the arena and make your way over to far side. If you missed any of the Gun towers or Gun Pods in the Bombing Run, use Sniper Mode to head-shoot the Gun Controllers through the open front of the pods.

As you near the Exit in the far wall of the arena, collect the pick-ups and then throw the Dummy Decoy in front of you to

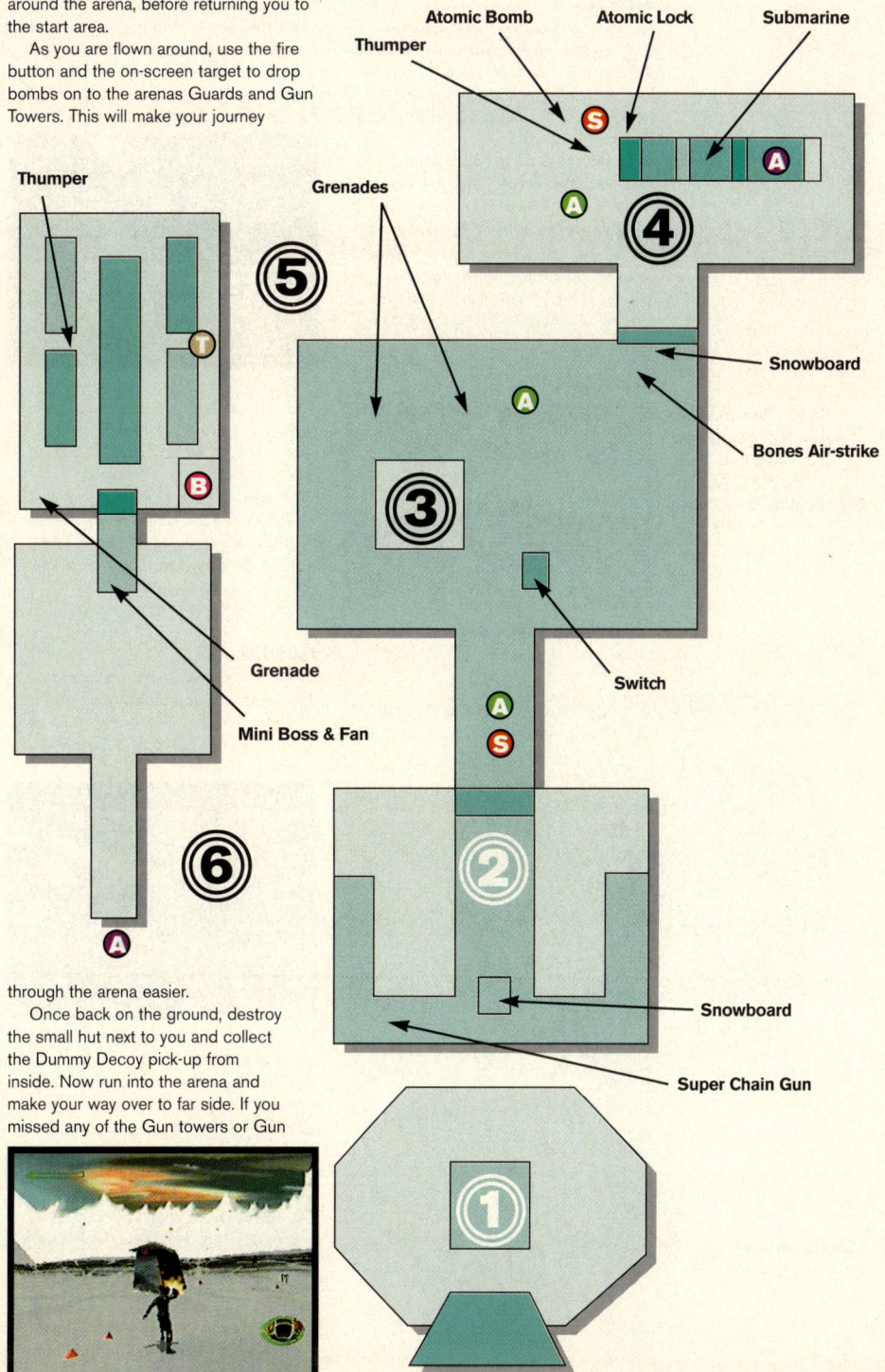

Map labels:
- Atomic Bomb
- Atomic Lock
- Submarine
- Thumper
- Grenades
- Thumper
- Grenade
- Mini Boss & Fan
- Snowboard
- Bones Air-strike
- Switch
- Snowboard
- Super Chain Gun

murder death kill

continued

distract the Guards and Sentry. While they are shooting at the Decoy, kill them with your chain gun. Once they have been destroyed, exit the arena through the cave and walk on to the next Snowboard.

Arena 4
As you snowboard down this tunnel, collect all of the Ten Bones to receive a pick-up at the end. Also, collecting the Earthworm Jim pick-ups will give the enemies a nasty surprise by dropping a cow on their heads!

When you reach the split level section of the tunnel, jump with your snowboard to land on the upper level. If you have collected all of the Bones in the tunnel, then when you reach the end a supply ship will fly down into the tunnel with a Twister pick-up hanging beneath it. Jump up as it passes over you to collect it.

Arena 5

Right: Take out that damn ugly guard with your chain gun. Then collect the World's Smallest Nuclear Bomb beside him.

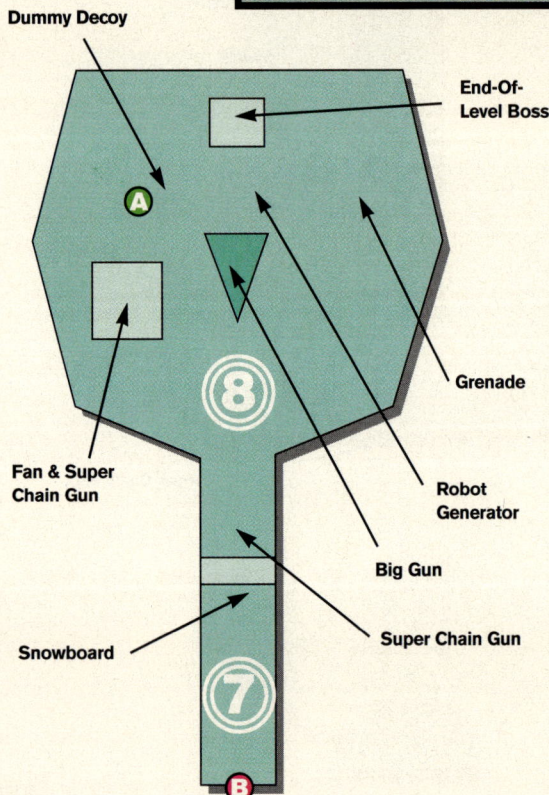

Dummy Decoy

End-Of-Level Boss

A

8

Grenade

Fan & Super Chain Gun

Robot Generator

Big Gun

Super Chain Gun

Snowboard

7

B

Float down into this arena and shoot the three Flying Drones as they approach you. Once these have been killed, climb up onto the Submarine and make your way along to the tail section to collect a Sniper Grenade. Use this to destroy the Guards and a Tank will be flown into the arena. Blow up the Tank, from either a sniper position on top of the Submarine, or from the ground with your chain gun. Once it has been destroyed, collect the World's Smallest Nuclear Bomb and kill the remaining Guards.

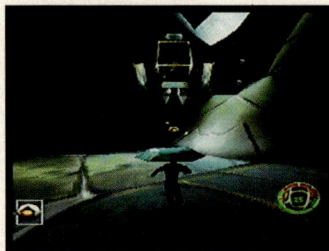

Now find the Atomic Lock on the Submarines door and use the Nuke to open it. Enter the Submarine, and you will come face to face with the Sub Boss. Destroy him by throwing Grenades into the air current that holds his Pod in the air. After the right amount, the Pod will blow up and allow you to float up the air current and into the passageway above. Follow the passageway to the next arena.

Arena 6
Destroy all of the Guard Generators in this arena with your chain gun, then kill all of the Guards. Blow open the crates to reveal power-ups and pick-ups to collect.

Approach the floating Gun Pod and either use the chain or throw Grenades into the air current to destroy it. Use the air current to float up to the next level, and then walk onto the Snowboard to exit the arena.

Arena 7
Like the previous snowboarding level, collect all Ten Bones for a Twister pick-up. When you reach the fork in the tunnel, take the path to the right to collect a Super Chain Gun pick-up. As you progress through the tunnel, collect the Earthworm Jim pick-ups to drop a cow on the enemy Gun Pods.

Arena 8
After landing in this arena, jump into the air current to float up and collect the Super Chain Gun pick-up. While you're floating, shoot down the enemy Ship and then drop down and collect the scattered pick-ups.

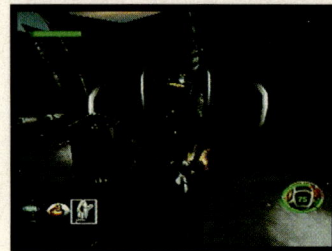

Run into the next section of the arena and destroy the Guard Generator with the super chain gun. Once destroyed, it will release a Most Cowardly Power Up. Collect this for a health boost, then enter the last room of the arena.

Avoid the Gun Pod Boss's bombs and destroy the crate to the left of the room. This will release a Dummy Decoy. Collect this and throw it to distract the Boss. Next, run over to the other side of the room and destroy the rest of the crates to receive a large supply of Grenades. Stand in front of the Gun Pod Boss and throw the grenades into the air-stream. Keep throwing the grenades until the boss is destroyed and you exit the arena.

MORE...

WORLD FIVE

Arena 1

From the starting position in this arena, enter Sniper Mode and wait for the Mothership to fly overhead. Follow it as it turns and wait for it to come to a stop. Now quickly shoot off each of the Gun Pods on its side to send it crashing down.

Exit Sniper Mode and run up into the arena. Use your chain gun to destroy all of the Guards in this area, and then find the ramp on the right which leads up to a secret Sniper Position, and a Dummy Decoy. Collect the decoy and enter Sniper Mode. Look through the slit in the wall and zoom in on the Alert Droid on the far side of the arena, in front of the Atomic Locked door. Kill it, then exit Sniper Mode and walk back into the centre of the arena. A ship with a World's Smallest Nuclear Bomb will fly into the arena and drop off two Guards. Destroy the Guards and then shoot down the ship to collect the Nuke. Walk over to the left of the arena and throw the nuke at the Atomic Lock to open the Exit Door.

Arena 2

Kill both of the Guards and the Alert Droid at the start of this arena, then use the sloping platform to jump across to the next platform. Run and jump off the end of this block to reach the edge of the passageway in front of you. Stop at the entrance to the tunnel and enter Sniper Mode. Now zoom in and target the Exploding Crate at the other end of the tunnel. Shoot it to blow up a Sentry hidden round the corner of the tunnel.

Move down to the end and collect the Sniper Grenade from the edge of the platform. Quickly enter Sniper Mode and use the Sniper Grenades to kill the Sentry at the other side of the arena.

When he has been destroyed, drop down into the arena and run over to the platform where the Sentry was floating. Climb up onto the platform and collect a Super Chain Gun pick-up. Use this to destroy the Gun Ship which takes off from the centre of this arena.

Once destroyed this will release a Forklift, which will try to ram you. Kill the driver by shooting the Glass Dome off it, and then use your chain gun to push it over to the yellow panel on the floor. This will deactivate the Force Field and allow you to drop down the Exit Hole.

Arena 3

Float up the air shaft and then drop down onto the ramp which leads up into the arena. Kill the two Guards and the Alert Droid at the top of the ramp and then face the far Control Room. Enter Sniper Mode and zoom in on the Technician in the control room. Shoot once to break the glass and then keep shooting at the Technician until he falls over backwards and hits the button on the wall behind him. Exit Sniper Mode and wait for the Support Arm to blow up and release the Ship. Once it does, shoot off each of the Gun Pods on the underside of the Ship, being careful to dodge the gunfire.

Once they have all been destroyed, run to the front of the Ship and use Sniper

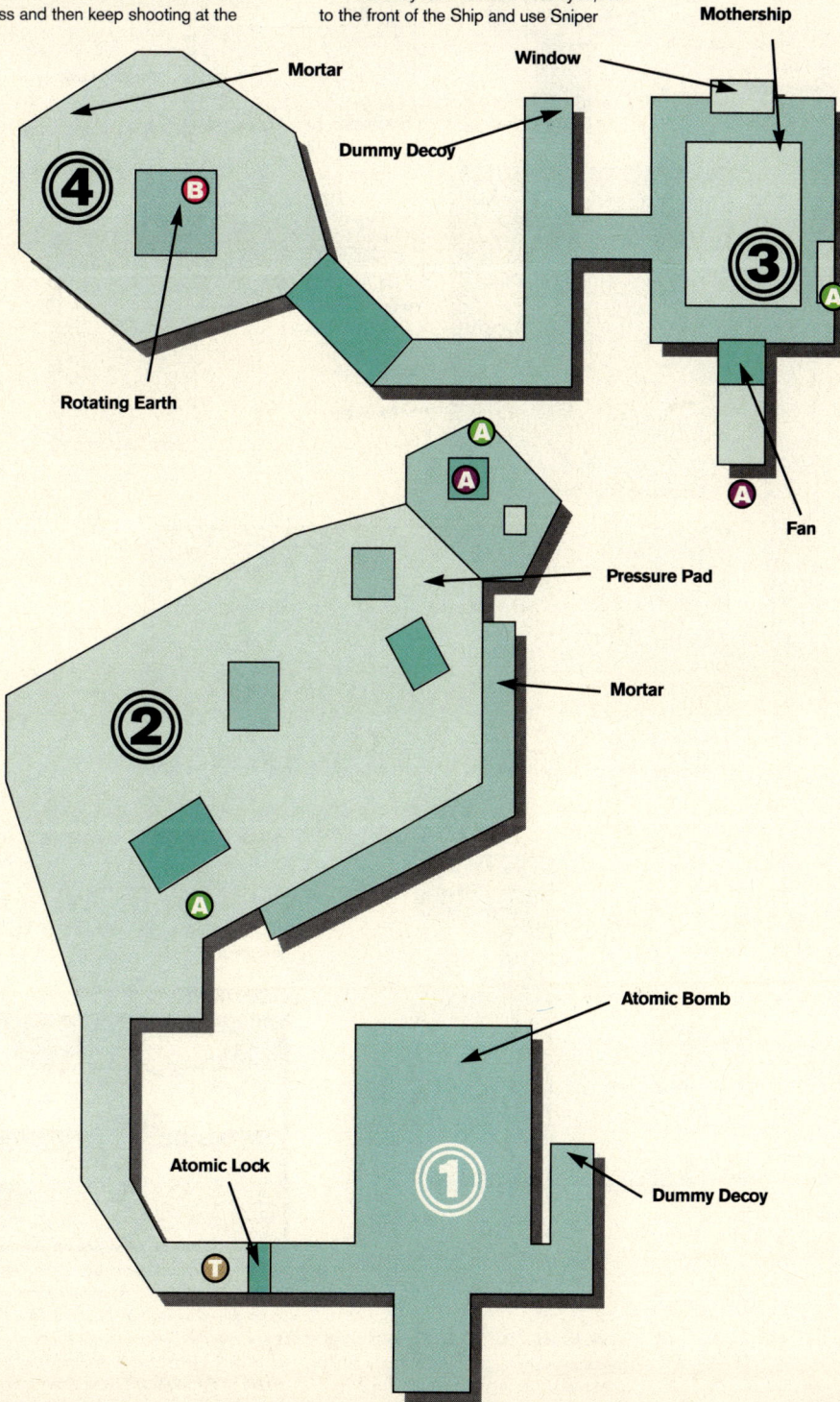

murder death kill

continued

Atomic Bomb

Super Chain Gun

Atomic Lock

Robot Generator

Atomic Lock

Atomic Bomb

Ⓐ

Ⓓ

Ⓐ

Ⓐ

⑥

Ⓒ

Thumper

Ⓐ

⑤

Ⓢ   Ⓢ

Ⓐ

Ⓒ

Mode to target the Ship's Pilot. Kill him and the Ship will lose control and crash into the right wall of the arena, breaking it open.

Exit Sniper Mode and kill all the Guards in the arena, then take out the Sentry. Now jump up through the broken wall and collect the Dummy Decoy to the right. Turn around and follow the left-hand path to the next arena.

Arena 4

Kill all the Technicians on the upper ring of this arena and then collect the Mortar pick-up on the other side of the room. Once the upper ring has been cleared, shoot repeatedly at the Spinning Globe in the centre of the room with your chain gun until

it drops down and breaks the glass floor of the room. Then jump off the upper ring and float down into the room below. As you near the bottom, use your chain gun to kill two of the Technicians working at their consoles. When two have been killed, the last one will run into the centre of the room and open a secret hatch in the floor. Drop down the hole to exit the arena.

Arena 5

Stop at the entrance to this arena and enter Sniper Mode. Then zoom in on the Alert Droid and kill it before it can raise the alarm. Next, zoom in on the two Sleeping Guards and use the head-shot technique to kill them quickly.

Now, run over to the doorway on the right and throw the Dummy Decoy out in front of you before you reach it. The Floating Guard in the room will now track this and allow you to take him out with the chain gun. After he has been destroyed, kill the two Guards in the room and collect the World's Smallest Nuclear Bomb and the Grenade pick-up.

Run back out into the centre section of the arena and enter the doorway opposite the one you just left. Kill all the Sleeping Guards and the Alert Droid in this room and then climb the ramp in the corner to reach the upper level.

Use the Grenades to blow up the three Guard Generators in the corner and then enter Sniper Mode. Zoom in to the other side of the arena and target the Alert Droid standing next to the Thumper pick-up. Kill it and then exit Sniper Mode.

Jump across to the small platform above the arena entrance, and then jump across to the other side. Collect the Thumper and the Mortars and then stand at the edge of the Green Ringed Hole. Use Sniper Mode to fire some mortars into the hole to kill the Floating Guard below, and then drop down.

Follow the corridor along and up, collecting the Sweet health power-ups as you go. The exit from the corridor is guarded by a second Floating Sentry, so use your chain gun and sidestep to kill it.

Once he has been destroyed, walk out onto the balcony and throw the Nuke onto the Atomic Lock which holds the Giant Stone Door closed.

Wait for the door to fall open and then float down and leave the arena.

Arena 6

Collect the Super Chain Gun pick-up hidden behind the first spike in this arena, then make your way forwards through the canyon. Destroy the Guard Generators, Guards and any Flying Drones until you reach the end of the canyon.

Quickly run into the last section and collect the Turkey health power-up and the World's Smallest Nuclear Bomb. Throw the Nuke at the Floating Guard standing in front of the Atomic Locked door and run back into the previous section of the canyon. Wait for the Nuke to explode and then kill the Floating Guard with your chain gun if it is still alive, before leaving through the Exit Door.

Arena 7

Run over to the blocks on the left when you enter this arena, and climb up to collect a Dummy Decoy pick-up. Turn to face the Guards which drop down into this arena and throw the Decoy into the crowd to distract them. Now take them out with either grenades, chain gun or sniper.

Next, jump down to the floor and run over to the blocks on the far side of the room. Then climb up onto the one with the Super Chain Gun pick-up. Collect this and then use it to clear the room of the second wave of Guards. Be sure to kill the four Alert Droids, then take out the three Forklifts by shooting the Glass Domes off the top of them.

Once this has been done, drop down to the floor and use your chain gun to push one of the Forklifts over to the block on the left of the arena entrance. Push up against the block, then jump up onto the Forklift. From here you can now reach the edge of the block and pull yourself up.

Jump over to the next platform and then again to the walkway which runs across the centre of the room. Follow this across to the other blocks and jump onto the sloping block. Stand at the very top of this and turn to face the upper platform which rings the room. Jump up onto it and go round anticlockwise until you're standing beneath a platform with an Apple health power-up.

Wait for a Forklift to drive round towards you, then shoot at it so that it stops next to the platform. Jump onto the Forklift, then jump across the platform. Collect the Apple power-up, then jump across to the platform in the middle of the room. From here, turn left and float across to reach the Exit Door.

Arena 8

Stand at the top of the long ramp at the start of this arena and enter Sniper Mode. Zoom in on the Gun Pod floating at the far side of the arena and shoot it once to get its attention. When it turns to face you, shoot through the open front to kill the Gun Operator.

Once this has been destroyed, walk down the ramp and kill all the Guards in the arena. Be careful to avoid the gunfire from the two other Gun Pods. After the Guards have been killed, destroy the second Gun Pod by facing the tower it floats over and firing your chain gun. Sidestep to dodge the incoming fire until it's destroyed, then run round to the other side of the tower.

Enter Sniper Mode and use strafe to move out from behind the tower shielding you from the last Gun Pod. Look up and zoom in on the open section of the gun to kill the Gun Operator. Now run back up to the top of the ramp and turn around.

Jump off from the highest point on the ramp and float down to the right-hand tower. As you float over it, you'll be lifted up to collect an Apple. Now, turn to face the middle tower and float over into the air current. Collect the next Apple, then float over to the last tower. Collect the last Apple and turn round to face the back down the way you came. Float across the arena into the door at the top of the arena.

Arena 9

At the edge of the cave, enter Sniper Mode and zoom in on Gunta, the large Mine Crawler Supervisor. Shoot at him a couple of times and he will jump up and activate a large door.

Drop down into the arena and land on the mound in the middle of the room. Now stand at the edge and wait for a large stone boulder to roll past in the gully. Drop down after it and keep shooting at it until it explodes. Once this has been destroyed, run around the gully and collect the pick-ups which drop down.

Find the path which leads back up to the top of the centre mound and wait for the large Mothership to fly overhead. When it does, enter Sniper Mode and shoot off all of the Gun Pods on its underside. When they have all been destroyed, the ship will explode and release a wave of Guards into the arena. Kill all the Guards and Gunta will open the door, jump out into the arena and kidnap Bones.

Above: You'll find the enemy can be killed twice as fast with this Chaingun upgrade.

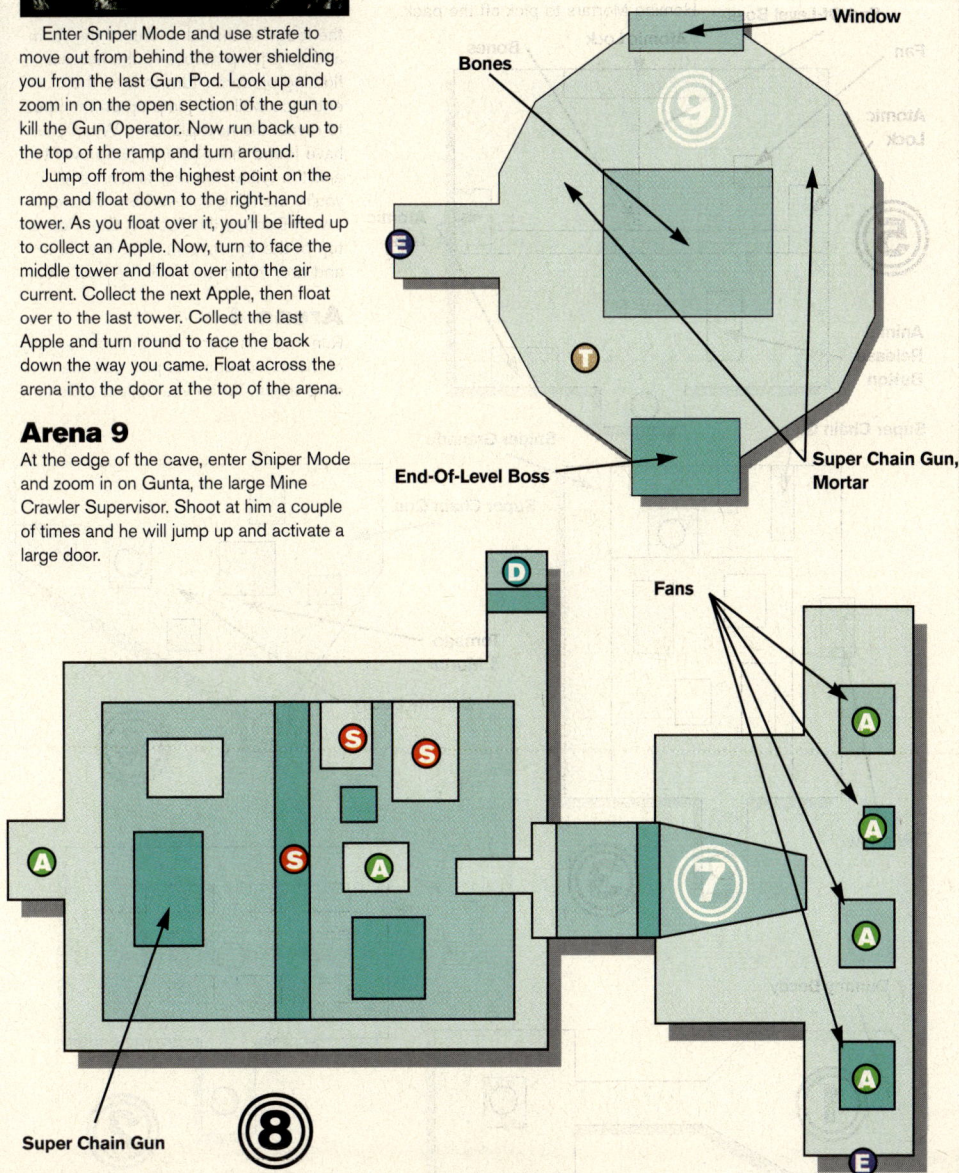

Window

Bones

E

Super Chain Gun, Mortar

End-Of-Level Boss

⑨

D

Fans

A

A

A

⑦

A

A

S

S

S

A

A

Super Chain Gun

⑧

E

murder death kill

Now sit back and watch as Gunta's greed gets the better of him.

WORLD SIX

Arena 1

Wait for the Dummy Decoy to land in this arena, then collect it. Next, wait for the Guard to roll through the Glass Wall and then run up the long sloping walkway until you reach a room with a Guard Generator and a Homing Mortar pick-up. Collect the pick-up and destroy the Generator with your chain gun. When it explodes it will leave a hole in the floor. Drop down the hole to exit the arena.

Arena 2

After landing in this arena, turn until you can see Gunta and his pack of Alien Dogs. Enter Sniper Mode and use the Homing Mortars to pick off the pack.

End-Of-Level Boss

Fan

Atomic Lock

Atomic Lock

Bones

Atomic Lock

Animal Release Button

Super Chain Gun

Sniper Grenade

Super Chain Gun

Tornado & Mortar

Dummy Decoy

Window

Dummy Decoy

Exit Sniper Mode and use your chain gun to finish off any that have survived.

When all the Alien Dogs have been killed, run up behind Gunta and chase him around the arena while firing your chain gun. After enough shots, Gunta will run into the centre of the arena and jump through the floor, leaving a hole. Drop down the hole to continue to the next arena.

Arena 3

Run down the length of the room and jump onto the lowest of the wall platforms. Climb the platforms until you reach the Super Chain Gun and collect it quickly.

Next, turn to the left and jump across to the ledge, then along the wall and collect the Homing Mortar. Run down the ledge to the other end of the room and then jump across to the nearest floating platform. Turn to face the entrance wall and jump up on the spot to reveal the next platform. When you have found this platform, jump over to it and the follow the rest around until you're standing across from the stone tower. Destroy the floating Gun Pod on top of the tower, then jump over to it and drop down to reach the next arena.

Arena 4

Run into this arena and collect as many of the power-ups and pick-ups that drop down. When you collect a Dummy

Decoy or Twister, throw it into the centre of the arena to distract the guards, then sniper Gunta on top of his tower. Shoot him enough times and he will fall off and hit the floor, causing the tall stone tower to fall over. Run back to the start of the arena and use the sloping platform to jump across to the fallen tower. Run up to Gunta's platform and drop down the hole to the final confrontation.

Arena 5

Float down into the arena and steer yourself over to the third room, with a Gunta Snack Dispenser. Jump onto the button next to the dispenser and a Gunta Snack will drop out of the machine. Collect this and throw it out into the main section of the arena. Gunta will chase after the snack, allowing you to collect the World's Smallest Nuclear Bomb from where he was standing. Once you have this, run over to the active air-vent and jump into the air current. When you're level with the platform, drop down onto it and use the Nuke to destroy the Atomic Lock.

Repeat this process for the remaining locks and Bones will be freed. After the animation has played, showing Bones jumping into the Snack Dispenser, run over and collect the Bones/Snack hybrid which drops out of the machine. Throw this at Gunta and he will run over and eat it hungrily.

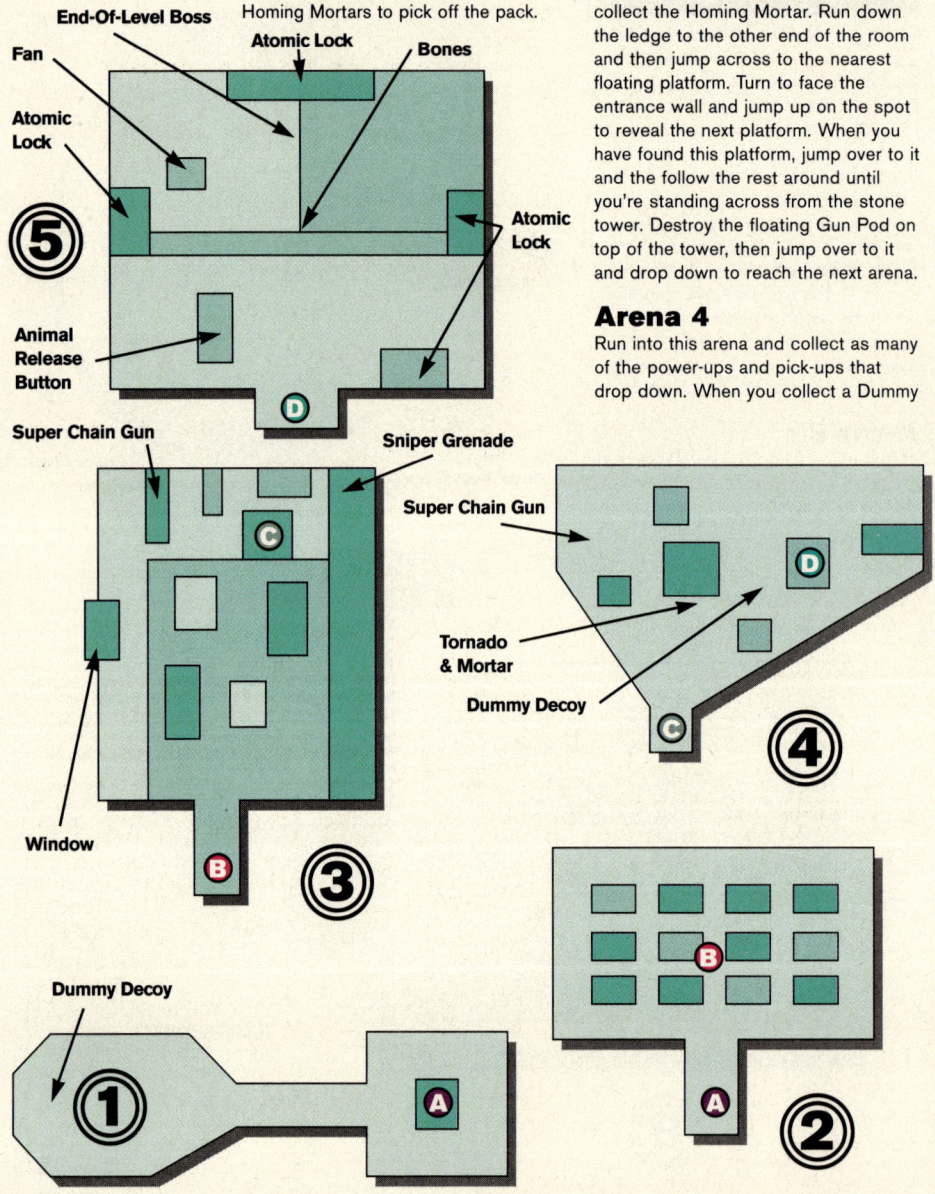

1 player	Memory	2 player	Multi-player	Split screen

RALLY CROSS

Rally Cross

Sony's latest **adrenaline-pumping racer** goes **off-road** to provide all the **thrills and spills** any **driver could want**. Following are a whole **bootful of cheats and top driving tips**. Read on and **put your foot down**.

CHEATS

All codes are entered as either the 'high score name' or (much easier) the 'new season name'. However, only one cheat code may be entered and activated at any one time.

From the starting menu, select 'one player'. Then from the subsequent menus select 'season', then 'normal'. Now enter one of the cheat codes below for the desired effect. Once the code has been entered, you can either start the season or exit back to the main menu and choose just a single race. *Note: '_' signifies a space.*

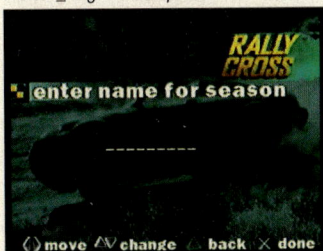

Cheat Codes

fat_tires
It doesn't take an Einstein to figure this one out. Your tyres double in width.

no_wheels
Wheels are usually an important part of the car's function. However, they're no longer needed with this cheat.

wheels
There they are. Those tyres have decided to have a race by themselves.

feather
As light as… This cheat enables your car to jump even higher than usual by making it weigh next to nothing.

stone
What goes up, must come down; and with a thud when this cheat is activated. Your car will barely lift off the ground.

float
You'll be flying like the birds when coming off any type of jump. Low gravity is a dangerous but thrilling way of racing.

spinner
You'll be able to turn on a two-pence piece when racing with this cheat as your car's tyre friction is severely reduced.

banzai
If colliding with the opposition seemed a frustrating setback, this handy cheat removes the collisions from the equation.

noviscous
You're moving along at a nice fast steady pace, then suddenly, oomph… You hit a muddy or wet patch. Not any more. Use this to avoid water and mud slowdown.

radbrad
This cheat seems to be pretty useless; unless you've just activated the float cheat. All this does is return gravity to normal.

Racing Season Codes

vet_me
Automatic promotion to the next season. This code gives you instant victory in the Rookie season.

im_a_pro
And if that's not enough, enter this code in and you'll be victorious in the Veteran season too.

weeoo
The ultimate code. Not only do you win the Normal, Head-On and Mixed Pro seasons, you also have access to all tracks and cars.

EXTRA TRACKS & CARS

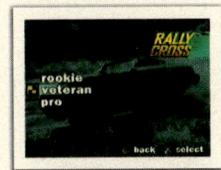

As you win each difficulty level you'll receive new tracks and cars, until finally you reveal everything – oo-er!

Once Pro level success is achieved you'll receive a fourth race type: Suicide. And they're not joking!

With each track comes three versions; a, b & c…

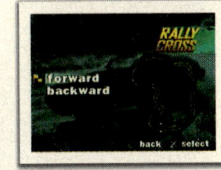

And each version lets you race forwards (normal) or backwards (mirror).

Publisher:	Sony Computer Entertainment
Price:	34.99
Format:	UK

Micro Machines v3

Never mind such **dirty tricks** as **unplugging your opponent's joypad**, or simply **thumping them** – just **follow our guide** to **come first every time**. We reveal the **special prize cars**, a **stack of cheats**, and all those **sneaky short-cuts** to stay **miles ahead of your rivals**.

1 player	Memory	Multi-player

MICRO MACHINES v3

GENERAL TIPS

• For a quick start, accelerate just after the second beep. Any earlier and you'll skid; later and you'll be left behind.

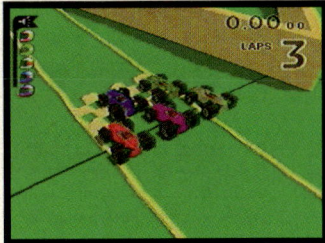

• If you're on a new track in the Challenge, take it easy on the first lap to familiarise yourself with it.
• Another way to get to the know the tracks better is to race them in Time Trial or Test Drive mode. Or use the Drone Car cheat in Debug Mode.

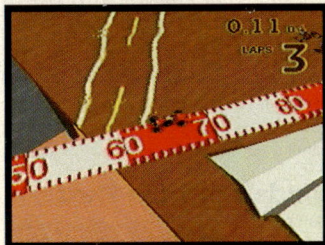

• You can repeat early races to upgrade your prize vehicles with ease, but you won't get the best ones till later.
• Experiment with short-cuts, particularly if you've no chance of winning the current race (or succeeding in the Time Trial).

THE TRACKS

There are 43 tracks in all, taking place in seven different zones, from the beach to the breakfast table.

SNOOKER

Swerve Shot

The easiest track of the lot, this is a simple circular circuit

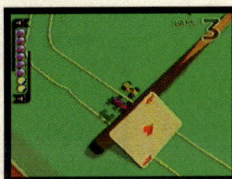

around the snooker table. Just make sure you hit the two card jumps and you should have no problems.

Rack 'N' Roll

Much trickier, this takes place over two tables. You get the second via a jump; and return through a pocket. The worst bit is driving along the cushion – be careful not to fall into the corner pockets.

Right On Cue

The trickiest part of this course is driving round the outside, so take care when going round the corner pockets and make sure you hit those card ramps up and down.

Pot Luck

A nightmare course, this takes you over three tables, linked by pockets and a huge jump – make

sure you've got enough speed. As usual, be careful round those corner pockets.

Love Triangle

Not featured in the main challenge, this features two table-to-table jumps, including one through a triangle – keep central to avoid hitting its sides. Watch out for the tricky bit around the balls.

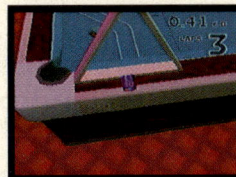

LAB

Periodic Park

A relatively easy course, following a circular chalk track. You can cut some corners to maintain your straight-line speed, including across the periodic table

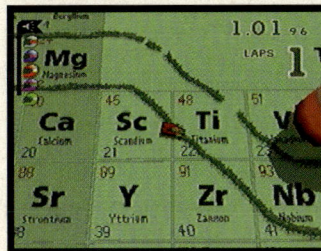

and the last bend of the lap. Line up with the tanks ahead to bomb them.

Stinky Sinks

Not too difficult. Even the bridge over the sink is wide, so you can put your foot down along this straight and bounce off the book round the

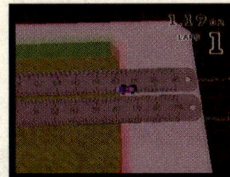

final corner. Hitting the red goo makes you invisible, while the green turns you into a fireball.

Pulling Power

A long course, the main hazard is falling off the edge of the table on the turns. There are also two double bridges (avoid the gap in the middle of the first) and a set of magnets to steer

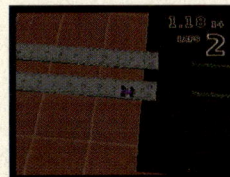

clear of (keep your speed up). Along the way, you get loaded into a teleport device – a good chance to catch up opponents in the same load.

Formula X

Part of this course involves being sucked up a tube and ignited by a Bunsen burner! The rest isn't too hard; just line yourself up for the right-hand ruler bridge

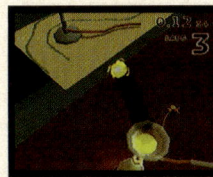

and don't turn too early on the final bend (you can bump round the outside).

Chemical Warfare

The trickiest part of this track is the climb up the ruler ramp – slam the

Big Bounce

During race, press:
□, ⇨, ⇨, ⇩,
⇧, ⇩, ⇩, ⇧, ⇩
A beep will indicate bouncy mode is enabled. To return to normal, re-enter the same code.

Double Speed

During race, press:
□, ✕, ○, □, △, ✕, ✕, ✕, ✕
A beep will indicate it's worked. Just watch those Micro Machines go like the clappers – especially the faster cars. To return to normal speed, re-enter the code.

Debug Mode

During the race, press:
□, ⇧, ⇩, ⇩, □, ○, ○, △, ✕
A beep will indicate it's worked. You can now do several things...
Select + ✕ – Quit the race and automatically win it.
Select + ⇧ ⇩ ⇦ ⇨ – Change camera angle
Select + L2/R2 – Zoom camera in/out
Select + □ – Turn players car into CPU drone
✕ + △ + ○ + □ – Blow up all cars

Tanks On All Tracks

Enter the following as a character name:
TANKS4ME
A noise will indicate the cheat's worked and you can now re-enter the player's proper name.
Note: If you try to use the tanks on the water they'll keep exploding!

micro machines v3

continued

brakes on when you reach the top (or you'll fall off the end) and turn right to go down the second ruler. The rest is pretty straightforward.

Interesting Voyage

This one includes being miniaturised to race through a microscopic sample. Back to full size, the only difficulties are two ramp jumps and a (fairly wide) bridge at the end of the lap. There are several weapons boxes lying around.

Bio-Hazard

A tricky track, this one has three bridges and three diagonal jumps – keep your speed up or you won't make it. There's also a teleport device – a good chance to catch up. The worst bits are the narrow sections by the table edges, so take care not to be rammed off.

BEACH

Pebble Dash

Someone's been having a nice picnic on the beach. This high-speed course has few difficulties apart from getting through the sand-castle tunnel and past a discarded bottle. Just try to avoid drifting out too far on the bends.

Bikini Blazer

Don't know who that discarded bikini top belongs to, but you can bounce over it! The main problem is the series of four sand-castle tunnels: you have to go through them all. Also, avoid drifting too wide on the first bend and don't try to take a short-cut over the seashell bend.

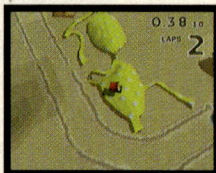

Beached Buggies

A simple high-speed course. Don't bother with the first right-hand bend – you can carry straight on and rejoin the track

without being penalised. However, don't try any short-cuts on the twisty section just afterwards.

Sand Blaster

The twisty sections round the picnic aren't too tricky. Just make sure you get through the book tunnel. The main hazard on this course is the large sand-castle at the end – be careful not to fall off as you climb round and enter the gate.

Bucket And Speed

This fairly long circuit has lots of obstacles around the edge of the track, so try to stay on the road. There's a big jump up the plank over some buckets at the end of the long straight (which you have to go over) – get ready to turn right as soon as you land.

Dunes Of Hazard

There aren't as many hazards as the name suggests, but this bumpy, bendy course isn't easy. Don't drift away from the road too much or you'll be penalised, and stay central for the plank bridge on the back straight.

DINNER

Baguette Balance

The main bloomer is to fall off the bready bridges, so make sure you line up centrally – too wide and you'll roll over the edge. You can take a nifty short-cut through the gap between the menu and candle, but you must go round the sundae. Take it easy to get round the tricky final plate and

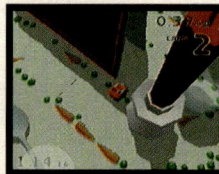

line yourself up for the first baguette again.

The Main Course

A simple circuit, the main danger is falling off the table on those two corner bends. There are no obvious short-cuts (yes, you have to go round that candle), apart from taking a straight line through the first couple of bends.

Tanks A Lot

A tortuous track with lots of sharp bends, complicated by the scattered mints (or whatever they are) which you can't jump over. The only short-cut is through the red sauce blob by the blue candle, but this slows you down anyway.

Vindaloo Drive-Thru

Be careful not to fall off on those tricky bends on the table corners and edges. The only real short-cut is going through the gap between the plate and knife by the third table corner.

Fast Food

This track only appears in Multiplayer Head To Head and Test Drive modes. It's an elongated elliptical circuit with two long straight and two very tight turns to skid round.

SCHOOL

Calculator Risk

This nightmare course includes narrow ruler bridges and long jumps over a binder and calculator. Just take care to line

up the bridges and get your speed up for the jumps. With practice you'll be bombing round.

Trucker's Luck
You need to line yourself up carefully for those two narrow ruler ramps. The rest is pretty straightforward, with felt pens to help you bump round. There's a short-cut between the piece of card and blackboard duster towards the end.

Learning Curves
Although there are no narrow ruler bridges or jumps to negotiate, it's all too easy to fall off the desk on the sections and bends near the edge. Take care to position yourself centrally to enter the book tunnels. There are no obvious short-cuts, so stick to the road.

Must Try Harder
The main difficulty on this 'figure of eight' is caused by the two long narrow bridges, so take care to line yourself up before zooming across. Be especially careful not to overcook it on the ramp just before the second bridge. The rest is pretty straightforward.

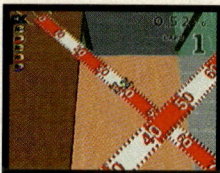

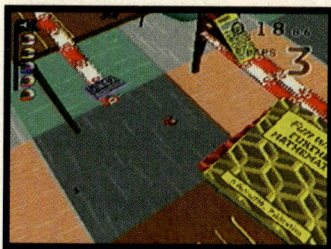

Text Book Manoeuvre
The final track on the Rock 'Ard level, this feature two bridges (the second one narrow) with long jumps at the end of them – so get lined up and put your foot down. You can cut the corner just before the first bridge, driving through the gap between stone and books. There's another narrow bridge later on, then a jump from a binder.

Turbo Returns
This Multiplayer Head-To-Head (and Test Drive) track is a simple elliptical circuit. It has no less than six wide bridges to try to ram each other off on – watch out, the final one on the back straight has the middle missing.

BREAKFAST

Cheesey Jumps
A high-speed circular course, the main hazard is falling off around the second and third corners. Start turning when you see the toast on the second bend, then take it easy on the third bend to line yourself up for the cheese jump.

Cereal Killer
This long course involves dropping off the table to go around a floor section, returning via an ironing board! On the table, you have to go over the Weetos ramp. There are no obvious big short-cuts, so don't even try sneaking onto the ironing board early.

Breakfast At Cherry's
No big hazards here. Just avoid falling off the first bend and avoid bumping the toaster if you don't want to get burnt – and penalised. You don't even have to go through the teaspoon bridge if you don't feel like it.

Wipeup
There's little chance of falling off the edge here, so you can put your foot down along the straights. You don't even have

to jump over the orange-juice cartons, although you may as well. Swerve round the maple syrup to avoid slowing down.

Brake-Fast Bends
Some tight bends give the track its name, but the main hazard are the jumps. There's a double one with a ramp and ironing board just after the start (so keep your foot down) to reach the breakfast table, plus another ramp jump later to return to the floor (via another ironing board).

Super Bowl
A fast circuit around the edge of the table, the main hazard is falling off. Timing the corners is crucial: on the first, start turning when you see the spoon; the second, just after the spoon; the third, when you see the syrup bottle (there's a banana to stop you falling); the last, once the juice jug comes into view.

Hair Of The Dog
Another track where you drop off the table for a stint around the floor (and the dog), returning via the toaster – so make sure you hit the lever. The table section is very twisty with no major short-cuts, apart from cutting inside the toast on the hairpin.

GARDEN

Destruction Dirtbox
The main danger is falling into the two pools – don't turn too early for the corner at the end of the second one. You don't have to go through the pipe, so don't worry if you miss the entrance. You can cut just inside the plant pots on the corners, but don't overdo it.

Beware Of The Dog
Try not to drift into the grass, which will

WEAPONS
You can nobble your opponents by picking up the bright green boxes scattered around the tracks. Note that you can't pick up another weapon until you've used up the current one.

Hammer
Use the wooden mallet to smash your rivals. It needs precision, so get close and hammer away.

Claw
This fiendish device pulls your opponent back so you can overtake. Just line up the target and fire away.

Mine
These can be very handy, especially if dropped in narrow sections of the track where they're harder to avoid!

Missile
If this connects with the target, it'll send them into a high-speed spin. Fire away down the straight.

Forcefield
If anyone is foolish enough to try to ram you, press the button to repel them with great force.

Flamer
Unlike other pick-ups this is activated on collection, leaving a flaming trail which blows up anyone on contact.

nuclear strike

continued

Shoot the buildings to make the agents come out, then winch them up quickly to avoid losing them in the gunfire.

CAMPAIGN 3

Peace Strike
Password: COUNTDOWN
Setting: Pyong Yang, heart of the North Korean capital.

Mission 1 Rescue agents
Description: Kym's security have arrested local agents. Three SIROK agents are being interrogated in separate security buildings. They hold vital information, so extract them before they crack under pressure.
Solution: Pick up the quick ladder from the fire station next to your home base, then go to each marked building in turn. Once there, shoot at the buildings to send troops scurrying into the courtyard. Amongst all the excitement, the agents will make a break for it, so watch out for them and winch them up before they come to any harm.

Mission 2 Stop transports
Description: Kym plans to kidnap the foreign dignitaries under the cover of his peace conference. Avoid a volatile hostage situation by stopping all four military transports before they can enter the conference grounds.

Solution: As your news chopper has no weapons, the idea here is to pinpoint each vehicle and then scoot on ahead to see what surroundings can assist you in destroying them. In most cases, they pass a petrol station, so get ahead of them and start shooting at the station – the idea being to make it blow-up just as they go past, thus taking them out as well. Electrical pylons can also be used as a means of destroying them.

Mission 3 Escort bus
Description: Evacuate the diplomats out of the city. Detonation of the nuclear device is imminent and Kym's security is on full alert. You must safeguard the bus and escort it through the hostile streets and to the French military frigate in the southeast corner of the map.
Solution: Shoot the troops that attack the bus as the diplomats are boarding, then stay closely behind it as it pulls away. After ramming Kym's statue, the bus will turn onto the roads. There will be two motorbikes hidden behind the roadside billboards to take out before they can cause any damage. Shortly into the journey, you'll be asked to shoot a road barrier to determine the route that the bus takes – make sure you shoot the one on the left! This is the safest route; the other one will result in certain death for you and the diplomats. Taking this

Campaign 03 **PEACE STRIKE**

route means that you have to tackle very little by way of danger – a couple of motorbikes and some boats is the maximum threat posed against you. Just keep following the bus to the frigate and winch up Andrea to complete the mission.

Mission 4 Get Cobra

Description: An attack chopper has been located (about time!). There is a Cobra Gunship stored at the war museum. Cover Andrea whilst she prepares the helicopter, then land at the LZ when she's ready.

Solution: Very simple. Go to the museum marked on the map and drop off Andrea. Then destroy the two tanks and the groups of soldiers that attack the building before landing your news chopper and transferring vehicles.

Mission 5 Cover airlift

Description: Evacuate the dignitaries. Strike has sent in two Chinook troop transport helicopters to airlift the dignitaries to safety. Drop Andrea at the city centre LZ and provide cover for these helicopters. They will be most vulnerable when on the ground.

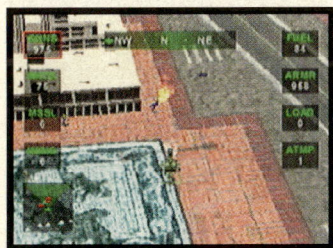

Solution: All is explained really: drop off Andrea and then pick off the red targets that close in around the building. As long as you get to the enemy targets quickly, they shouldn't pose too much threat to the allied helicopters.

Mission 6 Escort diplomats

Description: Get the remaining diplomats to the nearest bomb shelter. Seeing as the Chinooks won't be able to return for another pick-up before the bomb detonates, you must escort the remaining dignitaries to the shelter on foot.
Solution: Before dropping off Andrea at the LZ, first clear the immediate area of

enemy targets. Once the route to the shelter is clear, drop off Andrea and prepare for a hectic race against time. Andrea will escort the diplomats out of the building and down the road. However, they will come under heavy attack from enemy troops and tanks. Cover all sides and scoot ahead to clear the path. If too many diplomats are shot, it will result in a mission SNAFU, so be careful.

Mission 7 Collect supplies

Description: Seeing as the nuclear detonation is imminent, in the time left you must transport any remaining supplies to the football stadium in the bottom-right corner of the map. This isn't essential though because you certainly won't find yourself short later on. Simply make your way to the stadium and prepare to be rocked!

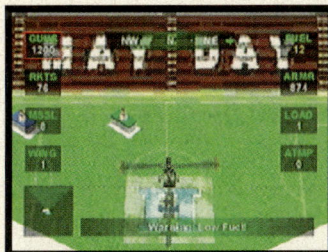

CAMPAIGN 3 PART 2

Password: PLUTONIUM
Setting: The remains of Pyong Yang, minutes after nuclear detonation.

Mission 8 Escort train

Description: The remaining dignitaries need to be escorted from the city. A northbound train is their only means of escape. Drop Andrea at the station and protect the train as it leaves the battle scene.

Solution: Scout around and clear the general area of all enemy activity, then drop off Andrea and hover over to the train. Straight away, an enemy train will pull up behind, se hit the engine carriage with missiles. Now the allied train will pull away and start proceeding along the northbound

line. Another train will strike on the first bridge, so use the same measures as before. Now things really start to hot up as enemy tanks and allsorts start closing in. At one point you'll need to shoot a switch to alter the lines, thus avoiding a head-on collision with an enemy train.

Drop Andrea at the station and she'll drive the train to safety. However, many obstacles cross your path along the way, so look sharp.

Enemy trains will surround you as you escape, so kill them quickly and effectively.

Mission 9 Destroy bridges/HQ

Description: Kym is moving his armoured reserve south to the demilitarised zone. Any forces that escape will appear at the DMZ. To delay their progress south, destroy the three southern bridges and the division's mobile headquarter vehicles.
Solution: Go south and take out the bridges, thus preventing the enemy convoys from escaping, then turn whatever firepower you have left onto the actual vehicles themselves. What better way to end a campaign than with mindless violence?

nuclear strike

continued

DMZ Strike
Password: PUSAN
Setting: The 38th
Parallel. A South
Korean airfield near the
demilitarised zone.

Mission 1 Collect Andrea
Description: Proceed to Camp Kitty
Hawk and pick up Andrea. From her you
will receive further orders. Don't, at any
cost, provoke the enemy by flying into
North Korean airspace.
Solution: Very straightforward. Go to
the US camp marked on the map and
winch up Andrea. You'll find the quick
ladder right next to her.

Mission 2 Main battlefield
Description: War has broken out. The

Pick up Andrea and the
battle will commence.
Brace yourself for the
fight of the century.

Korean People's Army is commencing a
full-scale invasion against the Republic of
Korea, and the United States' armed
forces stationed there. Keep the North
Korean heavy armour and APCs from
infiltrating the south. Select your battles
carefully and hold out until reinforcements
arrive.
Solution: All hell has broken out! This is
where things start to get really heavy, so
read carefully…
First of all, do what Andrea says and
head off the troop invasion that is
threatening in subs from the south/west.
Hit them before they moor, to eradicate
what little danger they pose. Next on the
agenda is a small troop of tunnel
commandos; again get to these quick and

shoot them all before the little buggers
can do any damage.
At this point the whole area will light up
like a Christmas tree with enemy activity
(though sadly without the chocolate coins
and Santas hanging from it). Go to each
allied camp marked on the map and
deploy the soldiers to the indicated
positions, then fly north into enemy
airspace and take-out the Scud-launchers.
Once done, fly back down to the
southwest LZ and transfer to the A-10X
plane. This has immense armour and
weapons, so start taking out the massive
fleets of tanks that start descending from
the north. By staying close to the bottom,
you'll be able to pick them off before they
head south, thus preventing the chances

Campaign 04 **DMZ STRIKE**

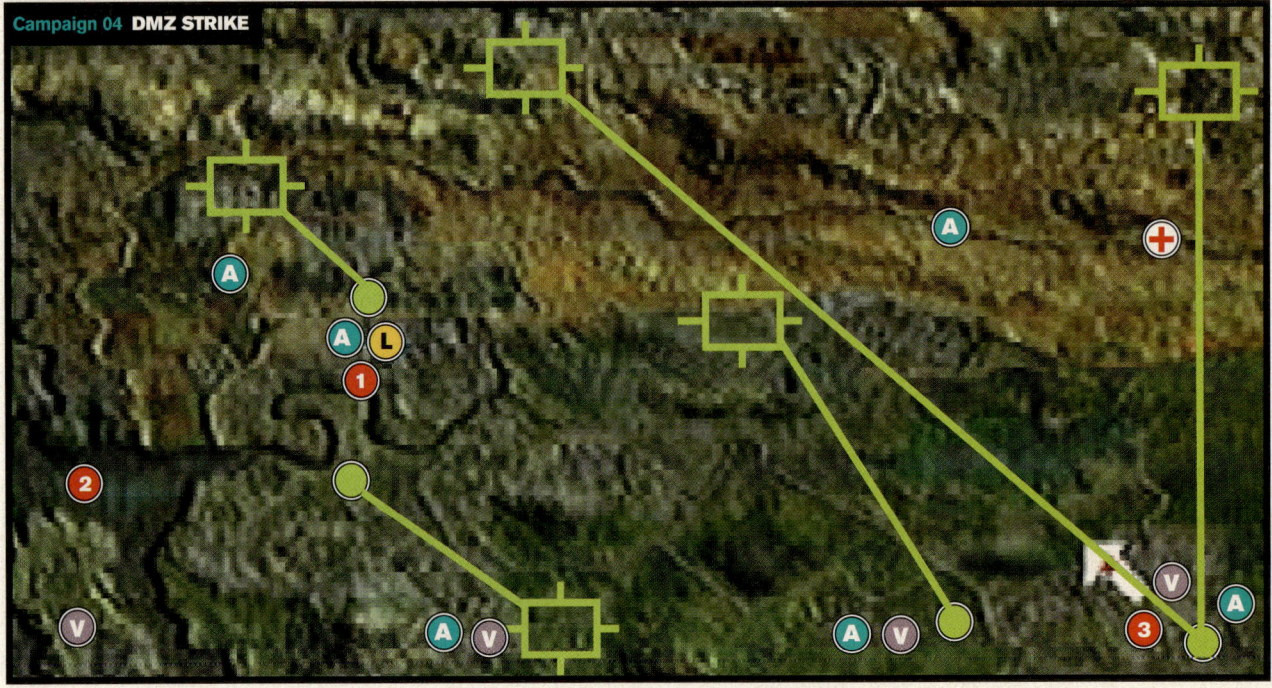

of a mission SNAFU.

There are a whole host of other ways to keep the enemy from attacking – such as changing signposts, crushing them by

shooting statues and dropping mines, bazookas and other high-powered weapons to your ground troops.

There are also tanks and rocket-launching vehicles that you can switch to, if desired. Each has good defences and cracking weaponry. Once you take control

of the situation though, keeping the enemy forces at bay isn't too hard. Just keep collecting the new weapons such as high-powered wingtips and tank guns, and keep obliterating each chain of tanks as they try to get past. Within 20 minutes, the allied bombers will arrive and wipe out the whole threat, so sit tight until then and try not to lose too many tanks.

Mission 3 Return to base
Description: Allied bombers have arrived over the battle zone in time to smash the enemy advance. Return with Andrea to the Comanche home base for debrief.
Solution: Make sure you collect Andrea (if you deployed her to wreck the tunnels) and return to your home base.

Well, that's another mission completed. So take some time out for a cup of tea and the obligatory Scotch egg!

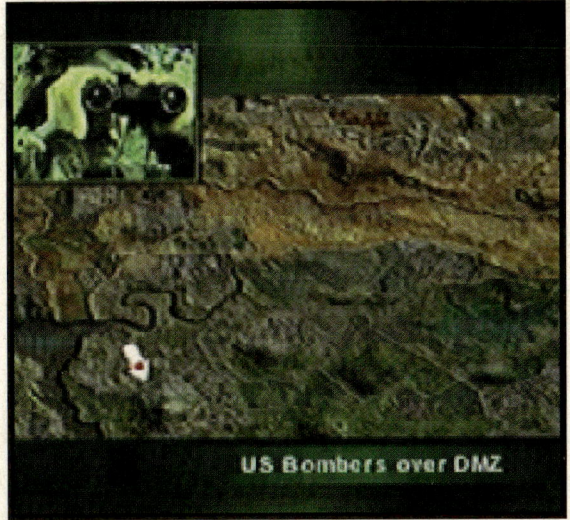

US Bombers over DMZ

PLANES, TRAINS AND AUTOMOBILES (OH YES... AND CHOPPERS AS WELL!)
Nuclear Strike does away with being cooped-up in one solitary vehicle throughout the game. Now you've got ten vehicles of destruction to wreak havoc on your enemies with. Here's what they are and when to find them...

A-10X CAMPAIGN 5
This heavily armoured plane is just the ticket for getting rid of tanks in a hurry.

COBRA CAMPAIGN 3
Compared to the news chopper, this seems like a godsend. Good all-round fire and strength.

COMANCHE CAMPAIGN 5
Good, agile fighter, but slightly lacking in armour and sufficient firepower.

HARRIER CAMPAIGN 2&3
The best attacker in the game bar none! This is the ultimate in enemy-maiming combat machinery.

HAVOC CAMPAIGN 1
Super-agile fighter that packs a real punch. Not quite as good as the Hokum, but not far off.

HUEY CAMPAIGN 1
Stronger and more dangerous than the helicopter you start with. Very slow in the air though.

HOKUM CAMPAIGN 5
The best helicopter in the game. Has plenty of armour points and can house many strong weapons.

HOVERCRAFT CAMPAIGN 1
Not good on land and limited in weapons. Not really worth bothering with.

M-1 CAMPAIGN 4
Powerful tank that is severely limited by speed and agility. Not worth the hassle.

MLRS CAMPAIGN 4
Spits out high-powered armour-piercing rockets like pips! Slow and not very agile though.

NEWS CHOPPER CAMPAIGN 3
Pathetic! This has only guns, tear gas, and smoke canisters as weapons. It's very fast though.

T-90 CAMPAIGN 5
This can be used to take out the gun turrets surrounding the fortress. Not much else though.

nuclear strike

continued

CAMPAIGN 5

Fortress Strike
Password: ARMAGEDDON
Setting: Tiger mountain, an undisclosed archaeological dig somewhere in eastern Siberia.

Mission 1 Protect agents
Description: Agents Naja and Cash are under attack by LeMonde's mercenary forces. Head over to the northeast sector and assist them in battle before they are lost for ever.

Radars are concealed inside ordinary buildings. Shoot the guns and then the building to reveal the main target.

Solution: Proceed to the sector in question and quickly take out the various T-55s, Gainfuls, APCs and BRDM-2s. Your agent will them clamber into the driller and head to the building where Naja is awaiting. Upon arrival, the building will blow and both of your agents will await pick-up. It is also here that you'll switch to the Havoc chopper.

Mission 2 Destroy towers
Description: Destroy six radar towers, and units covering the courtyard supply centre. Move quickly before LeMonde's border guards arrive to reinforce the inner fortress. You can deploy commando teams to assist in taking out the radar towers, setting up ambushes and cutting bridges.
Solution: Take out the nearest tower to the west and then fly back down to the commando camp in the Southeast. Deploy the chopper to take out the northern tower, and then use the ground units to block the eastern road. Now start taking out each tower in turn. Go clockwise around the map and deal with each unit as quickly and effectively as possible. Once you get near to Hack's ground base, you'll have to break off briefly and assist him by taking out a tank that is threatening. It is worth taking time out at some point to fly east and expose the hidden Hokum chopper that is concealed (see map): this has greater armour and weapons than the Havoc. The rest of the mission is very straightforward.

Mission 3 EMP Trucks
Description: Destroy the six relay trucks which transmit an electromagnetic pulse which disables all helicopter missile weapon systems. Use Naja to identify these camouflaged vehicles.
Solution: Don't follow the direct order of using Naja. By landing on the indicated LZ, she'll ride off on a motorbike and start dropping flares next to the relay trucks. However, each circle of trucks is guarded by T-90 tanks and these are very hard to take out with only guns – which means Naja will ultimately ride off and die with precious little you can do about it. Instead, simply fly into the fortress and

Campaign 05 FORTRESS STRIKE

take out every truck and the surrounding tanks. Hell, you may die, but at least it won't be a mission SNAFU.

Also, to get over the problem of not having any missiles, there is a super tank gun hidden inside a temple in the southeast. Winch it up and split open those tanks with ease!

Mission 4 Guardian guns
Description: Drop Cash at the LZ indicated on the map to assist you in destroying the guardian guns. Distract them whilst Cash gets to work and then take them out when they're vulnerable to attack.

Solution. Use the rest of your high-powered weapons to take out the enemy vehicle fleets, towers, and any other threats that remain inside the fortress, then drop off Cash. He'll go clockwise around the perimeter, so hover close to the guardian guns and strafe to avoid their fire. Once Cash hops inside and exits, hit them with a wingtip and missile to destroy them. Make sure that you have plenty of ammo, fuel, and armour before dropping off Cash.

Mission 5 Destroy ICBMs
Description: Destroy three SS-24 nuclear ICBMs. Go to each hilltop tower and deploy Andrea. She will manually initiate the launch sequence to expose the missiles – destroy them before they launch and then collect Andrea.

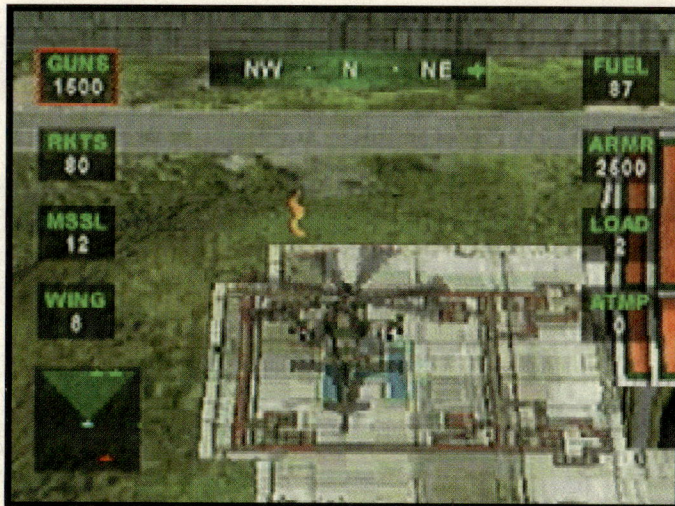

Solution: It is entirely random which towers contain the missiles, so it's a case of trial and error. One thing is for sure though: whenever Andrea exposes the silos in the top-right and bottom-left, reinforcements will arrive and start attacking, so winch up Andrea quickly before she can come to any harm. Otherwise, simply blow the missiles to smithereens before they leave the launch pad.

Mission 6 Shiva's Dagger
Description: Destroy Shiva's Dagger as it leaves the hardened silo. LeMonde is proceeding to launch the proto-nuclear warhead which will destroy the planet. Drop Andrea at the LZ. She will then pilot a Hokum to help you in destroying LeMonde's doomsday device.
Solution: Drop off Andrea at the LZ to the left and she will jump into a Hokum and follow you to the silo. Target the Dagger and fire everything you've got at it. After several missiles, wingtips and rockets, the Dagger will topple over and fire horizontally along the ground into the madman's base. Now simply take out the guns that surround the silo to complete the mission. Beware, the area is crawling with Havoc's, so pick them off before attempting this mission. When all danger is gone, fly back home for the poor ending. Oh go on, treat yourself to another Scotch egg and nice warm cup of tea...

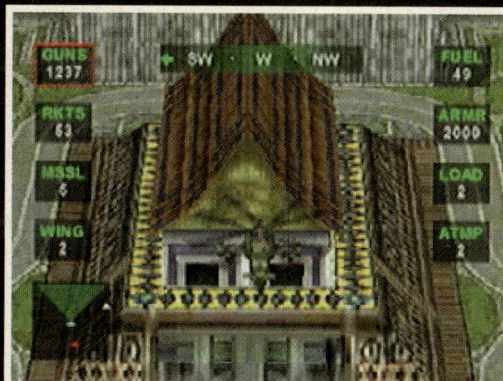

HOKUM
New vehicles are concealed inside buildings. Blast them to reveal new machines better suited to the missions.

rage racer

continued

Toggle Mirror on/off

Whilst racing in internal mode, pause the game at any time and then press and hold ▲ and then tap L1 to make the rear view mirror disappear and R1 to restore it again.

Mirror Mode

To enter Mirror Mode, whereby you reverse the tracks so that all of the corners and writing are reversed, select 'Race Start' from the main options and then hold L1, R1, Select and Start until the race begins. If the cheat has worked you will instantly notice the difference.

THE CAR SHOP (FINE TUNING)

Gnade Esperanza

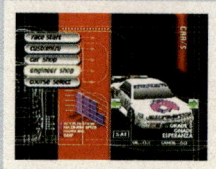

Engine:	1,927cc
Weight:	1,020kg
Power:	240bhp
Cost:	Free

Your first car, and it had better be, nobody in their rightful mind would pay money for this heap!

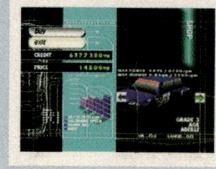

Age Aloutte

Engine:	1300cc
Weight:	580kg
Power:	160bhp
Cost:	2,300eg

Cheap, affordable whippet that will win you many, many races on the early classes.

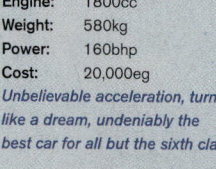

Age Abeille

Engine:	1800cc
Weight:	820kg
Power:	170bhp
Cost:	14,400eg

Looks like a Renault 5, sounds good and handles like it's on rails.

Age Pegase (manual gear)

Engine:	1800cc
Weight:	580kg
Power:	160bhp
Cost:	20,000eg

Unbelievable acceleration, turns like a dream, undeniably the best car for all but the sixth class.

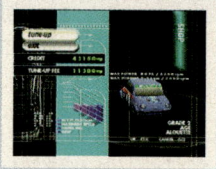

Lizard Instinct

Engine:	4,200cc
Weight:	1,160kg
Power:	285bhp
Cost:	4,000eg

Cheap to buy, but it is too big and handles like a lobotomised dog.

Lizard Bayonet

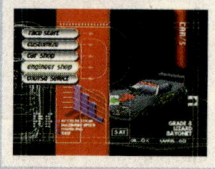

Engine:	4,800cc
Weight:	1,210kg
Power:	310bhp
Cost:	15,500eg

Like the Instinct only faster and better-sounding. It can be upgraded nicely too.

Lizard Hijack (manual gear)

Engine:	5,000cc
Weight:	1,260kg
Power:	340bhp
Cost:	136,700eg

A souped-up flatbed van with terrific torque but unresponsive handling. The modification is awesome though.

Assoluto Fatalita

Engine:	2 x 652cc
Weight:	1,130kg
Power:	325bhp
Cost:	20,000eg

Basically a racing Porsche that has been converted for road use.

Assoluto Instante (man.gear)

Engine:	3,500cc
Weight:	1,430kg
Power:	380bhp
Cost:	110,000eg

Way too fast for its own good – in fact we recommend it solely for The Extreme Oval. Now, is it a Lamborghini Diablo or a Venturi?

Assoluto Ghepardo (man. gear)

Engine:	5,000cc
Weight:	1,300kg
Power:	600bhp
Cost:	635,000eg

AKA The Beast, this will eradicate all comers on The Extreme Oval due to its Le Mans roots.

SPECIAL CARS

Once you reach the prestigious sixth class, you'll race against, and have the opportunity to buy three brand new speedsters.

Age Victoire 01

Engine:	3,500cc
Weight:	700kg
Power:	500bhp
Cost:	2,300,000eg

This is basically the Batmobile. It has incredible acceleration and speed – a belter.

Lizard Tempest (man. gear) 02

Engine:	9,000cc
Weight:	1,100kg
Power:	750bhp
Cost:	2,800,000eg

A scary-looking ZZTop mobile that goes like the wind.

Assoluto Dragone (man) 03

Engine:	Unknown
Weight:	Unknown
Power:	Unknown
Cost:	6,666,666eg

Due to the amount of sixes in the price, this has got to be the Devil car. This is by far the fastest, meanest, most evil car on the track.

Over Pass City

Scenery image:	City streets like San Francisco
Course Layout:	Course with steep ups and downs, and overpasses.

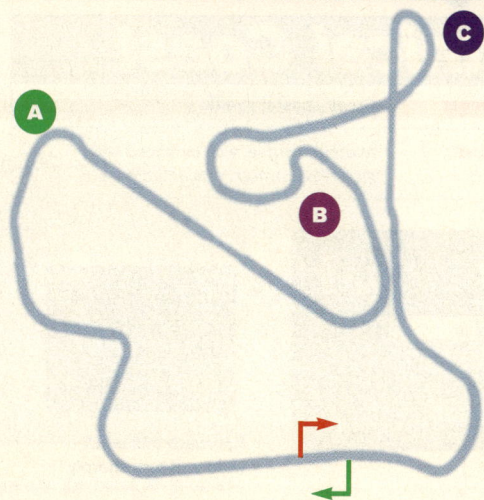

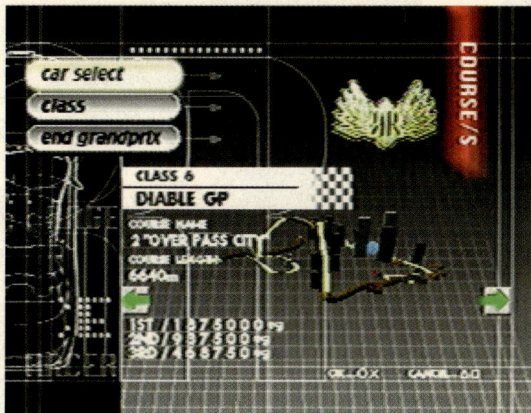

A1 With the faster cars, brake hard going in.

A2 Turn to the right to avoid ramming the kink.

C1 Accelerate out again like a mad young thing!

B1 Approach wide and brake hard whilst turning.

C2 Stay right then keep tapping the brake.

B2 Accelerate out of the next bend whilst turning.

Drifting

Unlike Ridge Racer, the 'powerslide' element in Rage Racer has been greatly reduced. Whereas before it was a means of tackling corners at full speed, now it just swings the back of your car around and allows you to tackle sharp bends more easily. In Rage Racer, the method of how to drift is different than before. Here's how you do it: (1) Approach the corner at a reasonable speed. (2) Turn slightly into the bend and then apply equal measures of both brake and acceleration. (3) Take your finger off of the accelerator for a second and then allow the back of the car to slide out, or 'drift'. (4) Finally, hit the gas and accelerate hard out of the bend, leaving the opposition gasping at your coolness!

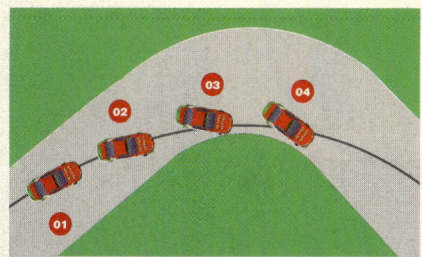

rapid racer

Publisher:	Sony
Price:	£34.99
Format:	UK

start

Rapid Racer

Subjected yourself to **high G-forces and excessive test depths** as you tackle the **treacherous waters** in *Rapid Racer*, the **new extreme racing game** from Sony.

1 player   Memory   2 player

Rapid Racer

COOL RUNNING

To maintain a healthy top speed, especially when you are turboing, keep the engines straight in relation to the boat. To help you come out of the corners like lightning, point the engines in the direction of the corner just before you have to turn. You can also do this while you are in the air to perform a tight turn when you land.

The calm stretches of track optimise your speed when you are accelerating. They also come in handy when you're using a turbo boost, as the engines stay in the water to give you maximum effect. So burn it down the straights, cap'n!

Views

As with most racing games on the PlayStation, you can switch between a variety of camera angles, some better than others.

Far

This useful 'over the boat' perspective is the easiest to get to grips with as you get a nice bird's eye view of the track. This enables you to see quite a long way into the distance, to better anticipate corners and other problems, and also helps you block opponents as they try to pass.

Close-Up

This is the standard 'in the boat' view. It's far harder to race with than the Far view. You can't see which way your rear-mounted engines are pointing and if you crash into anything it can be severely disorienting. The compensation is the improved speed effect.

Extreme Close-Up

Nothing to do with Wayne's World, this gives you a first-person perspective of the course. Known as the 'suicide view', only the most expert of racers will want to use this to experience 'in your face' action. Try this view to give yourself a white-knuckle ride.

CHEATS

Following is a comprehensive list of cheats. You have to input them on the name selection screen in one-player mode before they become available in the other game modes.

Extra Boats
_BOA (_ = space)
Makes all the hidden boats selectable.

Duck Mode

_QAK
This turns all the boats into giant plastic ducks with engines!

Hurricane

HURR
Gives you control of The Hurricane, a high-speed vessel that corners like it's on rails. It's got a horrible yellow paint job, though.

Unlock Day Tracks

_DAY
More cheats over page...

Pick-Ups

Turbo
The green pick-ups give you turbo boosts when you pick them up. Save them for the long straights or use them to recover when you crash. If you fill your turbo bar by collecting three green power ups, you can use them one after the other to give you a more powerful mega-turbo which can come in handy as you fight for the finish line.

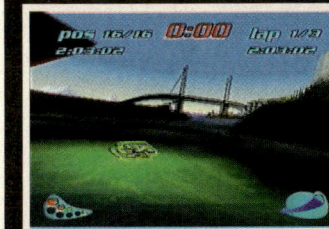

Time
These blue babies freeze the clock, saving you precious seconds as you race to extend your time. They are

essential on the bonus stages as you are never given enough time to complete them.

Upgrade
Yellow pick-ups are as precious as

gold dust in this game. Fill your special bar with seven of these pick-ups to upgrade your boat on the bonus stage. You also need a full bar of these to unlock the blanked-out tracks in one-player mode.

Slow
It's not easy avoiding these, but avoid them you must to stand any chance of victory. Not only do they slow you down, but they cancel out turbos you pick up. To dispose of them either collect three, which slows you down exponentially, or collect enough green pick-ups to cancel them out.

rapid racer

continued

THE BOATS

Take Chris de Burgh's advice and don't pay the ferryman – choose one of these powerboats instead. It's not all down to the wet, sloppy paint jobs either – read our guide to find out which boat is best for you.

Akula

Akula but definitely not a shaker, this boat starts with decent acceleration and an even keel. This is definitely the first choice for the discerning racer, not only because of its well-balanced performance but also because of the excellent octopus design on the front… if you have a fetish for eight-limbed sea beasts.

Waterhawk

A cool-sounding name and a mighty engine make this the professional's choice. It's a good idea to use this boat on the first track as the high top speed gives you the edge on the relatively smooth water and long straights. Such power can be a bit of a handful on other courses, though. So not recommended for the novice.

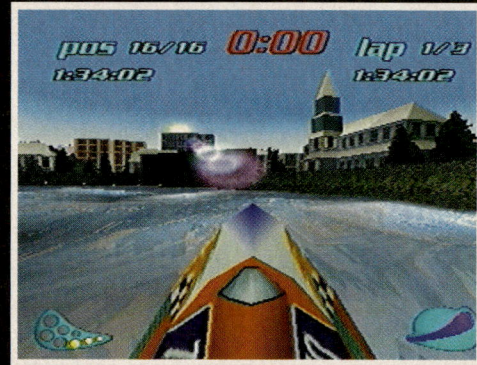

Wavehammer

This boat is a great one for the beginner, giving a good turning circle at the price of speed and acceleration. Use this one if you must, but upgrade it as soon as possible on the bonus sections, otherwise you won't stand much of a chance on the later courses. A bit of a slow boat to China.

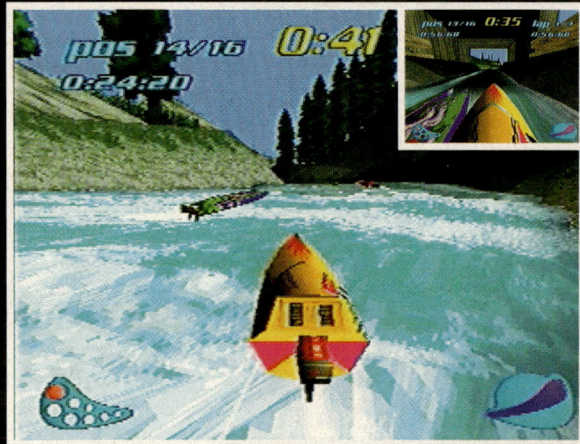

Americana

This stars and stripes special chews up the waves. A decent top speed and a sturdy hull give this an advantage over most computer-controlled boats, but make sure it doesn't run away from you on the corners. Brake early to stay afloat on the sharper turns, or sink like a brick.

Rapid Racer

Marlin

This fishily-named powerboat is one sleek speed machine that cuts through waves and choppy waters thanks to its pointed keel. If you hit another boat, however, be prepared to perform some swift manoeuvres to regain control as it's not particularly stable. In fact, you'll be rocking and rolling longer than Status Quo!

t550

This strangely-monikered boat is the master of cornering. It sweeps round sharp bends and chicanes with a very tight turning arc (talk about turning on a sixpence), allowing you to cut inside the corners and overtake most boats. The t550 is not good in rough water, though, so only use it on the relatively calm tracks.

Radioactive

As potentially fatal as it sounds (a bit like Def Leppard), this orange dream machine will really push your driving skills to the limit and then some.
Expect some easy victories in two-player mode if you can handle its immense power and speed – expect some spectacular crashes if not...

Black Widow

Like its namesake, it'll bite your backside if you go for a dump without looking under the seat. Only a champion racer can hope to control this engine on a stick. With maximum acceleration and top speed, your previous best lap times will be but a bad memory. Use it in two-player mode to ensure victory.

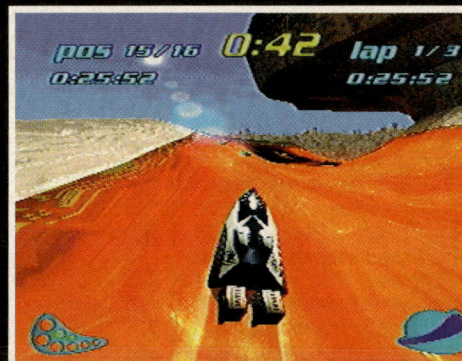

Unlock Night Tracks

_NIT

Unlock Mirrored Tracks

RRIM

Random Track Generator

FRAC

Win Race
WINR
Quit the race you are playing to be awarded first place.

Day Track Select
D__#
Where # equals the number of the track you want (from 1 to 6).

Night Track Select
N__#
Where # equals the number of the track you want (from 1 to 6).

Mirrored Track Select
M__#
Where # equals the number of the track you want (from 1 to 6).

Porsche Mode
BXTR
This enables the Porsche cheat, but it only works if you load in a *Rapid Racer* saved game from a memory card that also contains a *Porsche Challenge* saved game.

rapid racer

continued

Miami Golden Sands

The easiest track but still no pushover, Miami boasts some smooth water and gentle corners interspersed with sand dunes and jagged rocks. Use a boat with a pointed keel on this course as you will able to reach high speeds on the long straights.

1. Here you should cut to the outside of the waterway and keep the throttle high. If you do lose control, try and slow down using the marker buoys to steady your craft. Don't, whatever you do, hit the sand dunes as you'll probably be spun round to face the oncoming boats.

2. When you're past the first sand dune, cross to the inside of the waterway to set yourself up for the approaching corner. This crossover can be used as a good overtaking point: if you time it right you can cut off any pursuing boats as they reduce speed for the corner.

3. Be careful of the rocks that divide the corner as there is not much room to manoeuvre. Its a good idea to throttle down if you are behind another boat to avoid being forced onto the rocks.

4. To take the hard right, get the engine pointed in line with the current just before you reach it.

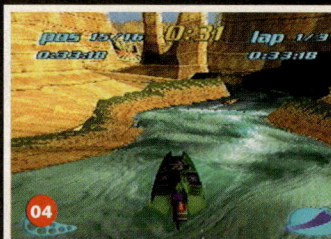

Arizona White Water Canyon

You will see that this course lives up to its reputation when you are dragged round by its wild currents. The tactic for this course is simple: point your boat in the direction you want to go and let the current take you there.

1. Keep the boat pointed straight for these chicanes – don't turn sharply into them, as you will get buffeted by the current and spun round.

2. Once again you will need to point the boat's engine in line with the water flow and let the current haul you round these rapids.

3. As you come out of the first tunnel, the water calms so you can quite safely fire off a few turbos before you take the sharp bend at the end of this section.

4. You will need to take the waterfall quite fast to avoid landing nose first. When you have landed, point the engines towards the next set of rapids and let your boat be carried round the corner. Stay on the inside of the long tunnel at all costs as the vicious current will pull you to the outside and onto the rocks. Save your turbos for when you exit the tunnel as the going is easy just before the finish line.

Alaska Glacier Bay

It's time to go roaring down river in this high-speed course. The channels on this level are thankfully wide, giving you some leeway if you make any mistakes. It also gets pretty dark when you go through the tunnels, so you will need to slow down.

1. It's best just to go with the flow on these excessively fast chicanes. If you are using a high-powered boat, be sure to throttle down to avoid bouncing off the sides like a billiard ball.

2. There are partially submerged rocks just before the second tunnel, some of which can be used as ramps to pull off cool jumps that will really wind up your opponent when you are ahead in two-player mode. However, make sure the rocks you jump are flat or it will be your opponent who's doing all the laughing.

3. Hit the turbos on this calm section to boost you right round the sharp bend that immediately follows.

4. Burn all your turbos when you see this bridge, as the finish line is only just around the corner. Luckily, if you are still behind in the race, this section is preceded by a long straight which is ideal for overtaking.

Rapid Racer

Canada Bear Lake

This course is fast-flowing and has huge jumps, so a boat with a sturdy hull is a must. You will need to power-slide through most of the corners, so the Wavehammer would be the best choice to complete this track.

1. The words 'reduce speed now' are highly applicable in this hairy situation. If you are in a boat with a powerful engine, slow down before you hit the jump or you will almost certainly lose control in the air – a bit like the food-poisoned pilot in one of those Airport movies.

2. Cut across the inside of this corner to give your boat a bit of a boost (rather than a Twirl or Wispa). The water is very fast-flowing on the inside lane so, for maximum thrust, get as close as you can to the edge of the channel without bouncing into the side. Go on, be a daredevil.

3. The current tries to beat you down as you approach the canyon, so use your turbos to maintain your speed as the computer-controlled boats nearly always try to sneak past at this point.

4. Straighten your boat up as you enter this turn and you'll be pulled round nicely into the next bend.

Costa Rica Lost Valley

Narrow channels, dark tunnels, and harsh jumps make this the toughest track of the bunch. You need to use a highly manoeuvrable boat with good stability, such as the excellent t550, to stand any chance on this wobbly waterway.

1. From the off you are faced with these narrow winding channels. So if you're a fat git, don't bother getting in your boat – eh, Mr Maxwell? Don't use your turbos here, however tempting it may be, or you will find your boat beached very quickly.

2. This corner is one of the few places that you can manoeuvre freely on this course. So make sure you use this breathing space to fire off a few turbos for maximum thrust down the next section.

3. The narrow channels on this section make the jumps difficult to negotiate. You can either throttle down and steer through them or, if you are a professional (like Lewis Collins), keep the boat straight and hit the turbos to carry you through.

4. This sharp bend is good for overtaking, as you come out of the previous section quite fast. So don't miss your chance when Bob says "Opportunity Knocks".

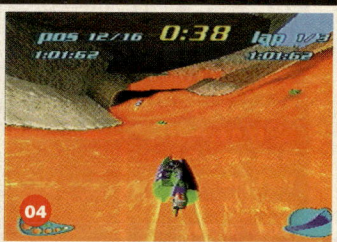

Hawaii Lava Trail

This track is almost totally calm and has many massive jumps and winding chicanes, so you can just pick a high-powered boat and burn it round. One of the most exciting courses available if you're a speed freak.

1. Just after you start you'll reach these chicanes, but don't bother slowing down – simply barrel on through them with turbos blazing and you should leave your computer opponents standing.

2. As you head out of the chicanes you will come to this slightly winding section. Use your turbos to overtake your opponents at this point, as you are just about to enter the tunnel where high speed is impossible.

3. Hey, who turned out the lights? Even the glow from the lava is not enough to illuminate this dark tunnel. There is a huge drop midway through the tunnel that changes at the bottom, so be prepared to slow down before you reach it.

4. Open the throttle up when you see this overhang, as the track is virtually straight with massive jumps that help you pass the opposing boats. A superb opportunity to leap to the lead.

street fighter ex plus

continued

Cracker Jack *Cracker Jack*

First Appeared: Street Fighter Ex Plus α
Speciality: Bat Attack

Special Moves
Dash Straight – Hold ⇦, ⇨ + any punch
Dash Upper – Hold ⇦, ⇨ + any kick
Final Punch – Hold and release 3 punches
Batting Hero – ⇨ ⇗ ⇩ ⇘ ⇦ + any punch
Football Kick – ⇦ ⇗ ⇩ ⇘ ⇨ + any kick

Super Combos
Crazy Jack – Hold ⇦, ⇨ ⇨ ⇨ + any punch
Note: Change attacks by pressing punch (straight) or kick (uppercuts).
Home Run Hero – ⇩ ⇗ ⇦ ⇩ ⇗ ⇦ + any punch
Raging Buffalo – Hold ⇦, ⇨ ⇨ ⇨ + any kick

The moves come hard and fast with this Texan Cowboy!

Raging Buffalo

Football Kick

Cycloid Beta *Cycloid Beta*

First Appeared: Street Fighter Ex Plus α
Speciality: Copying Other Fighters

Special Moves
Whirlwind Kick – ⇨ + ●
Front Direction Body Revolve – ⇩ ⇙ ⇦ + any punch
Beta Shoot Upper – ⇨ ⇩ ⇘ + any punch
Beta Justice Fist – ⇦ ⇩ ⇙ + any punch
Beta Purimu Kick – ⇨ ⇩ ⇘ + any kick
Beta Flying Swallow Kick – ⇩ ⇙ ⇦ + any kick
Beta Tornado Whirlwind Leg – ⇩ ⇘ ⇨ + any kick

Special Combos
Beta Kill Trump – ⇩ ⇘ ⇨ ⇩ ⇘ + any punch
Beta Refined Dragon Destroying Kick – ⇩ ⇘ ⇨ ⇩ ⇘ ⇨ + any kick (air)
Beta Devil Swallow's Flight – ⇩ ⇘ ⇦ ⇩ ⇘ + any kick
Beta Vacuum Tornado Whirlwind Leg – ⇩ ⇙ ⇦ ⇩ ⇙ ⇦ + any kick (air)

Sliding Tackle

Lightning Fist

Cycloid Gamma *Gamma*

First Appeared: Street Fighter Ex Plus α
Speciality: Copying Other Fighters

Special Moves
Gamma Heavy Stub Kick – ⇦ or ⇨ + R2
Gamma Sky Scraping Air Blade Leg – ⇩ + ●
Gamma Dance Wind – Any direction (except ⇘, ⇧ or ⇗) + ▲ or R1 (air) (close)
Gamma Buster Drop – Any direction (except ⇘, ⇧ or ⇗) + ▲ or R1 (air) (close)
Gamma Hundred Rending Kicks – Tap any kick repeatedly
Gamma Skullo Crusher – Hold ⇦, ⇨ + any punch
Gamma Sliding Arrow – Hold ⇦, ⇨ + any kick
Gamma Final Punch – Hold and release 3 punches or 3 kicks
Gamma Head Press – Hold ⇩, ⇧ + any punch
Gamma Somersault Kick – ⇩, ⇧ + any kick

Super Combos
Gamma Power Range – Hold ⇙, ⇘ ⇙ ⇗ + any punch
Gamma Double Somersault Kick – Hold ⇙, ⇘ ⇙ ⇗ + any kick
Gamma Roaring Fang – Hold ⇦, ⇨ ⇨ + any punch

There are a few holes in his technique!

Vertical Split

Darun Mister *Darun Mister*

First Appeared: Street Fighter Ex Plus α
Speciality: Hammer Punch

Special Moves
Gauge Head Thumber – Any direction (except ⇘, ⇧ or ⇗) + ▲ or R1 (air) (close)
Lariat – ⇨ ⇩ ⇘ + any punch
DDT – ⇨ ⇩ ⇘ + any kick
Brahma Bomb – Rotate 360° (anti) clockwise + any punch (close)
Indra Bridge – Rotate 360° (anti) clockwise + any kick
Darun Catch – ⇦ ⇩ ⇙ + any punch (use against airborne opponents)
Twilight Lariat – ⇩ ⇘ ⇨ ⇩ ⇘ ⇨ + any punch

Super Combos
Indra Bridge – ⇩ ⇙ ⇦ ⇩ ⇙ ⇦ + any kick
Super Suppressed Fierce God Bomb – Rotate 720° (anti) clockwise + any punch (close)

Brahma Bomb

Indra Bridge

Street Fighter Ex Plus α

Dhalsim — *Dhalsim*

First Appeared: Street Fighter II
Speciality: Yoga Flame

Special Moves
Drill Punch – ⇩ + R1 (air)
Drill Kick – ⇩ + any kick (air)
Yoga Teleport In Front – ⇨ ⇩ ⬊ + 3 punches (appear far away) or 3 kicks (appear close)
Yoga Teleport Behind – ⇨ ⇩ ⬊ + 3 punches (appear far away) or 3 kicks (appear close)
Yoga Fire – ⇩ ⬊ ⇨ + any punch
Yoga Flame – ⇩ ⬋ ⇦ + any punch
Yoga Blast – ⇩ ⬋ ⇦ + any kick (use against airborne opponents)
Taunt – ⬊ ⇨ ⬈ ⇧ ⇦ ⬋ + any kick (start move on ground)

Yoga Fire

Super Combos
Yoga Inferno – ⇩ ⬊ ⇨ ⇩ ⬊ ⇨ + any punch
Yoga Drill Kick – ⇩ ⬊ ⇨ ⇩ ⬊ ⇨ + any kick
Yoga Rejendo – ⇩ ⬋ ⇦ ⇩ ⬋ ⇦ + any kick

Not only does Dhalsim keep his old moves, he's got a few new ones to boot!

Yoga Rejendo

Doctrine Dark — *Dark*

First Appeared: Street Fighter Ex Plus α
Speciality: Mines

Special Moves
Knife Nightmare – ⇨ + △
Death Spin Kick – ⇨ + ●
Kill Blade – ⇨ ⇩ ⬊ + any punch
Dark Wire – ⇩ ⬊ ⇨ + any punch
Dark Spark – Press any punch (use after Dark Wire)
Dark Hold – ⇦ + any punch (use after Dark Wire)
Ex-plosion – ⇩ ⬊ ⇨ + any kick

Super Combos
Kill Trump – ⇩ ⬊ ⇨ ⇩ ⬊ + any punch
Dark Shackle – ⇩ ⬊ ⇨ ⇨ ⬊ + any kick

Dark Shackle

Dark Spark

Ex-plosion

Garuda — *Garuda*

First Appeared: Street Fighter Ex Plus α
Speciality: Fun With Spikes

Special Moves
Devil Murder – ⇨ + R1
Insane Serpent – ⇨ + R2
Dance – ⇨ ⇩ + 3 punches
Advancing Devil – Any direction (except ⬊, ⇧ or ⬈) + △ or R1 (air) (close)
Devil Slash – ⇨ ⇩ ⬊ + any punch
Serpent Slash – ⇦ ⇩ ⬋ + any punch
Attacking Fang – ⇩ ⬊ ⇨ + any punch
Thunder Fang – ⇨ ⇩ ⬊ + any kick (use against airborne opponents)
Roaring Fang – ⇦ ⬋ ⇩ ⬊ ⇨ + any kick

Super Combos
Devil Swallow's Spin – ⇩ ⬋ ⇦ ⇩ ⬋ ⇦ + any punch (air)
Devil Swallow's Flight – ⇩ ⬊ ⇨ ⇩ ⬊ + any punch

Devil Slash

Attacking Fang

Gouki — *(Akuma)*

First Appeared: Super Street Fighter II Turbo
Speciality: Air Fireball

Special Moves
Whirlwind Leg – ⇨ + ●
Sky Scraping Air Blade Leg – ⇨ + ● (air)
Front Direction Body Revolve – ⇩ ⬋ ⇦ + any punch
Ashura Sky Flash Forward – ⇨ ⇩ ⬊ + 3 punches (move to right) or 3 kicks (move to left)
Ashura Sky Flash Backward – ⇦ ⇩ ⬋ + 3 punches (move to right) or 3 kicks (move to left)
Great Wave Motion Fist – ⇩ ⬊ ⇨ + any punch
Great Rising Dragon Fist – ⇨ ⇩ ⬊ + any punch
Scorching Heat Wave Motion Fist – ⇨ ⇩ ⬊ ⬋ ⇦ + any punch
Killing Sky Wave Motion Fist – ⇩ ⬊ ⇨ + any punch (air)
Tornado Killing Sky Leg – ⇩ ⬋ ⇦ + any kick (repeat up to 4 times)

Super Combos
Deadly Great Surge – ⇩ ⬋ ⇦ ⇩ ⬋ ⇦ + any punch
Deadly Great Rising Dragon – ⇩ ⬊ ⇨ ⇩ ⬊ + any punch
Demon Great Killing Sky – ⇩ ⬊ ⇨ ⇩ ⬊ ⇨ + any punch (air)
Blink Hell Murder – ■, ■, ⇨, ✕, R1 (must have Level 3 Super Combo Gauge)

Gouki (Akuma) returns in super style, as ever!

Great Wave Motion Fist

street fighter ex plus

continued

Guile

First Appeared: Street Fighter II
Speciality: Sonic Boom

Special Moves
Spinning Back Knuckle – ⇨ + R1
Rolling Sobat – ⇦ or ⇨ + ○
Heavy Stub Kick – ⇦ or ⇨ + R2
Flying Buster Drop – Any direction (except ↘, ⇧ or ↗) + △ or R1 (air)
Sonic Boom – Hold ⇦, ⇨ + any punch
Somersault Kick – Hold ⇩, ⇧ + any kick

Super Combos
Rapid Punches & Kick – Hold ⇦, ⇨⇨ + any punch
Double Somersault Kick – Hold ↙, ↙↗ + any kick

Rapid Punches & Kick

Somersault Kick

Sonic Boom

Hokuto

First Appeared: Street Fighter Ex Plus α
Speciality: Neck Breaker

Special Moves
Deadly Elbow – ⇨ + R1
Deadly Leg – ⇨ + R2
Protect Against Attack – ⇦⇩↙ + any punch (use just before you're under attack)
Stream – Rotate 360° (anti) clockwise + any punch (close) (opponent undamaged, but open for attack)
Deadly Violent Elbow – ⇩↘⇨ + any punch
Crushing Palm – ⇩↘⇨ + any punch (use after Deadly Violent Elbow)
Vacuum Wave Attack – ⇩↙⇦ + any punch
Wave Leg Attack – ⇩↙⇦ + any kick

Super Combos
Trained Spirit Ball – ⇩↙⇦↙⇦ + any punch (hold & release punch to increase number of hits)
Phoenix Ability Attack – ⇩↙⇦⇩↙⇦ + any kick

Trained Spirit Ball

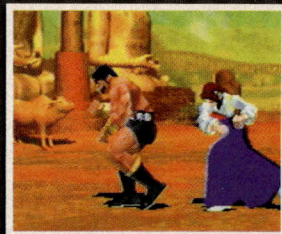

Stream

Evil Hokuto

First Appeared: Street Fighter Ex Plus α
Speciality: Neck Breaker

Special Moves
Deadly Elbow – ⇨ + R1
Deadly Leg – ⇨ + R2
Stream – Rotate 360° (anti) clockwise + any punch (close) (opponent undamaged, but open for attack)
Deadly Violent Elbow – ⇩↘⇨ + any punch
Leg Attack – ⇩↙⇦ + any kick
Phosphorous Palm Attack – ⇩↙⇦ + any punch (deflects projectiles)

Super Combos
Trained Spirit Ball – ⇩↙⇦↙⇦ + any punch (hold & release punch to increase number of hits)
Phoenix Ability Attack – ⇩↙⇦⇩↙⇦ + any kick
Connecting Rising Attack – ⇩↘⇨⇩↘⇨ + any punch
Connect Dance – ■, ■, ⇨, ✕, R1

Throwing a young school bird can't be recommended!

Phoenix Ability Attack

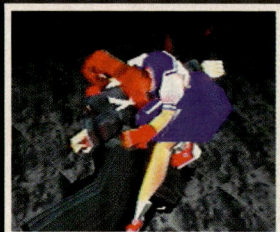

Connect Dance

Kairi

First Appeared: Street Fighter Ex Plus α
Speciality: Dragon Punch

Special Moves
God's Spirit Invoke – ⇩↘⇨ + any punch
Demon Dragon Destroying Light – ⇨⇩↘ + any punch
Nature Spirit Kick Rotation – ⇩↙⇦ + any kick (up to 3 times)

Super Combos
Devil God Discharge Motion – ⇩↘⇩↘⇨ + any punch (air)
Jackal Wolf Wicked Wind – ⇩↙⇦ + any punch
Refined Dragon Destroying Kick – ⇩↘⇨⇩↘⇨ + any kick (air)
Disastrous Omen Connect Dance – □, □, ⇨, ✕, R1

Disastrous Omen Connect Dance

Nature Spirit Kick Rotation

Demon Dragon Destroying Light

Street Fighter Ex Plus α

Ken Ken

First Appeared: Street Fighter
Speciality: Flaming Dragon Punch

Special Moves
Front Direction Body Revolve – ⬇ ↙ ⬅ +
any punch
Hell Windmill – Any direction (except ↘, ⬆ or
↗) + △ or R1 (air) (close)
Wave Motion Fist – ⬇ ↘ ⮕ +
any punch
Rising Dragon Fist – ⮕ ⬇ ↘ +
any punch
Tornado Whirlwind Leg –
⬇ ↙ ⬅ + any kick (up to 4 times)

Super Combos
Rising Dragon Render –
⬇ ↘ ⬇ ↘ + any punch
Great Dragon Fist –
⬇ ↘ ⬇ ↘ + any kick (tap any
button for extra hits)

Front Direction Body Revolve

Wave Motion Fist

Rising Dragon Render

Pullum Purna Purma

First Appeared: Street Fighter Ex Plus α
Speciality: Spiral Arrow

Special Moves
Femina Wind – ↘, ⬆ or ↗ (air)
Arakuru Wrist – ⮕ + ▲ (air)
Arakuru Wrist – ⬅ + ▲ (air)
Dance Wind – Any direction
(except ↘, ⬆ or ↗) + ▲ or R1
(air) (close)
Purimu Kick – ⮕ ⬇ ↘ + any kick
Teneru Kick – ⬇ ↙ ⬅ + any kick
Drill Purusu – ⬇ ↘ ⮕ + any kick
(air)

Super Combos
Somersault Kicks –
⬇ ↘ ⬇ ↘ + any kick
Twirl Kicks – ⬇ ↙ ⬅ ⬇ ↙ ⬅ +
any kick (air)

Purimu Kick

Somersault Kicks

Teneru Kick

Ryu Ryu

First Appeared: Street Fighter
Speciality: Fireball

Special Moves
Whirlwind Leg – ⮕ + ◯
Wave Motion Fist – ⬇ ↘ ⮕ + any punch
Rising Dragon Fist – ⮕ ⬇ ↘ + any punch
Tornado Whirlwind Leg –
⬇ ↙ ⬅ + any kick (up to 3 times)

Super Combos
Vacuum Wave Motion Fist –
⬇ ↘ ⮕ ⬇ ↘ ⮕ + any punch
**Vacuum Tornado Whirlwind
Leg** – ⬇ ↙ ⬅ ⬇ ↙ ⬅ + any kick
(air)

The one and only true Street
Fighter, Ryu. He's the man!

Wave Motion Fist

Vacuum Tornado Whirlwind Leg

Whirlwind Leg

Evil Ryu Evil Ryu

First Appeared: Street FighterAlpha 2
Speciality: Fireball

Special Moves
Whirlwind Leg – ⮕ + ●
Ashura Sky Flash Forward – ⮕ ⬇ ↘ + 3 punches (move to right) or
3 kicks (move to left)
Ashura Sky Flash Backward – ⬅ ⬇ ↙ + 3 punches (move to right)
or 3 kicks (move to left)
Wave Motion Fist – ⬇ ↘ ⮕ + any punch
Rising Dragon Fist – ⮕ ⬇ ↘ + any punch
Tornado Whirlwind Leg – ⬇ ↙ ⬅ + any kick (up to 4 times)

Super Combos
Vacuum Wave Motion Fist – ⬇ ↘ ⮕ ⬇ ↘ ⮕ + any punch
Vacuum Tornado Whirlwind Leg – ⬇ ↙ ⬅ ⬇ ↙ ⬅ + any kick
Deadly Great Rising Dragon – ⬇ ↘ ⮕ ⬇ ↘ + any punch
Blink Hell Murder – ■, ■, ⮕, ✕, R1 (must have Level 3 Super Combo
Gauge)

Ashura Sky Flash

Vacuum Wave Motion Fist

street fighter ex plus

continued

Sakura — *Sakura*

First Appeared: Street Fighter α
Speciality: Dashing Dragon Punch

Special Moves
Wave Motion Fist – ⇓ ⇘ ⇒ + any punch (3 times)
Cherry Blossom Fist – ⇒ ⇓ ⇘ + any punch
Spring Breeze Leg – ⇓ ⇙ ⇐ + any kick
Taunt – ✕, ✕, ⇐, □, R1

Super Combos
Vacuum Wave Motion Fist – ⇓ ⇘ ⇒ ⇓ ⇘ ⇒ + any punch
Cherry Riot – ⇓ ⇘ ⇒ ⇓ ⇘ + any kick
First Storm Of Spring – ⇓ ⇙ ⇐ ⇓ ⇙ ⇐ + any kick
Spring Hell Death – □, □, ⇒, ✕, R1

Cherry Blossom Fist

Taunt

Spring Hell Death (Honest!)

Skullomania — *Skullomania*

First Appeared: Street Fighter Ex Plus α
Speciality: Cannonball Attack

Special Moves
Stepping Upper – ⇒ + ▲
Heel Drop – ⇒ + ●
Skullo Dash – ⇒ ⇒ (press ⇐ once to stop)
Skullo Back Revolve – ⇐ ⇐
Skullo Head – ⇒ ⇓ ⇘ + any punch
Skullo Crusher – ⇓ ⇘ ⇒ + any punch
Skullo Slider – ⇓ ⇘ ⇒ + any kick
Skullo Dive – ⇐ ⇓ ⇙ + any punch
Skullo Power Stomp – ⇐ ⇓ ⇙ + any kick
Skullo Tackle – Skullo Dash into opponent
Taunt – Rotate 360° (anti) clockwise + R1

Super Combos
Super Skullo Crusher – ⇓ ⇘ ⇒ ⇓ ⇘ ⇒ + any punch
Super Skullo Slider – ⇓ ⇘ ⇒ ⇓ ⇘ ⇒ + any kick
Skullo Dream – ■, ■, ⇒, ✕, R1
Alternate Skullo Dream – Hold ⇓ + ■ + ✕ (use after Skullo Dream)
Skullo Dream Final – Hold ■ + ●, ⇓ ⇐ ⇒ ⇓ ⇙ (use after Skullo Dream)

Just when you thought there was no skeletons in the closet, out comes…

Skullo Tackle

Vega — (M Bison)

First Appeared: Street Fighter II
Speciality: Psycho Crusher

Special Moves
Vega Warp Forward – ⇒ ⇓ ⇘ + 3 punches or 3 kicks
Vega Warp Backward – ⇐ ⇓ ⇙ + 3 punches or 3 kicks
Psycho Crusher – Hold ⇐, ⇒ + any punch
Psycho Knee Press – Hold ⇐, ⇒ + any kick
Head Press – Hold ⇓, ⇑ + any kick (change leaping direction by pressing ⇐ or ⇒)
Somersault Skull Diver – Press any punch after Head Press

Super Combos
Psycho Cannon – Hold ⇐, ⇒ ⇐ ⇒ + any punch (hold & release punch to increase number of hits)
Knee Press Nightmare – Hold ⇐, ⇒ ⇐ ⇒ + any kick

The villain returns, but this time he's called Vega – Japanese humour surely!

Psycho Cannon

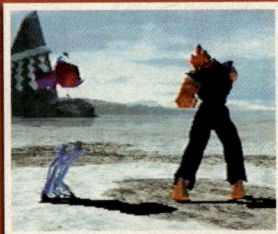

Vega Warp

Zangief — *Zangief*

First Appeared: Street Fighter II
Speciality: Spinning Piledriver

Special Moves
Flying Body Attack – ⇓ + R1 (air)
Stomach Block – ⇐ or ⇒ + any kick (behind opponent)
Double Lariat – 3 punches, ⇐ or ⇒ (pass through projectile attacks)
Screw Piledriver – Rotate 360° (anti) clockwise + any punch (close)
Russian Suplex – Rotate 360° (anti) clockwise + any kick (close)
Quick Double Lariat – 3 kicks, ⇐ or ⇒

Super Combos
Final Atomic Buster – Rotate 720° (anti) clockwise + any punch (close)
Final Atomic Buster Level 3 Version – Rotate 360° (anti) clockwise + 3 punches (close)
Super Stomping – ⇓ ⇘ ⇒ + any kick
Super Stomping Canceller – ⇓ ⇙ ⇐ + any kick (during Super Stomping)

Check out those rippling muscles!

Screw Piledriver

Super Stomping

Publisher:	GT Interactive
Price:	£44.99
Format:	UK

War Gods

Having **discovered a magical Ore**, ten humans have **evolved into War Gods. So what do they do** with their **new-found powers?** That's right: **knock seven bells out of each other** in the ring. This **guide** reveals **all the special moves** – though sadly **not the Tyson ear bite!**

This is where you enter the cheat you desire. To turn off the cheat, simply enter the off code.

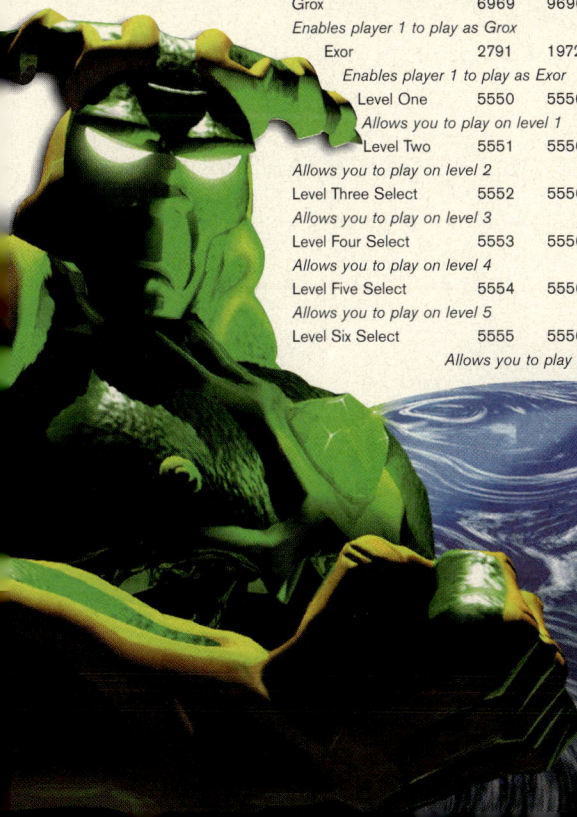

CHEATS

Cheat	On Code	Off Code
Enable Fatals	7453	3547
Enables fatalities (off by default)		
Free Play	0705	5070
Enables free play in options screen		
Player One Invincible	2358	8532
Player Two Invincible	1224	4221
Player One Extra Damage	7879	9787
Makes player 1 cause more damage		
Player Two Extra Damage	3961	1693
Makes player 2 cause more damage		
Quick Finish Game	4258	8524
Finish game after killing one CPU player		
Easy Fatalities	0322	2230
Pressing □ + ○ triggers a fatality		
Grox	6969	9696
Enables player 1 to play as Grox		
Exor	2791	1972
Enables player 1 to play as Exor		
Level One	5550	5556
Allows you to play on level 1		
Level Two	5551	5556
Allows you to play on level 2		
Level Three Select	5552	5556
Allows you to play on level 3		
Level Four Select	5553	5556
Allows you to play on level 4		
Level Five Select	5554	5556
Allows you to play on level 5		
Level Six Select	5555	5556
Allows you to play on		

level 6

Level Seven Select	5557	5556

Allows you to play on level 7 (secret level)

GENERAL HINTS

Blocking Throws
You need to press either ⇦ or ⇗ + R1 before counterattacking.

You Slide, You Win
The key to victory against all players, especially those who haven't yet come to grips with the game, is the 3D slide. Use this to knock the stuffing out of your opponent and annoy them like mad.

Getting Back Up With A Surprise
If, somehow, you get knocked to the floor, the 'Evasive manoeuvre' and 'Get-up attack' can be used to surprise your opponent before you suffer any more humiliation.

Shove Off
If your opponent is foolish enough to pause for a few seconds, run up to them and give 'em a shove. As the shove is unblockable, it leaves them vulnerable, so you can start a combo or other move. Then watch their health deteriorate fast.

Walk

GENERAL HINTS

backwards – ⇦
Walk forwards – ⇨
Crouch – ⇩
Jump – ⇧
High punch – □
Low punch – ✕
High kick – △
Low kick – ○
Block – R1

Flying punch – (⇧ or ⇗ or ⇖) + (□ or ✕)
Flying kick – (⇧ or ⇗ or ⇖) + (△ or ○)
Crouching low punch – ⇩ + ✕
Crouching low kick – ⇩ + ○
Uppercut – ⇩ + □
Roundhouse – ⇦ + △
Sweep kick – ⇦ + ○
Throw (close) – ⇨ + ✕
Run – ⇨ ⇨

Pounce attack – ⇧ + □, ⇧ + □, ⇧ + □
Evasive manoeuvre (on floor) – ⇦ + R1
Get-up attack (on floor) – ⇨ + □ + ✕

3D walk – 3D + ⇧ (or 3D + ⇩)
3D slide – 3D + ⇧, 3D + ⇧ (or 3D + ⇩, 3D + ⇩)
3D jump – 3D + R1 + ⇧ (or 3D + R1 + ⇩)

Start combo (close) – ⇦ ⇨ + □
Start combo (close) – ⇨ ⇨ + □
Start combo (close) (CY-5 & Ahau Kin) – ⇦ ⇨ + △

Finishing Moves
Auto combo – 3D + ⇦, 3D + ⇨, 3D + □

Auto combo (CY-5 & Ahua Kin) – 3D + ⇦, 3D + ⇨, 3D + △
Super kick – 3D + ⇦ + △
Super uppercut – ⇩ + □

syndicate wars

start

Publisher:	Bullfrog/Electronic Arts
Price:	£44.99
Format:	UK

Syndicate WARS

Are your cyborg agents forever **running off in the wrong direction?** Do they **always get slaughtered in gunfights?** Well, **fear not**. **Here we** reveal **top-secret tips** and **step-by-step mission guides** to help you **win those Syndicate Wars**.

1 player **Memory**

SYNDICATE WARS

WEAPONS

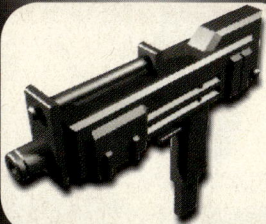

Uzi
Cost:	4,000
Damage:	0.5
Energy Used:	0.08
Delay:	–
Range:	50 yds
Effect Radius:	–

The classic machine gun is the most basic (ie, worst) weapon in the game. It's not very effective against anyone with armour, so you're better off selling your Uzis at the start and replacing them with the more powerful Miniguns.

Minigun
Cost:	12,000
Damage:	1
Energy Used:	0.2
Delay:	–
Range:	80 yds
Effect Radius:	–

A big step up from the Uzi, doing twice as much damage, the Minigun is a wonderful weapon that you should always have with you. Miniguns can even hold their own in battle against Pulse Lasers, due to the lack of firing delay.

Persuadertron/ Indoctrinator
Cost:	15,000
Damage:	–
Energy Used:	0.3 per point
Delay:	–
Range:	–
Effect Radius:	30 yds

The standard electronic device for persuading people over to your side. At least one of your agents should carry one. With enough followers, police and enemy agents can be persuaded, but you'll need the Persuadertron II to persuade Zealots.

Knockout Gas
Cost:	8,000
Damage:	–
Energy Used:	6
Delay:	3 secs
Range:	60 yds
Effect Radius:	25 yds

It's always worth carrying a few canisters of this on missions. It'll knock out a group of enemies for 15 to 20 seconds, rendering them sitting ducks for your guns. Just don't get too close to the gas yourself or you'll feel its effects.

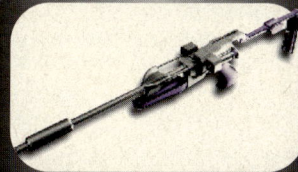

LR Rifle
Cost:	30,000
Damage:	13
Energy	Used: 2
Delay:	7
Range:	160
Effect Radius:	–

The ultimate sniper's weapon, this is great for picking off targets from distance: two shots will usually take out an agent. The only downside is the long reload delay, so use hit-and-run tactics to avoid being left vulnerable between shots.

Razor Wire
Cost:	10,000
Damage:	up to 10
Energy Used:	0.5 per sec
Delay:	–
Range:	–
Effect Radius:	–

This near-invisible wire can be laid across an area, heavily damaging any enemies that try to cross it. As it's difficult to lure enemies into such a trap, it's main use is for defence. You can see your own wire and not be damaged by it.

Disrupter
Cost:	20,000
Damage:	–
Energy Used:	–
Delay:	–
Range:	–
Effect Radius:	10 yds

An anti-Persuadertron, this can free people persuaded by enemies. You have to get close to the persuader.

Flamer
Cost:	16,000
Damage:	10 per sec
Energy Used:	0.7 per sec
Delay:	–
Range:	40 yds
Effect Radius:	5 yds

Although great fun to use, frazzling enemies to a cinder, it uses a lot of energy and costs more than a Minigun. Even worse, any agent carrying a Flamer is slowed to half speed. However, it can come in very handy when surrounded by a crowd of enemies.

Grenade
Cost:	100,000
Damage:	100 + fire
Energy Used:	6
Delay:	3 secs
Range:	60 yds
Effect Radius:	40 yds

It detonates on contact with any solid object, so take care you're not standing too near any lampposts when throwing one!

GENERAL TIPS

* In general, keep your agents together: their combined firepower makes them much less vulnerable to attack.
* Make sure you've got the necessary equipment to complete the mission – eg, it's no good trying to capture personnel without a Persuadertron.
* Steal a car whenever you can: it makes getting around the map a lot easier and lets you pass through barriers. However, don't stay in the car if under heavy attack – if it blows up, you're almost certainly a goner.
* Pick up weapons from dead enemies to sell when you get back to base.
* You'll need to rob banks to get more cash, so look out for them during missions.
* If outnumbered, use knockout gas to paralyse the enemies so you can blast them with ease.
* If you hear a warning siren or see a red glow, run for it: a bomb is about to explode.
* Don't stand near lampposts or grey bins: they explode when hit by any weapon.
* Don't use explosive weapons in confined spaces, as you're likely to get caught in the shockwave.

syndicate wars

Pulse Laser

Cost:	37,000
Damage:	2
Energy Used:	0.2
Delay:	0.5 secs
Range:	90 yds
Effect Radius:	

Its shots do twice as much damage as the Minigun (and can be supercharged), but then you don't get the same constant stream of fire. If you find any Pulse Lasers on dead enemies, you're probably best off selling them for lots of cash.

Electron Mace

Cost:	42,000
Damage:	2
Energy Used:	0.02
Delay:	5 secs
Range:	90 yds
Effect Radius:	–

The Zealots' favourite weapon, this electrically charged 'whip' packs all the punch of a Pulse Laser (and can also be supercharged). However, it takes longer to recharge and is more expensive, so you're best off selling any Electron Maces you find.

MISSIONS

EuroCorp Mission 1

London: Eliminate Unguided citizens

Recommended Equipment: Miniguns

Before starting the mission, sell your Uzis and equip all your agents with Miniguns. Stroll west, killing the Unguided indicated on your radar, then northwest. Return to HQ when all targets are killed. You can pick up Uzis from dead enemies to sell later. That's the first mission over!

Get your Miniguns out and splatter those Unguided citizens all over the pavement. Pick up their Uzis to sell later.

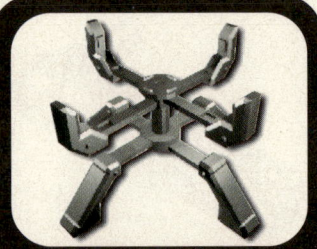

Cerberus IFF

Cost:	65,000
Damage:	5
Energy Used:	6
Delay:	0.25 secs
Range:	–
Effect Radius:	70 yds

Another defensive device, this robotic drone can be placed to guard a position, using its Pulse Laser on anyone coming within range. Used well, you can double your firepower, but make sure you remember which drones are yours.

Launcher

Cost:	75,000
Damage:	8 (+10 shock)
Energy Used:	3
Delay:	30 secs
Range:	120 yds
Effect Radius:	30 yds

Now we're talking! A Launcher may be heavy and expensive, but then just one of its rockets can fry a whole group of agents – while four will blow up a car. Just don't use them in a confined space or you may get caught in the blast!

Clone Shield

Cost:	50,000
Damage:	–
Energy Used:	0.5 per sec
Delay:	–
Range:	–
Effect Radius:	–

This clever little device disguises you temporarily as a civilian, so you can walk right past enemy guards unnoticed. However, you still have to watch out for punks who go around shooting civilians!

Explosive

Cost:	48,000
Damage:	50
Energy Used:	2
Delay:	3 secs
Range:	–
Effect Radius:	40 yds

This time bomb takes about 12 seconds to detonate once placed, although you can also set it off by shooting it. Great for blowing up gates and banks, just make sure you stay well clear of the blast. and the resulting fireball. The damage caused is catastrophic.

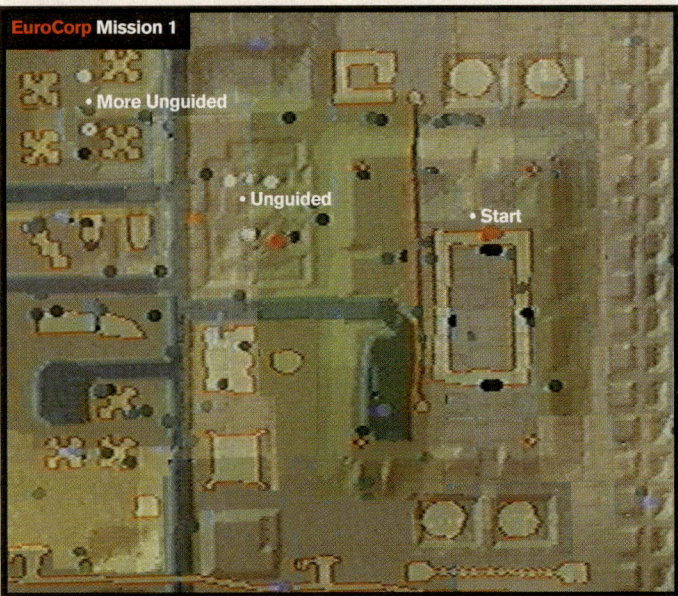

EuroCorp Mission 1

• More Unguided

• Unguided

• Start

SYNDICATE WARS

BODY PARTS

You'll need to keep upgrading your cyborg agents with the latest body modifications to make them tough enough for the later missions. If you've got the money, go for the best body bits you can get. Also, be on the lookout for advanced skin types during missions – they can't be bought.

ARMS 1
Cost: 2,500
Power Output: 7
Resilience: 20
Effects: +1.25 health, +33% throw range

BODY 1
Cost: 5,000
Power Output: 8
Resilience: 0
Effects: +1.25 health, +0.5/sec recovery, + stamina, +5 energy
You'll need this first body mod in order to buy any other parts.

BRAIN 1
Cost: 4,500
Power Output: 5
Resilience: 100
Effects: +1.25 health, +5 shield, x2 persuade range

BRAIN 2
Cost: 18,000
Power Output: 4
Resilience: 100
Effects: +2.5 health, +10 shield, x3 persuade range

BRAIN 3
Cost: 45,000
Power Output: 4
Resilience: 100
Effects: +3.25 health, +15 shield, x4 persuade range

ARMS 2
Cost: 10,000
Power Output: 8
Resilience: 60
Effects: +2.5 health, +66% throw range

ARMS 3
Cost: 25,000
Power Output: 6
Resilience: 60
Effects: +1.25 health, x2 throw range

BODY 3
Cost: 50,000
Power Output: 4
Resilience: 100
Effects: +3.25 health, +1.5/sec recovery, + stamina, +15 energy

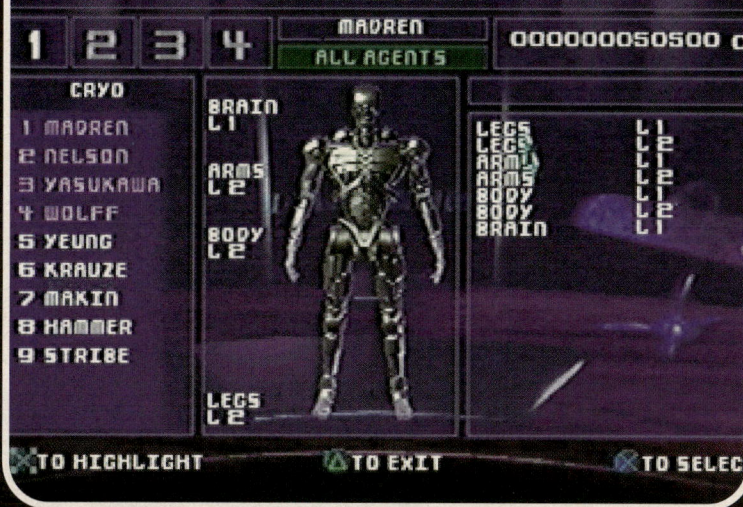

BODY 2
Cost: 20,000
Power Output: 4
Resilience: 100
Effects: +2.5 health, +1/sec recovery, + stamina, +10 energy
Required for other higher level modifications.

LEGS 1
Cost: 3,000
Power Output: 5
Resilience: 5
Effects: +1.25 health, + stamina, +2 speed

LEGS 2
Cost: 12,000
Power Output: 8
Resilience: 20
Effects: +2.5 health, + stamina, +4 speed

LEGS 3
Cost: 30,000
Power Output: 7
Resilience: 20
Effects: +3.25 health, + stamina, +6 speed

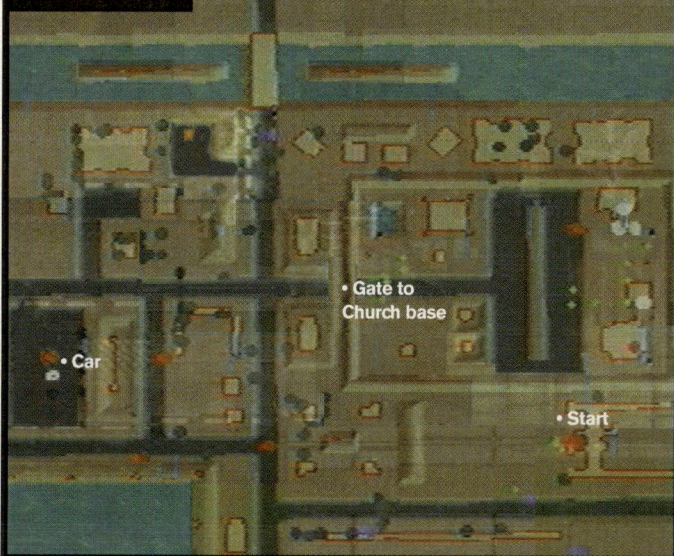

EuroCorp Mission 2

- Gate to Church base
- Car
- Start

EuroCorp Mission 2
Detroit: Eliminate Zealots
Recommended Equipment:
Miniguns

Kill the swines which attack you at the start, then head west so you can turn the corner past the wall and go north. Keep a lookout for cop cars.

Steal a car so you can get around faster – you can even run over targets and do drive-by shootings, though you're vulnerable to attack if the car's badly damaged. Watch out for cops near your base when evacuating.

If you want to get ahead, get a car. There's one in the southwest corner for you to steal. The gate to the Church base may be blown up by punks anyway. Go in and kill those Zealots.

syndicate wars

continued

EuroCorp Mission 3
Hong Kong: Persuade Yamaguchi technicians
Recommended Equipment: Miniguns, Persuadertron

Kill the agents which attack in the car park near the start. Then steal a nearby vehicle and drive into the fusion plant.

Once you've blasted the enemy agents in the car park, you can nick any of the vehicles.

Get out of the vehicle quickly to kill the guards which attack. When they're all dead, equip the Persuadertron and chase the target technicians in the plant. Get back in the car (and wait for the technicians to get in) and head to the Evac point.

Once you've driven into the fusion plant and killed the guards, persuade the technicians and evacuate.

EuroCorp Mission 4
Matochkin Star: Persuade Bluesky Tendencies scientists
Recommended Equipment: Miniguns, Persuadertron, Explosives

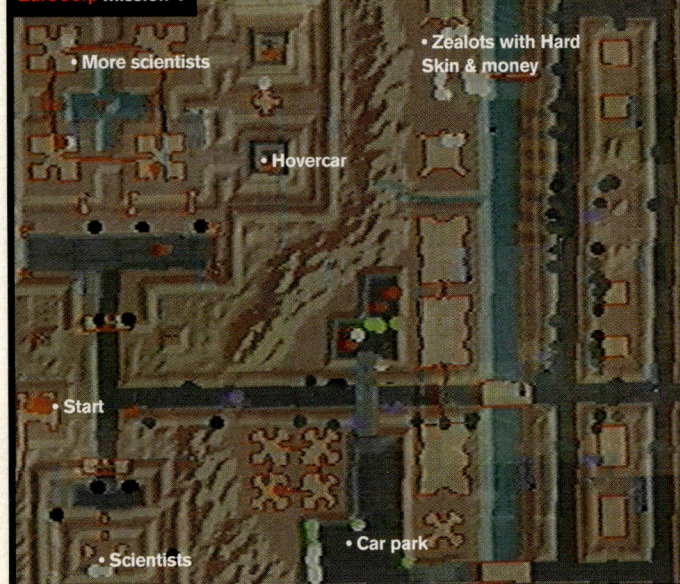

Go up the road in the southeast corner to reach the south car park – run past the armoured car. Eliminate any Unguided in the area, then steal a vehicle.

Drive into the target compound. Get out and kill the guards (if your car is destroyed in the melee, you'll have to blow up the gate to exit). Then enter the building and persuade the scientists.

Drive to next target: a complex in the NW corner. Get out and kill any guards, then enter and persuade the remaining scientists. Get back in the car and drive south through the barrier a little way. Get out and walk to the Evac point.

SYNDICATE WARS

EuroCorp Mission 5

Singapore: Deliver bullion to Evac zone

Recommended Equipment:
Miniguns, LR Rifles, Knockout Gas, Explosives

You have to hijack a bullion car from outside the bank and drive away with the loot. Note that if the target vehicle is destroyed, the mission will fail, so be careful not to damage it. From the start, kill the rifle sniper who attacks you. Then grab the car from the nearby parking bay (wait for the guy to park it there).

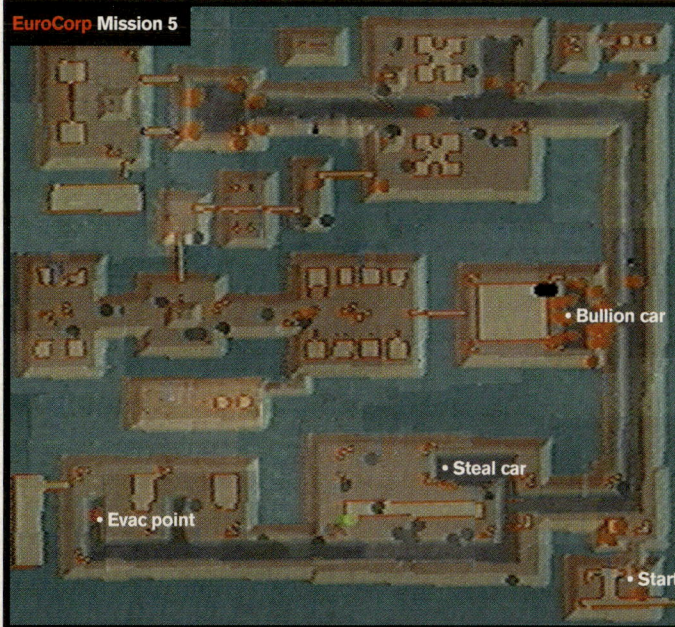

Drive outside the bank – where the white radar signal is emitted from. Get out of the car and ambush the guards which rush out of the compound – use Knockout Gas, if you want. Then blow up the armoured car blocking the entrance.

If the coast is clear, just run in and get into the bullion car (Bullfrog truck) and simply drive it away to the Evac point. Hurrah, you now have a million extra credits to play with.

EuroCorp Mission 5

- Bullion car
- Steal car
- Evac point
- Start

Once you've eliminated all the guards, steal the bullion car and drive it to the Evac point.

EuroCorp Mission 6

Phoenix: Penetrate defences of cult's temple and steal technology

Recommended Equipment:
Miniguns, LR Rifles, Knockout Gas

On the way to the temple, you may want to rob the bank first. Use Knockout Gas on the guards and punks, then Minigun them down and grab the loot.

Approach temple and kill the angry mob of Zealots, keeping out of range of their Electron Maces (pick one up to take back, and a Disrupter). Again, Knockout Gas is recommended.

If a flying APC attacks, run for it, then use LR Rifles and Miniguns to shoot it down. Shoot all the Zealots which pour out of temple and search their bodies for the secret technology. Once found, take it back to the Evac point.

EuroCorp Mission 6

- Church base
- Bank
- Start

syndicate wars

continued

EuroCorp Mission 7

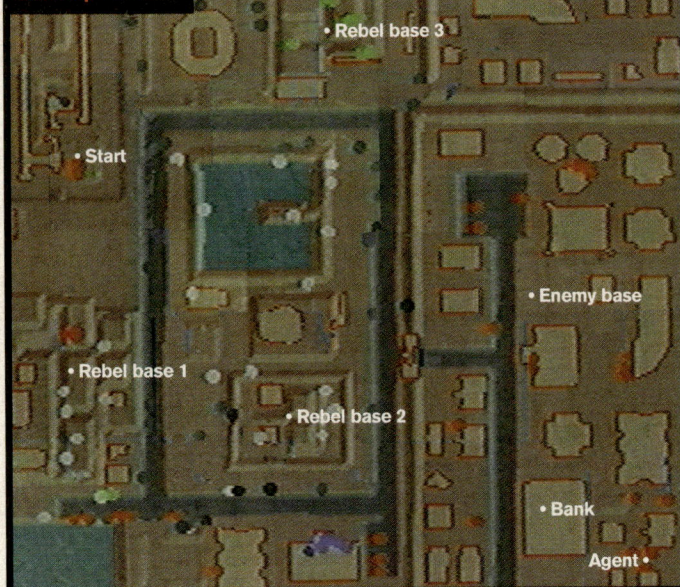

Rome: Eliminate all Unguided citizens and kill enemy Agent
Recommended Equipment: Miniguns, LR Rifles, Knockout Gas, Explosives

This one's a real riot! Head towards target building and use LR Rifles on approach to knock out a couple of punks. They'll soon retaliate with Satellite Rain, so leg it across the street to avoid the explosions.

EuroCorp Mission 7

- Rebel base 3
- Start
- Enemy base
- Rebel base 1
- Rebel base 2
- Bank
- Agent •

And the weather forecast for today… there'll be satellite rain in the downtown area, causing huge explosions.

Shoot any surviving targets, then head over the street to the nearby rebel building. Watch out for spider droids – run away from their lasers and use LR Rifles to pick them off.

Once you've eliminated the targets, you need to quell a riot in another building on the other side of the city. Watch out

for more explosions on approach, and Knockout Gas: it's best to send one man in and drop your own Knockout Gas to lure the targets out.

Steal a car to get into the base and use LR Rifles to pick off laser-wielding guards. To make it easier to reach the agent in the corner, blow up the bank. Watch out for more laser-wielding guards as you enter the compound to kill the agent. Once he's dead, drive to Evac point.

FUTURE WARS

Befitting such a supremely polished game, Syndicate Wars starts with a stunning Full Motion Video intro sequence in the dark cyberpunk style of Blade Runner and other sci-fi classics. Panning down through a futuristic city, the scene shows a hovership zooming away from a downtown building, the latter exploding mere moments later. The police soon give chase in their hovercars, darting between city skyscrapers in hot pursuit until they finally nail it.

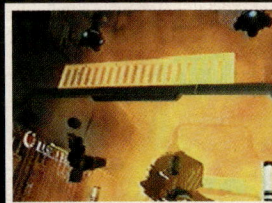

SYNDICATE WARS

EuroCorp Mission 8

Phoenix: Neutralise rogue agent
Recommended Equipment:
Miniguns, LR Rifles, Persuadertron, Knockout Gas, Explosives

A group of zealots attacks immediately, so be ready with Miniguns. Use LR Rifles to wipe out all the zealots in the city first, then go and take on the Unguided in the corner – lure them out, then run away to recharge your rifles.

You can now steal a vehicle where the Unguided were. But first, go and persuade a small army and get them all into your car! (Alternatively, you can do this beforehand to try and persuade all the Unguided instead of killing them, but it's trickier.)

Now it's time to go after the rogue agent. Drive into the base and run after the guards to persuade them. Run round to the target agent and persuade him before he can get into his car. Then go back to the car park and drive/fly out of there to evacuate.

EuroCorp Mission 9

New York: Persuade Jennifer Taks
Recommended Equipment:
Miniguns, LR Rifles, Persuadertron, Launchers, Explosives

Pump up your red mist and kill laser guards just to the south of the start point with LR Rifles. Pick up their Pulse Lasers to sell later. Use Launchers to blow up the two flying vehicles which attack. If the

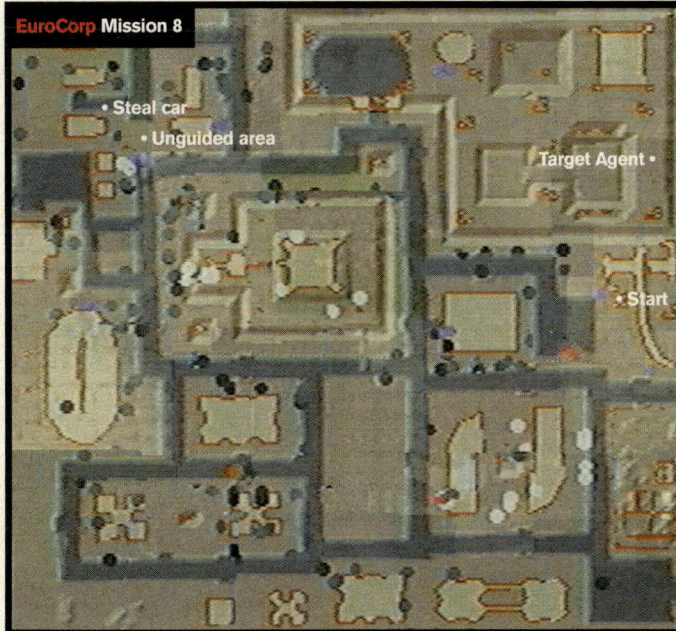

taxi lands, more guards will get out – note that is also packed with explosives, so keep clear once you destroy it.

Head towards the target until you see a large number of enemies appear on the scanner. Back off and take out as many as you can with LR Rifles or Launchers. Some are carrying explosives, so don't get too close!

Watch out for the civilian approaching the car: this disguised enemy will lay some explosives and run towards you unless you shoot him first. You can then steal his Clone Shield.

Now go inside and persuade the target: the executive who'll help you infiltrate the NAR building. Get in the car, equip your men with LR Rifles, and drive just inside the target compound. The place is crawling with police so get out ASAP and chuck a can of Knockout Gas, then shoot them with LR Rifles. Make sure the executive is

safely behind your men (it helps if you have a crowd of persuaded people).

Once the police are all dead, switch to Launchers to destroy the flying vehicle which attacks. Now go and persuade Jennifer. Get in the police car and fly to the Evac point – you'll easily survive the fire of chasing vehicles.

Note: You can also rob the bank on this level, but it's risky doing this when Jennifer is with you, as four flying police cars will attack.

Left: Watch out for laser-wielding guards in the car park. Back off and snipe at them with LR Rifles.

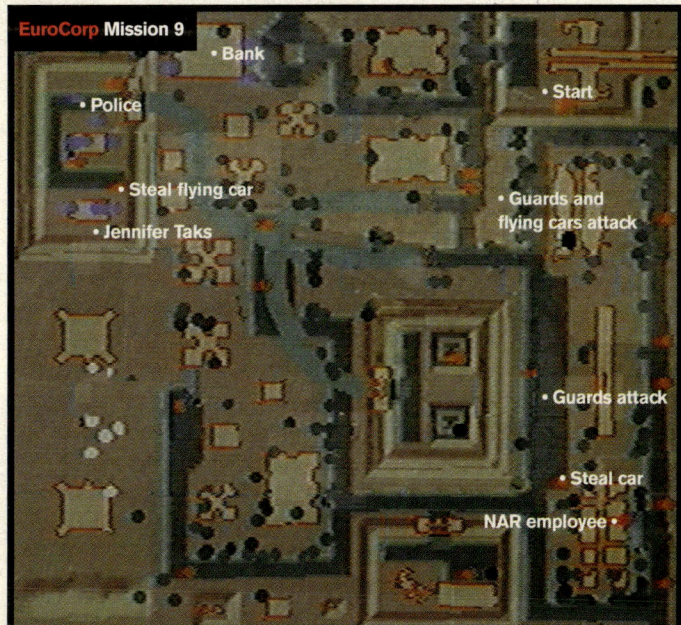

syndicate wars

continued

EuroCorp Mission 10
Cape Town: Persuade scientist
Recommended Equipment:
Miniguns, LR Rifles, Persuadertron,
Launchers, Explosives

At the start, the area is swarming with punks and police, so be ready with LR Rifles, then Miniguns. Many punks are carrying explosives, so watch out for explosions after you kill them. Destroy the two police cars with launchers.

EuroCorp Mission 10

Scientist • • Blow hole in wall
Church base • • IML Link
• Start

You're attacked at the start by police and punks. Watch out for explosions.

Once you've massacred the enemies in the vicinity, head north through the gap up the side of the Church base. Plant explosives to blow a hole in the middle of the east wall. Get launchers ready for a flying vehicle attack.

Enter the compound through the hole, then use LR Rifles to pick off all the

ESCORT SCIENTIST TO IML LINK

This one starts with a fierce shootout. Get your Miniguns equipped to deal with the rifle-wielding punks and laser-firing police which attack in large numbers at the start. Activate supershields and blast away until the coast is clear. You can then steal one of the police vehicles, if you want.

Zealots, retreating through the hole if necessary.

Only once they're all killed (including the ones by the gate), you should go and persuade the scientist. You'll then be able to escort him through the hole to the nearby IML Link without further attacks.

EuroCorp Mission 11
Adelaide: Persuade scientist
Recommended Equipment:
Miniguns, LR Rifles, Persuadertron,
Launchers

Head towards the Zealot temple in the east part of the city. Use LR Rifles to snipe at the Zealots from the road (do drive-by shootings, if you prefer). If a Zealot flying car attacks, switch to Launchers and run for it until it's downed. Only once all the Zealots are eliminated should you go in and persuade the scientist (inside the pyramid). Now steal a car from the nearby parking bay and head straight for the IML Link.

Blow a hole in the east wall of the Church base, then get ready to fight the angry Zealots.

EuroCorp Mission 11

- Start
- Unguided & police attack
- Church base
- Scientist

you can sell later.

Gradually make your way over to the east part of the city, luring out enemies (preferably one or two at a time) from the buildings and picking them off with LR Rifles. Watch out for the pair of flying cars which attack as you near the east side – leg it and use Launchers. Finally, you need to kill off a spider droid – use LR Rifles with hit-and run- tactics.

Equip with LR RIfles and use hit-and-run tactics to pick off the Zealots.

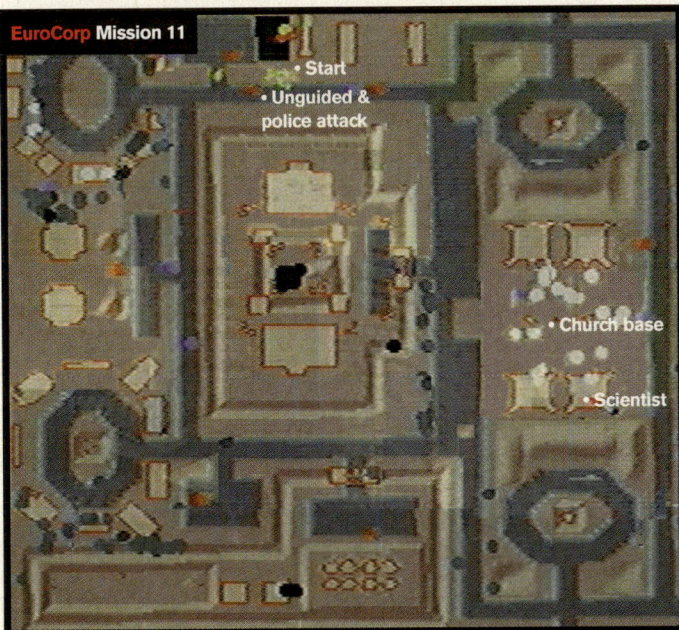

EuroCorp Mission 12

Nuuk: Conduct full sweep of city, eliminate Zealots

Recommended Equipment: Miniguns, LR Rifles, Launchers, Knockout Gas

There are an awful lot of Zealots on this level. The best thing to do is equip with LR Rifles and pick them off as they approach, running away to recharge. Knockout Gas may come in handy if attacked by a large group.

Switch to Launchers if a flying vehicle attacks. Watch out for ambushes as you

walk around the city. Particularly try to avoid getting enemies on either side of you. Frisk dead bodies for weapons which

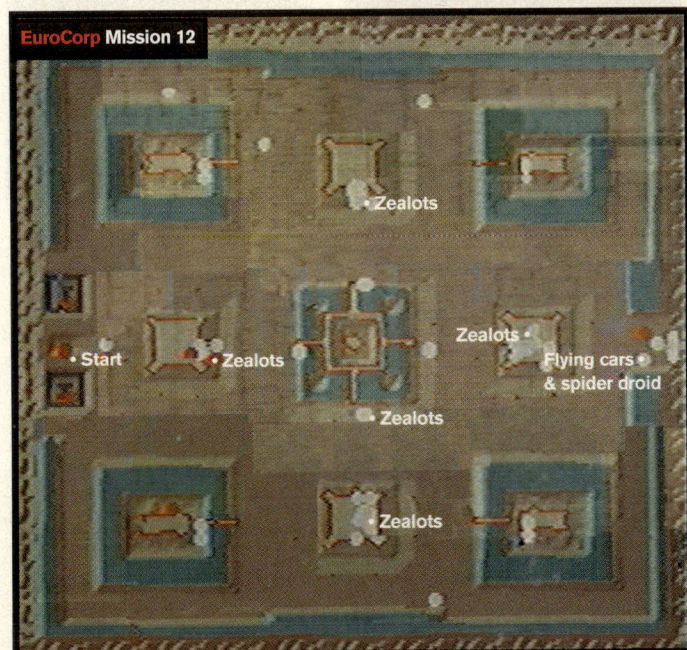

EuroCorp Mission 12

- Zealots
- Start
- Zealots
- Zealots
- Zealots
- Flying cars & spider droid
- Zealots
- Zealots

PERSUASION

Why go around killing everyone? Peace, love, electronic brainwashing. Civilians, police, and even enemy agents can be persuaded to join your side. At the end of a mission, the latter are added to your Cryovat. However, to capture agents you'll need to accrue enough persuasion points from civilians and others: this table shows how many you need, and how many each follower is worth.

TARGET	POINTS REQUIRED	POINTS WORTH
Civilian	0	1
Scientist	0	1
Police/Guard	6	2
Unguided	10	2
Government Official	15	3
Agent	20	5
Zealot	20*	1

*Note: Zealots can only be persuaded using Persuadertron II.

syndicate wars

EuroCorp Mission 13

Tokyo: Rescue Professor Drennan from cultists

Use Launchers to shoot down the flying car which attacks at the start

Recommended Equipment: Miniguns, LR Rifles, Launchers, Explosives, Knockout Gas

You're attacked by a flying car at the start, so use Launchers to destroy it (if you're getting hammered, you can always hide under a building until recovered – a good general tip).

If you really need some more cash,

Robbing the bank is tricky as the police soon arrive in flying cars

EuroCorp Mission 13

- Start
- Destroy flying vehicles
- Drennan
- Twin lasers
- Church base
- Bank
- Unguided march from north
- Unguided

head towards the city bank and plant some explosives beneath it. Then leg it because the cops will arrive in force, including two flying cars. Use hit-and-run tactics on them, then return to the bank to pick up the loot.

Try to avoid the Unguided marching from north to south and stay well away

from the southeast corner of the city as it's crawling with Unguided, some armed with Launchers.

Move your men just to the west of the cult stronghold and shoot down the two flying vehicles which attack. The Zealots should then pour out of the temple, so run for it (chuck a can of Knockout Gas if you think it'll help) and switch between Launchers and LR Rifles to snipe at them from distance. If they get too close, activate supershields, then leg it.

When all your pursuers are dead, enter the temple (stay on the east side of the road to avoid the twin police laser turrets opposite the entrance. Use LR Rifles to shoot any remaining Zealots inside, then rescue Drennan and head for the target IML Link.

EuroCorp Mission 14

Bangkok: Escort Professor Drennan to EuroCorp campus
Recommended Equipment: Miniguns, Launchers

Immediately arm with Miniguns and kill the first Zealot which attacks, then use Launchers to eliminate the ones inside the IML Link.

Once you've killed the first group of Zealots, Drennan will begin walking north to the campus. If he gets hit too many times, he'll die and the mission will fail. So if Drennan comes under attack, get between him and the Zealots, activate supershields, and gun them down.

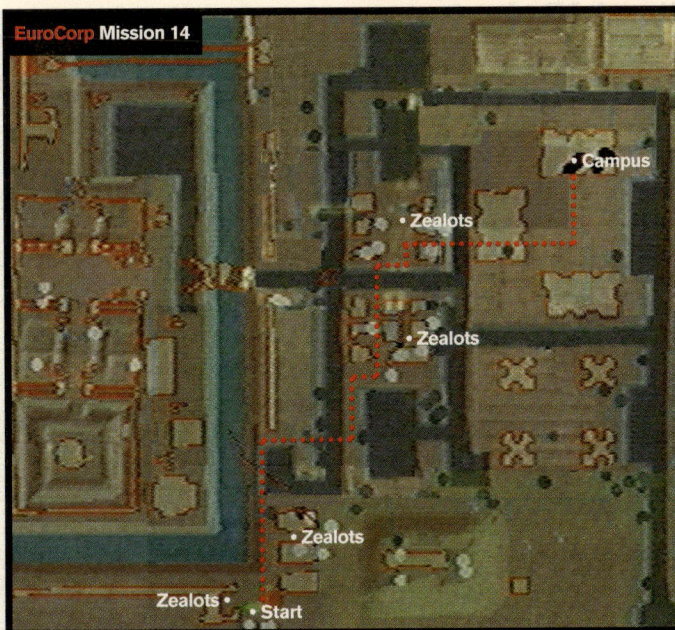

EuroCorp Mission 14

Watch out for a couple of Zealots trying to sneak around the back – locate them on the radar and go and kill them. Make sure the coast is clear, then run northeast to kill the four Zealots who are hiding in the cluster of buildings. In the buildings to the north (by the hotel) is another group of Zealots, so go and gun them down when your energy has recharged. The rest of the journey should be safe.

Get back in the car, drive out of the complex and straight to the Evac point. There, that wasn't so difficult, was it?

Steal the police car from near the start and drive into the EuroCorp base.

Walk slightly ahead and eliminate the Zealots who try to ambush you. Kill the ones in the first alley and the ones ahead.

Church Mission 1

Detroit: Capture EuroCorp substation
Recommended Equipment: Miniguns

As with the EuroCorp missions, before you begin you should sell all your agents' Uzis and replace them with the far more effective Miniguns. Eliminate the guards and police which attack at the start, then steal the police car to the west of the start point and drive it into the EuroCorp base. Get out an kill all the guards showing up as targets on the radar. Then simply walk into the target bunker to automatically plant the virus.

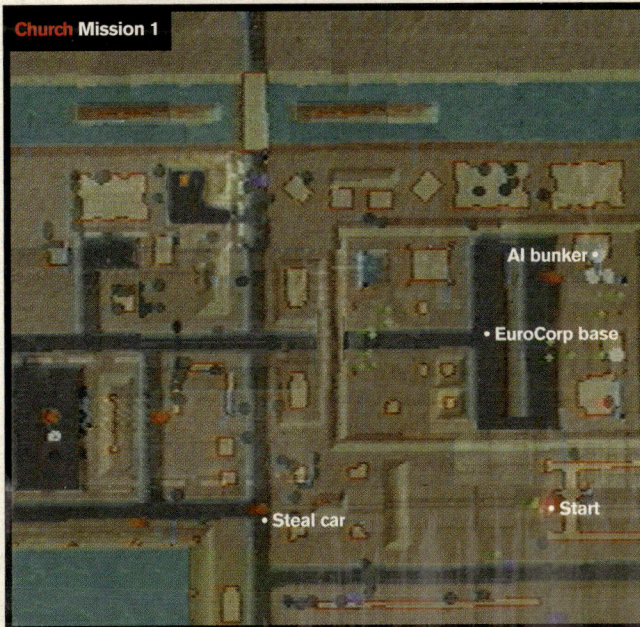

Church Mission 1

syndicate wars

start

EUROCORP MISSION 15

Extra Tips

Just a few extra pointers for that tricky escort mission…

As before, eliminate the first wave of Zealots by laying Trigger Wire in the

Lay loads of Trigger Wire in the entrance to the reservoir, then lure the Zealots to their death.

reservoir entrance, finishing off survivors with Launchers. Then do the same for the punks on the east side.

The best way to destroy the tank is to chase it southwards once it turns round, repeatedly firing Launchers as it exits the top of the screen – it's far easier to hit when moving away from you.

Put the executives in the far corner, well away from the conflict. Lay down tons of Trigger Wire in the reservoir entrance and up the road, then lure in the Zealots. Make sure you shoot down the flying APC with Launchers. Use the same Trigger Wire technique for the Zealots in SW of the crossroads and the punks near the IML Link (although you could try legging it past the latter). If any enemies get through the wire, finish them off with Launchers. Once the route is clear, take the executives to the IML Link.

EUROCORP MISSION 16

Johannesburg: Persuade Mirabelle Lucy DeSaxo
Recommended Equipment:
Whatever you can steal!

You start this mission with just one agent, armed with a Persuadertron and LR Rifle. De Saxo is impossible to catch, so you have to keep scaring her into moving on.

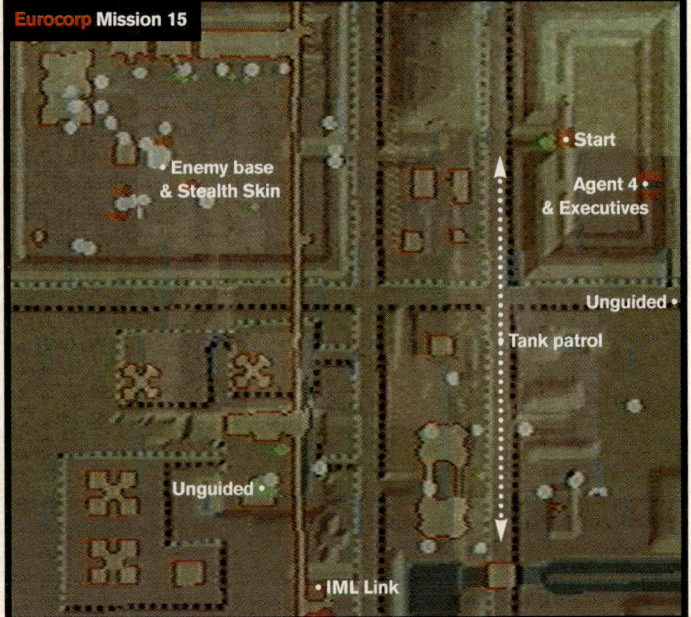

Eurocorp Mission 15

- Enemy base & Stealth Skin
- Start
- Agent 4 & Executives
- Unguided
- Tank patrol
- Unguided
- IML Link

SYNDICATE WARS

A Zealot immediately attacks you, so shoot him and nick his Minigun. If you want, you can steal an Electron Mace by killing another of the Zealots in the area (walk north and one will attack you).

Now go up the transporter tube just to the east of the start point. Once you arrive at the top you'll be attacked by lots of Zealots. You've no chance of defeating them all, so just use your supershield and leg it for the exit tube. The point of going

up there was to spook De Saxo into moving. Run for it and pick off the Zealots which chase you.

When the coast is clear, grab the nearby bike (on the corner just to the northeast) and head to the car park next to the roundabout in the northeast corner. Get out and walk south across the road and pick off one of the Zealots using the LR Rifle. More Zealots will come out and chase you. Run away and pick them off, then go and grab a Launcher off one of the dead bodies. Go back into the compound where the Launcher Zealot was and pick off any more Zealots (one of whom has a Flamer).

Head up the ramp at the east end of the car park. Proceed through the buildings to the south until you reach a garden. Lure out the Zealots (one of whom has a Launcher), then run away, picking them off one by one. Now head through the shuttle tube and either use the Flamer on the three Zealots, or activate the supershield and run for the

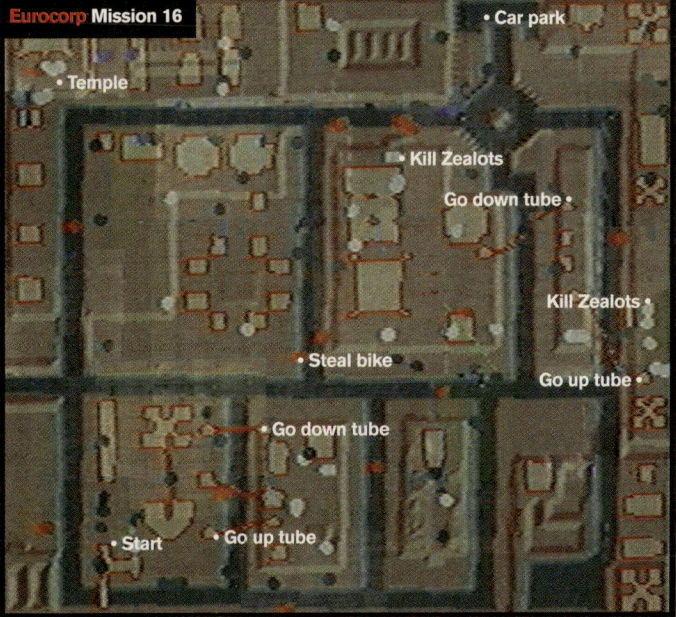

Eurocorp **Mission 16**

- Car park
- Temple
- Kill Zealots
- Go down tube •
- Kill Zealots •
- Steal bike
- Go up tube •
- Go down tube
- Start • Go up tube

exit tube. The lower compound should be clear, as you shot all the Zealots earlier.

De Saxo will now have moved to the temple in the northwest corner. As soon as you approach it, she'll get spooked again and run for the IML Link. Now go there yourself to complete the mission.

In this mission you have to keep chasing DeSaxo around the city until she runs for the IML Link where you started.

EUROCORP MISSION 17
Cairo: Eliminate Mirabelle Lucy DeSaxo
Recommended Equipment: Pulse Lasers or Miniguns, LR Rifles, Automedikits, Launchers

As you weren't able to persuade DeSaxo, you'll just have to eliminate her.

From the start, equip your men with Launchers or Pulse Lasers and stand firm to eliminate the first group of attackers.

Now head north along the road and use Launchers to shoot down the

Eurocorp **Mission 17**

- Kill VIPs for money
- Church base •
- Steal flying car •
- Car park
- Tank
- Tank
- DeSaxo's car •
- Start

flying vehicle which attacks you on the downward slope (try to shoot it down so it destroys the road).

Carry on towards the Zealot building and use LR Rifles to pick off the Zealots which rush out as you run away. When they get close, switch to Miniguns, Pulse Lasers, or Launchers. Return to the building to lure out a second group of Zealots

and repeat the same method. If you want some money and a Plasma Lance, attack the building in the northwest corner. As you shoot at the bodyguards, the VIPs will run for their cars, unaware that the road is destroyed up ahead (where you shot down the flying car earlier), so go and kill them. Now enter the building which you previously cleared of Zealots and steal the flying vehicle (run past the laser turrets). Head straight towards DeSaxo's car, to make her fly off around the city. She'll eventually land in the northeast car park – so try to head her off there. You'll come under heavy attack from Zealots and spider droids when you land: just activate supershields, chase after DeSaxo, and assassinate her with Launchers. Then quickly jump in a flying car and head straight for the Evac point.

syndicate wars

continued

EUROCORP MISSION 18

Bahrain: Neutralise rogue Agents and destroy Unguided assaults before they reach the AI building.
Recommended Equipment: Plasma Lances, LR Rifles, Launchers, Cerberus IFFs, Grenades, Automedikits

Use LR Rifles to wipe out any enemies in the vicinity, then send one Agent round to throw a Grenade into the middle of the large group of enemies behind the semicircular building to the south. Many of them are carrying explosives, so be ready for more explosions. Pick off survivors with LR Rifles, along with the tank and lorry.

Throw a Grenade at the punks behind the building, then finish off the tank and lorry.

Now head west for the path across the river (not the road). Shoot the punks the other side, then run across before their explosives detonate. You'll now be attacked by a couple of flying vehicles: use Plasma Lances to see them off (hide inside a building if you're low on energy). Next head south down the road to the stone pyramid. Run into the corner and steal the tank. Drive it out and shoot at the pursuing enemy Agents. When it's low on energy, get out.

When all the enemy Agents are dead, you'll be attacked from the north by a couple of tanks and lots of troops. Place your Cerberus IFFs on the road between the AI building and the harbour. Pick off

Eurocorp Mission 18

- Blow up temple to steal money
- Path
- Pyramid
- Steal tank
- AI building
- Start
- Tank & Lorry
- Flying vehicles

any survivors that get through, then destroy the two tanks. The safest way to do this is hide behind the stone pyramid, firing Launchers across at the tanks from the opposite bottom corner (if a flying car attacks during this laborious process, switch to Plasma Lances to shoot it down).

You'll then be attacked by up to four flying cars! Deal with them using the Plasma Lances, hiding in buildings if you're getting hammered. Once you've destroyed them, you can evacuate. But before doing so, you may as well pick up the money from the Zealot temple in the northwest corner. Just blow the place up with a Grenade, then take one Agent in to get the four cases of money – watch out for Satellite Rain if you hang about, though.

EUROCORP MISSION 19

Colombo: Retake control of the orbital elevator facility.
Recommended Equipment: Plasma Lances, LR Rifles, Trigger Wires, Grenades, Stasis Fields, Automedikits

Before starting, you may as well blow all your cash on mods and equipment, as you won't get a chance to re-equip for the subsequent mission. You'll need to save the Grenades for that.

This time your Agents each have four guards to protect them – and they need all the help they can get on this tricky mission.

Lay Trigger Wires on the path to the northeast corner. A couple of flying cars will attack, so stand firm with Plasma Lances to shoot them down – but make sure you get out of the way! More flying cars will attack, then some Zealots from the south (though you may have to lure them). Finish off any survivors with Plasma Lances, but watch out for explosions. Once they're all dead, lay more Trigger Wires, then lure the rest of the Zealots from the south.

Now head down the northern edge. Lay Trigger Wires up to the northeast corner, then lure out the Zealots from the U-shaped building. Use a Stasis Field and Plasma Lances to eliminate any survivors. Watch out for explosions.

Carry on westwards along the northern edge until you encounter another Zealot attack. Deal with this using a Stasis Field and Plasma Lances (or lure it back into Trigger Wires if you prefer). Then head further west and eliminate the Zealots

around the police station. Carry on round the western and southern edges of the level, picking off groups of Zealots.

Now start luring out the Zealots from the centre, using LR Rifles to pick off the ones around the edge. If flying cars give chase, use Plasma Lances to down them.

You'll need to send an Agent up the ramps to lure out the central Zealots. Watch out for them lobbing Grenades which detonate at the bottom of the ramps – activate the supershield as you run back down to your comrades, then use a Stasis Field and Plasma Lances to eliminate your pursuers.

Once all the Zealots and flying cars are eliminated (don't bother with the two large vehicles on the east side), go up a ramp and into the elevator – ideally you want all four Agents intact.

Short Method: There's an alternative to shooting all the Zealots, but it's riskier. Once you've killed the Zealots around the police station, you can steal

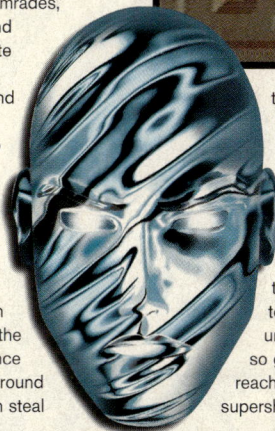

the unoccupied tank. Before doing so, take your men on foot towards the bottom of the northern ramp and kill the three Zealots guarding it (if you haven't already). Get in the tank and drive it to the top of the ramp. It'll come under heavy bombardment, so get out as soon as you reach the top, activate supershields, and run for the

elevator. It's easy to lose an Agent or two in the confusion, so you may be better off using the standard method.

To save time you can drive the tank up a ramp, then activate supershields and try to leg it to the elevator as all hell breaks loose!

Eurocorp Mission 19

GAME OVER

After all that fighting, the end-of-game sequence is a bit disappointing. The camera pans around one of your Agents standing on the moon. Erm, that's it!

EuroCorp Mission 20

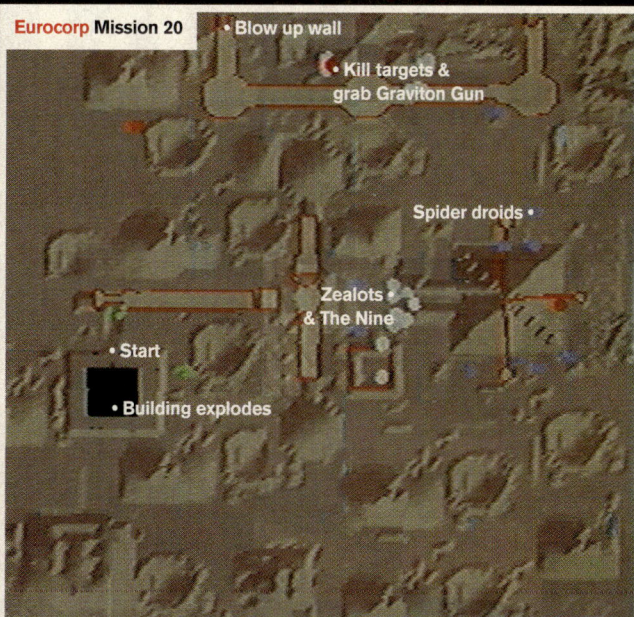

The Moon: Stop the Nine before they use the Ion Gun to destroy Earth.
Recommended Equipment: Whatever you have left from the previous mission – Grenades a must.

Arm your Agents with Plasma Lances and one with a Stasis Field, to take on the Zealots and spider droids which attack. Once they're dead, go towards the northern target and blow a hole in the west wall of the compound. Again, use a Stasis Field and Plasma Lances to eliminate the Zealots inside, and two of the Nine. Search around for the Graviton Gun, then head towards the main complex in the east. Get ready for the fight of your life as loads of spider droids attack – retreat into the west passage and use the Stasis Field and keep firing that Graviton Gun, as its shots home in on enemies.

Next head straight into the fortress: you need to assassinate the remainder of the Nine before they get to the Ion Gun, so there's a time limit for your success. The best method is to chuck in a couple of Grenades, activate supershields, and go all out to eliminate each target. Then simply run for the exit.

Eurocorp Mission 20

the lost world

Publisher:	Electronic Arts
Price:	£44.99
Format:	UK

Huge **lumbering giants** with **brains the size of a walnut…** but **enough about the team**, the dinosaurs have **escaped from Jurassic Park** and are **running riot**. This **survival guide** features an **illustrated walkthrough** for every stage. **If only the real dinosaurs** had **read these tips**, they might **never have died out!**

THE LOST WORLD
JURASSIC PARK™

Compsognathus
Levels 01-09

The Compy is a joy to control as he darts around the scenery at speed. He's hopeless at fighting though, so the best survival technique is to leg it away from enemies who quite fancy a bite of your tasty dinosaur flesh.

1 High Ride

1. Go left from the start to collect the 1UP on the steps. Just jump over the small dinosaurs.

2. Jump from the steps to the platform and over two more platforms. There's no need to go down the bottom.

3. Jump carefully down the platforms at the end, avoiding the plants, and leap over another dinosaur to finish.

SECRET: Walk into the right end of the log bridge to drop down through the hole and get the claw. Head left and across the platforms to get the tooth. Drop down and jump left over the leptoceratops. Jump up the platforms, being careful not to fall into pit (or it's curtains for you). Head right at the steps – they lead back to main level. Go through the hole to collect the DNA. Head right and go back past the leptoceratops and jump up platforms and the steps this time.

2 Rain Forest

1. Keep going right, jumping over the tree roots, plants, and dinosaurs. You're better off running away from these large dinos instead of fighting.

2. After jumping over the plants in the pit, scramble up the bank quickly before a dinosaur arrives to knock you down.

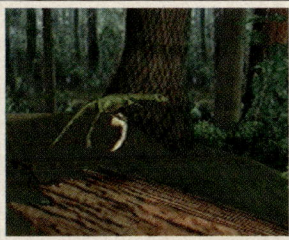

3. Grab the instinct claw on top of the log. Head right, past more plants and dinosaurs. Run right into the pit to finish.

SECRET: Walk into the left end of the log and through a hole. Head right, past the dinosaurs, to reach a pit with a leptoceratops and DNA. Then go back through the log hole.

3 Creek Bed

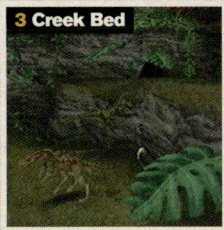

1. Go to the right, jumping over the raptors, to get the partial tooth.

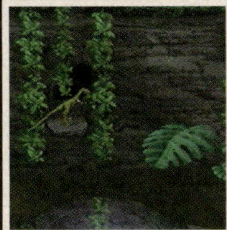

2. Return to the left. Jump onto the rock platform and enter the hole. Jump over the two raptors and through the next hole. Drop down the slope – carefully does it or you'll fall too far. Jump over the raptor at the bottom.

3. Jump over another raptor and up the steps at the end, then jump left and again. Jump up the steps until the raptor appears, then jump back over the gap to the right. Wait for him to drop down the gap, then jump back left and up the steps. Jump right, past two raptors, and into the hole.

4. Run past the raptors and pterosaurs. Jump onto the lowest rock platform in the background, then over to the left, into the hole and through the tunnel to get the 1UP.

5. Return right through the hole and jump to the right along the platforms, into the next hole. Leap over the raptors and through another hole.

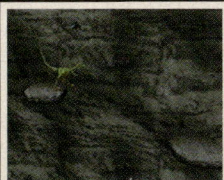

6. Jump right, along the platforms (don't fall onto plants) to finish.

SECRET: After point 5, head left (make sure you've exited the hole) and jump straight up for the DNA above the ledge. Watch out for the dinosaur behind you. If you fall off the ledge, you'll have to jump across the platforms again, into the hole.

the lost world

continued

9 Tidal Cavern

1. Run right, into the hole, where you'll be targeted by a hunter. Run right to exit the hole, then head left to get the DNA.

2. Run back to the right and jump round the rock ledge, avoiding the shots. A good technique is to stay still and wait for him to shoot before jumping out of the way – don't move if the laser is aimed ahead of you. Jump over the platforms.

3. Drift left from the platform to collect the partial tooth, then go left and up round again onto the platforms. You can't reach the 1UP (from here at least), so keep jumping right along the platforms – miss one and you'll fall to your death. Enter the hole at the end to complete the final Compy stage.

1 Enter Carefully

1. Jump over the spikes and shoot the first baryonyx from the (relative) safety of the rocks.

2. Fire the piton up and swing right to collect the rapid fire.

3. Fire piton and lower yourself slightly, then build up momentum to swing right and collect rocket grenades (while still attached). Release to sail over spikes.

4. Kill the baryonyx with the rocket grenades – now that's a weapon!

5. Fire piton up to swing right over rock wall (but don't swing left into the stalactites!).

6. Head right, killing another baryonyx. Fire the piton up at the stalactites to swing right, then forward-roll through the tunnel, collecting rapid fire.

Hunter Human
Levels 10-15

After being the hunted, it's time to be the hunter. Initially you're only armed with a rifle, but can collect power-ups for nerve gas, rockets, flamethrower etc. You can also fire a piton at ledges to swing around on a rope. This is often needed to reach secret areas, power-ups, and DNA. Move left/right to build up the swing.

7. Fire the piton at the stalactites (which crumble) to swing onto the right wall. Roll through the tunnel, collecting health.

8. Jump up and fire downwards to kill the baryonyx. Head right through the water, killing another baryonyx. Swing left from right-hand rocks to collect the rocket grenades. Roll through the tunnel and quickly kill baryonyx at the end!

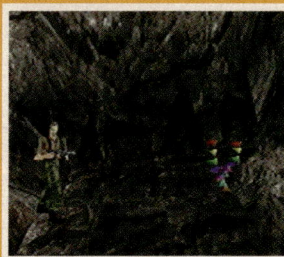

9. Fire the piton straight up from the right of tunnel, raise yourself, then swing right – fire piton again to swing onto the ledge with DNA. Drop off and head right, killing another dino. Shoot down at the baryonyx at the end of the rocks, then head right and kill the next one – and a third!

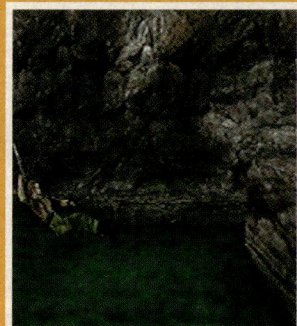

10. Run right and fire the piton at stalactites to get a good long swing right, then fire piton again and release quickly to land on the ledge. Swing via stalactites onto the next ledge and exit right.

The Lost World

2 Arid Canyon

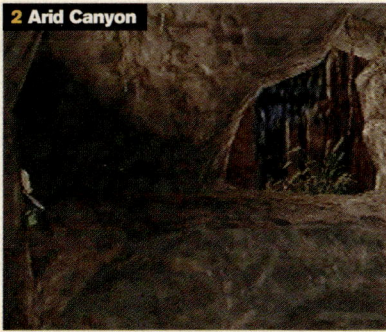

1. Go left from the start to collect the hidden nerve gas.

2. Fire piton up at the small rock near ledge, then do a double swing left via another small rock to reach the ledge on the left for rapid fire.

3. Shoot diagonally at the orodromeus on ledge before swinging over via small rock. Kill pterosaur and another oro. Head right and kill another oro by the cave, then a pterosaur – jump over it and use gas.

4. Kill another oro on the ledge (shoot it from below), then roll into the tunnel and kill a second oro – jump over it, then shoot it up the jaxi!

5. Fire piton at the tunnel roof to swing right and collect the 1UP. Then do a double swing right from the bottom of the 1UP platform, onto the ledge to collect rapid fire.

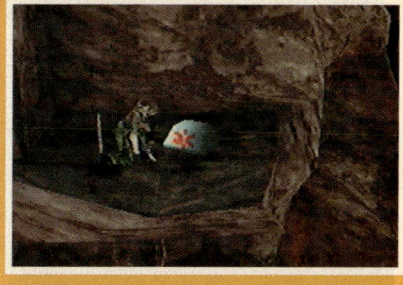

6. Return left through the tunnel and jump onto the top of the roof. Jump right and swing right via the small rock to land on a ledge. Drop directly onto health (or you'll die), then get rocket grenades.

7. Get ready for an ambush by a herd of oros. Shoot them with rockets or rapid fire and head quickly right before more appear.

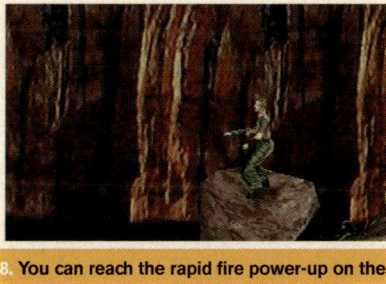

8. You can reach the rapid fire power-up on the platform above, by swinging right from the bottom of it, then immediately firing the piton at the ledge to the right and swinging left onto the platform.

8A. From here you can repeatedly swing right. By building up momentum, you can grab the (hidden) lower 1UP in mid swing, then release on the rise to grab the upper one. Immediately reattach and swing right to land on the platform with rocket grenades.

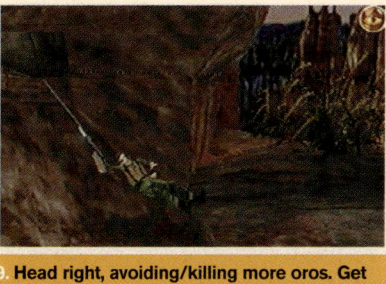

9. Head right, avoiding/killing more oros. Get the health, then head left. Jump and swing right from the small crumbling rock to land on the platform. Shoot the baryonyx up top. Fire the piton straight up and swing right onto the top ledge.

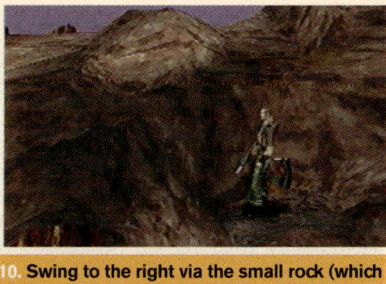

10. Swing to the right via the small rock (which looks uncannily like a Scotch egg, yum…) Shoot the baryonyx and avoid pterosaur, then swing right from the platform above, and swing left from the ledge onto the platform for rocket grenades.

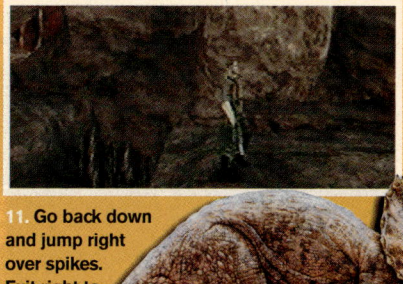

11. Go back down and jump right over spikes. Exit right to finish the level.

the lost world

5 Geothermal Centre

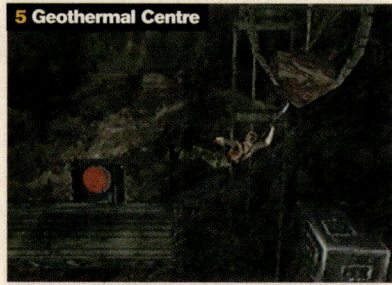

1. Shoot raptor when it jumps down, go right over crate (don't bother shooting it). Shoot two raptors to right, then come back and swing via rock/claw onto platform to activate machine.

2. Attach to claw and swing right near end of line and quickly attach to the second claw. As it moves right, swing right onto top platform. Shoot raptor, then jump right to next platform. Jump right again, then attach to ledge and build up swing to collect health on right.

3. Drop down to long platform and shoot the two raptors which attack (one from above on right).

4. Attach to static rock above and build up a really high swing, then release at right and attach to platform, then to rock/claw. Now swing and attach to roof on right (you seemingly can't reach that 1UP below without falling to your death).

5. Keep swinging right and reattaching to roof. When you see ledge, lure raptor over edge before getting rockets, then swing to ledge. Stand next to crates, shoot top one (explosives), then bottom one and grab time grenades.

6. Swing via roof to platform on right, but get ready to blast raptors which attack (shoot diagonally down as you fall). Then shoot crates and grab health (crate on top platform contains rockets if you can get it).

7. Drop off left side of bottom platform and quickly reattach straight up to underside. Pull up and swing right to land on the switch platform. Reattach to right and drop down and attach to claw as it descends. Let it take you down, then swing left to get 1UP. Then swing onto platform on right.

8. Drop to next platform, then jump and attach to rock/claw on right (you can swing left from here to lower platform for nerve gas if you want). Then swing right to the switch platform. Jump from left side onto rock/claw, then let it take you down. At end, jump right onto platform with crates.

9. Drop to right platform, then attach to high platform on right. Swing to right platform (you can attach to underside of this to get 1UP). Kill raptor and run right to exit.

SECRET 1: From top platform after claws in 2, jump left and attach to ledge, swing left to collect rockets – but reattach to something quick or you're a goner! If you swing right from ledge, you can reattach to ledge above. Swing long from right edge of this and you can attach to platform to get rapid fire plus 1UP above. Then swing back left and drop onto platform – or right to next ledge (by health).

SECRET 2: From end of 3, drop off right side and attach to underside, then drop to the switch platform. (You can drop off and attach to bottom of this to get flamethrower, if you reckon you can get back up!) Activate machine, attach to claw to be taken left. Lower yourself to collect rapid fire. Near top of claw path, swing right onto platform.

6 Ingen Complex

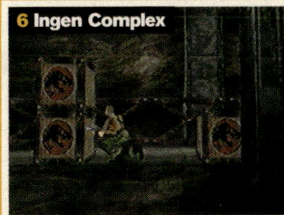

1. Jump onto the right crate, then onto left crates to get DNA above. Shoot bottom left crate for rockets (others contain explosives).

2. Head right, blasting raptors (two rockets each). Jump over to platform and get rapid fire from crate.

3. Keep running right, using rockets/rapid fire. Grab health from the crate.

4. Roll under the platform to collect more rockets.

5. Make sure you get the health from the crate under the second long platform.

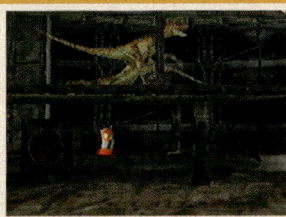

6. Get flamethrower fuel from the two crates under the platform – roll under to get it.

7. Use the flamethrower on more raptors. Jump from the right onto the high platform for a 1UP.

8. Run to the right to go through the door, which drops shut behind you to keep those deadly raptors at bay. Phew!

1 The Way Out

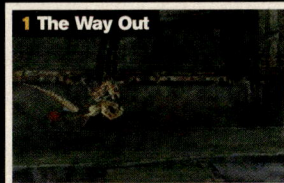

1. Head right, attacking any hunters you see. Use the lunge attack to pin them to the floor, then lunge/snap repeatedly.

2. Watch out for the trapdoors on the platforms. Most of the crates contain explosives, so steer clear unless there's a hunter nearby.

3. Beware hunters firing gas grenades, which can take a large chunk off your health.

4. Get the claw from the bottom of the second pair of crates under the platforms. Get the 1UP from the top crate of the third pair.

Velociraptor

Levels 16-20
Now this is a bit better than the little compy. At last, you can run around, ripping the guts off unfortunate hunters who cross your path. Simply lunge at them from behind to floor them, then snap or lunge at the victim until they stop struggling – time for dinner!

5. Continue right. Watch out for stack of three explosives crates after the corner – open one, then retreat until explosions cease.

5A. Jump left onto the platform, wait till the hunter there approaches, then do a jumping lunge attack and flip up into the air to grab the DNA (very tricky).

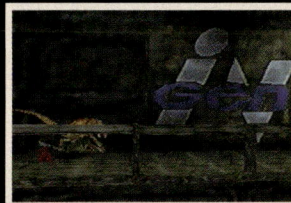

6. Quickly jump up to platform just afterwards, otherwise the hunters there will throw gas grenades down at you – avoid the trapdoor.

7. Drop down into the pit from the right side and grab the 1UP in the crate to the left. (By repeatedly dying and grabbing both 1UPs, you can build up your lives.)

8. Return left and onto top platform and jump over from right edge. Kill more hunters. The three stacked crates all contain explosives.

9. Continue right onto the bridge in the background to complete the stage.

the lost world

2 Raptor Ravine

1. Do a jumping lunge at the raptors to kill them – it's best to aim for their tails. Or jump over them and lunge/snap from behind. Kill the pterosaurs too.

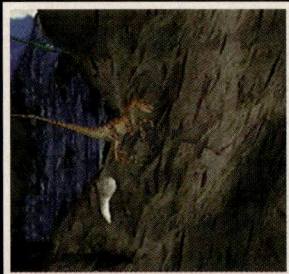

2. Jump over the platforms and down the slope, then jump over from the cliff edge to get tooth on crumbling ledge.

3. You can't reach the 1UP from here, so jump up to the right via the crumbling platform.

4. From the platform to the right of the crumbling one, jump up to the left to enter the hole. Go left to emerge on the ledge with the 1UP you saw earlier (aha!).

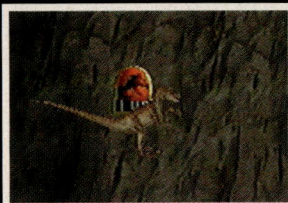

5. Return to the right. As the ledge starts crumbling, jump right when you see the 1UPs to grab them and land on the platform. (Again, you can use the 'dying and repeating' trick to build up your lives.)

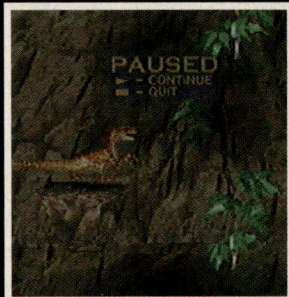

6. Jump to the right via the crumbling platforms (there are spikes below).

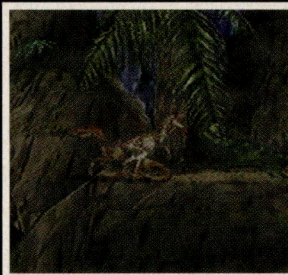

7. Kill the raptors and jump up the slope (when it's clear at the top). Jump over the spikes, kill a raptor, then up the platforms.

8. Kill the three raptors down the slope, then feast on their flesh. Jump up via the crumbling platform and kill the raptor and pterosaur. Walk right to complete the stage.

3 The Burn Zone

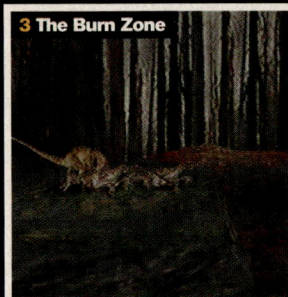

1. Kill or jump past the raptors at the start – watch for the one coming out of the background.

2. Jump over the lava, then the rocks, then more lava, killing the raptors along the way – some of them will jump into the lava.

3. It's best just to jump over the oros (when they duck their heads to charge). The DNA is above the log – to get it, you need to flip onto the log after a lunge attack, then jump up.

4. Jump over more lava and kill another raptor, then it's best to run/jump past the raptors by the log.

5. Jump over the rocks in the lava, then up the slope and leg it past the raptors by another log.

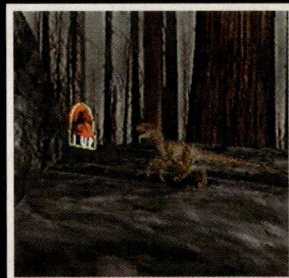

6. Jump up the slope towards the rock wall and kill the raptor, then head left and over the oro to grab the 1UP.

7. Lure the oro over and get him to headbutt the two tall rocks by jumping up at them! (You'll probably lose some energy in the process.) Jump over the raptor and lava.

8. Leg it past the raptors by the two logs – don't hang about, there's not far to go now. Finally, jump over the oro to complete the level.

The Lost World

4 Into The Fire

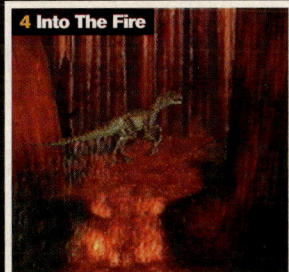

1. Jump over the fiery lava and avoid or kill the raptor – these guys are tougher than the previous ones.

2. Time your run past the falling ash to jump over the lava. Jump onto branch to collect tooth, then kill the raptors – when up against groups of them, lunge at one from behind to down it, then keep snapping away (don't get up) to kill the others which approach.

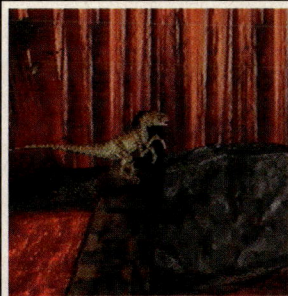

3. Jump onto branch above lava. Jump to the right via logs – don't fall in now!

4. Jump past or kill three more raptors. Then get ready for the deadly triceratops: jump onto the curved branch and wait for him to approach, then jump over.

5. Jump over some more lava and kill raptors arriving from the background (your instinct should still be red). Jump onto the branch to get the 1UP.

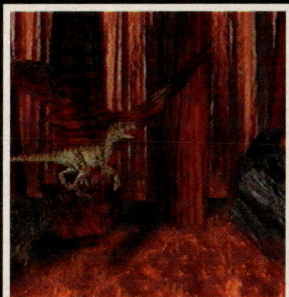

6. Kill a couple more raptors and jump onto the branch above the lava, then via the log to the right.

7. Now comes another 'horny' triceratops – so jump back onto the log, then over him. Leap the raptor behind – don't stop to eat it or that triceratops'll have you! Jump onto branch above lava, then to the right via the logs.

8. Run quickly right to avoid the triceratops coming from the left background – yes, another one! Jump past the raptors and lava, then jump onto the branch to collect the 1UP. You need all the lives you can get on this tricky level.

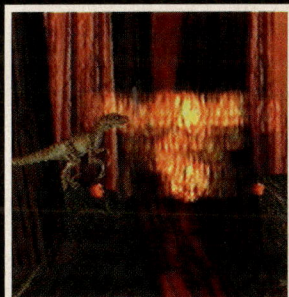

9. Run under the fiery branch, jump over the lava (watch out for falling ash) and more raptors.

10. Up the bank there's another triceratops: wait for it to charge, then immediately jump over from up close.

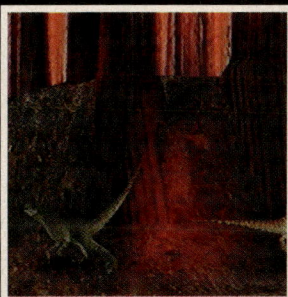

11. Jump over more lava and another couple of raptors to finish.

5 Eye Of Chaos

1. This stage is a simple battle with a big euoplocephalus. But first, head all the way right to collect the DNA.

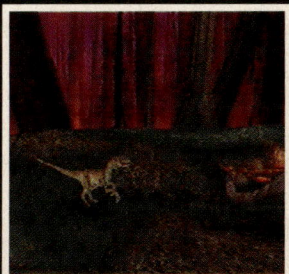

2. Approach the euo. Watch out for him turning around to try and lash you with his tail – keep out of range of it until he turns again.

3. When he's facing you, lunge at his head and keep snapping to turn him over onto his back. Now do (two or three) jumping lunges at his soft underbelly, but once he starts turning over, jump off.

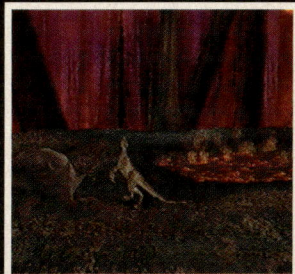

4. Repeat the process (three or four times) until he's dead. As the stomping starts, just leg it to the right to complete the stage.

the lost world

1 Aftermath

1. Jump precisely over the red-hot lava, then ram/lunge through the log.

2. Hold R1 as you walk right, to take alternative route into foreground.

3. Ram the log and head right, killing and eating raptors until you reach the 1UP.

4. Return left to the junction, then continue right. Jump over the pool and kill raptors, but don't hang about or you'll be attacked from behind. Jump over them if there's too many.

5. Smash through the next log (by junction) and continue right, smashing logs, jumping lava and killing raptors until you reach the dead end with the DNA. Lunge up to get it.

6. Return to the previous junction and hold R1 to go into the foreground for the tooth. Head right quickly before you're attacked from behind.

Tyrannosaurus Rex
Levels 21-27

At last, you get to play the king of dinosaurs. His powerful jaws can grasp enemies to swallow them whole, and you'll need a constant supply of food. The lumbering T Rex's lack of agility makes it a sitting duck for hunters' bullets and rockets.

7. Continue right, killing and eating raptors. Smash through another log.

8. Keep heading right to avoid attacks from behind. Exit right after the final lava pool to complete the stage.

2 Force Of Nature

1. Go left from the start to collect the claw by the lava pool – don't bother jumping over, it's a dead end. Head right and smash through the log. Jump over lava, kill the raptor hidden behind tree.

2. Hold R1 to go into the foreground before the second log. Head right, kill raptors, and get the tooth.

3. Smash through the log and kill lots more raptors, then attack the stegosaurus. Snap at his head, but retreat to avoid his swishing spiky tail. (You can try jumping over him if you prefer).

4. Head right at the junction (left road leads back to the start) to meet another stegosaurus. Get past to collect the DNA. Exit right to complete the level.

3 Sulphur Fields

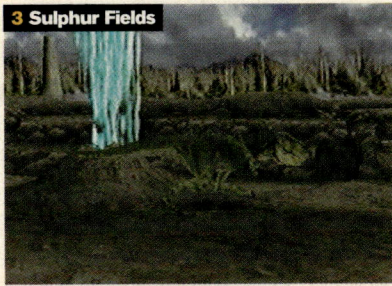

1. This is one of the trickiest levels in the entire game! First, jump the water pool, then time your run past the geyser.

2. If you want an extra life, hold R1 at the junction to go into the background. Jump over the pools and time your runs past geysers.

3. At the triceratops, retreat a bit and wait till he lifts his head up to charge you, then quickly jump over him – you have do it from the right distance away (not too close).

4. Collect 1UP at the dead end, then quickly turn left and jump past the triceratops. Return to junction and continue right.

5. Run past a couple more geysers, then get past the triceratops, by jumping over as previously (don't lunge at him as in this pic!).

6. Run quickly past geyser and jump over the pools (don't stop!), to meet another triceratops. Jump over him, as before – but quickly, before the other one comes back!

7. Don't press R1 at the junction – go right, past the pools and geyser to collect the DNA.

8. Return to the junction and press R1 to take the route into the background.

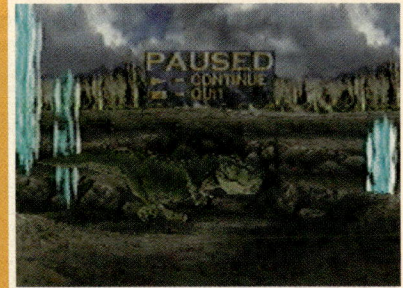

9. Jump over the pool and time your runs past the three geysers. Enter the cave to finish the stage.

4 Dinosaur Lairs

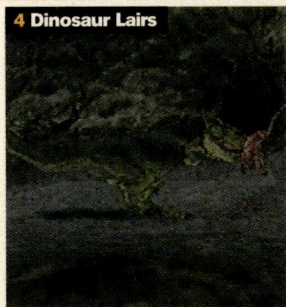

1. Eat the two raptors which emerge from the holes in background – easy peasy.

2. Hold R1 to go into the background at the first junction. Kill/eat lots more raptors as you head right. Get the DNA when you see it.

3. Keep heading right, killing an army of raptors. Watch out for those coming out of holes. If you get surrounded, it's often best just to jump ahead and leg it.

4. Eventually, you come out by the allosaurus at the end of the main route – get close enough to lunge in, then retreat to avoid his reply (repeat until victorious). Exit right to complete the level.

the lost world

continued

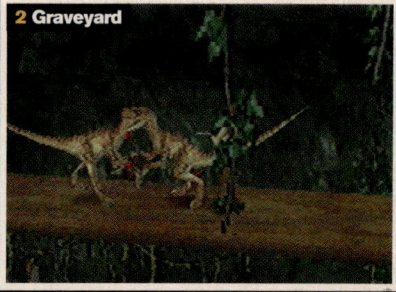

2 Graveyard

1. Collect rapid fire and shoot the nearby raptor and the ones as you run right. Return to collect health if you need it.

2. Drop off the right edge (by the T Rex) and collect the flares. Swing left over the crates and shoot the raptors to the left. Collect all the power-ups under the platform (leave health if not needed yet).

3. Head right back to the crates and fire a flare left to distract the T Rex, so you can get out safely to the right.

4. If you want the DNA, swing to the right from the platform and attach to the branch to swing right and collect it.

5. Continue right. Jump to collect flares, then blast the raptor with rockets. Swing right over the bones – hitting them is fatal.

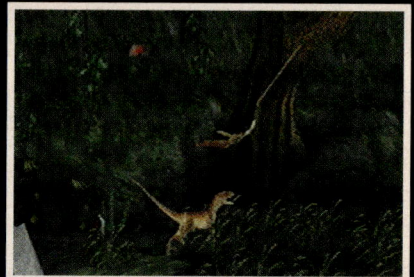

6. Collect rapid fire in the grass and swing left from the branch to collect health, then right over bones.

7. Best chuck another flare, then swing right from the branch to collect rapid fire. Swing right from next branch over more bones and collect the 1UP.

8. Swing right over three lots of branches (attaching to one after the other), collecting various power-ups and releasing over bones at the end.

9. You're now safe from the T Rex, so roll under mesh and shoot the raptors on the other side. Swing up on the metal tubing to get health, then right via tubes onto the wooden walkway.

Passwords

Only five level codes exist. So to make life easier, we have included standard ones and 99 lives versions.

Hunter
□□■△○×○△○□□×△

Velociraptor
□□△○□□△○×□×△

T Rex
△△□□■□□○××△△□

Sarah
××○○○○△△○×□○

Compy
99 LIVES, ALL DNA
××○■■×■×○■■

99 LIVES, ALL DNA
■■▲●×■■■■×○▲

99 LIVES, ALL DNA
××●▲■×■×■▲●

99 LIVES, ALL DNA
××○▲■■■×▲■▲■

99 LIVES, ALL DNA
■■▲●××■■▲×○▲

Finding all that DNA strands is hellishly tricky, so our special passwords give you all the DNA up to that point.

3 There Were Two...?

1. This is the final showdown between Sarah and two T Rexes (one appears later). Quickly shoot the crates to your left and grab the flares and flamethrower.

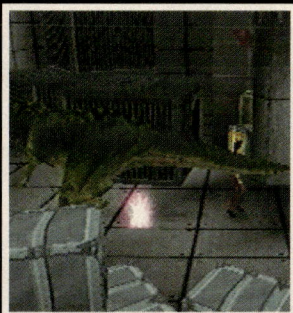

2. Go over to the left side to collect the DNA. Fire a flare left to get past the T Rex.

3. Quickly run over to the right side and swing up onto the platform for rockets – use a short rope, build up momentum, and release (best when swinging towards falling side of the floor).

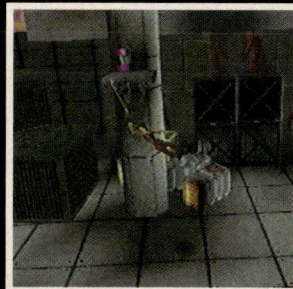

4. Shoot another flare on the right and run all the way left to swing up onto the platform for more flares – you'll need them.

5. Drop down and shoot the various crates (if the T Rex hasn't already smashed them open) to collect the weapons – beware explosives in a couple of crates.

6. Frazzle the T Rex with half your flamethrower (best to save the rest for the second T Rex), then use a flare to corner him and use rockets/grenades until he keels over and dies.

7. If you're low on energy, go to the right edge to collect the health there – or swing up onto the middle platform.

8. Watch out for another T Rex entering the scene (he may do so before the other one dies). Use flares and whatever weapons you've got left on it. If you're running out of flares or rockets, swing up to platforms to get more.

Game Over

After defeating the two T Rexes, the exhausted Sarah climbs out of the boat to make her escape. Climbing up the hill from the hunters' camp, she is picked up by a Mercedes off-road vehicle – now that's eaving in style. Followed by a helicopter with a searchlight, it zooms off into the countryside. Meanwhile a group of raptors look unperturbed as the chopper soars overhead. The camera then pans up to the moon, which is the Dreamworks logo. This is followed by a nicely polished credits sequence, featuring a rolling demo plus video of various programmers superimposed.

start

Time Crisis

Publisher:	Sony
Price:	£59.99 (with Guncon)
Format:	UK

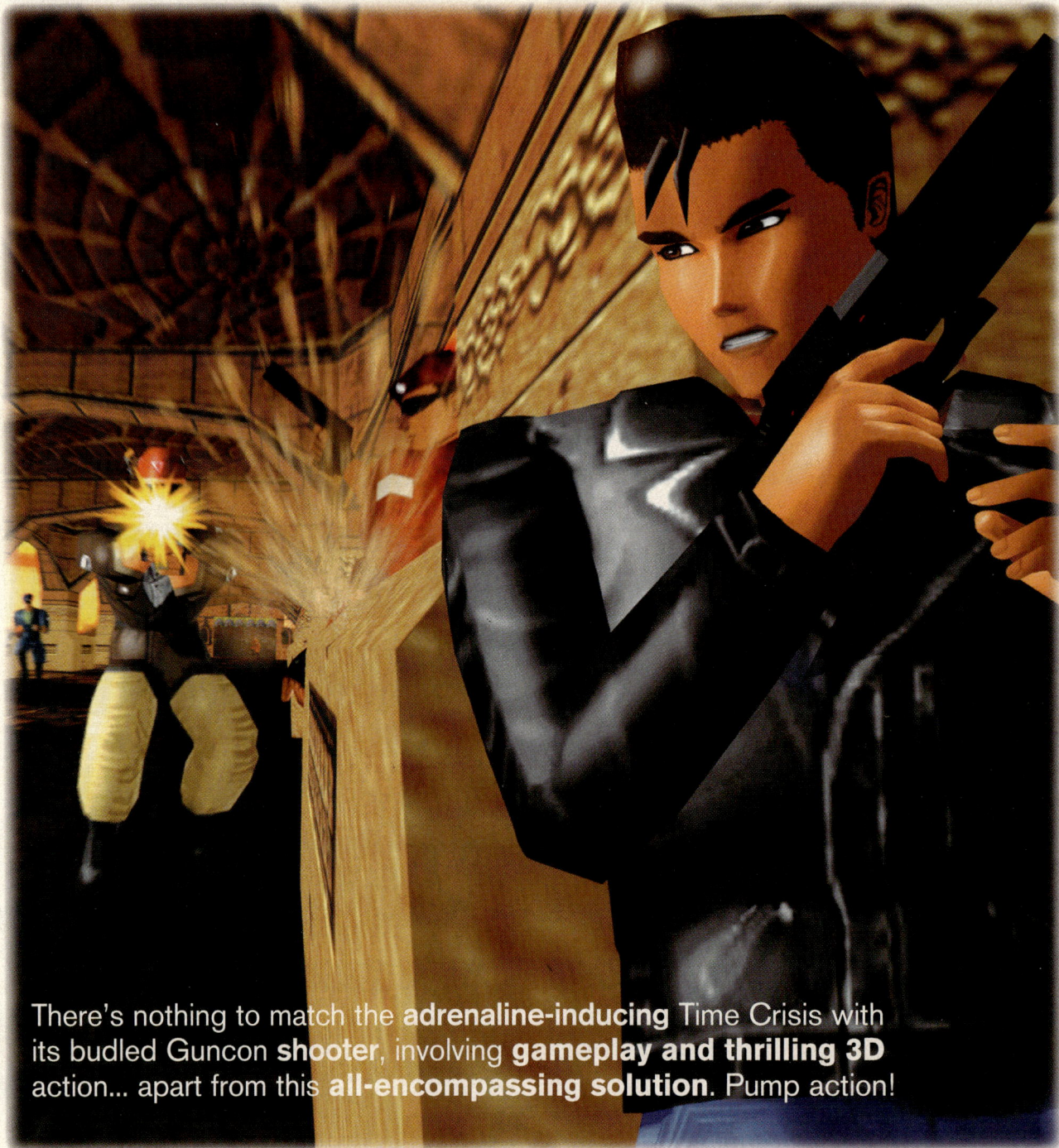

There's nothing to match the **adrenaline-inducing** Time Crisis with its budled Guncon **shooter**, involving **gameplay and thrilling 3D** action... apart from this **all-encompassing solution**. Pump action!

TIME CRISIS

1 player | Memory

HEROES & VILLAINS

The handy guide to who's who in *Time Crisis*, so you know who's getting shot...

Richard Miller

This is the hero of the caper, and somewhat fittingly, played by you. Richard dashes through the enemy complex in his tacky leather jacket, pulling seemingly unlimited rounds for his pistol from who knows where!

Rachel Macpherson

This is the damsel in distress, the President's daughter who has been kidnapped by the power-crazed hoods and held captive. It is your job to find her before the time limit is up, thus preventing you from having the embarrassment of presenting a stiff to the Pres!

Sherudo Garo

This is the brains behind the whole kidnap thing. A very sophisticated and well-spoken gent, who would no doubt be played by a British actor if Hollywood ever

felt the need to transform this gun-fest into a blockbuster. Oh yeah, he likes knives too!

Wild Dog

This is Garo's crazed sidekick, a deranged cigar-chomping psycho who will step in and run the show his way... if need be. You won't meet Wild Dog until much later in the game, but when you come up against him, you're gonna know about it!

LOOK OUT!

There are several points of interest in *Time Crisis*, so take note of the following before you embark on those treacherous missions.

Danger Objects

At various points throughout the game, you'll be warned about upcoming objects that will harm you if precautions aren't taken. Whenever one of these objects is coming, you'll be warned well in advance, as the picture clearly shows.

Explosive Objects

Both in Arcade and PlayStation mode, there are explosive crates scattered around. If these are hit with a succession

of shots, they will explode, wiping out a whole wave on enemies in the process. Cool!

I'm Hit!

If you don't watch your back, sooner or later you're going to get killed. You start the game with three lives, one of which

will disappear the moment you see a bullet hole or some other injury etched into the screen.

Extra Lives

Like in the coin-op, the player is awarded an extra life when hitting 40 enemies in a row – that's hitting 40 cronies without missing. If you miss, you'll have to start over again. You can score multiple hits on enemies by unloading a few shots into them before they hit the deck and disappear, but this can be construed as being risky. You can also shoot explosive crates and suchlike as they register as hits, but if you fire at any mechanised vehicles such as tanks and choppers, they don't count as hits, whether you score a direct hit or not. On the whole, though, attempting to get extra lives just isn't worth the hassle or heartache!

GENERAL HINTS

• Shoot through the doors. It is possible to shoot at doors and picture frames and hit enemies a split-second before they appear – thus saving time. To do this effectively, though, you need to know exactly when and where the enemies are going to appear.

• Firing two shots at each enemy in quick succession will increase your hit percentage and reduce the chances of missing, thus saving more time.

• Always shoot the coloured guys first as they are the most dangerous. It is very rare that the blue infantry will kill you, so concentrate your shots on the others to eradicate the main danger quickly.

• You duck to reload, so make sure that you remember to do it at regular intervals. There's nothing worse than taking out a stream of heavies with one round, getting to the last one and then... click!

Motley Crew

It is essential when playing *Time Crisis* that you know exactly who you're up against. That's why we've compiled this handy table to inform you how much damage you can take.

Name	Colour	Damage needed to lose life
Infantryman	Blue	6–8 shots
Squad Leader	Brown	6 shots
Rifleman	Dark Orange	1 shot
Time Soldier	Orange	n/a
Grenadier	Yellow/Green	1 shot
Marksman	Red	1 shot
Club-Wielder	Yellow/Green	1 hit
Machine-Gunner	Green	2 shots
Clawed Ninjas	Grey/Black	1 slash
Ninja Leader	Orange/Black	1 slash
White-Coats	White	Varies*
Sherudo Garo	Boss bloke	1 hit
Wild Dog	Boss bloke	2–3 shots

* Depends on what weapon they use. Some use pistols which don't pose much threat, but others may wield clubs or machine-guns which will need one or two hits to take a life off you.

time crisis

THE ARCADE GAME

Based on the hugely popular arcade game, this element comprises the main bulk of this package. Your aim is to blast your way through three huge stages against a very strict time limit before the evil blighters that have kidnapped the President's daughter subject her to a gruesome execution. Get to it, Dick, shoot the bad guys and get the girl!

AREA 1

Things start off very simple with harmless troops popping up to take pot shots at you. This is when you should go for the extra life.

When you take out the rocket-launcher geezer in the sub, he'll fall and blow the damn thing up. It doesn't effect play, but it sure looks good!

When you reach the final wave of enemies, aim for the explosive crate on the forklift. By hitting this with a succession of shots, it will blow, killing every guy on screen.

AREA 2

When the blue soldier jumps forward at you, keep shooting in the middle to take out the orange time soldier as he quickly pops up.

Take out the guy on the left before he hides and then pick off the harmless blue soldiers at your leisure. More follow afterwards.

You're confronted by a mini army as you turn the next corner. Take cover and then pick one off at a time, starting with the red bloke.

The last challenge of Area 2 is a simple three-way stand off. One guy will roll in from the left to provide cover for two more. Kill.

AREA 3

Take out the first wave and then aim at the door on the right. Three guys will run out. Shoot constantly and you should get the bonus time.

Straight after killing these two club-wielders, you'll have to shoot a helicopter. The key is to reload quickly and hit it with everything!

Don't pay too much attention to this car, it will roar around the corner and fly past, so just duck out of the way to avoid.

On this final wave, take out the cannon operators in the distance first, and watch out for two groups that emerge from the tower.

Area Boss

Things are looking nasty. You're trapped inside a room with hordes of claw-wielding ninjas. Your principle aim is to pick-off the orange guys (each one takes two shots), and then scatter your shots over the grey guys that pose a lesser threat. They will constantly keep coming forward at you, so when they do, duck behind the wall to avoid getting scratched. There are three waves to contend with, so pick them off quickly as they drop down and then concentrate on the last orange bloke. Killing him will mark the completion of the level.

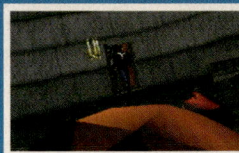

When the last orange ninja has been taken down, you'll briefly interrogate him before dashing off to Stage 2. Note that the fatally wounded ninja changes position three times during the sequence. Strange!

SECOND STAGE

Now that you're fully familiar with your weapon and the patterns in which the enemy attack, the challenge steps up a gear. In this stage you are required to pick off troops from a longer range and have many more attacking at once, so it is vital that you get your priorities right and determine who needs to be shot first. Easy enough...

AREA 1

The area starts with several short encounters around twisting passageways. So observe who is where, duck, and then attack.

Remember, always go for the coloured soldiers first. The blue guys pose little to no threat, and should be taken out last.

The final stand off takes place in this courtyard. There are two machine-gunners and a ninja to take out first. The others are easy.

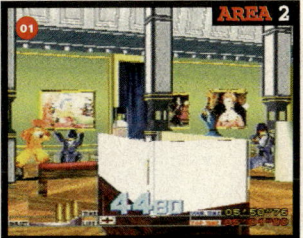

AREA 2

Watch out for the orange time soldier that sneaks in from the left. He won't stay long so shoot him quickly. Watch the paintings too!

A horde of re-enforcements will spill through the door and take cover. Shoot the pillar on the left to bring the house down!

Under the cover of darkness, you must take out several troops that cower behind the exhibits. Watch out for the orange chap on the left.

Finally, there are two green machine-gunners to kill before moving onto the next area. They pop up above the glass cabinet.

AREA 3

When battling through this wave, leave the shield guy on the right until last of all. Killing him triggers a time soldier to run along behind.

Loads to kill here. There's an orange time soldier if you're quick enough. Also, look out for the troops on the stairs in the distance.

Again, kill the troops that pose the highest threat first. There is a ninja amongst this wave that will jump up at you via the chandelier.

Watch your back! More of a fancy effect than cause for concern. This guy will foolishly blast your reflection, so turn and nail him!

Area Boss

Wow! You've got to the girl with time to spare... it looks as though your mission is going to be a complete success. However, the white-togged, knife-throwing boss, Sherudo Garo stands in your path, and he isn't such a pushover. Garo will emerge from behind the plant and proceed to bombard you with blades. So take a shot and then duck quickly to avoid losing a life.

After three hits, two cronies will pop up from behind the pillars, so take one out and then duck, and then aim your sights at the other for when he re-emerges. After another couple of hits on Garo, they will appear again, so repeat the same process as before.

After being wounded, Garo will hobble off behind the pillar, so duck behind the plant and get ready to fend off his blades once again. This time he will be backed up by men in white who will swarm the area. Sharp, precise shooting is required here to pick them all off as quickly as possible. The most lethal are the ones closest to you as they can take a life with one hit. So take one shot and duck each time until they have all been disposed of.

You'll now be one-on-one with Garo again so hit him with a few more shots to send him hobbling for cover elsewhere again. This time he will exit through the door and appear intermittently to throw more knives at you (where does he keep them all?).

Shoot Garo as he appears and then quickly duck for cover. He will be backed up by machine-gun-toting men in white – these are easily killed, so concentrate mainly on Garo. If you score another six or so direct hits, he'll tumble backwards in dramatic Hollywood style and crumple like a rag doll on the deck. Ha!

Mission accomplished... or is it?

Sherudo Garo has been successfully maimed, but his overloyal henchman, Wild Dog, has taken it upon himself to avenge his boss's death by snatching the girl and fleeing into another action-packed area. So stay tuned to see Wild Dog get his just deserts!

time crisis

continued

THIRD STAGE

By far the hardest stage of the bunch. It may be a good idea to practice on this level using the Time Attack mode, as it is so very difficult to complete.

area one

Shoot the blokes that drop from the helicopter and then another wave will appear from behind the battlements. Take out the grenade lobbers and red blokes first.

Aim your sights at the men operating the anti-aircraft guns first, and then take out the other foot cronies as they become visible.

After picking off the bloke in the tower, a helicopter will fly up and start firing. You'll need to pump about 40 hits into it to destroy it, so do it quickly and accurately.

area two

Inside the factory, there are loads of dangerous sharp-shooters to kill. They don't appear for long so you'll need to take them out fast.

Your view is obscured by bits of machinery, so just pepper the area with bullets and you're bound to hit someone!

Shoot the blues guys as soon as they appear because valuable time is taken up by having to dodge the crates that are moving your way.

The final wave of troops on this level will descend the stairs. But one bloke will fire through the hole in the walkway above. Be careful!

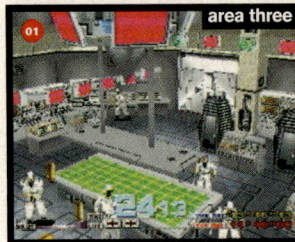
area three

You'll have a few seconds to start shooting before the guys down below notice you, so make the most of it. A grenade lobber will appear from behind the pods.

White guys will pop up from behind the table, followed by a red guy. He may appear on either side so try to spot him quickly before he can get a shot in.

The biggest threat here are the ninjas. If they get too close then duck, but otherwise keep blasting them. Time can get short here so accuracy is of the essence.

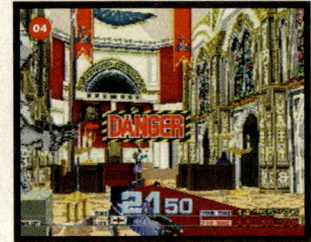

Various troops will come crashing through the windows, but keep your concentration because the armour in the foreground will keep taking swings at you.

Boss Intro

The final battle takes place on the rooftop. However, the stupid broad takes a bullet in the back... payback time!

Boss Guide

Wild Dog will first appear behind the fountain, so shoot him as he pops up. He will then run off and command his cronies to attack. Watch out for when he lobs grenades at the statues, as segments will break off and start rolling towards you. Finally, Wild Dog will dash off into the tower and start frantically fighting back. A smoke screen will disguise his movements whilst he lunges at you, so keep well hidden and then fight back when you catch a glimpse of him.

PLAYSTATION GAME

The hunk of dosh that you spend on this game seems incredibly insignificant when you start playing the new PlayStation missions. Far better than the arcade game, your mission is to infiltrate a multistorey hotel which is being used as a weapons factory and hunt down the arms supplier, Kantaris, a vindictive little tart you'll meet at various crucial points throughout the game.

The Lobby

When you reach the foyer section where the lifts are situated, the idea is to clear the entire area of enemies before the doors of the lift closest to you close. When the section begins, the lift will slowly descend to the ground floor – arriving by the time the fourth wave of enemies appear. Take them all out as quickly as possible, and if the doors are still open when the area is cleared, you'll hop in the lift and travel up to the Ballroom.

Shopping Mall

After you drop down the air duct into the storage area, you'll come across a loading crane that acts as a danger object. The idea here is to shoot the glass around the operating compartment of the crane: this will cause the thing to explode. When this is done, the mechanical arm will be severed and it will drop to the ground,

breaking a hole in the wall. Once the area is cleared, you'll make a break through this new hole into the Arms Factory.

Note: Despite trying various methods to avoid dropping down the air duct, it is impossible. We initially thought that by not hitting any glass, thus not triggering the alarm, you would be granted an alternative route. But sadly it's just a red herring!

Arms Factory

When you reach the last area of the Arms Factory, you'll notice three toxic waste storage tanks. Enemies will pop up all around them, so the idea is to pick each individual enemy off without hitting the tanks themselves. If they take a shot, the tanks will rupture and you'll have to exit via the emergency lift which will take you

to the Parking Lot. However, if you hit every enemy without damaging the tanks, you'll progress through the back door that leads you to the Lounge.

Parking Lot

Seeing as this is classed as the final stage on easy level, there aren't any

Route One

The main difference between the arcade and PlayStation games is that there are multiple routes through the hotel. You stick to the easy route as standard, but by shooting certain things that act as triggers, you can uncover hidden routes to other sections. The paths we've found are highlighted in the guide.

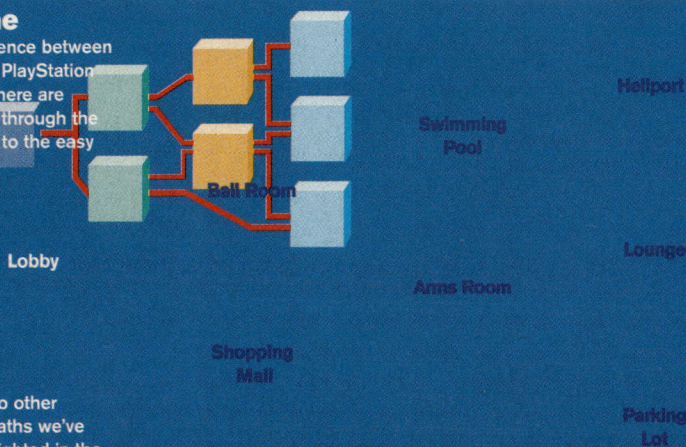

Heliport

Swimming Pool

Lobby

Ball Room

Lounge

Anns Room

Shopping Mall

Parking Lot

1 2 3 4

time crisis

continued

GAME OVER
Taking the easy route, you'll meet Kantaris in the Parking Lot. Shoot the car to kill her.

物語の最後は ハッピーエンドとは限らないものよ…

She gets away...

But not this time!

stage, a big tank-like monstrosity will bust through the wall and take you on. The aim is to shoot the windscreen. The tank will start by firing shots all over the place, so time your attack accordingly. It will then surge forward and try to head-butt you; again, duck to avoid it. After a while it will stomp off, only to appear a few moments later – killing troops for you in the process. This time it will fire rockets, bullets, and attack head-on.

Kantaris

Once the tank has been destroyed, you'll fight another two waves of enemy troops before Kantaris will try and make her getaway via a car. As it appears in the distance, unload several rounds into the body. If you score enough hits, you'll accomplish your mission; if not then you'll fail...

Ballroom

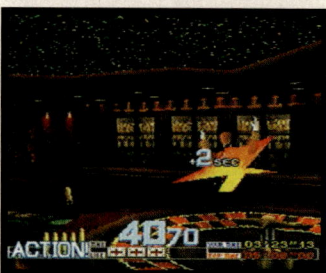

We stumbled across this purely by chance, but if you defeat the boss in as little time as possible, you'll be granted access to the swimming pool area. To do this you must hit the Web Spinner boss every time he pops up on screen without missing. If you are successful, you'll see Kantaris get the hump and storm off via a secret passage. Fail and you'll kill the boss and then exit to the Arms Factory.

alternate routes out of it. However, it's worth looking out for the explosive box on the ground. If you hit this, it will take out the entire wave of enemies in one fell swoop.

Boss

Once you battle through to the end of the

はじめまして リチャードカンタリスの城へようこそ

Boss

Typical! You've just barely survived a thick enemy onslaught and you have to face Keith from The Prodigy! This geezer is known as Web Spinner, and he's a real pain to defeat. He basically jumps all over the place like a nutter, stopping occasionally to chuck blades at you. The best bet is just to keep your pistol poised and then fire several shots as soon as he appears. Then duck to avoid any flying metal, reload, and get ready to pepper him once more.

Time Crisis
Cheat Mode

At the main screen, where you choose from the three boxes, shoot one bullet into the middle of the loop of the 'R' in 'CRISIS', then two shots right into the centre of the cross hairs (next to 'TIME').

It's tricky to do, so keep trying. If you get it right you'll be taken to a cheat menu where you can choose nine lives, no reload, and infinite continues. Well worth the trouble, if

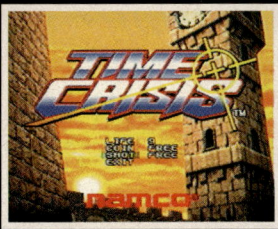

TIME CRISIS

Sharp shooting on the main menu is needed to get this cheat to work.

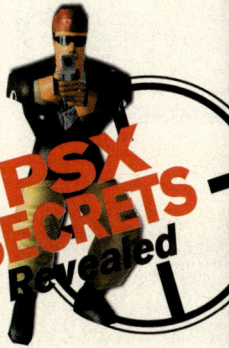

EASY ARCADE MODE

Select the arcade mission from the main selection screen and then, on the next screen that allows you to choose between Time Attack mode or the Story mode, shoot outside of the screen. If the cheat has worked, you'll see the word 'Easy' appear over the Story mode option. Now select it and start playing and you'll notice that you now have five lives and a lot more time with which to complete the game.

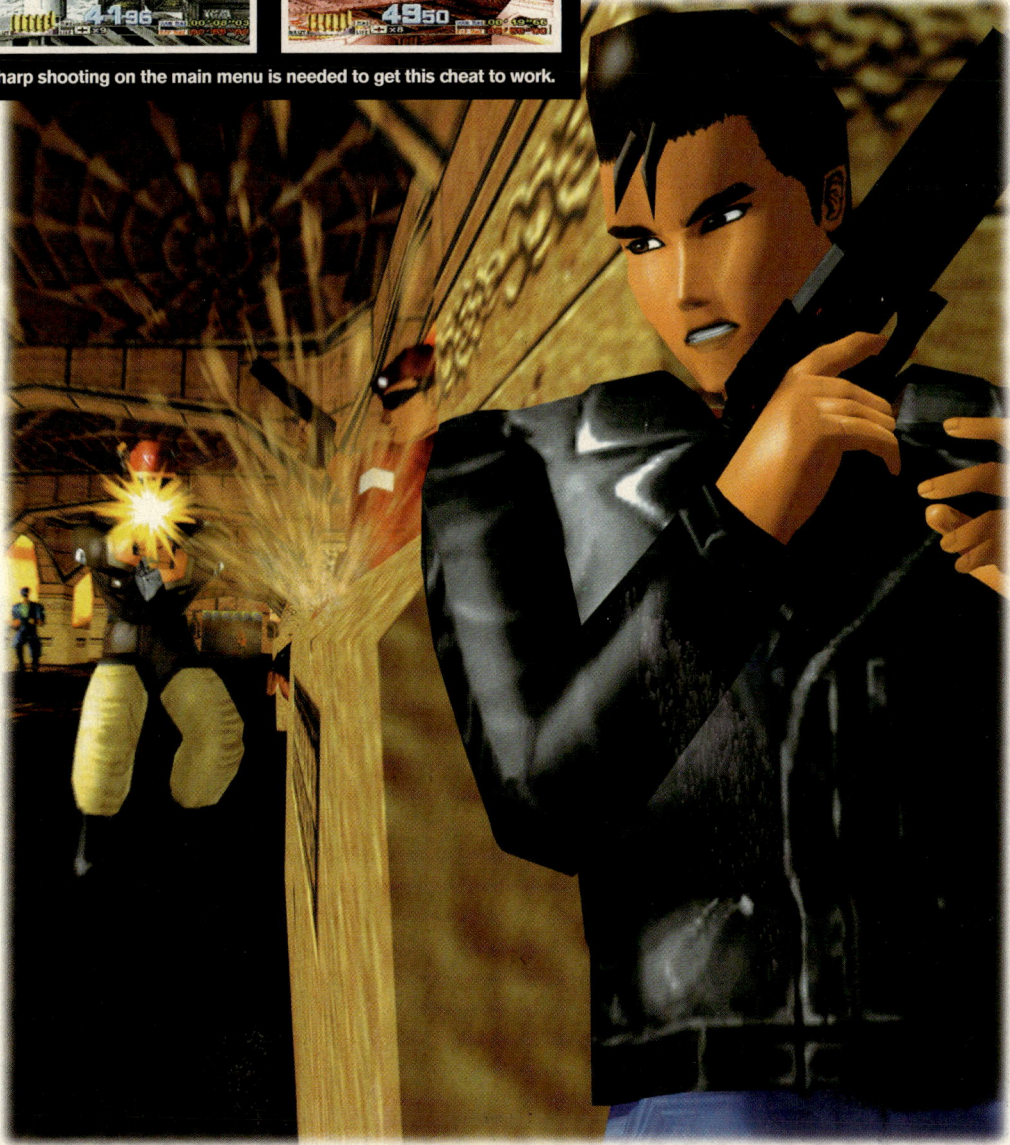

PSX SECRETS Revealed

time crisis

continued

GAME OVER

As endings go, this is a bit of a stinker. Make that a big stinker. Wild Dog ends up blowing himself up, like the daft twerp he is, and hero Richard Miller escorts the wounded hostage to safety via a handy helicopter – all of which is set against one of the worst soundtracks you'll ever get to hear.

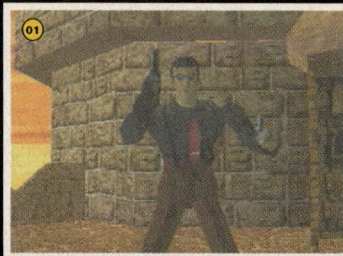

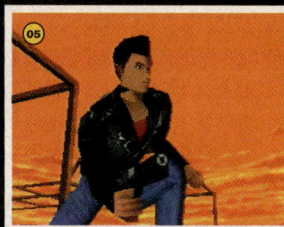

MANAGEMENT STAFF
KUNIO SAITOH
SEISUKE ISHIZAKA

PSX MISSIONS

Just before all the secrets and hidden sections are revealed in this epic shooter, following is a recap of what you're supposed to do in PlayStation game mode. You'll need to be familar with the various sections to get to the hidden stuff...

SECRET ELEMENTS

The Lobby

Once you're through to the final area in the lobby, where the lifts are situated, the lift closest to where you're standing will gradually descend and open. The idea is to clear the area of enemies before the doors shut and the lift ascends the building again. To do this you must try and memorise where each wave appears from and then take then out quickly before they take cover. Succeed in doing this and you will take the lift up to the Ballroom. Fail and you'll climb the stairs to the Shopping Mall.

Shopping Mall

After the gunfight around the shops, you'll dive through an air duct into the storage area. Once you get to the final section where there is a crane, you must shoot the glass cabin to blow it up. This will cause the crane arm to fall off and smash a hole in the wall that will provide an alternate route to the Arms Factory. If you fail to shoot the crane, you'll merely go on to the Parking Lot, where a poor ending will await you if you complete it.

Ballroom

As you may know, after battling your way through the Ballroom, you will end up facing the Web Spinner boss. Now, hard as he is to defeat, your aim is to destroy him as quickly as possible – the object being to have about ten seconds left on

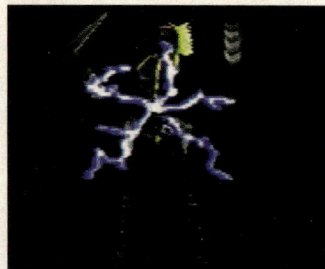

the clock after he dies, and thus time it so that Kantaris is still in the room with you. You'll know when you're on the right track because the boss will perform a dramatic flip as he keels over and croaks it. By doing this, Kantaris will get the hump and exit to the Swimming Pool via a secret tunnel, closely followed by yourself. If you fail to defeat the boss in time, you'll exit via a hidden tunnel and descend to the Arms Factory.

Arms Factory

When you get to the final area of the Arms Factory, the bit where you have to pick the enemies off three large and highly dangerous storage tanks, the idea is to kill the men without hitting the tanks. Easier said than done, we have to admit, and you'll need a very steady hand to pull it off. If you do manage to complete the level without rupturing the highly explosive canisters, when the level ends, you'll exit via the back door and ascend the building to the Lounge. If you fail and hit the tanks, they will explode, killing everything on screen, and you'll have no choice but to exit via the emergency lift which will take you back down to the Parking Lot. If this happens, only the easy and poorest ending will be available to you. So avoid those tanks at all cost!

New Areas!

Well that's us up to date with the many secrets contained within the hotel complex so far, so let us now continue hot on the trail of Kantaris by exposing the brand new difficult-to-find areas and bust the scum-ridden sanctums wide open!

01 The Lounge

The entrance into the Lounge is very straight forward. At first your path is blocked by a plethora of armed guards, so the idea is to take out the red guys cowering behind the shielded blue guys first. Once this wave has been disposed of, the doors will fly open as more and more troops come out blazing. Shoot fast and don't stay exposed for too long.

01 The Swimming Pool

Troops will attack in the foreground whilst more deadly adversaries will creep in from the back. Kill the rocket man in the distance for another 5 secs!

02

When the boat stops moving, baddies will pop up all over the place. Kill the red ones first and then look out for the orange man in the background.

03

You must stop the orange men from escaping down the back passage if you want to go to the Heliport. If you fail you'll go back down to the Lounge.

01 The Heliport

At every available opportunity, shoot the large helicopter with everything you've got. If it fires missiles, duck until the smoke disappears overhead.

02

It will keep dispersing troops, so take out the most dangerous first and then keep firing at the chopper before killing the others.

03

When all of the troops have gone, you're left free to concentrate on the chopper. Avoid the missiles and bullets and keep firing until it explodes.

Kantaris State

Use this chart to plot your route through the vast hotel complex. Taking the high route will take you through to the hardest, but best, endings. If you are unsure of how to get to certain areas, everything is explained in these pages. So there's no excuses for failure!

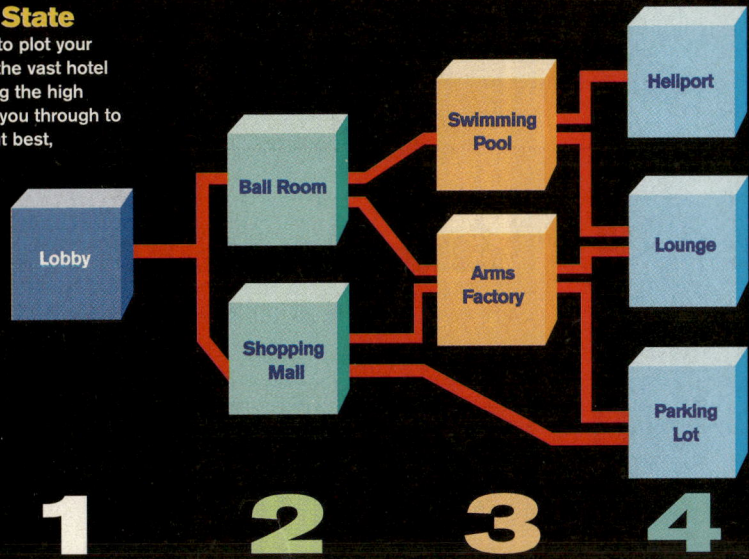

secrets · strategies · solutions PlayStation

time crisis

continued

GAME OVER: THE DOWNFALL OF KANTARIS

There are three final stages in which you must defeat Kantaris to finish the game. Which one you tackle depends entirely on which route you have taken through the game. The Parking Lot is the easiest, the Lounge is medium, and if you're brave enough to take her on at the Heliport, then you're facing the toughest challenge of them all.

As the red car driven by Kantaris hurtles into view, poise your sights and pump it full of lead. About three clips should cause sufficient damage to the vehicle to cause a nasty crash.

Easy (Parking Lot)

When the tank boss and all of the baddies have been shot, you'll see a red car spin around the corner in the background. Pump it full of lead and if you manage to score enough hits before it disappears off of the screen, Kantaris will panic and crash the damn thing into a wall – frying herself in the process. If you fail she'll merely drive away to safety. Seeing as this is the easy ending, it is rather lacking in the thrills department. So try harder for one of the decent ones!

This boss is very difficult to kill. You must aim your sights at the three lights situated in the centre of the robot, whilst taking care to avoid his bullets and charging assault. It is a good idea to score more hits by standing and shooting as he charges at you, but timing is critical. If you fail to destroy it in time, Kantaris will run off to safety.

Medium (Lounge)

The idea here is to shoot the three lights in the centre of the robot and do it as quickly as possible. If you are successful, the robot will turn on its heels and smash through the bulletproof glass, knocking poor Kantaris out of the window and to her grizzly demise several floors below.

After destroying the main boss gunship, you'll have one last stab at stopping Kantaris from flying to safety. She'll flee to an awaiting chopper which will be taking off just as you arrive on the scene. Waste no time and stand immediately and unleash everything you've got into the target. You'll need a nimble trigger finger because you need to empty three clips into the helicopter before it leaves. Do this and you'll get the good ending and credit pictures!

Hard (Heliport)

Dispose of the main gunship as quickly as possible, and then Kantaris will mumble something and dash off to an awaiting escape chopper. You don't get much time to stop her so fill it with lead as quickly as possible (you'll need to pump about three clips into it before it disappears off screen). If you are successful and don't miss, the helicopter will veer off and explode – sending poor Kantaris well and truly up in smoke. Fail on the other hand, and she'll fly away to safety, taunting you and badly damaging your macho ego!

Publisher:	GT Interactive
Price:	£44.99
Format:	UK

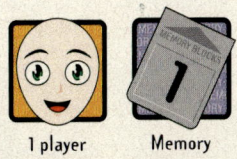

1 player

Memory

TIGERSHARK

Tiger Shark

With **most of Japan sinking** into the **murky depths of the ocean**, only **Tigershark can stop the Ruskies** from finishing off **the rest of the world**. Your mission is simple: **destroy all the undersea fault 'taps'** before they can rupture the **rest of the Earth's crust**. Put a **tiger in your tank** with our **cheats and passwords**.

CHEATS

Using your wits and skills may not be enough to advance through every level, particularly if you're not that good at the game. So why not try some of our many wonderful cheats?

Invincibility
Enter **KURSK** as a password.

You'll now be completely invulnerable to attack.

Infinite Ammunition

Enter **KIROV** as a password.
This gives you all the ammo you'll ever need.

Weapons Upgrade
Enter **RUBLE** as a password.
Power-up those weapons to really roast the Ruskies.

Low Gravity
Enter **SOYUZ** as a password.

It's like walking on the moon, as Sting would say.

Sea Hunter Mini-Game
Enter **SNEEG** as a password.

A special sub-game for you to enjoy.

View FMV Sequences
Enter **KIEV** as a password.
You can watch all the marvellous intro sequences in the game.

Preview Unreleased Game (Bug Rider)
Enter **BUGGY** as a password.
Check out a forthcoming game from the makers of *Tigershark*. Cool!

PASSWORDS

Still can't get any further?! Then enter the password for the level you want.

2	AKULA		
3	PASHA		
4	MIRAS	5	NAKAT
6	REZKY	7	TUCHA
8	ZARYA	9	VOSTA

abe's oddysee

Publisher:	GT Interactive
Price:	£39.99
Format:	UK

start

Abe's Oddysee
complete solution

You start Abe's Oddysee trapped in a **flesh farm** with **no gun, no explosives**, and no **discernible martial arts skills**. Sounds like it's **going to be a short game**. That is if **you don't read** this **comprehensive guide** that has been **paid for in blood**.

ABE'S ABILITIES

This alien may not have done over Sigourney Weaver but he isn't a pushover. Amongst his formidable talents is the ability to chant. Communication plays a big part of this game, so sound off regularly to make things happen. Abe can also roll himself into a ball to get through small holes, which comes in handy when he's trying to make a swift getaway. Taking possession of the finger-faced guards is also essential to make progress in this titanic adventure, so get them to kill each other rather than you.

RUPTURE FARMS

Hold R1 and sprint right to the next screen. Stop next to the sign marked directory and push up to activate a map that shows the location of Mudokons that need rescuing. Exit the map and keep running right. When you reach a ledge, push ⇧ to haul yourself onto it to avoid the armed guard.

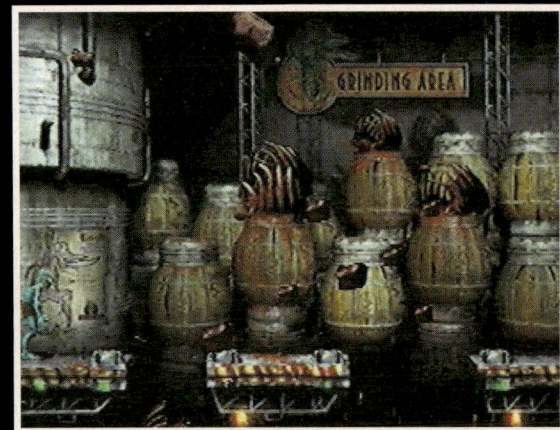

Proceed to the next screen and tap ⇧ to go through the door. Keep on running and head through the next two doors. Keep going right until you get to a message telling you how to jump. The mines at the bottom of the pits will make Mudokon flambé of poor Abe, so walk

close to the edges of the platforms before leaping across the gaps.

Go to the next screen, where there's a Mudokon wiping down a wall under the supervision of a guard. Take over the guard using Abe's chant and get him to flick the switch on the left that is marked with the electricity symbol. Run right through the next screen until you get to another guard. Fire over his head to wake him up, then when he stands up pepper him with bullets. Self-destruct the guard you are controlling (poor bugger) by holding the chant buttons.

When you have regained control of Abe, persuade the two Mudokons to follow you using the "hello" and "follow me" commands respectively. Run to the room where you gunned down the guard and get the two Mudokons to stand on the rope platform. Winch yourself to the screen below by holding ⇩.

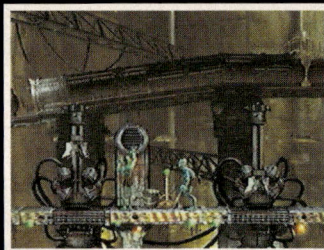

You should now be on a screen with a circle of birds to the left of it. Hold down the chant buttons and the birds will turn into a teleporter for your fellow Mudokons to run through. Head through the door at the right of the screen and walk right. You'll come across two more Mudokons: persuade these to follow you right to the bird portal and chant to send them through. Pull yourself up the ledge on this screen and go right. Attract the guard's attention and he will walk in your direction. When he is standing over the trap door, hit the switch next to you to

drop him down a hole. Jump off the platform and go right to the grinding area. There are two jumps to negotiate on this screen, but you have to avoid the rocks that are regularly falling down the gaps while you do so.

In the next section you'll have to disarm a bomb before you can pull yourself up the ledge. The bomb flashes red three times before turning green, so crouch next to it and press ■ when it is safe. When you have pulled yourself up, cross into the next screen, walk over to the switch and, by using skilful timing, throw the switch and dump both the guards below into a pit. Drop down, walk over to the right-hand platform and climb up to flick the switch and deactivate the lightning field. Drop back down and persuade the Mudokons to follow you back to the bomb room. When you get there the birds will have returned so you can send him home.

Go back right to the platform with the lightning switch and continue to the next screen. Before you crouch to roll under the door you'll need to kill the guard on the far walkway. Use the chant buttons to stir-fry his brain into oblivion. Persuade the Mod to follow you into the next room, tell him to wait, and climb onto the platform above the other Mod. Flick the switch to turn off the mincer and walk off the screen to the right. Walk back to the previous screen and the birds you scared away will have reappeared. Chant to send

Abe's Oddysee

abe's oddysee

continued

(Right) Run Abe! Run like the wind. Stay ahead of the Paramites or Abe will be on the menu.

and creep over to the noose on the next screen. Face right before you jump and grab it, so you can start running as soon as you hit the ground. Run off the ledge to the right and grab on to avoid the Slog. All you have to do now is get back to the exit door and head for the main temple.

PARAMONIAN NESTS

Walk right to the lift and winch yourself to the next level. Run left and jump to the platform before the Paramites catch you.

(Right) Don't be distracted by the nicely rendered graphics on the mines, as death is sure to follow.

Jump over the gap to the right and run to the next screen. Keep running and leap over the trap door that opens on the following screen. Run off the end of the platform and jump for the overhang on the next screen. You can dangle here out of harm's way as the Paramites don't have the ability to climb. When you feel you can continue, pull yourself up and start climbing.

Don't, whatever you do, mistime your jump into the bird portal or you will have to do the whole level again.

When you reach the next screen pull Abe onto the ledge then tap ⇩ quickly so that he is hanging from it. This should cause the two Paramites that drop in to run over Abe and fall onto the level below, leaving him unharmed. Get to the platform on the top right of the screen and pull yourself onto the next section.

Roll through the tunnel to the right and climb up to the top of the platform. Roll

quickly left and head for the next screen at full pelt. Jump across the gap and quickly jump up to the next platform. Burn it right and do two swift rolls to get under the outcrop of rocks. Run onto the next screen and chase the Paramite until you get to an overhanging platform. Climb up onto the platform quickly as the Paramite you were chasing has just met a friend. Leap into the hole before another Paramite appears and collect some meat from the bag on the next screen. Go through the second hole and chuck the meat down for the Paramites, leg it to the door, and make a speedy exit to stay alive.

Hit the chant buttons as soon as you appear on the other side of the door so there's no chance the birds will be scared away. Take a running leap through the portal to your initiation ceremony and pray that you never have to visit this b*****d level again.

SCRABANIA

Run to the left screen, jump over the mine and grab onto the ledge. Wait for the Slig to come over and investigate. When Slig turns his back climb onto the ledge and activate the bomb; roll off quickly before he can shoot. When the guard has been fragged walk to the left and hide in the shadows of the next screen. When the Slig here walks off to the right, scale the cliff above the shadows and wait by the switch. Throw the switch when the Slig walks back to the middle of the screen, to drop a large rock on him.

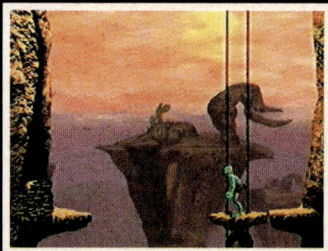

Lower yourself down and head left. When you come to a switch, walk round to the left side of it before you do anything. Hit the switch and a boulder falls to your right – it'll also open the well in the section where you began the level. Jump through the well and hit the switch when you emerge to open the hole on the screen with the mine.

Go through the hole and hold the chant buttons when you land to take over the Slig in the foreground. Dispose of him and return through the hole to get on the ledge he was guarding. Pull the noose to summon the Elum and descend to the bottom of the ledge. Get on the Elum and run left jumping over the holes on your way. You'll get a short bit of FMV before you begin the next part of Scrabania.

Ride the Elum to the lift and dismount so that you can descend. Repeat the password to the Mudokon you come across and he'll bless you with the power of the rings. Walk onto screen to the right and detonate the floating mines with the rings, then climb onto the ledge with the switch to activate another rope lift. Return to the Mudokon and collect another set of rings before heading down the lift again. Go down until you find a stone tablet that is protected by mines and use the rings. Collect the password from the tablet and return to the Mudokon to get yet another set of rings.

Get Elums to follow you down the lifts and use them to get as far down as you can go. Say hello to the Mudokon on the platform below and give him the password: he'll then throw the switch to activate the floating mines. When they're both on the right side of the screen, activate the rings, then use the Elum to jump over the gap. To get past the floating mines here you'll need to time your passage accurately as the slightest mistake will be fatal. Alternatively you could just go hell for leather and burn it through the mines and across the gaps (it worked for me).

When you reach the next section, walk to the right of the screen and head up the lift. Walk right and the Elum starts eating honey, leaving you without a ride. Lower yourself down the lift to the right and start running. There is a Slig sharpshooter in the background so don't

stop or you'll be cannon fodder. Throw the switch you come to and sky it back to the hole you passed on the way. Leap into it to be propelled to the bag with the rocks in. Pick up the rock that falls out and go back up the rope lift. Keep going up until you reach the tunnel with the land mine in it. Crouch at the end of the tunnel and throw the rock to destroy the mine. Roll through the tunnel and repeat the password the Mudokon gives you to get the ring power-up.

Go back through the tunnel and return to the room where you left the Elum and walk off to the right. Stand at the very edge of the screen and use the rings to detonate all the explosives in this room. Roll under the gap and climb up the cliff onto the next screen. Flick the switch and quickly drop down to the cactus and roll onto the screen where you left the Elum. The bees should start attacking the Elum and eventually it loses interest in the honey, allowing you to take him down the lift.

Mount the Elum and run back to the screen where the Slig was on guard. Run past him and leap the gap on the Elum. Keep riding the Elum until you reach a ledge with a bomb on the other side. Dismount and jump through the hole. Disarm the bomb and walk onto the right screen. Dive for cover behind the rock and wait until the Sligs have stopped firing before you make a run for the well. You should now be back on the screen with the Elum. Climb on its back and leap over the gap.

Return through the screen with the Sligs and stop on the edge of the cliffs. Get off Elum and jump down the hole. Collect the stone from the hanging bag and use it to destroy the mine on the lower ledge. Get the password from the stone tablet. Return to the Elum and leap over the gap.

When you reach a Mudokon, repeat the password and collect the ring power-up. Continue left. When you get to a gap that's blocked by a floating mine, dismount and lower yourself off the ledge. Flick the switch and climb back up to Elum so that the second mine doesn't crash into you. Get back on the Elum and jump the gap whilst dodging the now moving mine. Keep running and jumping until you get to a screen where a floating mine blocks your path. Dismount and

climb up to the ledge on the left. Take over the guard and walk him to the lift. Descend and shoot the guard sleeping to the right. Go down to the next screen and jump off the platform. Walk over to the switch and shoot the Slig next to it. Hit the switch and a mine will come flying towards you, killing the Slig which you are controlling.

Walk Abe back to the Elum and get on his back. Leap across the mine-free gap and run right until you reach a small gap. Dismount to jump across the gap. Tiptoe through the next screen and stop when you get to the floating mine. Jump and crouch quickly to dodge the mine whilst you are crossing the landmines. Go to the next screen and repeat the Mudokon's chant to get the ring power-up. Return to the mines and obliterate them. Go back to the hole and jump through it to reach a platform in the background. Take over the Slig in the foreground and walk him right. Eventually you'll come to another guard: blow him away and return to Abe.

Jump back through the hole, collect the Elum, and run right. When you get to a pillar that bars your path, leave the Elum and continue over the pillar on your own. Jump through the well and say hello to the Mudokon before rolling right. Quickly give him the password so you can return through the hole, away from that darned floating mine. After a lengthy tunnel ride you'll finally come to rest next to a Mudokon. Repeat his chant to get the red

rings and use them to blow up the mines. Cross the mine-free platforms and jump through the hole.

Walk onto the right screen and turn your back on the Slog standing next to the birds. Chant to open the portal and run for your life when the Slog comes at you. Leap into the well to avoid him and you'll be fired back out again. When you land, run back to the bird portal and leap through to finish the level.

SCRABANIAN TEMPLE

The first part of the temple is pretty straightforward. You have to avoid being gunned down by running left and hiding behind the rocks. Stop when you get to the flashing bomb so that you can defuse it, then clear the remaining mines with a running leap. Go through the door at the end to get to the main temple and begin

the trials. Take a hint from the stone tablet before you descend to the first trial.

Trial 1

Thankfully the Scrabs are too busy tearing each other apart to give Abe much hassle on this treacherous level.

Drop down and run to the switch. Throw it and climb back up to the entrance to avoid the Scrab lurking on the ledge. Drop back down on the right side and leap into the holes. Eventually you'll come to rest next to a stone tablet which you need to activate to get the bell password. Drop off the ledge when the Scrab is directly underneath you and run left. The Scrab pursues you at high speed so grab the ledge at the end of the section and pull yourself up fast. From this vantage point you can safely jump down the hole that takes you to the switch on the other side of the screen. Don't activate the switch yet – instead climb up the platform to the left and throw the switch there. Climb down and wait until the Scrab is directly beneath you before dropping down and running on.

Leap into the first hole you come to and you'll be transported to the flint switch. Hit the switch before lowering yourself back down to the ledge above the Scrab. Run past the Scrab as before and get back to the first switch you came to. This switch activates a trapdoor underneath Abe as well as opening the hole on the left of the screen, so make sure the Scrab is out of your way before you hit it. Leap into the hole you've just opened and climb onto the ledge above. You should now be just under the exit to this stage so hit the chant buttons to open the doors and leave. Go to the door on the left to begin the next challenge.

(Left) The Elum is useful for jumping long gaps but keep the greedy trog away from honey.

(Left) Take this guard over from a distance and walk him off the ledge for a laugh.

Run swiftly off this ledge and down the next before the quadruped below minces you.

abe's oddysee

Trial 2

If you get cornered like this, pray that another Scrab enters the screen or expect to die horribly.

(Right) Lure this Scrab into the hole to get to the switch.

(Right) Grab the lift and haul yourself up quickly to avoid becoming food for the Scrab that is jumping down.

This challenge is quite easy as all you need is good timing. Walk right to the hanging bag and collect a couple of rocks. Drop down the ledge until you get to a room with a Scrab lurking about. Jump down, run left, and fall off the edge to avoid the Scrab. When you land, keep going right until you get to a tunnel that is mined. Destroy the mine with the rocks you are carrying and collect the bell password from the stone tablet. Jump up at the spot on the screen where dirt is falling and haul yourself onto the ledge. Keep heading up and go left: you'll come to a flint switch. Pull the lever but don't roll under the ledge towards the Scrab. Instead, retrace your steps and get back to the first screen with a Scrab on it. Hang from the ledge until the Scrab is in the right corner of the cave, then haul yourself up and climb up to the ledge on the right. Now all you have to do is cross the gap on the next screen and chant to open the doors to complete the stage. Drop off the edge end enter the doorway to the left to begin the next trial.

Trial 3

When the Scrabs are fighting, don't stand and watch or you'll soon join in the melee.

Run off the ledge and you should avoid the floating mine on the first screen, don't worry about the drop as you'll grab the outcrop of rock on the following screen.

Drop off the ledge you are holding and walk to the right of the screen so that the Slig in the background cannot shoot at you. When the Slig in the background is out of the way, run to the switch and throw it to crush the guard nearest to you. Quickly run to the left and jump into the hole you come to. You'll appear in the background above a Slig. Take him over and walk him to the right of the switch. Flick it and hold down the fire button as a stream of Slogs run out of the tube to the left to attack you. Gun them all down before walking off the edge to the right. Shoot the guard on the next screen before returning to Abe. Walk Abe to the stone tablet and collect the chime password, then enter the hole. Use the chant buttons to open the door: go through it and head for the first trial on the right.

Trial 4

Drop down the ledges until you reach a screen with a Scrab on it. Drop down and keep running and you'll encounter another Scrab. The Scrab chasing you will attack it, enabling you to get to the ledge above you unmolested. While they are fighting, run back right until you get to a hole. Dive into it immediately so that the Scrab does not get a chance to charge. Flick the switch when you land and jump back into the hole when the coast is clear.

You'll appear in the background so just walk right and activate the stone tablet. Go through the door on the left and walk under the ledge with the Scrab. When it runs off, haul yourself up onto the platform it was previously occupying and take the lift to the screen above. Walk left off the screen and a lift will bring a Scrab up onto the ledge. Quickly run right to avoid the Scrab and roll under the tunnel. The Scrab will now be standing on the lift so just pull the lever to rid yourself of this pest.

Bring the lift back up and cross over to the left screen and activate the stone tablet. Return to the screen where you began this trial and run right. The two Scrabs on this screen will be too busy fighting each other so you should have a clear run. Jump onto the first ledge you find to avoid the Scrab being sent up on the lift. Flick the flint switch and proceed to the screen on the right where you should chant to complete and exit the

trial. When you have left, climb up the ledge and take the first door you come to on your way.

Trial 5

Run off the ledge and you'll grab onto the outcrop below. Continue descending and you'll end up on a ledge opposite a Scrab. The Scrab will jump off the ledge and walk towards you. When it is directly beneath the platform, run off the edge and jump up to the switch. Throw the switch to activate the flint and wait for the Scrab to walk beneath the platform. Run off the platform and head for the next screen. Grab onto the ledge with the stone tablet before the Scrab catches you and activate it. Run off the platform to the left and leap onto the ledge by the door. Don't worry about the Scrab guarding the door: he will fight the other Scrab that was chasing you, allowing ample time to use your chant and leave the section. Take the door on the right to continue your quest.

Trial 6

Walk right when you emerge. Jump across the gap and turn around when you find a Scrab. He chases you and you'll need to jump into the hole on the first screen. You end up behind the Scrab so start running as soon as you hit the ground. Run until you get to a lift: winch yourself down quickly so you don't become Scrab meat. When you get to the bottom screen walk right. Run back left and jump onto the ledge when the Scrab charges towards you. Wait until the Scrab is on the lift before you flick the switch and send him to the top of the screen.

Return to the screen with the chimes and flick the switch there. Jump into the hole on the previous screen and continue jumping into the holes. When you get to the platform above the Scrabs, activate the tablet on the screen and walk left to flick the flint switch. Go back to the section with the lift and the two Scrabs will start fighting, which enables you to make a getaway via the elevator. Head back to the bells and chant to exit. Clamber up the platform to get to the final trial.

Trial 7

First go left and collect the bell chant from the stone tablet, then walk off the

starting screen right and run through the next section to dodge the bats. Quickly climb the platform and proceed to the ledge on the next screen. Jump the gap in the middle of the screen and run right. Grab onto the ledge under the Scrab: this should make him jump down. Pull yourself onto the ledge and flick the switch to activate the hole. Jump through the hole and go right when you land. Eventually you come to a trap door switch. Throw the switch and the flint will light; you'll also drop down in front of the Scarab. Run left and roll through the tunnel to rid yourself of this menace. Jump the gap and proceed onto the ledge. You're now back in the room with the first Scarab. When it walks off the screen, run to the lift and haul yourself up. Chant when you have reached the bells and exit to finish the final trial.

SCRABANIAN NESTS

Start running right and leap the first three gaps. When you've leapt the third gap grab onto the ledge and haul yourself up. Climb up onto the next screen by standing under the falling debris: keep holding a when you reach this screen as you'll quickly climb onto the lift and dodge the Scrab. Ascend to the next screen and quickly run right. Grab onto the lift in the next section and pull yourself up.

Scrabs begin to arrive via the lifts so waste no time in running right. Continue running for another screen before climbing up the first ledge you come to. Jump the gap and roll under a low ledge to lose the Scrab chasing you. When you drop off the next ledge another Scrab will join the hunt so exit the screen right. Run and jump onto the ledge above the switch on the far side of the screen. When the Scrab is directly under the ledge jump off and climb onto the left platform with the switch on. Flick the switch and rocks will

start falling, opening up two gaps in the process. Dodge the rocks and flick the switch on the right side of the screen. This opens the exit door, enabling you to make good your escape.

STOCKYARD RETURN

With the two scars in place, Abe finally gets to turn into something viscous and kick some bad-guy ass. Run right and clear the gap to begin your return to Rupture farms. Go to the screen that's packed with mines and the Sligs. Hold down the chant buttons to unleash the mighty power of the Mudokon god.

Once all the guards and mines have been liquefied you can proceed through the bird portal and return to the stockyard. Scale the first two screens and take the motion-detecting beams slowly. When you get past them a Slog is sent after you so run right and grab onto the first ledge you see to avoid him. Creep to the switch whilst dodging the motion sensors and pull it. Run back left and jump off the ledge in front of the Slog: he starts chasing you so get rid of him by running through the first set of motion sensors. Drop off the ledge and the floating mine that's sent to kill you will obliterate the Slog.

Return to the screen where you deactivated the lightning field and collect some rocks from the bag below. Go back to the ledge just in front of the motion sensors, making sure you have activated the floating mine. Chuck the rock onto the screen and the mine will explode, giving you a safe passage through the detectors. Replenish your supply of rocks before continuing on your way right. Throw the rocks at the circle of floating mines that block the gap to clear your way to the next section.

Run off the ledge and get some rocks from the bag hanging on the tree – be

quick about it because the Slog in the cave isn't going to stay asleep for long. Run right when the Slog awakens and dive through the first tunnel you come to. Quickly scale the ledge on the next screen to avoid being shot by the guard. Cross onto the screen to the right and crouch on the ledge above the mines. Chuck a rock horizontally and the mines will all explode, vaporising the birds in the process. Walk off the screen and return to bring the birds back. Chant then leap through the portal to get to the second part of the stockyard.

The first screen is thick with mines and motion detectors. You need to time your jump down to the mines so you don't set off the motion detectors otherwise a Slig will run onto the screen and take you out. Once you have got safely down, deactivate the bomb on the right without setting off the motion detector. Now jump and grab onto the ledge on the right,

Achtung, land mines! I thought these things were banned.

(Left) You'll need a Slog for mine-detecting duties on this screen.

When the power of the Mudokon god is finally yours it's time for some payback!

(Left) This portal is the beginning of your daring rescue mission.

abe's oddysee

continued

setting off the beams as you do so. When the guard runs off the ledge to investigate, haul yourself up and he'll blunder into the mines. You can now turn off the lightning field using the uncovered switch.

Climb back onto the ledge and enter the screen where the guard emerged. Chant to get the Slog's attention and run back left. Jump down between the mines and leap onto the ledge to the left. Don't worry if you have not turned the electric field off as the Slog is running so fast he'll still be alive when he hits the mines. Walk through to the cave where the Slog was hiding and drop down the ledge. Chant to activate the bird portal and jump through it to reach Rupture farms.

RUPTURE FARMS 2

Zulag 1

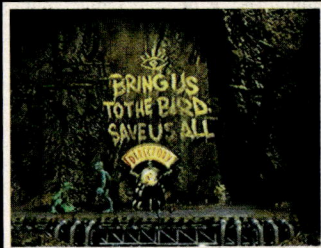

When you appear take the first Mudokon you find to the bird portal. When he has gone through, the lightning field deactivates allowing you access to the other part of the level. Run past the lift and you'll reach a familiar-looking area. Cross the gap on the next screen and collect some grenades from the machine. Now you can either dodge the slow-moving mine you have just activated or obliterate it with a well-placed bomb.

When you walk back into the screen on the right, an alarm goes off and your way is blocked by a lightning screen. To get through the screen you must chuck a grenade onto the ledge with the switch to dispose of the Slig guarding it. Stand near the ledge, hold the throw button, and

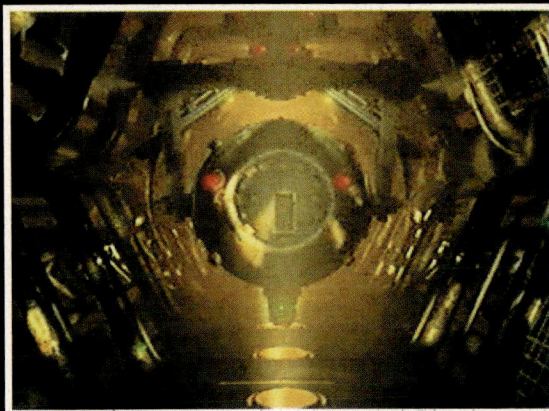

hold ⇦ to grease the mutha. You can then scale the platform and turn off the lightning field.

Go back to the lift, head through it, and start running left. A Slog will be chasing you so keep running and climb up onto the first ledge you find. Take over the Slig that has foolishly joined in the chase and use him to gun down the Slog. Walk the Slig right and eliminate all the guards that block your path. When you come to a pipe with snoring sounds emanating from the top, start firing your gun – don't take your finger off the trigger until every last one of the Slogs has hit the dirt or you'll be Slog food. Walk onto the screen to the right and flick the switch next to the Mudokon.

Return to Abe and walk left. Chant to send the Maudlin below through the portal before heading to the screen on the left. The Mudokon on this screen gives you the red ring power-up: use it to destroy the mines on the previous screen. Collect the remaining Mudokons and carefully transport them through the meat grinder to the bird portal. Send them through the portal and go through the door that you opened with the Slig. You'll be transported by capsule to Zulag 2.

Zulag 2

Walk through the door to the right when you emerge. Creep past the Slig and haul onto the platform above him. Use the chant buttons to take over the Slig and walk left. Say hello to the monitor in front of the lightning screen and repeat the noises it makes. The lightning field deactivates and another Slig enters the screen. Wait for the Slig to drop down before ventilating his bony butt.

Return to Abe and haul yourself onto the ledge which the second Slig emerged from. Go through the door at the top right of the screen to begin the first part of Zulag 2. Use the directory on the first

screen to take a look at the map, then proceed to the far right until you reach the bird portal. Climb onto the platform with the switch and activate it while facing left. A Slig drops in so you'll have to start running as soon as the lever is pulled. Stand under the platform and the Slig will drop off to find you. When he has done this, quickly haul yourself up to the platform and chant to take him over. Walk the Slig back to the screen with the lightning field and repeat the password to the monitor to deactivate it. Return to Abe and send all the Mudokons through the portal before climbing up the winch platform to the next section.

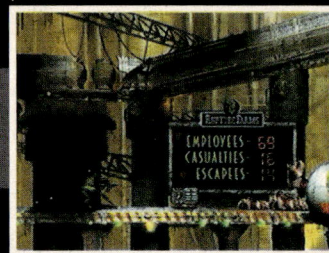

Flick the switch, cross into the screen on the right, and walk back to the lever. Remember those bombs you picked up? Now is the time to use them. Throw one from by the lever and you should destroy all the mines on the adjacent screen. Walk right and stand two steps away from the edge of the screen. If the floating mine is still about, it won't be able to get you at this point. Take over the Slig below and use him to waste the guard on the following screen. Return to Abe and head for the bird portal near the two Mudokons. Send them home and leg it back left as a guard is soon to appear. Jump for the platform and haul up.

Head back to the entrance to the section and go through the door to the right. Start running right when you appear as the Slig in the kennel above Abe soon

gets his scent. When you enter the next screen, grab onto the ledge and haul yourself up. Take over the Slig and command the Slog to come to you. Walk onto the screen to the right. Tell the Slog to attack and it'll run through the pipe to kill the other Slig. Command the Slog to come to you, then shoot it before returning to Abe. Roll through the pipe where the Slog killed the guard and continue through the next screen. Get the Slig to follow you onto the previous screen, then roll through the pipe and climb onto the ledge above the Slig. Take him over and walk towards the switch in the room on the right. Gun down the Slogs that run toward you, flick the switch, and return to Abe.

Walk Abe to the screen with the Mudokons and get them to follow you to the portal. Send them through the head to the final door in the Zulag. Walk right, jump over the mines, and creep onto the next screen. Continue along and haul yourself onto the ledge near the Mudokon. Collect some bombs from the machine, stand next to the switch, and rebound a bomb off the wall on the left. Quickly turn right and flick the switch: the bomb will fall through the hole and frag the Slig below.

Rescue both the Mudokons and flick the switch the Slig was guarding before heading up the winch platform at the far right of the level. Creep over to the guard and haul up to the platform above him. Walk left as far as you can go, then face right. Rebound a bomb off the wall to eliminate the Slig so that you can flick the switch and head to the next Zulag.

Zulag 3

When you enter the main section, creep left and attract the attention of the Slig. When he gets up, run left and haul up the platform there. Take over the Slig when he enters the screen, then command the Slog to come to you. Walk right and send the Slog to attack the Slig on the other side of the pipe. When the Slog has eaten the guard, put him down then return to Abe. Roll Abe through the pipe and deactivate the lightning field. Return to the far left screen and winch yourself up to the main doors of the Zulag.

Take the door on the right to begin the section. Walk through the screen with three Sligs and take over the Slig on the next screen. Walk him over to the switch on the previous screen, drop the Sligs through the trap door, and shoot them when they land. Return to Abe and roll through the pipe to get to the Mudokon. Get him to stand on the trapdoor you dropped the guards through, then hit the switch below so that you can get to the bird portal and send him through.

Go through the door at the far right of the section. Collect some bombs from the

bomb machine and descend to the screen below. Use the chant buttons to kill one of the guards on this screen and take the other one over. Flick the switch to the left and walk off the screen to the right. Shoot the guard here to sound the alarm. Three more Sligs drop in, so make a fight of it. If you don't kill them all they'll walk to the screen where Abe is, allowing him to take them over. When you have control of a guard, kill the others and walk right until you get to an electrical barrier. Kill the Slog and give the password to the machine. When you walk onto the following screen shout "look out" to the Mudokons. They'll duck, giving you a clear shot at the Slig watching them.

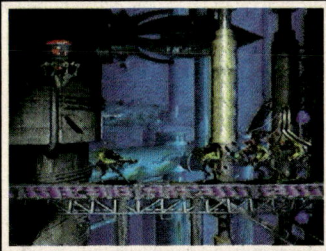

Return to Abe when you have disposed of the Slig and walk him to the Mudokons so he can send them home. Return to the main passage and head through the door on the right at the top of the screen. Dodge the floating mine in front of you to get to the switch below. Throw the switch then haul up to the platform above to get clear of the mine you've just activated. Run and jump across the gap, then go through the passageway that's now clear of obstructions. Run off the ledge with the Mudokon and clear the gap before the guard below has a chance to shoot. Run onto the following screen and haul up to the first ledge you find. The guard underneath you wakes up, so you'll have to wait until he has gone off the screen before you flick the switch and head up the platform.

Flick the switch on the next screen and collect some grenades from the machine before heading back down the lift. When the lift stops, it wakes the guard, so quickly run and jump onto a platform. Drop grenades onto the Slig until you kill him, then drop down and throw a grenade at the guard on the left screen. Stock up on grenades if you need them and return to the screen with the floating mines. Blow the mines to pieces and send the Mudokon through the portal before returning to the main section.

Go through the remaining door and jump across the gap on the right. Creep onto the next screen and collect some bombs if you don't have any, then climb onto the platform before the guard can shoot you. Frag the guard with a grenade

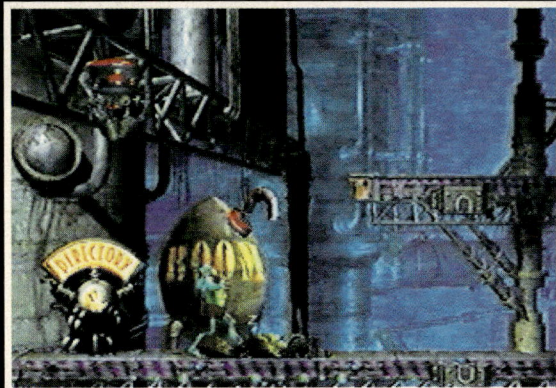

and walk right. Hold down the throw button, count to five, and chuck it at the floating machine at the top right of the screen. When you have destroyed the machine, take over the Slig below and kill him. Lower yourself down and flick the switch to deactivate the lightning field. Lower yourself down to the next screen and jump across the gap whilst dodging the meat carcasses that are constantly falling. Jump back right and drop to the screen below. Walk left so that you are above the screen with the two Sligs then eliminate them both by using your chant buttons. Walk Abe off the ledge and onto the screen to the left. Jump the gap, walk over to the switch, and face right.

As soon as you have flicked the switch, a guard is lowered in on a lift so start running right immediately. Grab onto the ledge and pull yourself up then take over the guard when he walks onto the screen. Kill the Slig, collect the three Mudokons, then go up the lift and flick the door switch. Collect the other Mudokon from the lightning switch and get him to stand on the elevator with the other Mudokons. Winch the elevator down to the bird portal and send the Mudokons through: you'll now get the blue ring power-up.

Lower the lift to the bottom of the shaft and walk right until you get to the section where the carcasses are being dropped. Jump across the gap and enter the following screen. Use the blue ring power as soon as you enter: this will deal with all the Sligs and the mines that block your path. Walk onto the next screen and send the Mudokons through the portal. With this section completed, you can simply return to the main passage and continue through the door to the final Zulag.

Zulag 4

When you have entered the main passage, climb off the top of the screen. Creep right when you reach the ledge on the next section to avoid the guard. Enter the open door at the bottom of the screen and get some information from the directory there. Run onto the screen to

Get past this guard in one piece and you can return to eliminate him later.

(Left) Top of the world ma! Take down as many Sligs as possible before you buy the farm. You know it makes sense.

abe's oddysee

the right and get the guard to follow you to the previous screen. When he enters the screen, haul up to the ledge above the door and take him over.

It may not look like it but there are half a dozen Slogs on Abe's tail. Jump onto the ledge to ensure they don't catch him.

Pull the switch and gun down the guards that drop from the ceiling – you don't need to do this, but I enjoyed it so much I wasted 20 of the fools! Walk the Slig right and shoot the other guard on the screen before descending to the level below. Shoot all the guards on the next

(Right) Lob a grenade from off the screen to give this guard an early retirement .

two screens: don't worry if the alarm goes off as the Slig reinforcements can't hit anything with their bandit-style shooting. When you have gunned them all down, walk off the ledge and head left. Shout "look out" to the Mudokon cleaning the floor before you grease the guard watching him.

Return to Abe and go to the screen where you left the Mudokon and send him through the portal. Walk right until you reach a screen with a sleeping Slig. Roll through the tunnel and quickly scale the ledge to avoid his bullets. Flick the switch to deactivate the lightning field, then got the Mudokon to follow you to the bird portal. Send him through and return to the ledge above the Slig. Destroy the floating drone using a bomb, then take over the guard below. Send him right and shoot the Slig there before returning to Abe. Walk Abe through the door at the end of the section to get to the kennels. Start running right as soon as you appear in the doorway. Keep running and you'll soon have an army of Slogs chasing you, so grab onto the platform at the end of the section and pull yourself up. When all the Slogs are gathered beneath Abe, run off the platform and

grab onto the ledge by the bomb machine. Haul up and equip Abe with some grenades. Chuck these down to frag the Slogs – there is usually one that follows you around, so to kill him throw a grenade as before then quickly drop down and haul up the other side and the Slog will run into the explosion. Drop down, walk left, and take over the Slig above Abe. Walk the guard right and execute all the Slogs that run from the kennels before activating the switch and returning to Abe. Collect all the Mudokons and send them safely through the portal.

Go back to the bomb machine and collect three more bombs, then return to the main passageway. The door above Abe should now be open: to reach it you must use the three grenades you picked up on the Sligs that are patrolling. Creep onto the screen to the left. The Slig on this screen should walk off right, so use this opportunity to chuck a grenade at him. When the other Slig walks onto the top platform, give him a grenade to the face for his trouble. With the way ahead clear, you just need to head to the top platform and flick the switch.

Drop through the gap on the bottom of the screen and collect nine more bombs (count 'em) from the now unprotected bomb machine. Then proceed through the newly opened door.

Walk onto the screen to the right and take over the Slig. Walk him over to the switch, flick it, and quickly turn around: Slogs will spill out of the kennels. Use semi automatic shots to kill them so you don't get forced off the screen. Walk the Slig left and flick the switch: more Slogs attack but it doesn't matter if the Slig you are controlling buys it, because he has done his job.

When you get back to Abe, leap the gap and enter the right screen. Drop down and attract the attention of the Slig there. Quickly hoist yourself back onto the ledge and off the screen. You'll hear two satisfying explosions that signify the demise of your pursuers. Go back to the screen on the right and walk through the door at the end of the section to enter the boardrooms.

That's right, there's just one more level to go, but it's a real toughie. If you don't have the patience of a saint, turn off your PlayStation now, otherwise…

THE BOARDROOMS

Speed is of the essence here. You have only two minutes to complete this final section, so roll wherever you can to increase your speed.

Roll left and drop to the screen below. Drop to the next screen and defuse the bomb. Jump down and leap the mines. Cross into the next screen and dodge the mincers. You'll need to hit the jump button as soon as you land to leap continuously and stay alive. Climb up to the top screen and roll under the ledge.

Throw the lever, then return through the mincers to the switch in the far right corner and flick it to activate a winch

platform. Go back through the mincers and descend via the winch platform. Roll through the tunnel and stop short of the mines. You'll need to do a running jump to clear the mines before heading through the tunnel to the next set of explosives you need to avoid. Leap these with another running jump and drop down to the platform below.

Go left and defuse the three bombs in front of the Mudokon. Get him to follow you back to the portal and send him through to get the blue ring power-up. Swiftly pull the noose when he has gone and descend into the boardroom. When the Glukkon commands the Sligs to attack Abe, hit the chant buttons. Sit back, relax, and watch the outstanding end sequence.

Tomb
Raider II

Expert cartographers have been busy drawing exclusive maps for *Tomb Raider II* to help you navigate around the huge levels – from the Great Wall of China, through the scenic canals of Venice, to sea-battered oil rigs and submerged shipwrecks. Naturally there's also a step-by-step walkthrough, including how to find all those hidden areas – three per level. All Lara Croft's secrets exposed!

tomb raider II

Publisher:	Eidos
Price:	£44.99
Format:	UK

The Great Wall

TEETERING ON THE BRINK

As in the first game, Lara often needs to do a running jump right from the edge of a platform. To do this successfully every time, simply safe-walk to the edge (by holding R1), then take one step back (in normal run mode). Now run forward and quickly press jump to get Lara to leap from the very edge.

Once Lara has slipped down the slopes into the cavern, head for the shallow pool in the corner. Climb up the rock on the left and look down to shoot the tiger below.

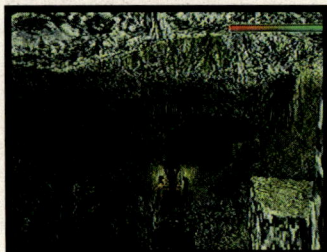

Run up the path to the dark corner (there's nothing there). Turn left and do a diagonal standing jump to the next platform. Jump over to the adjacent pathway and continue round it. Climb up the platform at the end, roll round and jump over to the platform above the path.

(See Secret 1.)

Climb up the rock to the left and over to the far wall. Turn right and run to the wall. Roll around and do a running jump to reach the opposite platform. From here you can turn right and climb up into the room.

Drop through the trap door in the corner to splash into a pool. Swim over to the platforms and go up the steps in the corner. Do a running jump and grab the opposite platform. Pull yourself up and flick the switch there to open the door. Go through it to emerge on top of the Great Wall.

Keep moving to shoot the three ravens which attack. Slide down the slope to splash into the pool below. Swim down into the dark tunnel to collect the Guardhouse Key.

Watch out for the tiger when climbing out of the pool: somersault backwards while shooting it. Now climb up the green

platforms by the wall to the right of the pool. From here climb back up onto the Wall. Use the key to open the door.

Swim into the tunnel to get the key

Inside it's pretty dark and the place is crawling with spiders, so get shooting. Climb up the ladder to the platform above and shoot another spider. Grab the Rusty Key and climb back down. Use the key to open the door at the end of the dark corridor.

Go through and walk down the cobwebbed corridor. Shoot the spiders which drop down – watch out for one behind you. Collect the shotgun ammo and large medikit by the skeleton. Pull the block out to reveal a corridor behind. Go through and slide down the slope.

In this pool room there are pipes on the sides and far end firing darts. The best way to avoid them is to grab onto the crevice to your left and shimmy all the way to the right.

Drop down and quickly swim to the exit and haul yourself up. Run across the crumbling tiles (with spikes below) and turn right. A couple of boulders will start rolling towards you, so keep running and leap over the spikes at the end.

Cripes, Lara gets away from the spikes just in time

You'll slide down into a room with a twin set of sliding spikes. So immediately somersault left (to grab the ammo if you

1 player   Memory   01

dare) and pull yourself up into the corridor to avoid being impaled – move forwards a bit too, otherwise you may still get hit by the spikes.

Now comes another tricky bit. Hug the right wall and keep running forwards over the crumbling tiles, timing your jumps over the three blades. You enter a room with more spikes and that tempting green dragon. **(See Secret 2.)** Upon exiting, keep to the right side to avoid the spikes sliding in from the left and run forwards over the crumbling tiles. At the end you slide down a slope and drop into a room – quickly head left and stand on the crumbling tile to drop through before the spikes get you.

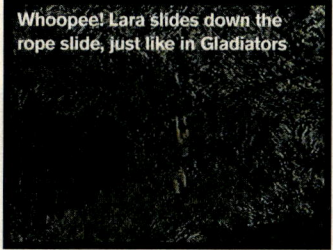

Whoopee! Lara slides down the rope slide, just like in Gladiators

At the end of the corridor is a cavern with two large circular blades rolling from side to side. Walk forwards to grab the small medikit before timing your run past. You emerge in a large cavern with a sheer drop to the right into the dark valley below. **(See Secret 3.)** Blast the spiders which appear, then grab the handles of the rope slide and hold X (to avoid falling off) as you whizz to the other end of the valley.

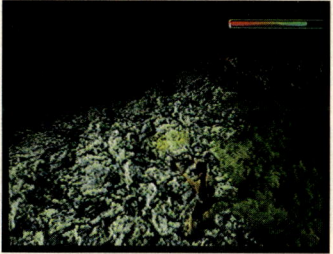

Land on the ledge, but get ready for the two tigers which leap out at you.

Once they're dead, run into the corridor which takes you round to the final room. Simply head for the large door to complete the level. If you managed to get all three secrets, you'll be awarded a grenade launcher.

The final cut scene shows Lara duffing up a bad guy

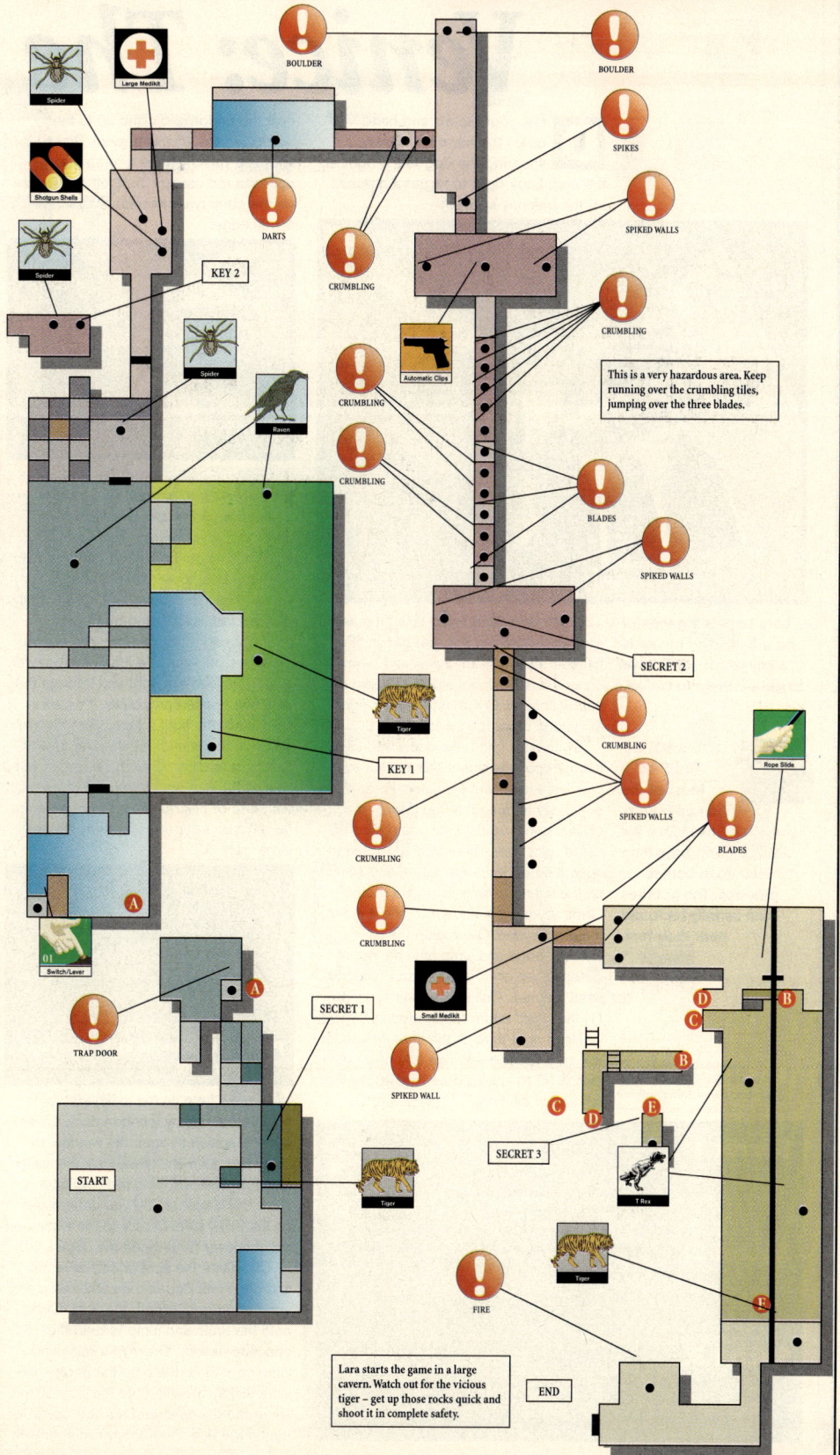

Map labels:

Spider · Large Medikit · BOULDER · BOULDER · SPIKES · SPIKED WALLS · Shotgun Shells · DARTS · CRUMBLING · CRUMBLING · KEY 2 · Spider · Spider · Automatic Clips · CRUMBLING · CRUMBLING · Raven · CRUMBLING · BLADES · SPIKED WALLS · Tiger · SECRET 2 · KEY 1 · CRUMBLING · SPIKED WALLS · BLADES · Rope Slide · CRUMBLING · CRUMBLING · A · A · Switch/Lever 01 · TRAP DOOR · A · SECRET 1 · Small Medikit · D · B · C · SPIKED WALL · B · C · D · E · SECRET 3 · T Rex · START · Tiger · Tiger · FIRE · END

> This is a very hazardous area. Keep running over the crumbling tiles, jumping over the three blades.

> Lara starts the game in a large cavern. Watch out for the vicious tiger – get up those rocks quick and shoot it in complete safety.

tomb raider II

continued

Bartoli's Hideout

Drive the boat through the gate and jump out onto the dock. Shoot the rats and head left up the stairs and round to the right. Shoot the rats and the gangster at the end of the corridor. Flick the switch (1) to open the front door to the building. However, this releases another gangster, so have your guns ready. Keep your guns drawn as you enter: there's a gangster up on the balcony to the right and another in the far right corner.

As you enter the front door you're fired at by a gangster up on the balcony. Shoot the swine, Lara.

Once you've popped them, head to the left of the room and smash the windows. Kill the dogs which jump out, then go through the windows to find some goodies. Return to the large room and keep to the right as you time a run past each of the three chopping statues in the corridor. At the end is a dark room: light a flare and hit the switch (2) to open another door above the canal.

Back in the large room, jump and pull up the high end of the sloped block and, as you start to slide, jump and grab the opposite wooden platform. Head right onto the ledge and push the block twice. From here, do a running jump to land on the balcony. Climb right via the ladders to reach the outside balcony.

Secret 1: Stone Dragon
From the room entrance turn left and walk towards the corner. Just before you reach it, there's a switch (10) hidden on the wall.
Flick it to open the door at the top of the staircase. Go through to reach the balcony with the gangster you shot earlier and the first secret.

Secret 2: Gold Dragon
Pull the lever (9) to open the nearby door. Swim forward and surface to light a flare, then swim down and round to the right. Make you way past the pillars and through the holes to the end. In the far right corner you'll find the gold dragon. You'll be running out of air soon, so pull the nearby lever (8) to open a trap door above. Swim up (to where the fires are) to catch your breath. Go back down, grab the grenades in the other corner and make your way back through the tunnel to the original pool.

Secret 3: Jade Dragon
Before using the Detonator Key, climb onto the right wall and go over to the opposite end of the water. Climb up and onto the roof, then go through the window to find the final secret.

Shoot the gunman who appears on the balcony to your right. Now do a running jump from the open end of the balcony to slide down the red canopy and grab the edge. Shimmy left, pull up, and jump back to land on the opposite balcony. Do a running jump to grab the small platform to your left, then to the opposite canopy. Finally, jump and grab to sail through the open doorway.

Shoot the two dogs and go upstairs. Go through the doorway and shoot the gunman in the room. (See Secret 1.) Smash the window and blast the gangster on the long balcony. Head right and smash the next window, turn around, and jump back into the room so you can shoot at the gangster who appears on the balcony. Another gangster and his dog come through the door, so shoot them. Then push the block in the fireplace twice.

Climb onto the block, then left into the corridor, shooting the rats. Instead of sliding down the slope, past the blades, there's a better method. Walk to the edge of the slope, shuffle to the right, and jump forward, turning right to land in the water. Another tricky bit follows: getting past the fires. With your back to the wall, run forward and jump from the edge of the wooden section (at which point the fires go out), then immediately do a standing jump, followed by a running jump to reach the end safely.

As the door opens, get ready to shoot at a gangster and two dogs. Drop down into the room and use the nearest sloped block to jump and pull up to the lowest chandelier. Do a running jump to grab the middle one. Pull up, turn right, and do a running jump to the platform with the switch (3). Flick it to open the picture to the right of the fireplace.

Jump back to grab the middle chandelier, then do a running jump to grab the highest one. Pull up and jump up again to haul up to the high wooden section. Shoot the rats as you walk round to the right. Grab hold of the high beam and shimmy right to pull yourself up.

From here, jump over to the opposite wooden section. Get ready to shoot the gangster who emerges from the brick section. Jump forward from the brick wall to land on the high beam. Flick the switch (4) to reverse the position of the chandeliers. Jump back to the bricks and drop down onto the now-highest chandelier. Jump via the middle to the now-lowest chandelier. From here you can now do a running jump to grab the open picture ledge. Pull up to get the Library Key (1) there.

Now jump back to the low chandelier,

then do running jumps and grabs to the highest one. Turn towards the window and do a running jump and grab to land on the platform with the switch (7). Flick it to open the trap door behind the fireplace. Walk through the window and head right along the ledge. At the end, grab the edge and drop down through the opened trap door into a pool below. (See Secret 2.)

Shimmying across the high beam

Climb out by the doors and use the key (1) to open them. Entering the library, shoot the gangster and go straight through the opposite doors. Follow the path round the bookcases and climb up onto the far one. From here, shoot the rats before jumping over to the other side. Flick the switch (6) to open doors back in the first room.

Return and shoot the gangster, then enter the new room. Climb the left bookcase, then jump to the ledge opposite and climb the left bookcase to reach the very top. Shoot the window out and jump diagonally onto the sill. Turn around and slide backwards down the slope to grab hold of the edge. Now pull up and jump backwards onto the opposite balcony. From here, do a running jump to the opposite roof, then leap onto the right wall.

To get the Uzis, turn right and go to the white sloped end of the wall, then do a running jump over the canal to grab the lowest part of the hut roof. Stand just left of the far chimney and do a running jump to land on the middle of the wall under the arch. Drop down the other side into the shallow water to collect the Uzis. Climb up the ladder to get back out.

Just over this wall lie the Uzis!

Go inside the hut and shoot the gangster, then grab the Detonator Key. Outside, swim over to the door in the wall – when you pull up, a gunman will appear

END

SECRET 2

08
Switch/Lever

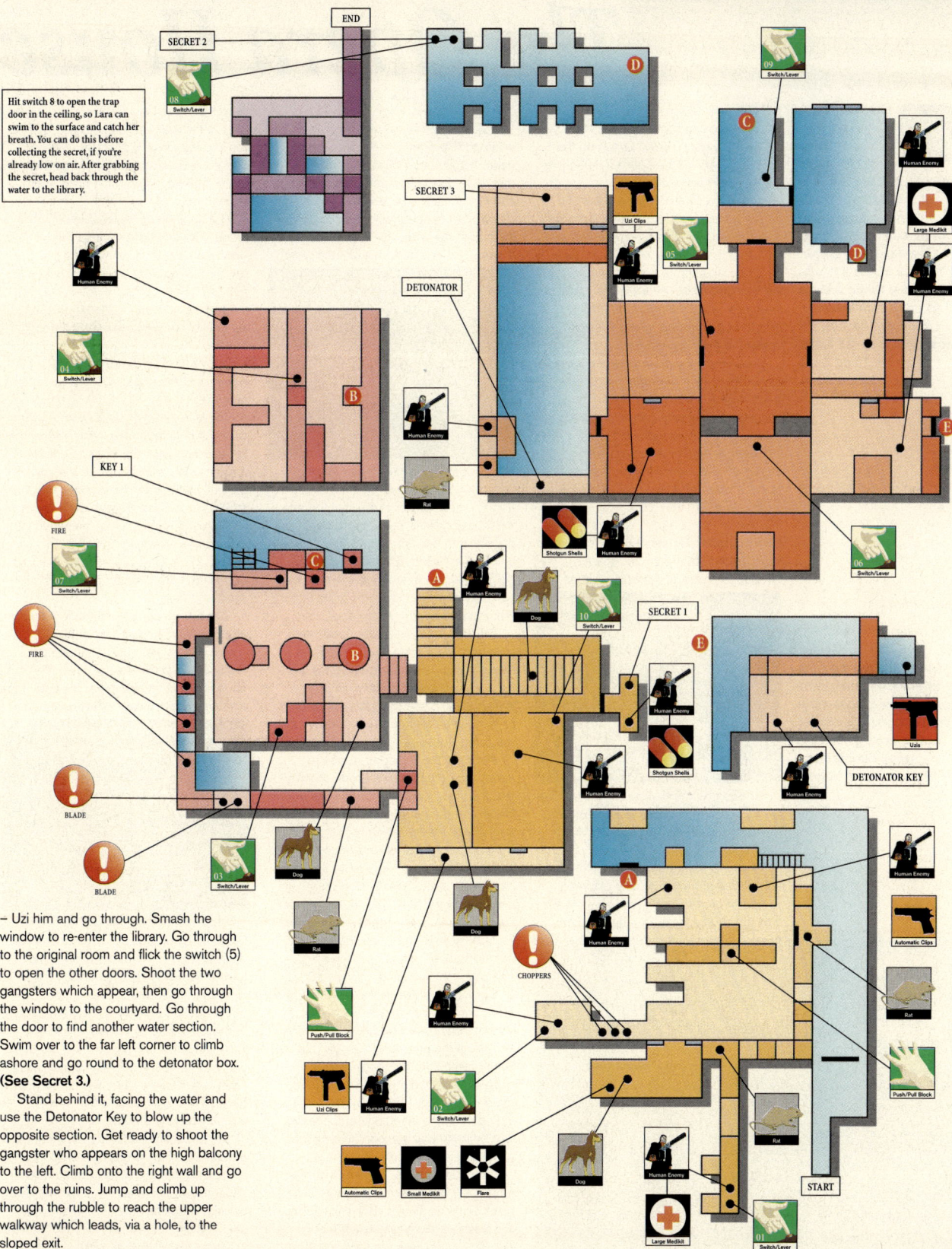

Hit switch 8 to open the trap door in the ceiling, so Lara can swim to the surface and catch her breath. You can do this before collecting the secret, if you're already low on air. After grabbing the secret, head back through the water to the library.

D

09
Switch/Lever

C

Human Enemy

Large Medikit

SECRET 3

Uzi Clips

Human Enemy

05
Switch/Lever

D

Human Enemy

Human Enemy

DETONATOR

04
Switch/Lever

B

E

Human Enemy

Rat

KEY 1

FIRE

07
Switch/Lever

C

Shotgun Shells

Human Enemy

06
Switch/Lever

FIRE

B

A

Human Enemy

Dog

10
Switch/Lever

SECRET 1

E

Human Enemy

Uzis

BLADE

Human Enemy

Shotgun Shells

Human Enemy

DETONATOR KEY

BLADE

03
Switch/Lever

Dog

Dog

A

Human Enemy

Human Enemy

Automatic Clips

Rat

– Uzi him and go through. Smash the window to re-enter the library. Go through to the original room and flick the switch (5) to open the other doors. Shoot the two gangsters which appear, then go through the window to the courtyard. Go through the door to find another water section. Swim over to the far left corner to climb ashore and go round to the detonator box. **(See Secret 3.)**

   Stand behind it, facing the water and use the Detonator Key to blow up the opposite section. Get ready to shoot the gangster who appears on the high balcony to the left. Climb onto the right wall and go over to the ruins. Jump and climb up through the rubble to reach the upper walkway which leads, via a hole, to the sloped exit.

Push/Pull Block

Rat

CHOPPERS

Human Enemy

Rat

Uzi Clips

Human Enemy

02
Switch/Lever

Push/Pull Block

Automatic Clips

Small Medikit

Flare

Dog

Human Enemy

START

Large Medikit

01
Switch/Lever

tomb raider II

continued

The Opera House

J ump to the right brick ledge, so you can shoot down at the gangster below. Drop into the drink and swim to the opposite left corner. Climb up the first ladder and climb up the ledge behind you to flick the switch (1).

Climb up the second ladder, onto the upper ledge and do a running jump over the canal to the white ledge. From here do a running jump to grab the ledge with the swinging crate. Avoiding the crate, do a running jump and grab over the canal to land through the trap door you've just opened in the opposite roof.

Shoot the gangster inside and collect the Ornate Key (1) near the entrance. Head up the stairs and shoot another gangster before exiting through the door to emerge on the switch ledge.

Return to the swinging crate ledge, then over to the small ledge, as at the start. Shimmy left along the adjacent roof to drop onto another small ledge. Jump left onto the sloped roof, and grab onto the window sill. Smash the window and safe-walk into the room and safely through the glass to reach the ladder.

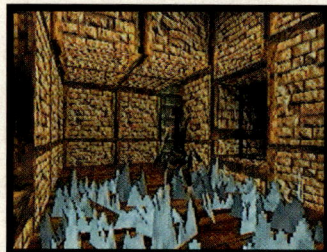

Looks like the morning after a Christmas party as the floor is covered in broken glass. It's deadly, but you can guide Lara safely through it by holding the R1 button.

Climb up to the dark stairs and use the key (1) to open the door at the end. Go round and climb up the ladder to reach the ledge.

Tricky bit ahoy. Do a running jump to the group of three crumbling platforms (second from the right), then again to the next threesome, and from the edge to grab the opposite ledge.

Pull up, head right, and climb up to the corridor. Turn right at the end to see the opera house roof. Shoot the gangster, then turn round, drop and grab the ledge, and immediately pull back up. This lures out another gangster and his dog. Shoot them from the ledge, then jump over to the roof. Run round to the left and shoot

Jump across the crumbling tiles

the two gangsters. See that swinging crate in the far corner? Do a running jump from the near corner of the roof to grab the ledge to the left of it. Pull up and drop through into the dark room. Light a flare and hit the switch (2) to open the trap door in the opera house roof. Shoot the two new gangsters from the crate ledge, then drop through the trap door.

Flick the left switch (3) to open the gate to the left. Drop through and run down the slope, climbing up to the left ledge to avoid the boulders. Hit the switch (5) to close the gate, enabling you to climb left from it to reach the inside of the opera house.

Avoiding the sandbag opposite, shoot the gunman who appears on the left, then head right to the double doors. Shoot the gangster and dog. Run into the hole to the level below and shoot down at the gangster and dogs. Drop safely to the ground and head to the back wall of the theatre. Use the box to climb up to the first floor platforms and head for the corner, to the large gap. From here jump and grab the ledge to pull up to the second floor where you can plug that gangster.

Drop safely down to the floor and run along the poolside to lure the boulders from the back wall. Wade into the water and shoot the gunman on stage. Use the box to climb onto the stage. Shoot the gangster and dog, then head left to a room with a switch (9) Flick it to open a high gate at the other side of the stage. Run over there and shoot those two gangster swines.

Climb up to the open gate and walk around the glass and over by the raised plank. Do a running jump to the middel of the crevice and shimmy left to pull up onto the ledge. Flick the switch (10) to

drop the plank. Do a running jump back over to the walkway, being careful not to run into the glass. Cross the lowered plank and do a running jump from the end of the walkway to grab the plank in the left corner.

Pull up, then up again to the brick ledge. Turn around and shoot the rat opposite, then do a running jump to grab the high ledge. Time your jump past the first swinging sandbag – you can safely bypass the second, on the left. Hit the switch (11) to drop a sandbag through the trap door on the stage. To drop into it, slide backwards down the middle of the slope, grab the edge, then pull up and jump back.

You land in a dark water pool – light a flare. Wade through the left entrance, turn left to swim down the stairs to emerge in a room with a switch (12) by the shallows on the left. Flick it to open a door on the second floor. **(See Secret 1.)** Return right and through the entrance, then head left through the wide gap to surface in a room with a ladder. Collect the Relay Box at the bottom of it, then climb up through the opened door.

Climb back up to the third floor and go right round to the passage in the opposite corner. Shoot the dogs and insert the Relay Box in the broken panel by the elevator to get it working. Hit the switch (6) and the doors will open. **(See Secret 2.)**

Insert the relay box to get the elevator working again

Step inside to be taken down to the large room below the crumbling tiles you crossed earlier. Shoot the two gunmen and hit the switch (13), but don't get in the elevator. Once it's gone up, enter pool at the bottom of the shaft. Swim through to the left and up the steps to find the Circuit Board. Swim back down the stairs and through the opposite doorway into a room with a lever (14) in the corner. Pull it to open the cage door to the right and swim through to surface.

Climb out and shoot the rat, then turn around and jump to grab the ledge. Pull up, roll around, and draw your guns to shoot the gangster above. Jump and grab the high ledge and pull up the second floor passage.

Shoot the rat and dog, then head

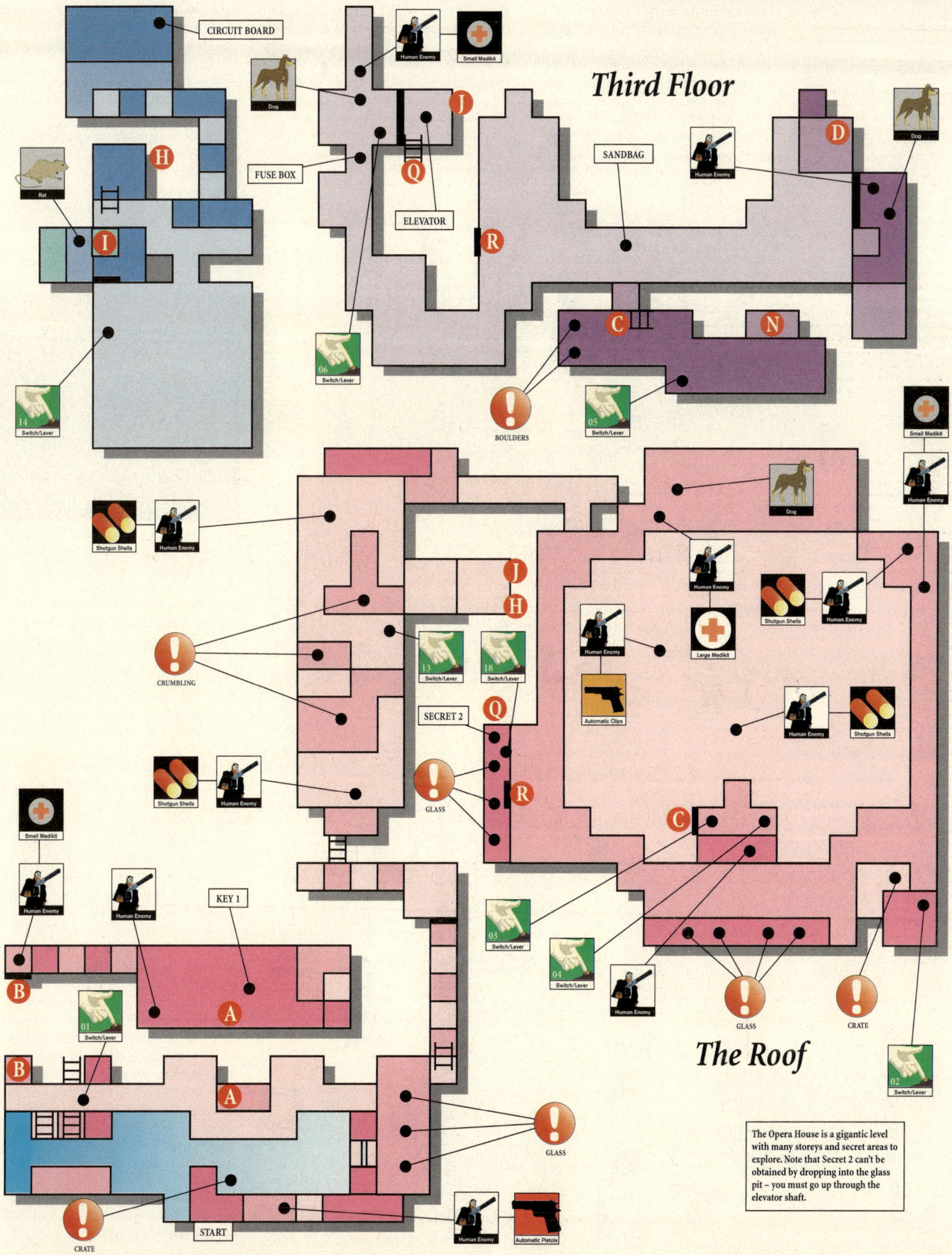

Tomb Raider II

Third Floor

CIRCUIT BOARD

Human Enemy

Small Medikit

Dog

FUSE BOX

J

Q

ELEVATOR

R

SANDBAG

Human Enemy

D

Dog

H

Rat

I

14
Switch/Lever

06
Switch/Lever

C

N

BOULDERS

05
Switch/Lever

Small Medikit

Human Enemy

Shotgun Shells

Human Enemy

J

H

CRUMBLING

13
Switch/Lever

18
Switch/Lever

SECRET 2

Q

GLASS

R

Human Enemy

Large Medikit

Shotgun Shells

Human Enemy

Automatic Clips

Human Enemy

Shotgun Shells

C

Shotgun Shells

Human Enemy

Small Medikit

Human Enemy

Human Enemy

KEY 1

B

01
Switch/Lever

A

B

A

03
Switch/Lever

04
Switch/Lever

Human Enemy

GLASS

CRATE

02
Switch/Lever

The Roof

GLASS

CRATE

START

Human Enemy

Automatic Pistols

The Opera House is a gigantic level with many storeys and secret areas to explore. Note that Secret 2 can't be obtained by dropping into the glass pit – you must go up through the elevator shaft.

tomb raider II

continued

down the passage and smash the window. Go through and hang and drop into the dressing room. Press the switch (15) to open the door. Another tricky bit: slide down the slope and jump from the end to miss the fan and grab the ledge. Pull up and collect the Ornate Key (2).

Turn right and climb up the blocks to the corner. Jump across to the slope and

jump to the opposite passage. Shoot the rat and walk to the edge to jump over the gap. Turn around and jump backwards from the edge to the higher ledge. Repeat this trick for the next fan. **(See Secret 3.)** Enter the room with the crate and pull it out to reveal a switch (16). Press it to open the door.

Push the crate through the doorway

into the dressing room. Climb onto it and smash the lower windows. Go through and push the block there onto the first one. From the sill, jump and grab the top crate and pull up. Shoot the gangster above, then climb up to the upper window and go through.

Return through the passage and jump up to grab the higher ledge which leads to the second floor. Use the key (2) to open the door, leading back to the original boulder trap. Jump through and hit the switch (5) to reopen the gate to the roof. Climb up into the room with the two switches. Insert the Circuit Board into the panel by the cage door to activate the right switch (4). Flick it to raise the curtain at the back of the stage.

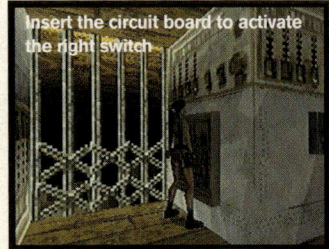

Insert the circuit board to activate the right switch

Make your way down to the stage and shoot the gangster. Go through the revealed doorway and shoot the gangsters and dog – best retreat to the pool. Inside the room they came from, pull the crate out twice (see map) and enter the passage to hit the switch (8) to lower the stage curtain again. Return to the room and climb the crates to reach the high doorway leading to a white ledge. Head right to the balcony and shoot at the gangster who appears below you.

Drop down into the wooden section to the right. Jump over the hole to grab the high ledge and pull up to enter a room with a swinging sandbag. Flick the switch (7) to open the far door. Jump to the slope on the right, then time your run past the sandbag. Turn around and hang below the swinging crate and immediately pull up. Turn around and fire down at the twin-gunned Bartoli.

Drop down to shoot the dogs and gangster, then collect Bartoli's grenades – and launcher if you haven't got one. Climb the low crate near the end, turn right and pull up. Turn right and jump to the next stack and pull up to the high part. Step to one side and time your running jump forward past the swinging crate. Turn right and jump to the L-shaped stack. From the opposite edge, turn left and do a running jump to the crate near the entrance. Hit the switch (17) to open the final door, but draw your guns for another gangster. Drop down and go through the door to find a walkway to the seaplane. Enter it to complete the level.

continued over page

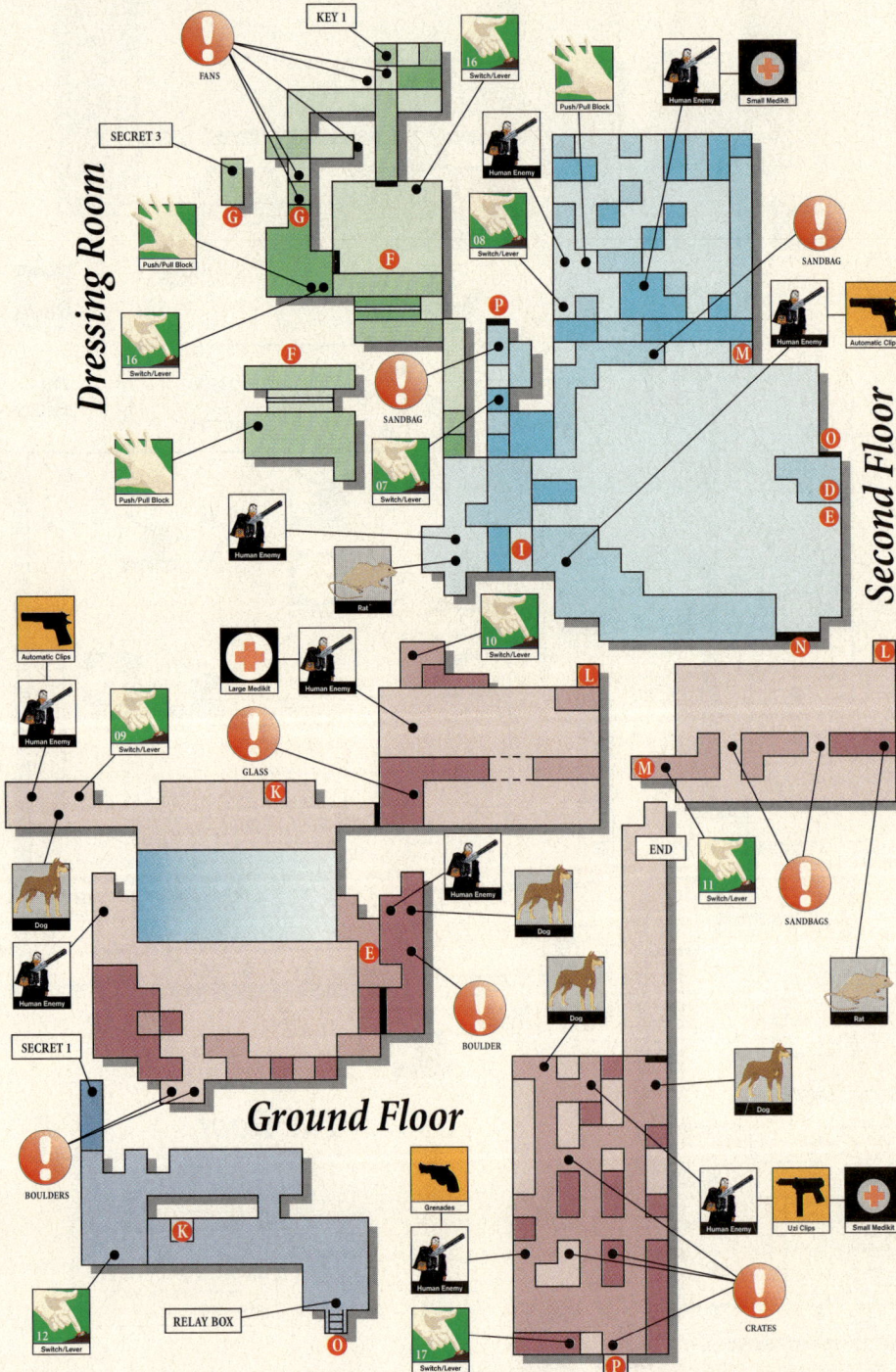

The section with the fans (not Lara's) is tricky. You have to jump backwards over a couple of them – try it forwards and Lara's dangling legs will get sliced to ribbons. Don't forget to collect the secret on the way.

Dressing Room

Second Floor

Ground Floor

KEY 1 · FANS · SECRET 3 · Switch/Lever · Push/Pull Block · Human Enemy · Small Medikit · SANDBAG · Automatic Clips · Rat · Large Medikit · GLASS · Dog · SECRET 1 · BOULDERS · BOULDER · END · SANDBAGS · Grenades · Uzi Clips · CRATES · RELAY BOX

tomb raider II

continued

Offshore Rig

THE ART OF PULLING

Lara's impressive pectorals enable her to push large crates and blocks around. Note that she can't pull one right to an edge where she's standing – else she'd be squashed flat! So sometimes you need to go round to the back to push it that extra space forward.

Lara wakes up in a locked room with all her weapons gone. Pull the rear crate three times to reveal the passage with the switch (1). It opens the door for only a few seconds, so you need to clear a path to the latter by pushing and pulling more crates. Push the one near the window right twice, then pull out the crate that was behind it and push it right to the previous crate.

Push the crates around to create a clear path from switch to door

Once you've escaped, head left into the room, running past the guards. Run past the slope to avoid the rolling barrels. Continue round to the right and lure the gunman into smashing the windows so you can escape. Turn right and drop off the ledge to hit the switch (4) which

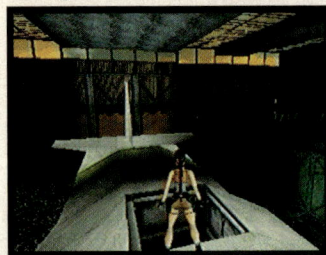

Once Lara jumps onto the plane, she can drop through the hatch to collect her pistols.

Secret 1: Jade Dragon

Jump left from the window ledge and follow the passage to the small pool. Jump in and pull the underwater lever (3), then climb out again. Return along the passage and jump into the water. Head for the lever (2) near the fan in the corner. Pull the lever to open the nearby door, then head well back from the fan to avoid being sucked in. Hug the right wall to swim right through the doorway. Swim down through the opened trap door and through to the fan room. Collect the secret carefully, then return to the passage and exit via the door near the fan, heading along the left wall to avoid its suction. Make your way back to the Yellow Pass Card door.

Secret 2: Stone Dragon

A dead easy one. After plugging the guard with the Red Pass Card, simply climb the nearby ladder to emerge on the rig deck and collect the secret.

Secret 3: Gold Dragon

Swim to the large pillar to the right of the starting walkway and climb onto its base to collect the secret. Upon doing so you're attacked by a couple of guards, so swim off.

opens the trap door under the plane. Dive into the water and enter the plane to hit another switch (5) which stops the plane's propellers. Climb out and go back round through the broken windows to do a running jump onto the plane's nose. Head down the fuselage and drop through the trap door to find your pistols.

Exit and climb out of the water to shoot the guards. One of them holds the Yellow Pass Card. **(See Secret 1.)** Use it to by the smashed windows to open the opposite door. Go through and flick the switch (6) to turn off the alarm, then head right up the stairs. Open the door, go through, and roll around to shoot the guard who appears behind you. Enter the next room with the ramp and shoot the guard who comes down the ramp (you can't get through the door above it) Open the door to the right, go through, and shoot the guard.

Go through to find a dormitory. Get the Automatic Pistols from the top middle-right bunk, then the Harpoon Gun from the last bunk on the left.

Lara finds a harpoon gun in her bed

Hit the switch (7) on the top first left bunk to open the trap door in the ceiling. Jump to grab it from the top far right bunk before it closes. Follow the passage and slide backwards down the slope to grab the ladder and climb down. Pull the left block out and pull/push it past the other one. Pull the latter once, then get behind to push it next to the fires. Climb onto it and do a running jump to grab the ladder.

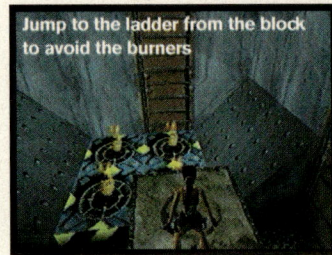
Jump to the ladder from the block to avoid the burners

Climb up and plug the guard in the passage to get the Red Pass Card. **(See Secret 2.)** Return, via the hangar, to the room with the alarm switch (6) and head up the left stairs. Shoot the gunman and

dog in the room, then run past the end of the slope to trigger the barrels. Go up the slope to open the Red Pass Card door.

From the entrance, shoot the guard in the next room. Then go in and kill the two guards who rush to the scene. Push the block on the ledge into the corner. Go round and pull it out the other side, then get behind it and push it to the edge. From the opposite ledge, do a running jump to grab it. Pull up and leap to grab the high passage on the left.

After moving that block round, jump and grab the high ledge

Follow it round and shoot the guard. Hit the switch (8) in the room to fill the first water tank. Go back round and swim to the other side. Climb to the right to flick the switch (9) to open the trap door in the room with the Green Pass Card door. Go back round and drop through it.

Slide down the slope to emerge in a huge room with water below. Heading left to the end of the walkway, you can jump across the platforms to your right, but if you want the secret you may as well drop into the water. **(See Secret 3.)** Avoid the divers and climb up onto the one of the pillar bases to shoot them. Climb up the ladder in the far left corner to reach a ledge. Do a running jump to grab the next walkway, upon which a guard will start shooting. Pull up and blast the swine, then nick his shotgun. Continue round, jump to the next walkway, and shoot the guard. Jump to the walkway by the wall and shoot the guard over the other side, then leap over to the L-shaped one by the large pillar. Jump over to the walkway where you can smash the glass to collect the Green Pass Card.

Return via the L-shaped walkway to the one by the wall. Above it is an entrance, so climb up and follow the long passage to find a ladder. Climb up and drop down the other side to emerge in the corridor to the room with the Green Pass Card door. Shoot another guard, then use your card to open the door. Before going through it, flick the switch (8) again to refill the second pool. Dive into it and swim down the underwater passage. Pull the lever (10) to open the gate, then swim through, get out, and climb the stairs to the exit.

Tomb Raider II

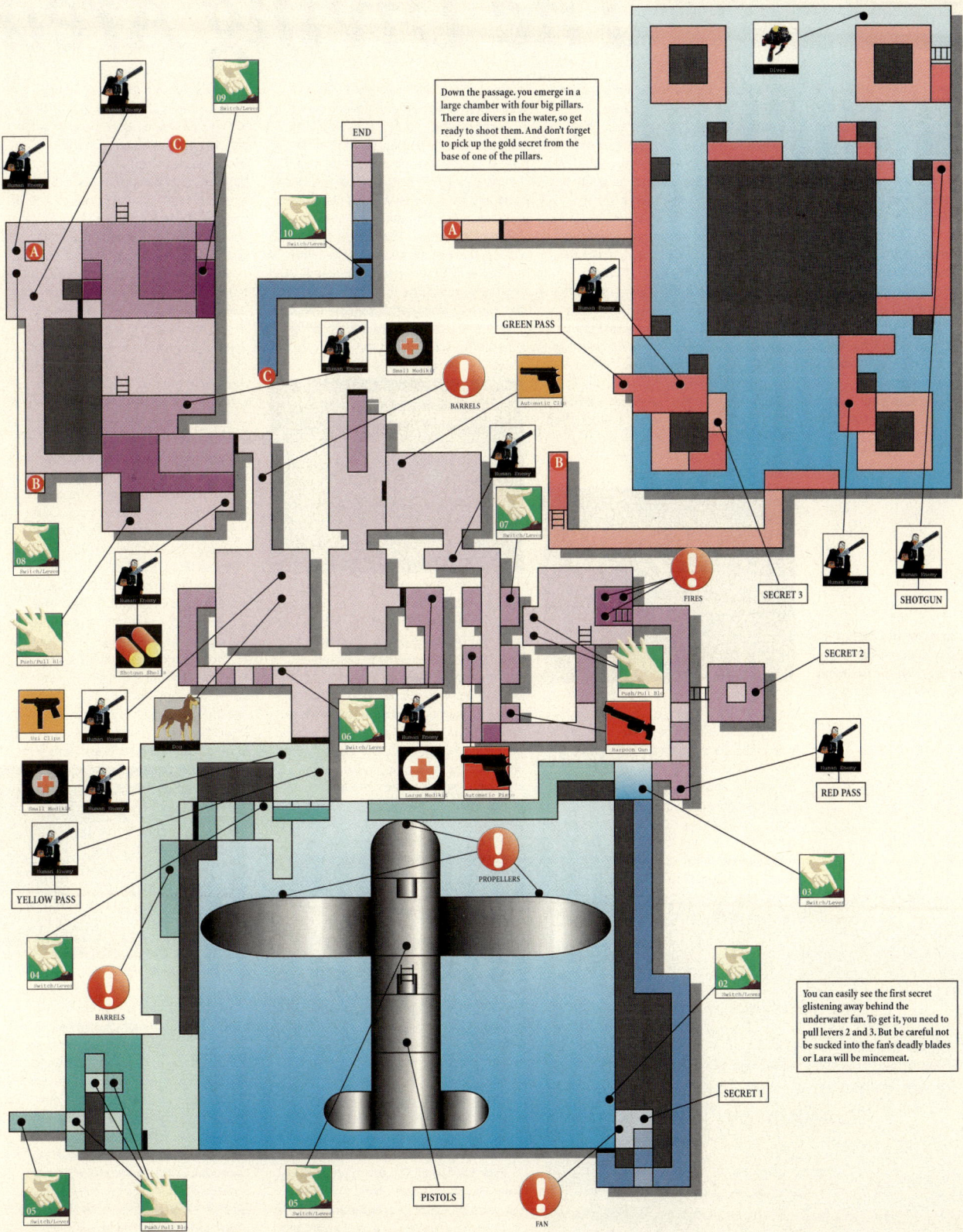

Down the passage. you emerge in a large chamber with four big pillars. There are divers in the water, so get ready to shoot them. And don't forget to pick up the gold secret from the base of one of the pillars.

Diver

Human Enemy

09 Switch/Lever

C

Human Enemy

END

A

10 Switch/Lever

A

C

Human Enemy   Small Medikit

BARRELS

Automatic Clip

GREEN PASS

Human Enemy

Human Enemy

B

B

08 Switch/Lever

07 Switch/Lever

Human Enemy

FIRES

SECRET 3

Human Enemy

Human Enemy

SHOTGUN

Push/Pull Bl.

Shotgun Shell

Uzi Clips   Human Enemy

Dog

06 Switch/Lever   Human Enemy

Push/Pull Bl.

SECRET 2

Harpoon Gun

Small Medikit   Human Enemy

Large Medikit   Automatic Pist.

Human Enemy

RED PASS

Human Enemy

YELLOW PASS

PROPELLERS

03 Switch/Lever

04 Switch/Lever

BARRELS

02 Switch/Lever

You can easily see the first secret glistening away behind the underwater fan. To get it, you need to pull levers 2 and 3. But be careful not be sucked into the fan's deadly blades or Lara will be mincemeat.

SECRET 1

05 Switch/Lever

05 Push/Pull Bl.

05 Switch/Lever

PISTOLS

FAN

tomb raider II
continued

The Diving Area

Climb the stairs and do a running jump to grab the ladder opposite. Climb up and press the switch (2) to turn off the fan in the pool. Jump into the water and swim down the long dark tunnel behind the fan to find some grenades. Return and surface before pulling the underwater lever (1) to open the door on the ledge. Go through and immediately jump back to shoot the dog and two guards – one of whom carries Uzis. Shoot the guards opposite if you can, then jump via the platforms to the other side of the pool – avoid the hooks by standing to the side. If you fall in, return to the original ledge via the underwater tunnel.

Go through to the room with a slope and a pool of oil – the latter is lethal. **(See Secret 1.)** Slide down the middle and jump at the last minute to land on the opposite walkway.

Jump at the end of the slope to leap over the oil and land on the walkway.

Head round to the left and climb the ladder all the way to the top. Drop off to the right and follow the passage to see a hole in the floor. Go to the left side of it, turn your back to it, and step back to slide backwards down the slope – so you can grab the edge. Now drop and catch the ledge below, then pull up and shoot the guard. Below to the left you can see a recess in the slope, containing the Blue Pass Card. Do a running jump through the gap in the walkway railing to slide back into the recess and collect the card.

Climb to the nearby passage. Follow it to the end and jump back to the ladder. Climb back to the top and drop down the hole and grab the ledge, as before. Head right and open the Blue Pass Card door.

Keep away from the flame-thrower bloke on the left as you enter the next door and shoot the pack of dogs. Now shoot the flamer from a safe distance, then head round the the opposite side of the square hallway and open the outside door. Go down the stairs and shoot the guard by the pool. Push the crate to reveal a panel by the door.

Do a running jump through the gap to slide into the recess

Jump into the water and enter the tunnel. Lure the diver out to the pool, then climb out on the low platform and shoot him from the shore. Jump back in and swim through the tunnel to pull the lever (3) which opens one of the nearby gates. Swim through it and round to pull another lever (4), then continue round to the right and through the next gate to return to the pool surface. Return up the stairs to the large square hallway with all the doors. Head left and open the outside door. Go up the stairs to the newly opened door and shoot the three guards – you can't do anything to stop that chopper taking off.

Shoot the guards on the helipad

Go through to the next room and flick the right switch (6) to temporarily turn off the nearest fire in the narrow corridor. Quickly go through, fall through the trap door, collect the M16 (yes!), and return to the room before the fire restarts.

Flick the switch (6) again, press the other switch (5), then quickly run down the corridor, jumping over the trap door, to collect the Machine Chip. Roll around and return before the fires relight.

Now return all the way to the room with the pool and insert the chip in the panel to open the door. Go through and shoot the guard in the next room from the passage. Run through and shoot at the flame-thrower from the opposite side of the pool. **(See Secret 2.)** Over by the scuba equipment, you'll find the Harpoon Gun (if you haven't already got one).

Jump into the pool and swim through the tunnel. Harpoon the divers (or lure them to the pool and shoot from the shore), then swim through to surface in another pool. You can only climb out on the small platform in the middle on the right. Shoot the two guards before climbing the ledge to flick the switch (7).

Return to the pool room with the saw and shoot the two guards. Go through the opened left door and hit the switch (8) to move the block over the middle of the pool. Use it to jump to the other side, but don't go near that saw yet. Climb over the crates in the corner and drop into the passage to hit the switch (9).

Head back to the helipad, shooting two guards and dogs on the way, and you'll find the middle of the floor has dropped. Go down in there and through the passage to drop down into the room in the middle of the square hallway. Shoot the flame-thrower and guard – who carries another Machine Chip. Go through any of the doors and return to the saw. Insert the chip in the nearby panel to stop it, then grab that Red Pass Card.

You can't get the Red Pass Card till you've turned off the saw

Return to the central room with the four doors and use the Red Pass Card to open the door in the middle. Toggle the switch (10) to the left of it twice before entering. Drop down the hole and shoot the guard there. Follow the passage and climb the ladder to emerge in the pool room where you couldn't climb out properly before. Enter the opposite passage and follow it, via sections of water, to reach a walkway above the final room. Shoot the guards from up here, then go down round the steps. **(See Secret 3.)** Walk to the body in the middle of the room to exit the level.

Secret 1: Stone Dragon
Slide backwards down the slope to land in the hole where the secret lies. Climb back out the short side to continue the slide down the slope.

Secret 2: Jade Dragon
On the opposite wall from the entrance, step to the right of the orange tank to open the nearby panel, revealing a passage. Flick the switch (11) at the end to open that trap door under the pool. Dive down to get the secret.

Secret 3: Gold Dragon
Since you flicked the switch (10) near the Red Pass Card door twice, the door to the right of the final room will be open. Just make sure you don't go near the dead body in the middle of the room as you go to enter it, or you'll complete the level. Through the door you'll find the last secret.

Tomb Raider II

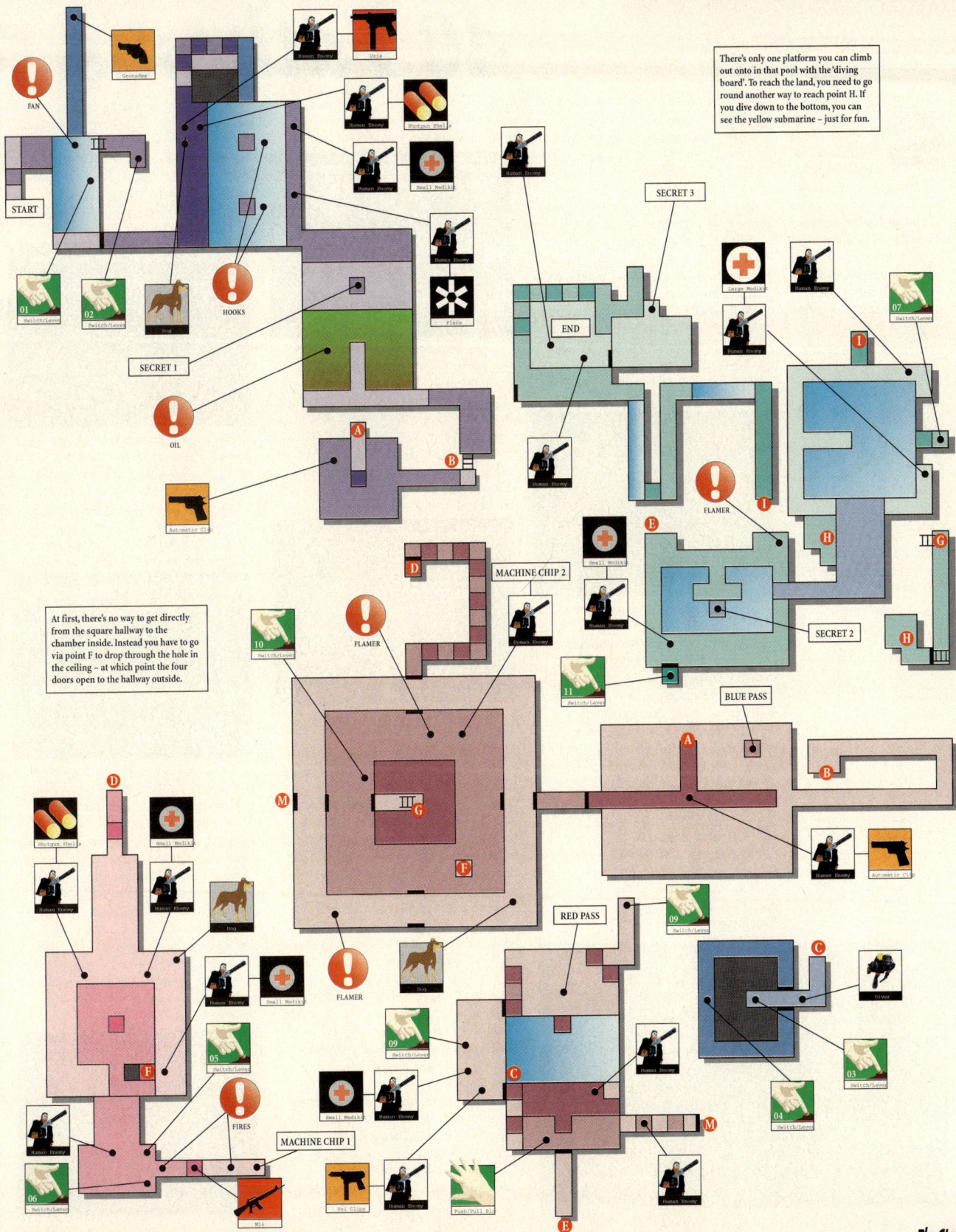

There's only one platform you can climb out onto in that pool with the 'diving board'. To reach the land, you need to go round another way to reach point H. If you dive down to the bottom, you can see the yellow submarine – just for fun.

FAN

Grenades

Human Enemy

Uzis

Human Enemy

Shotgun Shells

Human Enemy

Small Medikit

Human Enemy

SECRET 3

Large Medikit

Human Enemy

07
Switch/Lever

START

01
Switch/Lever

02
Switch/Lever

Dog

HOOKS

Flare

Human Enemy

END

I

SECRET 1

Human Enemy

FLAMER

I

H

G

OIL

A

B

Automatic Clip

D

MACHINE CHIP 2

Small Medikit

E

H

At first, there's no way to get directly from the square hallway to the chamber inside. Instead you have to go via point F to drop through the hole in the ceiling – at which point the four doors open to the hallway outside.

10
Switch/Lever

FLAMER

Human Enemy

Human Enemy

SECRET 2

11
Switch/Lever

BLUE PASS

A

B

Human Enemy

Automatic Clip

D

Shotgun Shells

Small Medikit

M

III

G

F

Human Enemy

Human Enemy

Dog

RED PASS

09
Switch/Lever

C

FLAMER

Dog

Diver

Human Enemy

Human Enemy

Small Medikit

05
Switch/Lever

09
Switch/Lever

C

03
Switch/Lever

F

Small Medikit

Human Enemy

04
Switch/Lever

FIRES

MACHINE CHIP 1

M

Human Enemy

06
Switch/Lever

M16

Uzi Clips

Human Enemy

Push/Pull Blo

E

Human Enemy

tomb raider II

40 Fathoms...

SUBAQUA SKIRMISH

Lara can collect a Harpoon Gun which lets her do battle underwater. However, it's nearly always better (for your health) to lure enemies near the surface, then climb out and shoot them from dry land. So do this if you can.

Lara starts this level deep under the ocean with her oxygen rapidly running out. Worst still, the local sharks have taken a fancy to her!

Turn right and follow the trail of debris to find the shipwreck. To enter it, swim down the hole by the rusty anchor in the corner to emerge in a pool .Surface to catch your breath, but don't hang about: those sharks are still on your trail. Swim through the underwater hole into the next chamber, then through a small hole (high up) to another. Quickly swim through the next hole to the next room. Pull the lever (1) on far left to open the trap door. Swim down and round the passage, then through the hole in the ceiling to surface in a long pool.

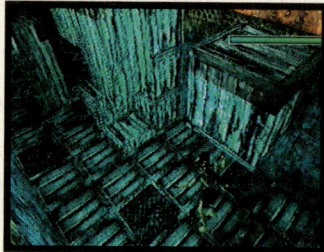

Surface in the room with the crates. Then hit a switch (2) to drain it.

Swim through the hole under the stack of crates to surface in a small pool. Climb out the other side and follow the passage round. Flick the switch (2) at the end to drain the water from the long pool. Return to the latter and jump via the crates to the high ledge, leading to a square room. Jump backwards into it and pull back up to the ledge to lure out the guard, then shoot him from above. **(See Secret 1.)**

Step backwards onto the large trap door, ready to grab onto the edge and pull up when it opens. Now shoot down at the guards below.

Drop down and climb up the crates to do a running jump and grab the high opening. **(See Secret 2.)** Go down the wide passage, jumping over the pipes. Take the first right and climb up by the

Secret 1: Stone Dragon
Call this a secret? After killing the guard, just go round the trap door to collect it.

Secret 2: Jade Dragon
After climbing out of the shallow water room, flick the switch on the left: you have only 16 seconds to reach the secret door. Run down the corridor, jumping the pipes, and round to the left to get through it. Swim into the underwater cavern to collect the prize.

Secret 3: Gold Dragon
Swim down to the bottom again, and collect the secret to the right of the switch passage. Be prepared to avoid barracudas as you swim back up to the surface.

ladder (in the dark) into the small room. Flick the switch (3) to open a door elsewhere.

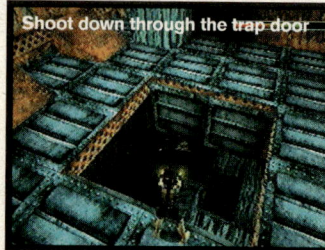

Shoot down through the trap door

Drop back down and continue along the narrow corridor. Turn right to head down the wide passage (notice the fires in the corridor on the left). Follow it round to the right to find the newly opened door. Inside, flick the switch (4) to turn off the first two fires in the corridor you bypassed earlier. It's on a timer, so get back there fast and flick the switch (5) by the second fire before jumping left out of there.

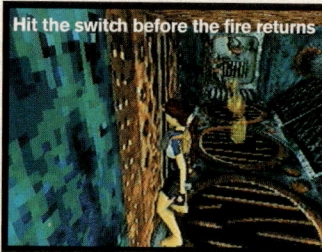

Hit the switch before the fire returns

Now head right from the fire corridor and round to the shallow water. Climb through the newly opened door and flick the switch (7) which turns off the second set of fires. It's on a timer, so quickly head back round the corridors to the earlier switch (4) which turns off the first two fires, then leg it back to get past the fires before they relight – you've only just got enough time. Flick the switch (6) at the end to open the door.

Jump into the water and lure the barracuda out, then shoot it from the shore. Now swim through the trap door and quickly up through the other holes (just keep turning so you spiral nicely upwards) to pull the lever (8) near the top. Swim all the way back down, through the opened door to flick the switch (9). Swim like Sharon Davies up through the shaft again to surface and catch your breath. **(See Secret 3.)**

Climb out and run into the hole at the end of the passage. You fall into a rocky room. Go round to the left and drop down another hole to emerge in a huge room. Go to the corner and pull out the crate twice: use it to climb up to the high ledge. Pull the switch there (10) to drop the

rocks through into the huge room. When you return, jump up the rocks to go back through the hole you entered by (by the right ladder) – jump forward and grab from the wall. Head left round the corner to climb up to the ledge. Follow the passage and hit the switch (12) which opens a door later on.

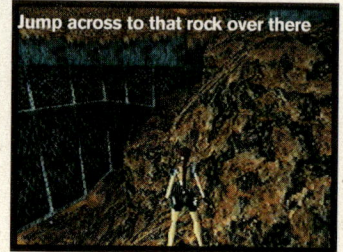

Jump across to that rock over there

Return to the room, drop back down, and jump up through the other hole in the ceiling (by the ladder) to reach another rocky room with lots of slopes. Head right and jump onto the right side of the sloping rock by the wall and walk left up the next two. Now do a running jump diagonally left to land on the high rock.

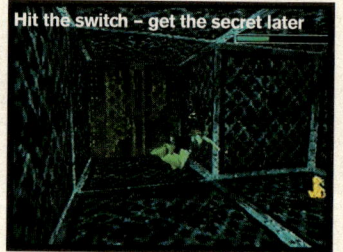

Hit the switch – get the secret later

Climb up the next rock and up into the passage. Go down it and flick the switch (11) which fills a pool later on.

Drop and slide back down the rocks, then through the hole into the huge room. Walk along the rocks, past the large trap door, to the small high opening. Follow the twisty passage round and jump into the deep pool. Watch out for the diver as you swim down into the underwater tunnel – best just swim past him. Climb out at the end of the tunnel and get ready for a battle with two guards. Now hit the switch (13) to open the final door. Go through to exit.

Tomb Raider II

Flicking switch 10 kills two birds with one stone – literally. It opens the trap doors to drop a load of rocks from the room above into the long room. For the latter, this enables you to get back up through holes F and G, as well as climbing up to the high passage at the right end. Going back up through F to the original rocky room, most of the rocks will have fallen through, enabling you to reach switch 12.

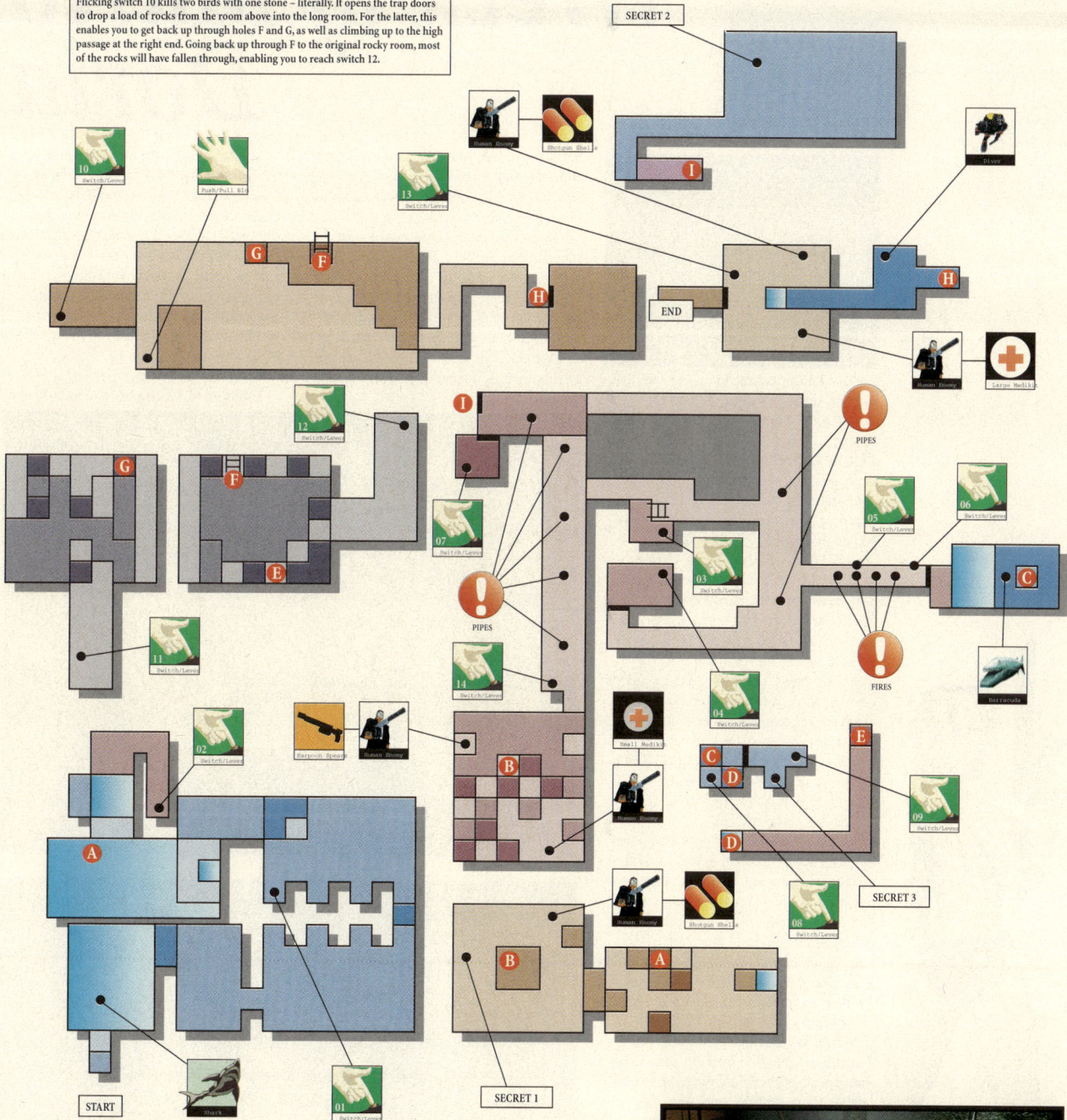

SECRET 2

Human Enemy
Shotgun Shells
Diver
I

10
Switch/Lever

Push/Pull Bl.

13
Switch/Lever

G
F
H
END
H

Human Enemy
Large Medikit

12
Switch/Lever

G
F
E

I

07
Switch/Lever

05
Switch/Lever
06
Switch/Lever

PIPES
C

03
Switch/Lever

11
Switch/Lever

!
PIPES

14
Switch/Lever

!
FIRES

Barracuda

02
Switch/Lever

Harpoon Spear
Human Enemy

Small Medikit

04
Switch/Lever

B
Human Enemy

E
C
D
D

09
Switch/Lever

A

SECRET 3

Human Enemy
Shotgun Shells
08
Switch/Lever

B
A

START
Shark

01
Switch/Lever

SECRET 1

Lara starts the level under the ocean and must quickly get to the first pool to surface and catch her breath before she drowns. It's easy enough to find: just follow the trail of barrels and other debris from the yellow sub, until you see the shipwreck. Swim to the anchor in the corner and go down through the hole to emerge in the pool. Take a breather, but don't hang about too long – those sharks are on your trail!

tomb raider II

continued

Wreck of Mario Doria

Go round and drop into the water. Get the harpoon spears/gun from the bottom. Kill or avoid the diver. Go through the underwater passage. Surface and get the large medikit. Slide backwards down the slope and grab the edge. Drop onto crumbling tiles and grab as you fall through – you're bound to lose a lot of energy. Shoot the two guards and go through into the room with the upturned furniture. (See Secret 1.) Pull the block out once, go round and push it, then push it twice into the dark corridor. Do the same with the next block, so you can pull out the third, opening up two corridors.

Go down the right one and drop down with guns drawn, ready for the three guards who arrive – including one behind you. Once they're dead, go through into the large room and shoot the guard on the walkway above. Go over to the far right sloping platform next to the upper walkway and jump up to grab it. Pull up, then go round to the left and jump back and grab to shimmy left to the dead baddie. After grabbing his automatic ammo, shimmy further left and pull up the other side. Run round to the end and do a running jump to the ledge in the corner. Pick up the first Circuit Breaker (there are three to find), then drop down. Head left, then into the right passage. Safe-walk through the glass to the near edge of the hole. Jump back and grab, then drop and grab the lower ledge.

Pull up to collect the Rest Room Key. Turn around and jump from the edge to grab the opposite side of the hole and pull up. Safe-walk through the glass and back round to the large room. Then return through the first passage to the room with the blocks.

Head down the other passage to reach a brown room. Insert the key in the far-right corner to open the windows there. Go through and push the button to open the opposite windows – roll around to shoot the guard who arrives through it. Hit the switch there to open the upper door

in the room with the upper walkway (by the dead baddie). Before going back to shimmy over there, hit the opposite switch again to close the windows.

Go through the upper doorway and round to the passage with the doors. Open the second wheel door and hang-drop in. Pull/push the block round to the other corner, so you can pull the upper one out. Hit the switch and climb up onto the block and through the open door. Follow the passage to a room, then the next passage, shooting the guard.

Go through into the next room and pull the block to find the Rusty Key. Then move the block under the switch in the corner – climb up and hit it to open the door, then exit back to the door corridor. Head left and use the key to open the door. Hang-drop into the room and move the block to the end of the ledge, so you can pull the upper block out twice. Go through the passage into the next room and run over the crumbling tiles, jumping over the barrels which roll in from the right (See Secret 2).

Climb up to the room entrance and shoot

the guard. Drop through the hole, onto the wooden raft. Swim down to the lever and pull it to temporarily open a door in the room above. Quickly climb back up via the hole (from the raft side is easiest) and go through it to flick the switch there. Go through the next door, then slide backwards down the slope onto the opening trap door and grab the edge to pull up just before it closes (if you're too early, keep jumping from slope to slope). Climb into the passage and hit the switch to open a door in the other passage above the raft room. Jump up the slope and get up there.

Go through into the large room and shoot the three guards (two below). Hitting the switch opens a trap door, but you can get down to the lower ledge by simply jumping back from near the switch and grabbing. Go and get the second Circuit Breaker in the corner. Hit the switch down here to drain the raft pool. Approach the corner where you found the Circuit Breaker and the trap

door round the other side will temporarily drop – run round and climb up. Return to the raft room and hang-drop through the hole to lessen the damage.

Open the wheel door in the corner and follow the passage up to climb into a red passage. Drop down at the end to find the third Circuit Breaker. Hit the switch in the corner, then climb back up to the passage and take a right turn to drop through the opened trap door, back into the brown room and shoot the two guards. (Note: if you can't get to the Circuit Breaker, do this first, then hit the switch in the brown room to close the doors.)

Return via the room with the blocks to where you first dropped in through the crumbling tiles. Jump into the small pool and swim round and up to pull the lever, then up to the surface. Climb out quickly to shoot the three guards. Insert each of the Circuit Breakers, in turn, to turn off the fires.

Pull the block out three times, then use it

Secret 1: Stone Dragon
Light a flare and jump up in the near-left corner to reach the dark passage. Shoot the guard and follow it to the end. Drop down to collect the secret. Climb back up and shoot another guard on your way back.

Secret 2: Jade Dragon
Climb up to where the barrels came from and prepare to dodge some more – flip back and jump left/right. Go back up there and grab the secret.

Secret 3: Gold Dragon
Instead of heading round to the right, go straight on towards the bright pillar. Swim up behind it to surface in a cave with the secret. This place also provides a useful breather when getting the Cabin Key.

to climb up to the passage above. Shoot the guard, then hit the switch. Return down the passage and do a running from the edge to the opposite ledge. Do a running jump to grab the next ledge, then repeat and jump to the passage at the end. Drop down (it's a long way!) into the water. Swim through to the flickery passage. Shoot the barracuda from the shallows, then swim through the large pool to the far left passage. Shoot the guard and enter the large room looking out to sea. Open the far door and go through. Flick the switch, then quickly head back through the sea-view room to the opposite door before it closes. Push the block to reveal a switch. Flick it to open a trap door. Head back through the sea-view room and turn left at the end. Light a flare and go down the dark passage to find the opened hatch.

Now comes the tricky bit. Drop into the water and swim past the sharks and barracudas. (See Secret 3.) Follow the cavern round to the right (outside the sea-view room) to find the Cabin Key. You've got just enough time to grab it and get back through the trap door before running out of air.

Return to the sea-view room and go through the far right passage. Light a flare and use the Cabin Key to open the door. Flick the switch inside to drop a trap door in the sea-view room. Return there and drop into the new hole to push the crate down the trench. Climb on it and hit the switch to open a trap door in the cabin ceiling. Go back there and climb up. Follow the passage and drop into a large room with glass and water at the bottom. Shoot the two guards below, then drop from the right gap (looking from entrance) onto the non-sloped platform to reach the lower walkway. Get the goodies from the dead guards and go down the dark passage to find three M15 clips.

Now slide into the water, avoiding the glass. Avoid the divers and head for the brown barrel. Swim down to the left of it and through the wide opening. Follow the narrow twisty passage, avoiding the eels. Surface in the small blue room to catch your breath, then drop back in and swim to the rusty section to complete the level.

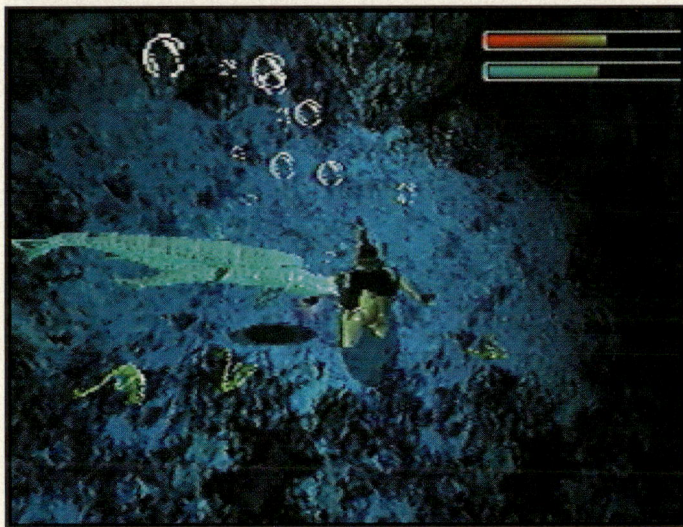

tomb raider II

Living Quarters

Swim through the hole and pull the lever on the left of it to open the trap door above. Surface through it and climb out. Shoot the guard who arrives. Go through to the large room and jump up and over the other side of the engine. Enter the far right red passage and follow it round. Drop into the lower passage and shoot the two guards. Go to the end and turn left to see a room, but jump left to avoid the barrels and get ready to shoot another baddie.

Go through to the room with the fires. To get past the latter, jump to from the top of the slope to the crevice and shimmy right. Hit the switch at the end to turn off the fires, then climb up to your left to a small room, then up again. Follow the passage and hit the switch before dropping through the hole. Return to the engine room to find the pistons have changed positions. Climb up to the right and jump to the piston. Jump via the others to the last one. (See Secret 1.) If you can, shoot the guard in the opposite passage before jumping across. Follow the passage and push the block three times. Go round down the stairs and push the next block. Drop down and flick the switch up (which you hit before). Climb back up and return to the engine room.

Jump across the pistons and do a running jump from the far one to grab the ledge on the right. Hit the switch there to flood the fire room. Jump back to the piston to drop safely down to the floor, then go round to the flooded room. Pull the lever to the right of the entrance to open the far door. Swim through and down through the hole. Avoiding/shooting the diver, surface through the next hole to catch your breath in a small blue room. Drop back in and swim through

the gap by the weeds. Go round to flick the switch – avoiding the giant sea serpent near it! Swim back to the chamber and up through the opened trap door to surface in a large room.

Shoot the guard above. You can skip this next section, if you want (see Short Cut). Jump up to the middle ledge and hit the switch to open the opposite door. Go through and hit both switches to temporarily raise the opposite trap doors, then roll round and do a running jump to the left one. Quickly shimmy right before they fall again.

At the end pull up and hit the switch. Go back to the previous room, where a trap door has fallen in the corner. Face the lower sloped block and jump forward, jump twice again to grab the upper blue girder and pull up. Pull then push the block out, so you can shimmy left to the other side. Go up the slope, turn left, and leap to the high passage.

Short Cut: Instead of doing all that, you can reach the upper area of the room directly from the middle ledge. Standing at the opposite end from the switch, walk to the

grilled platform above the third cog. Turn right and jump from the edge to grab the blue girder (if you're standing too far left you won't be able to jump). Pull up and make your way up the slope, turn left, and jump to the high passage.

Follow the passage down and shoot the guard. (See Secret 2.) Take the second right turn and slide down the slope, jumping over the crumbling tiles. Shoot the barracuda in the shallows. (See Secret 3.) Wade through the water to reach the sloped room. Save your game here – the next bit can be tricky. Run forwards from the entrance to the sloped block, then do a running jump diagonally into the gap, turning left in the air to face the left side of the pillar. Pull up quickly before the tile crumbles or you won't be able to reach it – if so, reload your position.

Shimmy right until you can pull up. Go over the slope through the opposite passage to reach an ornate room with a stairway – shoot the guard who comes down it. Go upstairs and shoot from the balcony at the guy on the chequered marble floor below. Go round and pull the crate twice, then jump down to the chequered room. Shoot another couple of guards as you go round to the left.

Drop down and pull the block out to find the Theatre Key. Climb back up and shoot another guard before going upstairs. Head right down the passage and shoot the guard, then use the key to open the windows. Head left up the stairs into the theatre and shoot the guard. Head right across the seating and shoot the guy on the balcony.

Jump up there and shoot another baddie. Flick the switch to open the left part of the stage curtain. Head down there and shoot another thug as you go behind the curtain. Pull the block out from the end of the dark corridor and use it to climb to the high ledge. Drop the other side and light a flare, then jump over the glass pit.

Flick the switch at the end to flood the low section of the chequered room. Head back to the stage and up through the theatre. Another gunman awaits on the stairs down to the chequered room. After shooting him, go round to swim over the pool to the doorway to exit.

Secret 1: Stone Dragon
From the last piston, do a running jump to the grab the right ledge where the secret is in plain view.

Secret 2: Gold Dragon
Take the first right turn and jump from the edge of the glass pit (you can see the secret below) to grab the dark high ledge. Pull up and drop through the crumbling tile to get the secret. Safe-walk through the glass and climb out.

Secret 3: Jade Dragon
Step on the crumbling tile in the shallows. Avoiding/shooting the barracuda, swim through the hole and round the passage into a large underwater cavern where the secret awaits.

tomb raider II

continued

The Deck

Watch out for the flame-thrower to your right. Keep your distance as you shoot him and a guard. Go through to the open area where the baddies came from. Follow the building all the way round to the right to find the grenade launcher in the corner. Return to the corridor where you started and climb into the opening above the pool.

Jump into the water and swim left, avoiding the barracudas, to climb out. Shoot the barracudas from the shore, then climb up the sloped block and jump/run all the way around the wall to find the Stern Key. Drop back into the water and swim down to the left of the rusty ship, through the opening into an underwater cavern. Head right and follow the passage to find a hole to surface. Climb out and shoot the thug, then drop down and head right to shoot the flame-thrower. Carry on round to the left to find some crates. Push the nearest one, then climb onto it and push the upper crate. Jump back down and pull the first box, then go round and push it, enabling you pull the next low crate out to reveal some flares and a door. Use the Stern Key to open it.

Go through and jump into the water. Light a flare and swim forwards through the underwater chamber to find a lever near the far right opening. Pull it, then swim back and climb out. Leave by the crates and head right to shoot a gunman on the ledge where

the flamer was. Drop down the nearby trap door, follow the passage, and climb the ladder to find a switch. Flick it to drain the pool you've just been swimming in. Climb out and go back there. Hang-drop into the drained pool and head right at the end to find a crate in the wall. Pull it out to reveal a passage. Turn right at the end and climb out into a grotto. Go through it to find a pool with an orange raft. Swim towards it, then left and climb out by the crates to blast the thug before shooting the divers from the

shore. (See Secret 1.) Jump in and swim left to the corner to find a small opening near the bottom. Go through and follow the passage, avoiding a barracuda, to surface and climb out – may as well shoot it now. Follow the passage round to the snowy section and shoot the gunman. Carry straight on and grab the large medikit by the hole. Make sure you've got full health before hang-dropping through it onto the highest crate below. You can now grab the Cabin Key on the raft.

This releases a couple sharks and a barracuda into the pool. Lure them back to the shore with the crates and shoot them from there. Now go through the underwater tunnel again. Climb out and follow the passage round to the snowy bit where you shot the gunman earlier. This time take a left turn, light a flare, and climb up all the rocks at the end to emerge in a cavern. Drop through the opening to the upper deck. Head down the opposite passage and shoot the two guards who arrive. Head left at the end and hang-drop down to the side of the pool. Get ready to shoot the flame-thrower and two thugs, then the gunman below. (See Secret 2.)

Drop down to the next deck (above the one where you started the level) and save your game. From the ledge above the corner where you found the grenade launcher, do a running jump to the nearby platform.

Do a running jump to grab the white ledge (to the right you can the jade secret, but it's better to get it later). Do a running jump from the high right side of the ledge to the orange roof. Head to the far side and hang-drop to grab the crevice just below, then shimmy left to pull up.

Turn left and do a running jump to the rock ledge. Follow the twisty passage round to reach a sloped room. Jump via the pillars to climb the slope, then shoot the two thugs at the top.

Follow the passage round and do a running jump to grab the opposite roof. Go to the far left corner and do a running jump over the gap to reach the ledge with the trap door. Drop through and kill the thug who arrives, then follow the passage round to a crate and door. Pull the crate out and hit the switch to open another door. Go through the doorway onto the upper deck and head right down the corridor, then right past the next alley to find the newly opened door. Inside, get the M16 ammo in the dark corner, then use the Cabin Key to open the door. Enter and head left across the crumbling tiles to hit the switch in the corner. Jump back over and return to the upper deck to shoot another thug. Go back to the narrow corridor, where the second door has now opened. Enter and go upstairs to climb to a rocky passage. Follow it to the wall where you can't jump up high enough: turn around and jump forward to grab the opposite pillar, then do a running jump to the high ledge. Drop through the hole to get the Storage Key.

Climb back out and return to deck. If you want the final secret, jump over to the white ledge, as before. (See Secret 3.) From the deck with the white ledge on, you can shoot down at the two flame-throwers by the crates. To get down there, don't drop – follow the original path through the very first corridor and the drop into the pool. Go round past the crates to find a locked shed. Use the Storage Key to open it, then pick up the Seraph to complete the level.

tomb raider II

continued

Barkhang Monastery

Secret 1: Gold Dragon
This is found in a nook behind the big statue. Go round the grey walkway and jump up the ramp, then pull up into the nook to grab the secret.

Secret 2: Stone Dragon
Dive into the water and swim to the opposite wall. Past the ladder, look up and left to see an opening: swim through it to find the secret.

Secret 3: Jade Dragon
Go down the passage with the rolling blade, using the nooks either side to dodge it. Enter the passage on the left with the snapping doors. Roll through two sets of these to find the secret.

Follow the dark passage round to the open area where some monks are fighting a couple of gunmen. Don't shoot the friendly monks – if you kill one, they'll turn against you for the rest of the level! Help them defeat the gunmen, by carefully targeting the latter.

Climb up the ladder opposite the staircase and shoot the crow at the top. Jump over to the platform by the ladder, then over the hole to grab the opposite ledge. Drop to the ledge, then jump onto the flat rock at the end, watching out for more crows. Jump to the sloped rock above the crevice on the other side, to slide down and grab the edge, then drop to grab the crevice. Shimmy left until you can pull up.

Smash one of the windows nearby to enter the building. Follow the corridor to the junction and wait for a monk to come from the left passage to enter the room ahead (containing the door to the Strongroom). When a gunman jumps through the window, help the monk defeat him. Return to the passage junction and take the right turn (the locked doors at the end lead to the Main Hall). Approach the first opening on the left and let the monk run past you to take on another gunman. Through that door, climb the ladder to a walkway above the Main Hall. Head right and then first left to find the Main Hall Key (the monk doesn't seem to mind you taking it).

Continue around the walkway and drop into the passage. Jump sideways to avoid the boulder rolling down the narrow slope. Follow the passage and jump back from the junction to avoid another boulder.

Go past where it ends up and climb down the ladder and push the block in the corridor. Climb back up the ladder and go all the way up the boulder slope. Follow it round to find a pool. The hole in the middle

of it will suck you down, so swim around it to enter the passage on the far side.

Surface in the next pool and wade out to drop a long way to another pool. Wade out to the right and light a flare to see those snapping doors. Walk as close to them as you can, then simply roll through when they're open.

Repeat this for the next two sets and follow the watery passage round to a ladder. Climb up to the room and help the monk kill the gunmen. Go through to the dark area to

see the first of five Prayer Wheels (in the corner) which you have to collect. Once you grab it, the two rows of burners light. To get past them, turn left on the prayer wheel platform and jump forward from the right side of the edge. Then jump forward between the burners on the second row.

Back in the other room, pull the red crates out to reveal a passage. Head right along it and climb the ladder back to the second boulder. Return to the walkway above the Main Hall, climb down the ladder,

and return to the main hall door. Use the key to open it, then go through and over to the railing – at which point, the monks start battling with more gunmen by the doors.

Once the battle's over, go through the first door on the right – when entering the main hall. Pass through the room into another corridor with swinging blades. Run and jump over the first and turn left to get the Strongroom Key. Return all the way to the Strongroom door and open it to find the Rooftops Key. Use the latter in the nearby room with the rolling blades (right from the passage to the main hall).

Go through and look behind the first gold statues to find a switch. Flick it to temporarily turn off the fires in the next passage, then quickly go through. At the end is a door which requires a Gemstone to open. Take the left turn, enter the room, and climb the ladder on the right to watch the monks and gunmen fight it out below. Flick the switch in the courtyard to open two trap doors,

revealing a glass case: smash it to get two Gemstones. Use the switch round the corner to exit, then insert a Gemstone between the second set of gold statues to open the door behind (which you saw before). Enter and pull the box twice to get the second Prayer Wheel.

Back in the Main Hall, take the second entrance on the right (as you enter from the main doors) and climb up the ladder. Up top, do a running jump to grab the statue's hand, then climb to the upper hand, then do a running jump to grab the head. Cross to the next hand, then over to the high ledge. Insert the second Gemstone to open a trap door in the room below the statue. Head back to its base and go down the nearby wide passage. (See Secret 1). You can rearrange the crates in the room on the right to find some ammo.

Exit to the wide passage and head left, then right. Take the first left into the pool room. (See Secret 2). Return to the trap-

door under the statue and drop through it. Follow the passage and flick the switch to open the door. Inside, push the crate across the stream to drain that pool room. Go there and push the box on the ledge to find the third Prayer Wheel.

Return to the wide passage from the statue and go through the entrance on the far left. Go through the room and follow the passage to reach the Gauntlet. Shoot the gunmen who attack as you cross the room, then get ready for more hazards. The fire goes out as you approach, so jump over it into the passage below. Avoid the spiky balls and climb up to the ledge. Wait for the rolling blade to go past, then jump across the hole in the floor. The fire ahead will go out, so you can run into the next tunnel. Climb to the right ledge and time your run past the rolling blade to the opposite doorway to discover the Trapdoor Key. (See Secret 3).

Go and use the key on the lock to the right of the closed doors near the trap door. Drop down the trap door and pull up. Flick the switch to open the double doors leading to the statue, then close them again. Follow the outdoor path and go round to the left of the rocks to climb the ladder. Shoot the eagle and gunman as you approach the bridge. Cross over and kill some crows. Get to the top of the structure via the ledges and enter to grab the fourth Prayer Wheel.

Return to the wide passage by the big statue room, shooting more gunmen. Past the room with the crates is a passage with a trap door. Run across it, then quickly grab one of the ladders.

Go right, then left to find a staircase leading to a window. As you ascend, some gunmen appear behind you: jump out of the window, then flick the switch to let the monks out. Close it behind them.

When you've killed any gunmen remaining, climb the long ladders to grab the final Prayer Wheel. Head back to the big statue and go round to the left to the room to insert all the Prayer Wheels. This opens the double doors there. Climb the slope and insert the Seraph to open the level exit.

tomb raider II

continued

Catacombs of the Talion

Drop off the side of the stairs to avoid the deadly icicles falling onto you.

Go through into the room with the slope. (See Secret 1.) Slide down and kill the yeti which attacks, keeping your distance.

Flick the switch by the bars at the bottom, then climb the ladder from the dark area. Then slide down the slope again and jump to grab the ledge. Shoot the leopard, then drop off the stairs (to avoid icicles) and follow the passage round to a large cave with a pool.

As you near the pool, gunmen appear on the stairs above. Then watch out for leopards around the pool. From the stairs, go up the snowy slope to the left of the pool and jump right into the latter to avoid the snowballs. Return to the slope and jump diagonally right to a lower ledge. Run over the crumbling tiles and climb the ladder. Backflip from the top, then turn around and jump up to flick the switch which raises the cage over the Tibetan Mask.

Go over and get it, at which point the pool drains. Go down there, hang-dropping through the hole. Do a running jump over the spike pit and insert the mask to open the gate. Run up to the left of the slope and pull up the ledge to avoid the snowballs.

Get ready to shoot four leopards, but don't go back to the slope until another set of snowballs have rolled down. Go the stairs on the left and jump from the lowest one to grab the opening in the rock. Drop into the large cave and head towards the ice, at which point four leopards appear. Bag the cats, then go through the archway and shoot some more. Climb the rock ledge just to the left and drop into the pool below to find the second Tibetan Mask.

Climb out and up the rock ledge again. Down below, shoot the two gunmen, then trek back to the snowball slope. Follow the

wide passage to the right and insert the mask to open the door. Drop down into the dark room – there are yeti cages at the bottom.. Head round the walkway to the left and jump over two gaps to reach the switch. Flick it to light the room (a bit) and open the cages. Get shooting those yetis, circling round to keep your distance.

Once they're dead, get the goodies from the cages. Then go back up top and move the block in the corner (right of the switch). Push it beneath one of the sets of bars next

to the switch (to stop them closing) before entering the other one. Flick the switch at the back, then exit back to the outside, shooting the gunmen who appear.

Return all the way to the opening in the rock wall, by the snowballs slope. Go through the opened door and up the first rope bridge. At the start of the second, move to the left to dodge the snowballs.

Continue up the second bridge and do a running jump to grab the ladder. Climb up and follow the passage to a hole with a

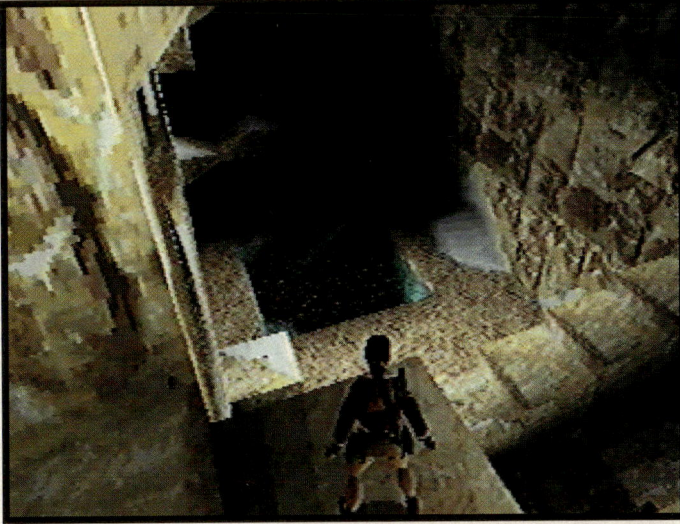

large pool below. Jump into the water and climb out to avoid the barracudas. Shoot them from the shore, then swim/wade to the next cave. Swim to the left. (See Secret 2.) Carry on left to where the cavern opens out and turn right to head towards the closed doors. Climb the pillar opposite, then do a running jump to grab the ladder.

Climb up and jump back at the top to land on a ledge with a switch. Flick it to open those closed doors below. Jump back in the water and go through them. Shoot the leopard, then flick the switch to open the large doors near the snowballs slope. Hang-drop down to the ice sheet, then go back through the opening in the rock.

Enter the doors and do a running leap over the pit. If you want some goodies, shoot down at the leopards before dropping down and grabbing the stuff in the far left corner. Flick the switch to open the doors, then shoot the leopard which appears.

Return upstairs and jump over the pit again. Jump forward, back, then forward over the snowballs ahead. Then lure the snowballs from the smaller side slope. They smash through the door, enabling you to enter the small room. Step on the left floor switch to open a door. Go through to a room with spikes on the floor. (See Secret 3.) Head towards the door on the near right and jump through, then over the snowballs. Turn around and run over the other floor switch, jump over the snowballs, and jump back through the right door, then through the opposite exit before it closes. Stop as soon as you enter, to avoid the drop. Jump to grab the ladder and climb down.

tomb raider II

Ice Palace

Secret 1: Gold Dragon
Return to the narrow cage and pull the block out (the second from the left when entering through the bars), then push it sideways to reveal an entrance to a large room.

Secret 2: Stone Dragon
It's in the dark passage to the right of the cave. Light a flare and jump forward over a ramp to grab it.

Secret 3: Jade Dragon
Before grabbing the Talion, drop down to the ice field and head for the ladder near the far left corner. Jump over to grab it, then climb down. Light a flare and turn left. Drop down via two platforms, then turn around to find a switch. hit it to open the hut near the palace. Climb back up the ladder and jump back to the ice field. Then head for the hut (which also proves a useful hideout when facing the guardian).

Shoot the bell to open the door and go through. Watch out for those panels on the floor which spring Lara upwards – they can be fatal. Go round to the right and line yourself up with the springboard under the long hole and bell above. Draw your guns beforehand and keep firing as you run forwards and bounce up – you need to hit the bell to open of the area exit gates in the room near the slope you slide back down.

Now run towards the double springboard, in the direction of the exit gates and grab as soon as you're airborne to reach the ledge above. Flick the switch there to lower the yeti cage – and release them. Drop down and shoot all three. From the upper wooden section, jump over into the long narrow cage. Shoot the yeti at the end, then go round and flick the switch to raise the nearby trap doors. (See Secret 1).

Go back to the room with the gates and

run towards the new ledge, onto springboard, grabbing as soon as you're airborne. Turn towards the bell and jump to shoot it, which opens the second gate below.

Jump to the slope on the left to slide down. Go through to find another springboard. Run at it from the left to grab the ledge above. Pull up and jump back, holding the jump button so that Lara keeps leaping from slope to slope. Hold c to drift right and shoot the bell there, then hold g until she bounces over to the ledge on the left.

Climb up through the opened gate and climb the ladder to the right ledge. Climb up the next ledge and jump over to the left. Shoot the yeti, then climb up through the opening to the right. Ahead you'll see a large cave: the right rocky path leads to a sealed door. (See Secret 2.) Drop down to the floor and follow the passage to another large cave, shooting the three white tigers.

Grab the Tibetan Mask from the block on the far side. Return to the right rocky path in the previous room, where the door has now

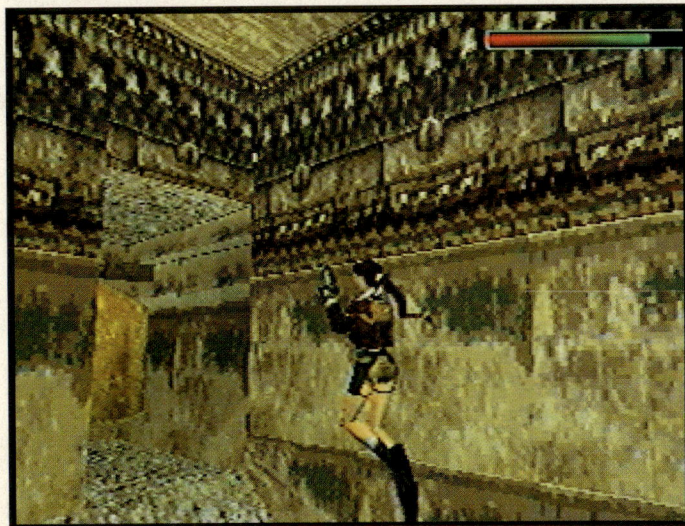

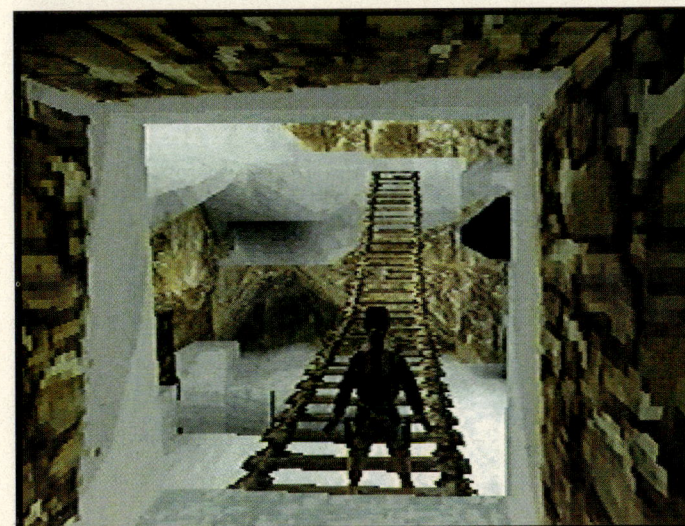

opened. Go through and follow the passage, shooting the yeti when you drop by the brickwork. Shoot another yeti through the holes in the floor. Hang-drop from the middle of the last hole to avoid the spikes.

Light a flare and head out onto the balcony on the left. To the left of it, insert the mask to open the door just to the left of the balcony from the dark room. Go through and cross the rope bridge.

Follow the passage to emerge above the ice sheet from the previous level. Jump over to the switch and flick it to melt the ice. Drop down and shoot the to white tigers. Swim past the Gong Hammer to the next pool and shoot the three yetis from the shallows. Go and get the Gong Hammer now, then quickly get out of the barracuda filled pool where you shot the yetis.

Head down the right passage and shoot the yeti. Climb the steps and go through the door. Turn right to see some snowballs: lure some down, backflipping out of the way, then make a run for it down to the doorway.

Phew. Go through to the left and slide backwards to grab the edge. Shimmy left until you can see a ledge behind you (using L1). Pull up and jump back to land on it. Do a running jump to grab the ice wall, then climb up to the entrance above. Slide backwards and grab the edge of the slope, then hang-drop by the gong. Use the hammer to hit it and open the palace doors. (See Secret 3.) Jump and pull up the left slope to slide down. Drop and enter through the doorway. Grab the Talion and exit, at which point the giant guardian attacks you. Now's the time to use your grenade launcher – it takes eight to ten hits to kill him. Keep mobile, but don't fall off the edge! When he'd dead the level is completed.

tomb raider II

continued

Temple of Xian

Secret 1: Gold Dragon
As you slide down the wide tunnel, jump back to twist in midair and slide backwards. Grab the edge of the waterfall, shimmy left, and pull up to the secret.

Secret 2: Stone Dragon
Don't just drop from the ladder above or you'll die. Head down to the left and shimmy right along the low crevice to reach the secret.

Secret 3: Jade Dragon
From a platform by the angular structure, jump to the white bricks and slide down to the springboard. Push forward in the air to land on a rafter. Do a running jump to grab the ledge with the secret. From here you can jump to a ledge by the angular structure.

Go through the torch-lit rooms to emerge in a large chamber. Run along the walkway to drop through a trap door to a long slide section. Jump over the blade on the way down to the waterfall. (See Secret 1.)

You end up in a pool with fighting fish. Climb out on the ladder ledge and shoot them. Then swim down through the large opening to emerge by the temple doors. Shoot the two tigers which leap out at you, then go round to the left to find a springboard. Step onto it from the left, then push forward in midair (not too early) to land on the roof. Go round to the other side to flick the switch which opens the trap door above the ladder in the previous pool. Shoot the eagle which appears.

Hang-drop down and swim back to the ladder and climb up to the passage, shooting the spider. Go through to the large room with the long drop to red gunk – fatal to touch. Turn around and hang-drop to find a ladder. Climb down it and drop to grab the next ledge. Pull up and shoot the spider as you follow the path. (See Secret 2.) Jump from the edge of the walkway to reach the ladder and climb up.

Follow the path up to the spike-pit room. Climb the wall opposite the pit, then right, against the wall – jump to backflip to a slope, then immediately jump to land on the wall. Walk across the top to see a crumbling plank – jump onto the furthest end of it, then drop straight down to the block with shotgun shells. Do a running jump from the left side to the slope and jump quickly to land on another slope: jump and turn right in the air to land on a third slope. Slide down it to land by some grenades between the spikes.

Climb up the nearby blocks, then grab the ledge above and shimmy left to pull up

by the switch. Flick it to open the temple doors back by the pool. Follow the path and jump out by the waterfall to return there. Get ready to shoot the four statues which have come to life, then go through the doors.

In the room with another red gunk pool, do a running jump from the ledge to slide forward down the sloped platform. Jump near the end to reach the next slope and slide before jumping. Jump twice again to grab a ledge and pull up. Climb the blocks

to the top of the room and do a running jump to grab the exit passage.

Run down it towards the switch and fall through the trap door. Push forward from the bottom of the slope (don't jump) and run to the switch when you land. Flick it and roll round to run back down the path to avoid the spikes and get through the door.

Follow the passage and jump back, then left to avoid the first boulder. If you go near the top left corner of the long ramp, another will roll down. For the final boulder, run

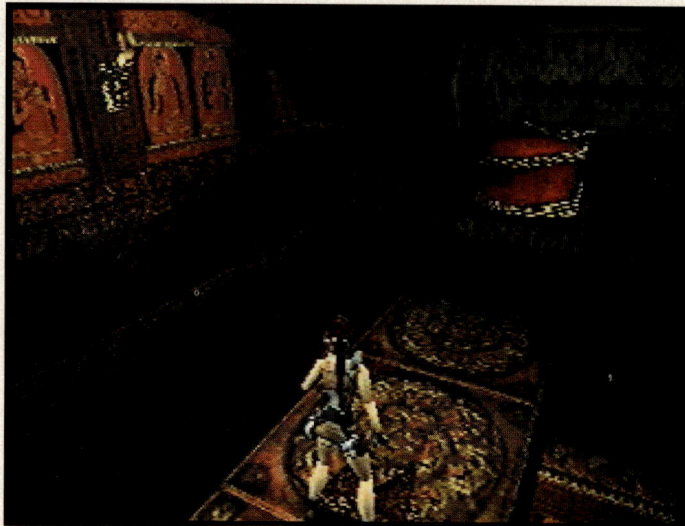

across the short ramp below the ladder, down to the long ramp below. Climb the ladder to a dark room, so light a flare. Flick the switch to the right of the exit to open it, then shoot the tiger which attacks. Pull up into the passage, then turn your back to the rolling blades and head left to drop and grab a ledge, then drop down again to a safe corner. Time your move past the blades below to reach the exit opposite.

You emerge high above the first room in the temple. Shoot the two eagles, then push the button on the left to temporarily open the large doors on the other side. To get through, immediately roll after pushing the button, then run and jump along the rafters.

Keep to the side of the walkway and time your runs past the swinging spikes. Push the right button, then quickly jump left to hit the other one. Press L1 to break out of the cinematic view, turn right, and keep running down the hallway to reach the exit.

As you go outside, a boulder drops behind you, so quickly run to the end of the walkway an jump to grab the far ledge. Go to the platform under the statue to find the Dragon Seal. Jump to the platform by the head, then climb the blocks to the dark room. Flick the switch to create a walkway in the gunk, then go through the opposite side of the head to exit. Hop along the platforms over the gunk. Turn left and do a running jump to the slope in the middle of the room, then jump to grab the block. Pull up, slide down the other side, and jump to the flat ledge.

On the tall pillar, turn right and do a running jump to grab the ledge by the wall. Do a running jump down to the platform by the springboard. Jump onto the latter, then push forward in the air to land on a platform by the angular structure – quickly step back and grab the edge to avoid the boulder which rolls down. Jump up the platforms, then to the right and run to the white bricks to avoid the boulder. (See Secret 3.)

Continue up the structure and shoot the eagle near the top. Jump to grab the next platform, then do a running jump to get near the door, before jumping through it. Pull the crate twice to reveal a passage. Go through and flick the switch to open a trap door. Drop down to a slope, chased by a boulder: run left at the end to slide down a slope to the rafters above the temple. Shoot the tigers below, then hang-drop to the floor. Insert the Dragon Seal near the door to open it.

Go through and follow the passage, avoiding the rolling blade. Slide down the slope and quickly flick the three green-handled switches to open the exit before you're crushed by the spiked ceiling!

Go via the platforms to the ledge over a large pool. Shoot some more fish, then jump in and pull the lever to raise the water level. Surface to catch your breath, then swim through the wide tunnel, but ignore the lever on the left. Turn right into a narrow tunnel and pull the lever there, then swim back to surface near the door. Swim back to that lever and through the door it opened. Pull the lever inside to open the big door back in the pool. Surface to catch your breath again, then swim down and through the door. Pull the lever there to open the door above. Go through it and grab the ammo, then wade into the small room and flick the switch. Run from the sliding spikes and drop through the trap door. The water current will carry you to the Gold Key, so grab it and exit through the nearby grating.

Go back to the ladder ledge with the lock, from near the start of the level. Use the key to open the grating. Swim through the passage and turn right at the junction. and through the opening. Pull the lever on the left of the second pillar, then exit and swim through the opened passage to surface in a large cave. Climb out and shoot the giant spiders along the dark tunnel, and more in a large cavern. Climb round the ledges to

reach the pillar in the middle. Do a running jump to grab the pillar near the doorway. Jump over to grab it and follow the passage.

At the other end, do a running jump to grab the pillar by the rocks in the middle. Climb the rocks to grab the Silver Key, then jump into the water and return to the temple doors. Use the key to open the locked door. Inside, jump forward and grab to climb the slope, avoiding more boulders. Turn left at the top and cross the bridge, shooting a tiger and eagle. Shoot the tiger in the next room, then climb the low sloped pillar and jump backwards onto the taller one. At this junction, one route leads to some springboards, while the other features a rolling blade. Jump past the latter to find a room with another blade by a bridge. Dodge the blade and hit the button at the far end of the bridge to open a door above the springboards. Make your way back there and, facing the wall, backflip onto the first springboard and let the springboards propel you upwards – only push forward on the last bounce to grab the ledge.

Shoot the eagle and jump to grab the wide ledge. Go through the door, cross the walkway, and jump to the small platform by the lock. To avoid a spiky death, jump to the left crate, then climb up the left side of the ladder. Drop to the ledge and quickly do a running jump from the edge to grab the ladder to avoid some more spikes.

Climb up and follow the path to find a switch. Flick it and turn back to the open grating. Drop through to the pillar below to get the Main Chamber Key. Slide down the serpent to land on a low pillar. Jump over to the lock and use the key to open a grating behind you. Turn around and do a running jump to grab the wide ledge. Climb the long ladder and drop off to the right. Jump over the spikes and climb the ladder. Don't touch the switch on the right side.

Above is the chamber where you got the Main Chamber Key, but another grating has opened, leading to an even taller pillar with a serpent. From the ledge through the grating, turn left and do a running jump to grab the next platform. Upon landing on the steep slope, jump towards the serpent. You'll slide down a way, but stop on a flat bit. Climb up the ladder until a blade stops you, then backflip to a slope and jump again to grab another ladder. Climb up to reach another blade. Backflip and push forward to twist and grab the climbable wall behind. Climb up to the passage to complete the level.

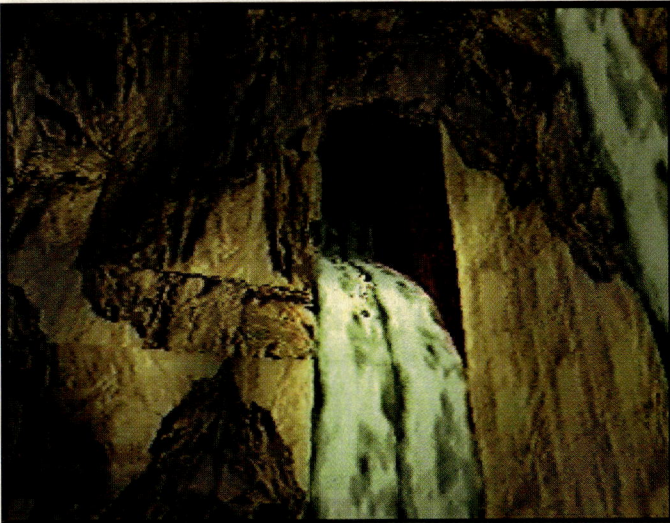

tomb raider II

continued

Floating Island

Look right to see the sparkly trail of a flying warrior. He's dead slow, so you've got plenty of time to target him and shoot him down with just pistols. Walk forward to the edge of the island. Step back a bit and jump to the slope to slide down forwards, jump halfway down and turn slightly right to start sliding forwards down the next – immediately jump and grab the ledge. Pull up into the lattice-covered section. Flick the switch, then go down the narrow passage and slide down the ramp. Draw some big guns to face the first statue guardian. Another comes to life when you approach the front of the island. Shoot them in turn, then climb up through the trap door. When you grab the Mystic Plaque the other statue awakens

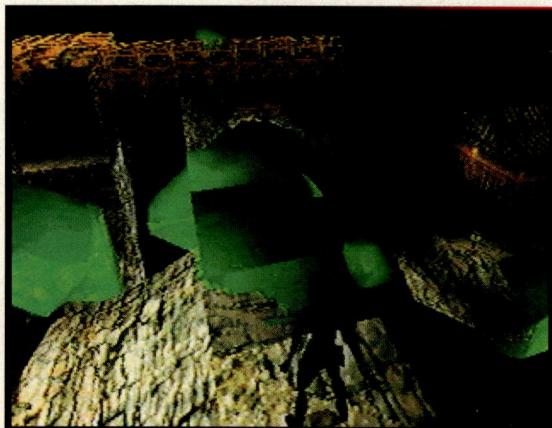

below. Go down and smash him. (See Secret 1.) Hang-drop from the side opposite the ramp you entered and grab the edge of the room below. Turn left to flick the switch and run jump through the gate.

From the edge, do a running jump to the next island. Walk forwards and turn left to jump to the upper part. Turn towards the green staircase island, and do three running jumps and grabs to reach the lowest step. Climb the stairs and turn right. Do a running jump to the wonky stairs island. Climb up and turn round near the top to see another warrior coming. Shoot him then turn around at the very top to shoot down another.

Walk along the lattice to above where you entered before. From the left corner, do a running jump diagonally left to slope which you first jumped onto. Slide backwards and grab the edge to drop onto the ledge below. Do a running jump from here to the platform with the second Mystic Plaque. Do a running jump to grab the right side of the next platform, then jump to the island.

Follow the route round again to bottom of the wonky stairs, then turn left to see where the island where the plaques must be inserted. From the left side of the step (important, as the right side's too short), do a running jump to grab the island ledge. Insert both plaques to open the doors.

Guns drawn, go through to the walkway and keeping jumping back to shoot the warrior who appears. (See Secret 2.) Take a step back from the large green boulder and turn around, then jump backwards twice. Grab the edge as you slide back, then drop down and shoot the warrior above. Climb onto the sloped green block in the building. Turn around at its top to jump forward and grab the roof. Climb through and up to a narrow passage in the sandy rock to return to the upper section. Slide down the slope where the boulder was, then jump forward to a slope. Go up and turn right at the brickwork. Do a running jump to the island with the top of the rope slide.

Use it to slide down and drop off over the lower bridge. Enter the building and shoot the warrior, then flick the switch to open the large door obstructing the rope slide. Shoot two more warriors, then go through to the next room and use the rope slide there to reach the opposite wall – grabbing when you fall. Climb the lattice there and head right. Shimmy left from the green edge and drop down.

Return to the top of the main rope slide

and take a ride down, through the opened doors, all the way to the end. Ignore the two rooms by the hallway and jump to right area by the push-block. When you touch it another warrior appears, so shoot him. Now move the block and jump up tot he ledge above. Flick the switch on the pillar and climb the stone wall towards the lava pit. Turn right as you approach it and drop into the corner to avoid the blades. Step back and jump over to the bridge. Flick the switch to open the trap door in the lava. Climb back up to the stone wall: to reach the trap door, you have to do a running jump and grab.

Wade to the end of the room and flick the switch to open a door in the main room above. Then wade back and swim down through the passage on the left. Surface to the side of the wide area to avoid the blades. Go through the passage and climb up to hit the switch to stop the blades swinging. Go back through the blade passage and return to the main room with the newly opened door above. Push the crate to the pillar near the door, then dive (using R1, to avoid the low ceiling) from the middle of the crate into the doorway. Through the passage is a barred door, opened by a switch above the spikes room. Jump forward to grab the crevice and shimmy left to pull up. Return to the upper passage via a running jump at the left of the opening. Go through the opened door to find two more closed doors guarded by statues. Drop through the hole and grab the edge of the slope.

Drop down into the cage and flick the switch, then roll round and run back to the ledge and climb up to one side of the pillar. Get behind the latter, draw your guns, and pick off the ninjas, jumping sideways to avoid their fire. Now approach each statue in turn, then climb the wall and shoot down at it. Grab the goodies, then hit both switches: one opens the exit, the other a door in the room above.

Exit and head upstairs, shooting another ninja. Flick the switch upstairs to open the ornate door and awaken the two warriors. Once they're dead, go through and climb to the top of the lattice. Jump off and push forward and grab in the air to twist and grab the lattice behind you. Repeat this trick several times to reach the slope. Jump backwards from it and hold the button to keep leaping to and fro. Push g to reach the flat area, then shoot the ninja there. Move the box to reach the rope slide. (See Secret 3.) Ride down it to complete the level.

Dragon's Lair

It's time for the big showdown. Shoot from by the statue into the large room to kill the awakened warrior. Enter and flick the switch opposite to activate the original statue. Once he's dead, flick the switch by where he came to life to awaken two more warriors – and open the exit. Go through it once they're smashed and lure the ninjas out to the large room to kill them. Back in the darkened room, killing one of the ninjas near the large closed door will net you a Mystic

Plaque. When all the foes are dead, insert it to open the door and go through to meet the dragon.

This fire-breathing giant is an awesome adversary, but there are some tricks you can use to defeat him. For a start you can hide behind pillars. If he does manage to flame you, quickly jump in the water below, making sure you surface in a different place. His other main weakness is that he turns slowly, so you can run past, then roll and run past the other side.

Once he falls, you must run over and grab the dagger from the wound on his belly to win the battle. When this happens, the lair starts to collapse, so run through the gate which opens and through the passage to complete the level.

Lara's Mansion

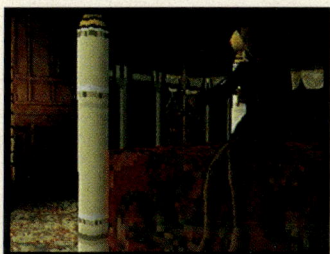

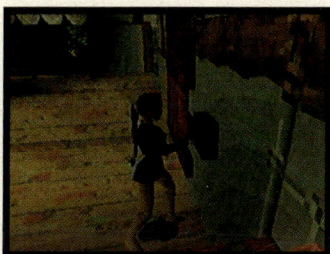

Dagger in hand, Lara can finally relax. Admiring the dagger it took so much trouble to collect, she surely feels like a bit of a snooze in the bedroom of her mansion. But hold on a minute, isn't that the alarm ringing? Better unlock that bedside cabinet to grab the shotgun and ammo before the goons arrive. When they're dead, light a flare and exit through the front door to kill the baddies outside, then the boss. You've made it. Now for Tomb Raider III...

a-z of cheats

start

A-Z of Cheats

the biggest database of tips, cheats and codes anywhere

2 Extreme
Ramp Tricks
Note: Certain ramps give you more air, so do hard tricks to get more points. You can do more than one trick on a ramp.

Skate Board	△, ✕, □, ○
Snow Board	△, □, ✕, ○
Roller Blade	○, □, ✕, △
Mountain Bike	✕, □, △, ○
	✕, ○, □, △

Actua Soccer
Secret Team
When the FMV title screen is displayed, press Select + ↻ together and then go to Exhibition. Now by flicking through the teams, you'll see the Gremlin Showbiz XI are available in a tasty black football strip.

Adventures Of Lomax Lemming
Level Skip
During the game press: ⇩, Start, ⇧ (hold), L1 (hold), △, ○, ✕, □. A number appears left of Lomax. To skip a level, press and hold: ⇧, L1, Select + Start.

Helicopter Mode
Note: This only works when the Level Skip cheat is activated.
Select the chopper, then press L1 + □ to fly around the levels, just like Anneka Rice on Treasure Hunt.

Air Combat
Infinite Planes
If you complete the game on the Normal difficulty setting, when you play again you'll be rewarded with an infinite stash of every aeroplane. This comes in especially handy for attempting to play on the Difficult setting.

Loading Game Cheats
Just before the game switches to the loading screen, press and hold R1 and ○. The loading screen will now change to lots of jumping CDs. Whilst in this screen, press any of the following button combinations for the desired effect…

Loading Game
Whilst on the jumping CD screen, press ⇧ ⇦ ⇩ ⇨. If this has been done correctly, a small green monster will appear in the bottom left-hand corner of the screen. Now the next time the game loads, you'll be able to play a very strange bonus game. Allegedly, if you complete this bonus game, you can employ wing-men in the actual game for nowt.

Alternative Paint Jobs
On the jumping CD screen, press ⇧ ↓ ⇦ ⇧ ⇩ ⇧ ⇨, R1. If the code has worked, a small jet plane will appear in the bottom left-hand corner of the screen. You'll now be able to alter the colour of your plane.

Agile Warrior
Passwords

Level 2: 5433	Level 3: 0007
Level 4: 1213	Level 5: 1224
Level 6: 7154	

Cheats
Pause the game to enter the following:
Invincibility
⇦, □ x4, △ x3, ○, ⇩, ✕, △ x3, □
Makes you invulnerable.

Maximum Fuel & Armour
⇦, □ x4, ⇧, △ x3, ⇨, ○, ⇩, ✕, △ x3, ○
Gives you full fuel and armour. Rather handy.

Max Weapons (999)
⇦, □ x4, ⇧, ⇩, ✕, ⇨, ○, ⇩, ✕, R1 x4, L1 x4, R2 x4, L2 x4
Gives you an unlimited supply of all the weapons.

B1 Airstrike
⇦, □ x4, ⇧, △ x3, ⇨, ○, ⇩, ✕ x6

Colour Of Wingmen
On the jumping CD screen, press Start 10 times followed by R1. You will now have the added bonus of seeing your wingmen fly around in jazzed-up planes. Pointless but fun.

Different Paint In Two-Player
You can also alter the colour of your planes in two-player mode (if you're both petty). Input the following code on the jumping CD screen: ⇦ ⇨ ⇨ ⇩ ⇧ ⇩ ⇧ ⇧ ○ ○ △ △ △.

Air Combat 2
Model Display
By completing the game with a ranking of General, you'll open up this new feature on the options screen. Basically, it allows you to view every single aircraft in the game by bringing up a picture and letting you zoom in and rotate it around. It even tells you if it is an enemy or allied craft – which makes it easier for you to tell if you've found every single flyable plane in the game (there are 24 in total!).

Secret Missions
Upon accessing the Free Mission mode,

Brings on the Stealth bomber for a devastating strike.

Mesh Fog Editor
⇦, □ x4, ⇧, △ x3, ⇨, ○, ⇩, ✕, ⇩ x3, △ x3
Lets you alter the graphical shading, using □, △, ○, and ✕.

Overhead Map Translucency
⇦, □ x4, ⇧, △ x3, ⇨, ○, ⇩, ✕, ○ x5
Lets you seethrough the overhead map.

Mission Complete
⇦, □ x4, ⇧, △ x3, ⇨, ○, ⇩, ✕, △ x3, ⇩, ⇩, ⇩
Instantly completes all mission objectives.

New Camera Angles
⇦, □ x4, ⇧, △ x3, ⇨, ○, ⇩, ✕, ⇧, ⇩, ⇦, ⇨
Enter this code repeatedly for various new views.

if you play through the familiar missions again and complete them all on Easy, Normal and Hard modes, you'll be rewarded by two bonus missions that aren't in the normal game. These two can only be accessed in the Free Mission mode, so enjoy!

Dirty Dancer
⇦, □ x4, △ x3, ⇨, ○, ⇧, ✕, ⇩, ✕, ⇩, ✕, ⇩, ✕, ⇩, ✕, ⇩, ✕
Enter this code, then complete the current mission. On the next mission briefing, you'll see a sexy blonde girl dancing just for you!

All Missions Available
⇦, □, □, □, □, □, ⇧, △, △, △, ⇨, ○, ⇩, ✕, △, △, △, △, ⇧, ⇧, ⇧

Enable Ground Crash
⇦, □, □, □, □, □, ⇧, △, △, △, ⇨, ○, ⇩, ✕, □, ✕, ✕, □

Figures On Display
⇦, □, □, □, □, □, ⇧, △, △, △, ⇨, ○, ⇩, ✕, L1 + R2

All Missions Complete
⇦, □, □, □, □, □, ⇧, △, △, △, ⇨, ○, ⇩, ✕, Select, ✕, ✕, ✕, Select, △, △, △, Select, ✕, ✕, ✕

adidas Soccer
Female Commentary
Go to the in-game options screen by pressing Select during an Arcade match. Now go to the Audio option, highlight Commentary and press the □ and ○ together. If the cheat has worked, you'll have the choice of French, German or good ol' Blighty babes to offer their uneducated match opinions as the action unfolds.

Arcade Special Moves
Attacking
Back-heel (□ + ✕)
Back flick (△ + ○)
Predator shot (✕ + △)

Receiving A High Ball

Heading (hold □ or ○)
Bicycle kick (✕ + △)
Hand of God (△ + ○)

Receiving A Low Ball
Mega volley (✕ + □)
Diving header (✕ + △)

Defending
Nudging (△ + ○)
Two-handed shove (△ + ○)
Kung-fu kick (✕ + □)
Mega tackle (✕ + △)

Flashy Stuff
Juggling (✕ + □)
Mega run (□ + ○)

Dream Team
Select a Friendly match and press □ + ✕ + L2 + R2 on the Tactics screen. At the top of the screen it'll say 'Dream Team' to confirm correct entry.

Andretti Racing
Car Editor
While racing, press Start to pause the game, then move the cursor to Race Statistics. Now press and hold L1 + L2 + R1 + R2 + ✕ + ○ + Select. This will bring up a secret car editor menu,

3D Lemmings

Fun Level	Tricky Level	Taxing Level	Mayhem Level	
LEWISIAN	CINGULUM	ZOMBORUK	CHORIAMB	CAATINGA
BLIMBING	BESLAVER	SKILLING	GARGANEY	PENSTOCK
FANAGALO	ANABLEPS	WOBEGONE	KAOLIANG	SPRINGAL
DRICKSIE	QUINCUNX	BINDIEYE	MAROCAIN	BABIRUSA
KURTOSIS	TARLATAN	FRAXINUS	OBTEMPER	
GREGATIM		LINDWORM	TASTEVIN	**Animations**
WALLAROO	**Tricky Level**	CURLICUE	VELLOZIA	Enter at the
AVENTAIL	CABOCEERGE	HANEPOOR	BORACHIO	password screen
GAZOGENE	ROPIGA	IDEMQUOD	JACKAROO	and end-of-game
JINGBANG	BONTEBOK	BLANDISH	COOLAMON	animations:
DIALLAGE	EMPYREAL	MALAGASY	BANAUSIC	SPACEAAA
BUNODONT	LANGLAUF		FABURDEN	EGYPTAAA
NAINSOOK	NANNYGAI	**Taxing Level**	RECKLING	ARMYAAAA
YAKIMONA	SARATOGA	CHORIAMB	MIRLITON	MAZEAAAA
FUMITORY	QUINTAIN	GARGANEY	OPAPANAX	
	MUSQUASH	KAOLIANG	BIMBASHI	**Level Select**
		MAROCAIN		LAMPWICK

Other column entries:
ZOMBORUK, OBTEMPER, Mayhem Level column: TASTEVIN, VELLOZIA, BORACHIO, JACKAROO, COOLAMON, BANAUSIC, FABURDEN, RECKLING, MIRLITON, OPAPANAX, BIMBASHI, CAATINGA, PENSTOCK, SPRINGAL, BABIRUSA

enabling you to change many settings such as downforce, fuel consumption and tyre wear. Note that some of them can be reduced to below zero – try making the centrifugal force negative for a laugh!

Different-Coloured Cars
Start a new race and select the Begin Career option. At the Register screen, enter the following passwords:
Go Bears! – For stock cars
Go Bruins! – Formula One cars
At the car selection screen, you'll see cars with different paint and logos.

Alien Trilogy

The Ultimate Cheat
For all the weapons, unlimited firepower, invincibility and complete access to every level, enter this password:
1GOTP1NK8C1DBOOTSON

Jump Levels
In the password section, type G0LVL then a level number.

Xenomania Setting
2)**J3BBBBBBDWP8903BBBBBB BBMBBBXJBBB**
3)**LZBBBBBKCPB9N3DBBBCGB BMBBCD1BBB**
4)**FBBBBBBBMCPB9XLDBBBFB BBMBBCX1BBB**
5)**7LBB7BBB84PB9K3GBBBDLB LMBBDB1BBB**
6)**1LBBBBBB6WPB7F3GBBBJ2B BBBBDX1BBB**
7)**YGBJLBBB70PB9R3CQVCBG9 BBDBQFJ9CLB**
8)**WGBBBBBB0HPBJLBLL3BTGB LMBVFX9DVB**
9)**XQBJLBBBMHPBJNVFQVBTGB LMCBGD9HBB**
10)**4BBBGBBBFWPBQHLPN2BT LBLJCGG29FBB**
11)**3ZBJLBBB4HPBQQ3PQVBTL BLJCGHJ9FBB**
12)**03BJGBBBHWPB9BB0H3BTL BLDCBHZ9GVB**

Section 2
1)**Z3BBSBBB74PB9GVTJVBBBB BDB7JG9BVB**
2)**4BBLGBBBB8PB91B4PVBBBB BMB3JZ9C3B**
3)**4GBKVBBBZRPB9BB5QVBBB BBKCGKG9GLB**
4)**2BBQGBBBSRPBBBBB5BBB BBBBBBBKZ9GVB**
5)**0ZBBBBBD9V8PB9QWDHBBT LBLBCGLH9G3G**
6)**03BQVBD9VHPB9QWJM7BTLB LGCGL09HBD**
7)**1LBHXBD354PBJBCLPQBTBBL BB3MH9HBD**
8)**RQBBBBD988PBJCCVDBBTBB LBBVM09CBH**
9)**4BBQVBFGX4PBJJMVQGBTLBL BCGNH9FVK**
10 (QUEEN)
77BQVBDMYMPBJ24XPQBRLBLB BZNY9HBD

Section 3
1)**8ZBCLBC8RMPBDKMPBD3BS 1BLBB3PF9HBF**
2)**H7BBBBCSFRPB9DWLP3BC7B BLBLP09GVB**
3)**NQBBBBCSLMPBQHCLP3BC7 BBLBQQH9GVB**
4)**0GBBBBFGK8PBLH4KK2BBB BBLB7Q09CBC**
5)**KBBBBBFGCWPBLH4KJVBBB BBLB3RH9B3C**
6)**KVBBBBBRL0PB9BBBCLBSQ BBMB3R09CLB**
7)**03BBBBBB8CPB9BBXDQBSQ BBMCBSK9CLB**
8)**WVBBBBBBY8PB9BBXL33BN3 BLMB7509CBB**
9)**TQBBBBBB4MP9P3BDQBBBB BMCGTH9BBB**
10)**4VBJLBFGDMP89XVNQVBJLB BMCBT49F3J**
11)**4VBFNBCSZ4PB94BNF7BQV BBMB7VH9F3J**
12)**S3BBBBFGS0PB94BNKZBQV BBMBZV09HBL**
13)**Q3BQVBDXRCPB94BNQVBTL BLMBGWH9GBL**

Area 51

Control Boss
Go to the first level of the game. Shoot nothing but the first three STAAR members. The game should restart and you will be controlling the alien boss.

Shotgun Cheat
At the pause screen press △, □, △, ⇦, R1 to start with a shotgun.

Ballblazer Champions

Shrinking Rotofoil
On the password screen enter:
×○××○×
××××××
××△△××
□××××□
×□□□□×
Note: Code resembles a smiling face!

Master Dome
On the password screen enter:
○, L1, L1, R1, R2, L2
×, □, □, R1, R2, R1
R2, △, L2, R1, L2, ○
L2, R2, R1, ×, L1, R2
□, L2, R1, ×, R1, R1

Bases Loaded '96

Cheat Mode
Play a normal game and press △, □, ×, ○, ○, ○ on controller 2 .You will hear a piano noise, indicating that you have activated a cheat mode.

Any Inning
While in the cheat mode press × and the words 'lets go inning' will appear in the upper left-hand corner of the screen. Now press × repeatedly for the desired inning. For example: ×, ×, ×, × would bring you to the 4th inning.

Homer
While in the cheat mode press L1 – you will hear a voice say "home run". This lets you hit a homer every time.

Computer Takeover
While in the cheat mode press L2 – the computer will now play a game.

Battle Arena Toshinden 3

Random Select
Hold L1 + L2 + R1 + R2 at the character select screen. Press □, △, ×, or ○ while the selection box is moving.

Remove Display
Pause a fight. Hold ○ + △ + □ + × and press Select. This removes the continue, options, and reset selections. While continuing to hold all four buttons, press Select again. This removes the Life and Over Drive bars. To return the display to normal, repeat the code while pressing Select once.

Play As Sub-bosses
Beat the game with each basic character at level 3 or higher to unlock his or her sub-boss.

Play As Shou
Unlock all the sub-bosses, then beat the game with Vermilion at level 3 or higher.

Play As Abel
Beat the game with Shou at level 7.

Play As Veil
Beat the game with Abel at level 7.

Play As Naru
Beat the game with Veil at level 7.

Alternate Costumes
Beat the game with Naru at level 7. Use □ or × to select a character.

Instant Secret Moves
Beat the game with Naru, then set two or more of the shoulder buttons to special moves. Press all special move buttons at once to perform a secret move.
Note: This does not work for all characters.

Manual Camera Control
Enter the button configuration menu, highlight any shoulder button, and press L1 + L2 + R1 + R2. The controls for the shoulder buttons will change to camera view controls. The view may now be rotated manually.

Assault Rigs

Invincibility
Fancy blasting your way around without getting hurt? If so, pause the game and then press: ⇦, ×, ⇦, ×, ⇦, ⇦, ×, ⇨, ×, ⇨, ×, ×. If you see a message on the screen, you'll know that it's worked.

All Weapons
Again, press pause and input this code and you'll gain access to all the weapons in the game: ⇦, ⇨, ⇦, ⇦, ⇨, ⇦, ⇨, ⇨, ⇧, ⇩, ⇧, ⇧, ⇩, ⇧, ⇩, ⇩.

Codes
Here are the codes you'll need to get to the other levels…

02	■, ×, ■, ×, ▲, ■
03	▲, ■, ■, ●, ●, ▲
04	▲, ■, ▲, ▲, ●, ▲
05	■, ▲, ▲, ▲, ×, ▲
06	▲, ■, ●, ●, ×, ■
07	×, ■, ■, ■, ●, ▲
08	▲, ■, ×, ■, ▲, ▲
09	■, ▲, ■, ×, ▲, ×
10	▲, ▲, ●, ■, ×, ■
11	▲, ▲, ×, ▲, ●, ■
12	●, ■, ▲, ▲, ▲, ×
13	▲, ■, ●, ×, ▲, ■
14	▲, ▲, ×, ■, ■, ×
15	●, ×, ▲, ▲, ▲, ▲
16	●, ■, ●, ●, ●, ■
17	▲, ▲, ▲, ●, ▲, ■
18	■, ●, ■, ×, ■, ▲
19	×, ×, ■, ×, ▲, ●
20	×, ■, ×, ▲, ▲, ■
21	▲, ■, ▲, ■, ▲, ▲
22	■, ■, ▲, ●, ■, ▲
23	●, ×, ×, ×, ×, ▲
24	▲, ■, ■, ▲, ▲, ▲
25	▲, ●, ▲, ▲, ●, ■
26	■, ●, ●, ×, ■, ×
27	×, ●, ■, ▲, ▲, ■
28	■, ●, ■, ■, ■, ■
29	▲, ■, ●, ×, ●, ●
30	■, ●, ×, ●, ×, ■
31	●, ■, ×, ▲, ●, ▲
32	▲, ■, ×, ●, ■, ×
33	×, ×, ▲, ×, ×, ■
34	×, ●, ■, ●, ●, ■
35	●, ▲, ×, ▲, ×, ▲
36	×, ▲, ▲, ×, ×, ■
37	×, ▲, ▲, ×, ▲, ■
38	●, ×, ▲, ▲, ■, ●
39	■, ▲, ■, ▲, ■, ×
40	■, ×, ▲, ×, ×, ▲
41	▲, ×, ▲, ●, ■, ×
42	●, ×, ▲, ●, ×, ■

Battle Arena Toshinden

Play As Gaia
To play as the deadly warrior, Gaia, simply input the following code very quickly on the title screen when the text to highlight the option flows-in from either side of the screen: ⇩ ⇗ ⇦ □ (□ represents weak slash; if you have changed your button configuration, press the corresponding button). If the code has been entered correctly, you should hear a voice say "Fight!". Now go to the character select screen and highlight Eiji, and then press ⇧ whilst you select him. If all is well, Eiji's portrait will turn blank and the name "Gaia" will appear underneath.

Play As Sho
To play as the hidden Master of Darkness, input the same code you entered above and then let the game run into the demo mode. Whilst the demo is running, press Start on controller two to bring up the title screen again. Now press the following code very quickly on controller two whilst the text to highlight the options flows-in from either side of the screen: ⇦ ⇨ ⇦ ⇨ ⇦ □(□ represents weak slash, if you have changed your button configuration, press the corresponding button). As before, you should hear a voice say "Fight!" to indicate that the cheat has worked. Now go to the character select screen and highlight Kayin, and then press ⇩ as you select him. If all is well, Kayin's portrait will turn blank and the name "Sho" will appear.

Instant Special Moves
After entering the codes to play as Gaia and Sho, wait until the game switches to demo mode and then sit through the whole thing until the title screen comes up again. As the text to highlight the options flows in from either side of the screen, press ⇗ and weak kick on controller one. If the code has worked, you'll hear a voice say "Fantastic!" and the option text will turn white. To make the most of this feature, go to options and change you control type that that the L1, L2, R1, and R2 buttons are used for special moves. Now start fighting and marvel at your special moves at the touch of a button. If you press all four buttons and Select during a fight, you'll unleash your character's desperation move. Nnote that this cheat only works on Easy & Very Easy modes.

Config Select
After inputting the instant special moves cheat, wait for the demo to start and then press Start. As the text to highlight the options flows-in from either side of the screen, press the following combination very quickly on controller two: ⇦ ⇨ ⇦ ⇨ ⇦ □ (□ represents weak slash; if you have changed your button configuration, press the corresponding button). If done correctly, you'll hear a voice say "Fantastic!" and the option text will turn yellow. This cheat will allow you to use any control configuration on any difficulty setting.

Battle Arena Toshinden 2

Last Boss
At the title screen press ⇧, ⇩, ⇧, ⇩, ⇧ + ▲ to access the last boss.

Select Bosses – The Hard Way
Complete Battle mode on skill level 4. Then, when you go to pick your character, the random select will show the normal two bosses, Uranus and Master, which can now be selected. Complete Battle mode on skill level 6 (with no continues) and two more bosses will be selectable: Sho and Vermillion.

Now, to get the last secret guy, Grim, you have complete Battle mode on skill level 8 using Vermillion. Then on the title screen, press ⇦, ⇦, ⇨, R1, ▲, L2 and ■. You'll know if you've done it right, because you'll hear a bell.

To select a boss highlight the ? on the character selection screen and hold down the Select button to slow the scrolling. Now press ■, ▲, ● or × when the required boss appears.

Easy Select Uranus & Master*
On the title screen, as the menu items fly in from the left, quickly press (on controller 1): R1, L2, ×, L1, R2, ●. You'll hear a jingle if it's worked.
Now go to the character select screen and highlight the random box. By timing your button press, you'll be able to select Uranus or Master.

Easy Select Sho & Vermilion*
Once you've activated the Uranus & Master code, wait until the menu items fly in from the left again, and quickly press (this time on controller 2): ●, R2, L1, ×, L2, R1 (the reverse of the previous code). You'll hear a jingle if it's worked. Now go to the character select screen and highlight the random box. By timing your button press, you'll be able to select Sho or Vermilion.

Secret Moves
After beating the game when Sho and Vermillion are available, the menu box should turn green. This indicates that the instant secret moves feature is enabled and you can now perform them by simply pressing the R1 and R2 buttons together.

Armoured Gaia
It seems that this one only works on the Japanese import version. Select Gaia and before it says "Fight", quickly press ⇧, ⇧, ⇧, ⇩. If done right, about five huge chunks of armour will fly all around Gaia and mould to his body: you now have Armoured Gaia! Hits only cause half damage to him, but he is slow-moving. He also has a spectacular new desperation move.

Candid Camera!
On the options screen set all R1, R2, L1 and L2 to 'NOT USED' and then set the camera option to 'CONTROL'. Cycle through the R1, R2, L1, L2 options again until all of them are set to 'CAMERA'.

Now you can rotate the camera by pressing R1, R2, L1 and L2 when paused or fighting.
You can turn off the gauges by pausing the game and pressing ■ + ▲ + ● + × + Select on controller 1. The options menu will disappear. Press them again and the energy and overdrive gauges go. Press them again to get back to normal or Start to play without them! When you have no gauges selected you can control the zooming and vertical scrolling with R1, R2, L1 and L2.

***STOP PRESS:** Many thanks to the Welsh bloke who phoned up to correct our boss select cheats. He just called again to tell us you can hold Select to slow down the random box, making it easier to select the bosses. And guess what? Yes, we forgot to ask his name again! Cheers, mate, whoever you are.

Blam! Machinehead

Passwords

Level 2 (1.2)	SQDZFO5TJJ
Level 3 (1.3)	HYM7GODECM
Level 4 (1.4)	WFHIHOPOJC
Level 5 (2.1)	I54FHOD5BF
Level 6 (2.2)	E94FHOLLKJ
Level 7 (2.3)	MHLFHODTCM
Level 8 (2.4)	ALLFHOXGPU
Level 9 (2.5)	BDNJHOLLPU
Level 10 (3.1)	8JGIHO9B4V
Level 11 (3.2)	E9GGHOJIQH
Level 12 (3.3)	9F0JGOLZJD
Level 13 (3.4)	SKAGHO9P40
Level 14 (4.1)	JJ0BNN9FCM

a-z of cheats

continued

Level 15 (4.2)   EYWJHOP7BF
Level 16 (4.3)   JQNFHOT7BF
Level 17 (4.4)   7G9DAOMOCE
Game Over   6H9DAOQJ2F

Ammo Code
On either the title screen or main menu, enter this code:
○ x4, L1, ○, L1 x2, ○, L1, ○, L1 x2, ○, L1, ○, L1 x4
An 'infinite ammo engaged' message will scroll across if you've done it correctly.

Black Dawn
Pause the game and enter Select, L2, Select, R2 before the relevant code for each cheat:

Max Fuel & Ammo
△, △, △, ○

Max Weapons
L1, L2, R1, R2

Summon Wingman
□, □, □, ○

Mission Complete
△, △, △, ⇧, ⇩, ⇩

Screen Mode Toggle
⇩, R1, R2 (bypasses pause menu)

Upgrade Current Weapon
L1, L1, R1, R1

Blast Chamber
Infinite Lives
Go to the Main Menu screen and press the following: □, ⇨, L1, ⇨, ○, ⇧, ○, ⇧.
Now go into Games option and choose Solo Survivor. You'll have chosen the one-player mode, but your lives will never go down.

Level Passwords
Ziggurat	NAEMMAAB
Backstab	MAGDIEAH
Fall N Arch	NINKPDME
Fugitive	MJKKAMKC
Rainbow	JODPIGEH
Lavapalooza	ICJABNA

Blazing Dragons
Password
If only Flicker could win the tournament and marry the princess…
V?U5MK 4N6LUL OHW5CB.

Blood Omen
During the game, input the following codes for a bundle of goodies.
Blood Refill: ⇧, ⇨, □, ○, ⇧, ⇩, ⇨, ⇦
Full Magic: ⇨, ⇦, □, ○, ⇧, ⇩, ⇨, ⇦
All FMV: ⇦, ⇨, □, ○, ⇧, ⇩, ⇨, ⇦

Bogey Dead 6
Access All Fighter Jets
Go to the plane selection screen and enter the following code:
⇨, ⇦, ○, ⇧, ⇧, ⇩, ⇩, Select. You'll hear a shout to confirm that the code was entered correctly.

Access All Missions
Choose Mission Select from the Game Menu and press the following buttons: ⇧, ⇩, ⇨, ⇦, ⇦, ⇧, ⇩, △.. Once you've entered this code you should hear a shout to confirm that it was entered correctly.

Bubsy 3D
Secret Passwords
Choose Load Game from the main menu and enter these codes as the password.

XMUCHOLIFE – 99 Lives

XTOOROCKER – All rocket parts

XBNSCHTMMM – Go bonus rounds.

XLVLCHTMSB – Level select

XZOOMMERKB – Level warp (during the game, press ⇦ and Start to warp to different bits of level)

XDBUGLOCNC – Pause screen coordinates

Burning Road
Mirror Mode
Select Practice, pick your track, car and

Brahma Force: Assault On Beltlogger-9

Easy Mode
Hold ♫ + ✕ + □, then press Start at the 'Press Start Button' screen.

Hard Mode
Press L1, R1, L2, R2, □, ✕, △, ○ at the title screen.

Flight Mode
Complete the game in less than 1:30:00. Hold L2 + R2 and press ✕ on

controller 2. Then, during play, press R2 on controller 1 to climb, and L2 to dive.

Bonus Options
Use a memory card and complete the game in less than 1:30:00. Press Start after the title screen appears again. Choose the 'Special' selection on the screen to access level selection,

view FMV sequences, enter sound test mode, and other options.

End Game Bonus
After completing the game, regardless of time required, hidden areas will be visible on the map. Additionally, you will retain weapons and ammunitions. However, SAPUs will be reduced by half.

Casper
Drift Over Walls
This cheat enables Casper to glide over any walls so that you can get to unobtainable areas without having to painstakingly get the necessary keys and suchlike. To activate it, simply go to the top-left corner of any room and press the following code: ⇩ + L1 + R1 + Start. You should now notice that instead of pausing, the game will merely freeze. Keep those buttons held down and press ▲. The game will unfreeze and by pressing R1, you'll be able to float up over the walls.

Mega Secret Room
Now this is incredible! This cheat will allow Casper to stumble upon a hidden room that contains every morph icon, plus item needed to defeat his uncle bosses, plus loads of keys and other useful objects. In the main entrance, activate the drift-over-walls cheat and then go up the left-hand flight of stairs leading up to the first floor. Once on the first floor (the one with the blue doors), turn and face the staircase you just climbed and then press R1 to float upwards. The aim is to float high above and over the beam above the staircase and then keep drifting downwards until a new room comes into view.

Turbo
To make Casper travel faster than a speeding bullet, simply press ▲ + ✕, R1, R1, R1 at any point during play to make the mischievous ghost get his little white arse into gear! Please note that whilst accessing this cheat you will go into the inventory screen, so after you've finished pressing R1 for the third time, press ▲ again to return to the action.

Crash Bandicoot
Super Password
At the main menu enter the Password screen. You'll notice that there is only one line: don't fret, because as soon as you enter the first two triangles it will expand to three lines. It gives access to any level, 100% complete score, both keys and all gems.

▲, ▲, ▲, ▲, ✕, ▲, ▲
▲, ✕, ×, ▲, ○, ▲, ▲
▲, ○, ■, ▲, ×, ×, ×, ×

transmission. Now as soon as the race starts, turn your car around and go the other way. As soon as you pass through a checkpoint you'll be placed in first, and the other cars will turn and follow, although it'll take them a little while to catch up. Now race as usual, but you'll have three more tracks to play with.

Bushido Blade
Spurting Blood
Use the Broad Sword and beat your opponent. Now stand beside his head and move your right hand over it. Get it right and you can watch the blood spray!

Get Character With Gun
To get all the character endings, beat the chambara mode without any continues. You'll able to get the character with gun. Unfortunately you can only play with him in the versus mode. Highlight the spot next to Kanuki to select him.

Bust-A-Move
(Puzzle Bobble 2)
Modified Levels
On the selection screen (where you get Game Start, Time Attack, etc) enter R1, ⇧, L2 and ⇩. The single-player 'story mode' should now have the words 'Another World' below it and contain modified versions of the original levels.

Credit Cheat
Go to Option mode and highlight Credit. Press ⇦, ⇨, R1, R2, L2, L1, ⇧, ⇩. Then press ✕ repeatedly to increase credits before the timer runs out – with rapid button pushing, you can get them up to 29.

Character Select
Start a Puzzle game. When the stage map appears, press ⇦, ⇨, ⇧, ⇩. Then press L1 + L2 + R1 + R2 and a Character Select screen will appear. Use ⇦ and ⇨ to select a character and press ✕ to continue. You'll still see Bubby on the Map screen, but your new character will appear!

Castlevania: Dracula X
Play As Richter Belmont
Save any game with 190% or greater completion. Start a new game with the name Richter: he may now be controlled when the new game begins.

Cheesy
Level Codes
1	WESTONMARE
2	FOUNDATION
3	PANTALOONS
4	POLYNESIA7
5	LANDSCAPES

Croc
Passwords
1-1	ULLLLDDULULURRU	2-B1	ULDLRLDULRRDRRU
1-2	ULLLLDDULURDRRU	2-4	RDDURLURLRDURUD
1-3	RULULUURLRURLUD	2-5	LUUULUDUDRULULD
1-B1	DLURLDRLRLRRDLL	2-B2	RULURDURURDRRUD
1-4	URDLLDDULRRDRRU	3-1	DLURRURLULLLULL
1-5	RDDULURLUURLUD	3-2	RUDURDURURDLRUD
1-6	DRRRLDRLRRRDLL	3-3	RUDURDURDRULRUD
1-B2	DRURRRRLLLLRULL	3-B1	RDDURDURDRDURUD
2-1	RDLURRURLRURLUD	3-4	RULURLURURDLRUD
2-2	DRURRLRLRRDLL	3-5	RULURLURDRULRUD
2-3	RLRRRRLLLLLULL	3-6	DRURRRRLULRLULL

Colonization
Cheat Mode
Enter 'CHARLOTTE' as the name of one of the cities. Your total funds will increase to 50,000 and the map will be fully revealed.

Contra
Enter all these codes at the title screen:
Weapon Select
L2, R2, L1, L2, ⇦, ⇩, ⇩, ⇧
Unlimited Continues
L2, R2, L1, R1, ⇦, ⇨, ⇩, ⇨

Command & Conquer
Covert Operations
Input the following password:
COVERTOPS

All Passwords
GDI
2 Estonia	IY2E4RGPK
3 Latvia	VMNMUJFZP
4A Poland	1NXZDC3MK
4B Poland	LHGHL19AI
4C Belarus	LHY8GYVDS
5A Germany	W1N457LJ4
5B Ukraine	OXL3NYNNO
6 Czech Rep	1MVDCPIIM
7 Czech Rep	OX3CS3D4G
8A Austria	WMJ8FPOQH
8B Slovakia	AAY1YZS9J
9 Hungary	CSGU0J7AQ
10A Slovenia	Z6J3CUD9V
10B Romania	W5741QXPJ
11 Greece	PZBVQGKQK
12A Albania	0M86O28IO
12B Bulgaria	LWO3SMF6F
13 Yugoslavia	YM3XI0625
14 Yugoslavia	WMJQ8C0HG
15A Bosnia	GTJ2PW403
15B Bosnia	4QLR9NRLA
15C Bosnia	C9RO0JST0

GDI Special Ops
1	8PHJTYIP1
2	SZ4VH22RY
3	878FR0G1M

GDI Covert Ops
Blackout	GT1BEQHY8
Hell's Fury	8PH1RPW9W
Infiltrated!	SHDZUI8ID
Elemental Imperative	8PZAIF13P
Ground Zero	GT1TAEXF9
Twist Of Fate	C9RO8NZGU
Blindsided	W15VEC3SQ

NOD
2A Egypt	C99FAXKW8
2B Egypt	KDTPX9WPE
3A Sudan	EDT4LLS9D
3B Sudan	JFBS8WWVM
4A Chad	JY2RPNB0L
4B Chad	4QHTTEY4B
5 Mauritania	W15DASRS8
6A Ivory Coast	9QYUCB63B
6B Benin	208F7432R
6C Nigeria	Q0WRYGFWX
7A Gabon	GTJKWOJDK
7B Cameroon	OX3UJ0V6Q

7C Central Afr Rep	C9R67C70W
8A Zaire	OH1Y3FSC2
8B Zaire	GTJKE8W7B
9A Egypt	Y4UMW1NWE
9B Egypt	3NJDSOKII
10A Angola	BBK5ONRL4
10B Tanzania	MILZJC113
11A Namibia	OX3UKOP94
11B Mozambique	GTJ26Z72A
12A Botswana	A9G1KD5FJ
12B Botswana	CSZZGEJ8H
13A South Africa	W3C6NH4OV
13B South Africa	AJ5CEQE7I
13C South Africa	25UJG3YHZ

NOD Special Ops
1	0LXRXJOY5
2	03O5MO802

NOD Covert Ops
Bad Neighbourhood	C99X6L0D9
Deceit	SHVQLLFOX
The Tiberium Strain	W1N4V4TK8
Cloak & Dagger	C99FJ8DM5
Hostile Takeover	C99F1A8VH
NOD Death Squad	0LF0D3T25
Under Siege: C&C	457E1D682

Map Code
On the title screen hold L1 + L2 + R1 + R2 + □ + ○, then press Start and select 'Password' or 'New Game'. Keep holding the six buttons until the level begins – including when you're entering a password!

Cheats
These codes work for both GDI and NOD sides. Enter during play:

Instant Nuclear Strike
⇨, ⇩, ⇦, ⇨, ⇩, ⇦, ⇨, ✕, ⇧, ✕

Instant Ion Cannon
⇨, ⇩, ⇦, ⇨, ⇩, ⇦, ⇨, ✕, □, △

Instant Air Strike
⇨, ⇩, ⇦, ⇨, ⇩, ⇦, ⇨, ✕, □, ○

Extra $5000
⇨, ⇩, ⇧, ⇦, L1, ⇦, ⇦, ⇩, ⇧

Reveal All Map
○, ○, ○, ⇧, ○, □, R1, ○, ○, ○

Descent
Cheat Codes
Input these handy cheat codes during play – NOT while the game is paused. A woman's voice will say "Cheater!" and an on-screen message will appear to indicate that each one's worked.

Full Level Access
△, ■, □, △, ✕, ○, △, ⇧, ⇦, □
After inputting code, quit the game and select new game from the main menu. Two extra difficulty levels will have appeared. When you reach the galaxy map screen, you can move

around and start the game at any stage – including secret ones.

All Keys
□, ✕, ○, △, ✕, △, ✕, △, ✕, ✕
You can go through any door on the current level.

Mega Weapons
△, □, ○, ✕, □, ✕, △, □, ✕, □
Gives you a huge supply of the most powerful weapons.

Invulnerability (on/off)
I, △, □, □, ⇩, △, □, □, △, △
Gives you invulnerability. When you reach the

You can't be harmed. To deactivate, enter the cheat again.

Turbo Mode (on/off)
□, △, ○, ✕, ○, □, ✕, ○, △, ✕
Makes the gameplay faster. To deactivate, re-enter the cheat.

Shield Recharge
△, △, ✕, △, ✕, □, ✕, △, △, ✕

Bright Display
■, △, ○, ■, ⇩, ✕, ○, △, ■, ○, ✕, △

Criticom

Level Codes
From the options screen, select Load/Save, then enter the following codes next to each character to increase their ranking and access more moves.

YENJI
Level 2: Spid
Level 3: Star

SGT EXENE DULALT
Level 2: Sphe
Level 3: Wing

DELARA ZERAL
Level 2: Phan
Level 3: King

DAYTON
Level 2: Sier
Level 3: Eter

DEMONICA
Level 2: Gone
Level 3: Worl

GORM
Level 2: Cham
Level 3: Marv

SID
Level 2: Odth
Level 3: Batm

SONORK
Level 2: Play

Animation Code
Use this for any character and it takes you to their end-game sequence:
TTAM

Movie Player
L2, L1, R1, R2, ⬆, ⬅, ⬇, ➡

Bamboo Arcade
R2, R1, ➡, ⬅, L1, L2

Bamboo Gyruss
L2, L1, ⬅, ➡, R1, R2

The Crow: City Of Angels

Level Codes
At the main menu, highlight the continue option to enter a password:h
Pier: △X△△□X○
Boat: XXXX△□X○
Tomb: △O△O□△△OX○

Dark Forces

Level Select
Select 'Restore Game' and enter the following code. Then select 'Start Game' and you'll have the choice of all 14 levels.
P3NDLDQNY2

Cheat Menu
To access the cheat menu, just press the following during play:
⬅, ●, X, ⬅, ●, X, ⬇, ⬆, X

If entered correctly a cheat menu will appear. The options are:
Invincible – Can't be killed (deflects weapon attacks)
Coords – Provides position coordinates
Supermap – Fills in HUD map completely
Pogo – Propels you to normally inaccessibly high places
Pal Mode – Changes Video Mode (Note: not recommended)
Max Out – Provides you with maximum weapons & equipment
Game Won – See 'Level Skip' cheat below
Ponder – Freezes enemies
Return To Game – Resume

Grave: X△X△□XX△□○
Church: △△△△△□□X○
Day o' Dead: X△X△□○○X□○
Club: △○△○○△X○□○
Tower: XX○X□□X△○
Borderland: △XXX○□△□
Finale: XXX○□□XX△○

Crusader: No Remorse

Mission Passwords
Select 'Load Game', then 'Teleport To Mission' to enter the level password.

gameplay (what else!)

Level Skip
When in the cheat menu (see above for how to access this), toggle the 'Game Won' option to on (green). Now exit the cheat menu and pause the game.
Another menu will appear with the following options:
Game Paused
Return To Game
Next Mission
Abort Mission
Choose 'Next Mission' to skip to the next level.

Passcodes
2. Talay: Tak Base Y7B5T7S183
3. Anoat City !VHDBMBMXZ
4. Research Facil. 9WJHBLCN00
5. Gromas Mines 8XKGBKDPZ1
6. Detention Centre 7YBKBJFL22
7. Ramsees Hed Y7C4L7Q193
8. Robotics Facility X8D3L6R2C4
9. Nar Shaddaa W9F635SZB5
10. Jabba's Ship V!Q534T0F6
11. Imperial City NVHL4LFQ1R
12. Fuel Station MYGM!KBR2S
13. The Executor LXFN4JCSZT
14. The Arc Hammer 205F6HJT0V

2	FWQP	3	PLRQ
4	SZNF	5	TD5S
6	J1BT	7	K2CV
8	N3DW	9	M4FX
10	X5GZ	11	C6HO
12	D7J1	13	F8K2
14	FGL3	15	JFM4

Crime Crackers

Animation Select
At the title screen press ⬆, ⬇, ⬇, ⬇, ⬅, ⬅, ➡, ➡, Select. The word 'Start'

will turn to 'Animation'.

Debug Mode
At the title screen, press:
R1, R1, L1, L1, R2, R2, L2, L2, ⬅, ➡, □, Select, Start

Cyberia

Three For All
Enter NEMROSIM as your name at the beginning of the game. This will enable three things…
1. You can select difficulty level 1 for both Arcade and Puzzle modes.
2. You can 'load' any game save point, as all passwords are automatically put in for you.
3. Blood. Not that much, but it is uncensored. The Slice-O-Matic death scene proves that.

Credits
At the terminal password screen ('GENIUS'), you can enter two different passwords to get the Sony developer's credits…

Destruction Derby 2

Passwords
Enter Race Type, then select Championship mode. Now enter your name as the following:

All Tracks
MACSrPOO

Animated Credits
CREDITZ!

FMV
ToNyPaRk

Note: After you type it in you'll have to go back and start a new Practice race to play the new tracks.

Descent Maximum

Cheat Mode
Enter the following information in the keys section to activate the cheat.

Effect	Keys	Nickname
Weapons, Energy & Shields	□▲○▲□X○△□X	ACE
Weapons, Energy, Shields, Keys & Level Select	△▲○X△▲△X △□X	$40
All Keys	□△X△○△X△X△	MIK
Toggle Invincibility	△X▲○X▲□△○△	DCD
Full Shields	△X○▲□X▲○X□	BUG
Toggle Cloak	X△○▲□△X△△○	RED
All Accessories	□△○XX△X○□○X	TOY
Turbo	△X○□○X□△○XX	SVT
Extra Life	△X▲○X△X△X○	+1 UP
Toggle 'Go Wingnut' Mode	△○△▲□△X△□X○	4AD
Fast Robots That Fire Slowly	X△□□△□○X△X	JAVA
Colours	△X○▲□△X△○X	LSD
Acid Mode	□△○□△□△X○X	ACID
Hello Minnie Mode	X○X○X○X○X○	XO

Die Hard Trilogy

Cheats
To activate any of the following, pause the relevant game and hold R2 while entering the code. Pressing the final button in the sequence should automatically unpause the game, so you'll know if it's worked.

Die Hard 1

Level Skip
⬇, ○, ⬅, □, ⬆, □, ⬅
Now press Start on controller 2 to access a level skip: press Right to cycle through the levels.

Invincible Mode
⬅, ⬇, ⬆, ⬆, □
It doesn't matter how matter times you're shot, you never die.

Unlimited Ammo
⬅, ⬆, ⬇, ⬇, □, ⬅

When first entered, this gives you a shotgun with infinite shells. Simply re-enter the code to switch to the other weapons, all with unlimited ammo!

50 Grenades
➡, □, ⬇, ○
Gives you 50 standard grenades to throw around.

Skeleton Mode
△ x 10, ➡ x 4
This turns all the baddies into skeletons, while the hostages appear blue.

Reverse Controls
⬇, □, △, ➡.
This reverses your controls, although why you'd want to do this is questionable.

Silly Mode
⬇, ○, ○, ⬇, △, ⬇
The baddies will bend over to fire between their legs!

Fat Mode
➡, □, □, ⬇
Puts pounds on Bruce and all the hostages!

Coordinates
⬅, ○, ⬇, □
Puts coordinates on screen, plus strange wire-frame objects.
Speech Speed
⬇, □, □, ○
Repeat to alter speed of speech, from ultra-slow to helium high!

Screaming Plants
○, ○, □, □, ⬅
The plants will scream in pain when you shoot them!

Floating Dead
⬇, □, △, ⬅

Dead enemies will now float to heaven.

Die Hard 2

Invincible Mode
⬇, △, ⬅, □
Although you still get hurt, you won't die when you lose all your lives. To turn off invincibility, re-enter the cheat.

Select Weapon/Map Editor
⬅, ⬆, ⬇, □
Now press △ during play to change your current weapon.
Press Start again to access the Map Editor. You can now scroll around a map of the current level with your and the baddies' movements shown by coloured lines. You can even move stuff around. Press Select to move around freely in 3D, using Up/Down to zoom in and out, and L1/R2 to look up and down.

Maximum Specials
⬅, □, ⬅, ○, △, ⬇
Gives you 99 grenades and 99 rockets to cause total devastation!

Fergus Mode
○, ⬇, ⬇, □, X, □
This makes all the people look like Probe Entertainment boss, Fergus McGovern – even the women!

Odd-Shaped People
⬅, △, ⬅, ⬇
The people are now either extremely tall or short and fat!

Skeleton Mode
⬇, □, △, ⬇
To return them to normal, enter the cheat again.

Die Hard 3

No Clock/Level Skip
⬅, ⬆, ⬇, □. Various letters and numbers should appear on screen. On the second controller, press Start and some cheat options will appear.

Press △ to toggle the clock off/on. Move Right on the D-pad to advance through the levels. Also while playing in this mode, pressing ○ on the second controller will advance to the next bomb.

Infinite Lives
⬅, ○, ⬆, ⬇, □, ⬅
Take as many attempts as you like to defuse the bombs.

Infinite Turbos
○, ○, □, ⬇, ⬇, X, X
Speed around town to reach the bombs with ease.

Infinite Super-Turbos
○, ⬅, ⬇, □, △, ⬇
Even better, keep jumping right over the traffic at high speed.

Giant Cars
⬅, △, ⬅, ⬇. All the cars are gigantic!

Extra View
⬇, ○, ⬇, ○. You can now select a new Chase Car view.

Flat Shade Mode
⬇, ⬅, ⬅, ➡, ⬅, ➡, ⬇, ⬅, ➡
Turns off the texture-mapping for flat-shaded polygon graphics.

Fergus Mode
○, ⬇, △, X, □
Not only do all the people look like the Probe boss, but hundreds of Fergus faces float around like balloons!

Slow Motion
⬅, ○, ⬅, ⬇, ⬇
Slows the action down to a snail's pace.

Odd Mode
○, □, ⬇, ➡
Repeat the code to switch between three very strange views: flattened, stretched, and extreme close-up.

Weird Buildings
⬅, □, ⬅, △, X, ⬇, ⬇
Causes strange slumps in some of the buildings.

Car Hanger
⬅, ○, ⬅, ⬅, □, ⬇
Makes a toy car hang above the windscreen on the Inside view.

Cloudy Sky
⬇, □, △, ⬇, □, □, △
The sky goes all dark and cloudy.

X-Files Mode
This cheat only works properly on the Central Park 1 level, so use Level Skip to get there. Once in Central Park, pause the game and highlight 'Quit'. Hold R2 on controller 1 and press ➡, □, △, ⬇, X, X, X and a 'Roswell' screen should appear.

Blue Pram
On Die Hard 3, you can get a new car that looks like a bright blue pram! To get it, go to level 12 (you can use the level skip if you want – see cheat above). Now pause the game, hold R2, and press ⬅, ⬆, ⬇, □ (the first part of the level skip cheat) to bring up the letters and numbers. If you hadn't worked it out already, the red and white numbers in the middle of the screen are coordinates which go up or down depending on which direction you travel: east moves the first number up; west moves the first number down; south moves the second number up; north moves the second number down. So you know where you are.
To find the pram, go to the coordinates 45, 122. So that's first right from the start, then straight on until the next right, then straight on until the second set of numbers reaches 121 or 122 and the car park is on your right. In it, your brand-new pram should be waiting.

a-z of cheats

continued

Dynasty Warriors
Reveal Bosses & Extra Character
Sun Shang Xiang (Extra)
At the title screen press the following: ⇦, ⇦, ⇧, ⇩, ▲, ■, L1, R1. You'll hear a chime signifying correct entry.

Nobunaga (Extra)
Complete the game with Lu Bu, then press the following at the title.screen: ■, ⇧, ▲, ⇩, ●. You'll hear a chime signifying correct entry.

Toukichi (Extra)
Complete the game with Nobunaga, then press the following at the title screen: ⇩, ⇧, ⇦, ⇧, ●, ▲, R1, R2. You'll hear a chime signifying correct entry.

Zhuge Liang (Boss)
Complete the game with Guan Yu, Zhao Yun, and Zhang Fei.

Cao Cao (Boss)
Complete the game with Xiahou Dun, Dian Wei, and Xu Zhu.

Lu Bu (Boss)
Complete the game with Zhou Yu, Lu Xun, Taishi Ci, Diao Chan, Zhuge Liang, and Cao Cao.

Note: All characters can be selected at the character select screen by moving off to the left or right of the screen once they have been activated.

1. TNRUB_SDC_NOILLIB_A ('_' = space)
2. _REEB_OROPPAS_KN IRD (that's a space at the front)

Cybersled
New Sleds
Once the game has loaded, on the screen saying 'Press Start Button', enter this button combination:
⇧, ⇦, ⇧, ⇦, ⇧, ⇩, ⇧, ⇦, ⇩, ⇦, ⇧, ○

Darklight Conflict
Cheats Menu
Go into the options menu and press the following:
⇩, ⇧, ⇦, □, ⇦, ●, L1, R1, ○
Now exit to the previous menu. You should now see an menu full of cheats.

Defcon 5
Hidden Game
Hidden deep inside this game you'll find a secret game. To find it, just go to any VOS terminal in the Defence Station and enter the 'Communications' area. Go to 'Local Communications' and when you come across a message about the option being unavailable, hit the △ button on controller 1.

Disruptor
Level Codes
1. □□▲✕○○✕✕○✕✕
2. ▲○△✕✕△○○□○○
3. △✕○✕△□○○✕△△□
4. △○○△✕✕✕□□□○
5. ✕□○○✕△△□✕○✕□
6. △○○✕○○✕○□
7. ✕✕△○○✕△△○□✕○
8. △○✕○✕△○□△✕□✕
9. ✕✕✕○○△□○✕△
10. ✕□✕△○□△✕○○○✕
11. △○○△✕✕○○✕✕□○
12. ✕△✕△○✕○□△○✕□

Cheats
Go to map by pressing Select and turn real time off by pressing L1, then enter the code:
△, ✕, ✕, ○, ✕, △, □, □   Full Life
✕, □, △, △, ✕, ○, △, ✕   Full Ammo
○, ○, □, ○, △, ✕, ✕, ○   Invincibility
□, △, □, □, ○, □, ○, △   All weapons

Double Dragon
Secret Characters
At the character select screen, put the cursor on Billy, wait 3 seconds, move it to Marian, wait 3 seconds, move it to Chung Fu, wait 3 seconds, move it to Jimmy, wait 3 seconds. Then you have Shuko and Duke.

ESPN Extreme Games
Money Round
Pass through all the gates on a course and enter the bonus Cash Course, which consists of $5 and $10 gates.

Extra First Race Money
229 013 066 016 000 000 000 000 031
After you use this password, complete the first race (Utah) to get $1,110.

All Vehicles
237 190 190 080 000 000 176 113 219
Gives you a super athlete, all possible vehicles and $5030, having won the first two races.

Excalibur 2555 AD
Cheat Codes

91MBL-9HHY2-0T98R-WHKG97

Descent 2
Secret Levels & Codes
Zeta Aquilae, Level 2: FYHTK-9WDBB-4B031-HC#0R-WHKG97
Quartzon, Level 6: 58WRH-90KBB-5C0HK-6H#6R-WHKG97
Brimspark, Level 12: BDR8F-9*QBG-6FQ32-KH##R-WHKG97
Limefrost Spiral, Level 15: GWTN#-9VFBL-7GHC1-WW#98-WHKG97
Baloris Prime, Level 17: 5PK5#-9V4BB-8B*MJ-TW#98-WHKG97
Puuma Sphere, Level 22: 83Y6W-

Fade To Black
Passwords
To access any level instantly, enter these passwords.
Level 1: □, ■, △, ✕, ■, □
Level 2: △, ✕, ✕, ○, ■, ✕
Level 3: ✕, ○, ✕, ○, △, ✕
Level 4: ✕, ■, △, ○, △, △
Level 5: ■, ■, △, ✕, △, ✕
Level 6: △, ✕, ✕, ✕, ✕, ○
Level 7: ○, △, △, ✕, △, ■
Level 8: □, □, ✕, △, ■, □
Level 9: △, ✕, ✕, △, ○, ■
Level 10: ✕, △, ■, □, △, ✕
Level 11: ○, ■, ✕, ■, □, ✕
Level 12: ✕, △, ✕, □, ✕, ■
Level 13: ✕, ✕, ○, △, ○, ■

Cheats
Ignore all 'Invalid Code' messages

when using them. First, you need to enter the…

Cheat Activation Code.
□, △, ✕, ○, □, △
Now leave the password screen and re-enter it. Enter any of these codes to produce the desired effect…

Play All Movies
□, ✕, ○, △, ○, ✕

Infinite Shield Code
■, ○, ○, ■, △, ✕

Invincibility Code
△, ✕, △, △, ■, ○

Level Select
○, ○, △, ✕, □, ■

Press Start to pause the game, then:
Full Health
△, △, △, □, □, □, □, □

Full Sword Power
△, △, □, □, ○, ○, □, □

Skip Level
□, ○, □, △, △, ○, △, △,

Show Collision Boxes
○, ○, ○, ○, □, ○, ○, □
Then select 'Continue' and press 'X' to active the cheat. Or press Start.
Note: You can only enter one cheat at a time, so pause, enter first cheat, unpause. Then pause again and enter second cheat, unpause, and so on.

Special Moves
Spinning Slice – ✕, △, ○, □
Roundhouse Swing – ✕, □, ○, △

FIFA '97
Alter Shadows
Start a match, then go to the instant replay mode. Hold R1 and move the D-pad ⇧ and ⇩. This lets you change the size of your players' shadows. Now exit out of the replay and continue.

Motty Playing
To see John Motson or any of the EA crew play football, go to a friendly match, choose the USA league and select Dallas or New York.

Motty Singing!
You can also hear Motty singing by selecting track six on the audio CD player!

Fighters' Impact
Alternate Costumes
Highlight a fighter ,then hold ○ + □ and press Start.

Small Characters
Highlight a fighter on the character selection screen. Then hold ⇩ + ✕ + ○ and press Start.

Deformed Characters
Push Select (x10) at the title screen. A chime will confirm correct code entry.

Paper Cut-out Style Characters
Push ⇦ (x10) at the title screen. A chime will confirm correct code entry.

Stick Figure Characters
Push ⇦ (x10) at the title screen. A chime will confirm correct code entry.

Hidden Characters
Complete the game four times to unlock the four hidden characters.

Firestorm:
Thunderhawk 2
Codes
South America 1: Arms Running
1   PVH7CVEVEBDU44I

Doom
All Weapons & Ammo
Pause Game, press ✕, ▲, L1, ⇧, ⇩, R2, ⇦, ⇦

Invincibility
Pause Game, press ⇩, L2, ■, R1, ⇦, L1, ⇦, ●

Level Warp
Pause Game, press ⇦, ⇦, R2, R1, ▲, L1, ●, ✕

X-Ray Vision
Pause Game, press L1, R2, L2, R1, ⇦, ▲, ✕, ⇦

All Map Plus Objects
Pause Game, press ▲, ▲, L2, R2, L2, R2, R1, ●

All Map
Pause Game, press ▲, ▲, L2, R2, L2, R2, R1, ■

Ultimate Doom

Level	Health	Armour	Weapons	Password	Title
02	125%	200%	All	CR!3WDD3DB	Plant
03	200%	200%	All	3JJCMK8W64	Toxin Refinery
04	200%	200%	All	03LTJ0Y!02	Command Control
05	200%	200%	All	H33!1HFTHK	Phobos Lab
06	200%	200%	All	04MSKZX9Z1	Central Processing
07	125%	200%	All	YTTLCXXLXV	Computer Station
08	200%	200%	All	09SMBY04YW	Phobos Anomaly
09	200%	200%	All	7KKBLD7V53	Diemos Anomaly
10	100%	200%	All	FM4217GSGJ	Containment Area
11	200%	200%	All	H!!3WDGLDB	Refinery
12	200%	200%	All	07QPDW26WY	Deimos Lab
13	350%	150%	12346	WTXQ9C3W12	Command Center
14	100%	200%	123456	RBR4G!LDLN	Halls of the Damned
15	300%	175%	1236	WTXQ9C3W11	Spawning Vats
16	50%	75%	1234567	548C7DFWYX	Hell Gate
17	100%	125%	1234567	JOC89DZPQS	Hell Keep
18	100%	125%	1234567	JGB9CT0NRT	Pandemonium
19	100%	200%	All	9QLTKR0!02	House of Pain
20	100%	200%	All	78M63QX921	Unholy Cathedral
21	200%	200%	All	S!61FHVQJG	Mt. Erebus
22	200%	200%	All	33QHFTT6WY	Limbo
23	200%	200%	All	VBGQPJ!Y46	Tower of Babel
24	200%	200%	All	ZYKTLW7V53	Hell Beneath
25	200%	200%	All	0DJSM4HW64	Perfect Hatred
26	200%	200%	All	LS5YPTCRKH	Sever the Wicked
27	200%	200%	All	ZDJSMVRW64	Unruly Evil

28	200%	200%	All	1YKTX4QV53	Unto the Cruel
29	200%	200%	All	XKF6R8LZ97	Twilight Descends
30	200%	200%	All	DJX07Q4HTR	Threshold of Pain

Doom 2

Level	Health	Armour	Weapons	Password	Title
31	200%	200%	All	C0W1!QNJQS	Entryway
32	125%	200%	All	VM!3V1D3DB	Underhalls
33	150%	200%	All	W394W2DMFC	The Gantlet
34	150%	200%	All	ZQ58ZKJRKH	The Focus
35	175%	200%	All	Z758ZKJ8KH	The Waste Tunnels
36	200%	200%	All	5C2V3DQBNL	The Crusher
37	200%	200%	All	NCKBLX7V53	Dead Simple
38	200%	200%	All	1Q580FCRKH	Tricks and Traps
39	100%	200%	All	HTMSKZZ9Z1	The Pit
40	200%	200%	All	WS58ZKCRKH	Refueling Base
41	200%	200%	All	CSNRG2W820	O of Destruction!
42	200%	200%	All	WT670JBQJG	The Factory
43	200%	200%	All	DQLTJ1Y!02	The Inmost Dens
44	100%	200%	All	2N94VFFMFC	The Suburbs
45	200%	200%	All	CQLTJ0Y!02	Tenements
46	200%	200%	All	WR492GDSGJ	The Courtyard
47	200%	200%	All	PFFGXH3777	The Citadel
48	200%	200%	All	JWCJV2X479	Nirvana
49	200%	200%	All	CJJTM35964	The Catacombs
50	200%	200%	All	M!T174XZXV	Barrels of Fun
51	200%	200%	All	5770MX2CDF	Bloodfalls
52	200%	200%	All	YJLW3PPCPM	The Abandoned Mines
53	200%	200%	All	DKKBLM58J3	Monster Condo
54	200%	125%	All	7L3!266DJK	Redemption Denied

Bonus Stages

Level	Health	Armour	Weapons	Password	Title
55	150%	0%	All	CKHDP33X35	Fortress of Mystery
56	200%	200%	All	OJ1W3PRCPM	The Military Base
57	100%	0%	1235678	WVX07TT0TR	The Marshes
58	250%	25%	All	XDV29SRKRT	The Mansion
59	150%	25%	All	644YL1Q9GJ	Club Doom

2	DRHVSV93EFDQ5LQ	
3	3BH3SV6QEJD24UA	

South America 2: Stealth Down
1	63G1SU4AAVTE5DQ
2	SFGTSU96AVTA4RI
3	U7GTSU96AVTM5M2

Cen America: Recapture Town
1	BFGPS1JUI7QE51Q
2	DRGPS1MQI7QA4L2
3	SFGPS1IMJBQMS6I

Middle East 1: Recapture Territory
1	4VHVS7TEQNDE4OA
2	77HBS6N6QNDA51A
3	23G1S69QQRDM4H2

Middle East 2: Oil Dispute
1	BFF9S1FU7HUE49Q
2	CJF1S1667LUA5DI
3	FFF0S16P7PUM47A
4	HRF0512L7TUISIQ

South China Sea
1	URGPS1IA3BUE5QA
2	M3F9S1LQ3FUA4NA
3	ONF9S1FU3FUM4JA

Panama
1	93G5SD9UNGGE4OA
2	VVG5SHUENGGA4SQ
3	JNGH4CPUNKGM5TI

Eastern Europe
1	L3GG4406VOEE5R1
2	F7GK5S2QV0EA41A
3	27GK50UMV4EM58Q

Firo And Klawd
Passwords
Back alley	MOOMIN
Back street	MOONPIG
Back street B	MOONPINGEON
Back roof	SNUFFKIN
Main street	LITTLE_MI
Main street B	LITTLE_MO
Vinnie's scrap yard	SOUP_DRAGON
Vinnie's scrap yard	BSUPER_DRAGON

Formula 1 '97
Arcade Hidden Tracks & '60s Mode
To reveal the hidden track in each arcade difficulty you must place first in every single race.

Goalstorm
Special Konami Team
To play with a top-notch Konami team, simply do the following cheat on the 'Press Start' screen, with the two footballers on it.
⇧, ⇧, ⇩, ⇩, ⇦, ⇨, ⇦, ⇨, ✕ and ○
By inputting the code on pad 1, the team will have the home strip on, and with pad 2, the players will be wearing the away strip. Now select any team and when they get on the pitch they'll have Konami strips on and look like they've got paper bags on their heads.

Gundam 0079: The War For Earth
Passwords
Scene 1	△△△△△□✕✕✕
Scene 2	□□△△△✕✕△✕
Scene 3	○○△△△△□△
Scene 4	✕✕△△△△□□△
Scene 5	○□△△△△□□△

View The Entire Game
✕○△△△△○□△
After inputting the code, be sure to select 'Playback' in options.

Gunship
Invulnerable Mode
1. At the loading screen (helicopter pic) after you get your mission orders, press and hold L1 + L2 + R1 + R2 for the entire load time.
2. When the mission begins you'll see the word 'CHEAT' in the top-left corner.

Hardcore 4x4
Select Time Trial from 'Race Type' on the menu, then start time trial. Select 'Edit Details' and then 'Edit Name'. Now enter the special codewords:

Choose Race Class
Enter 'MAINLINE' to choose the other race classes, pro and extreme. This also enables the Mother truck.

Raining Frogs!
Enter 'RAINFROG'.

Formula 1
Bonus Track
Choose a Single Race in either Arcade or Grand Prix Mode. Select any team, driver and track. When you reach the Race Qualify screen (Practice/Qualify/Race), hold down Select and press (quickly, as with all the following codes):
⇦, ○, ○, △, ⇨, ⇨, ⇨
A message will appear to indicate it's worked. Now start the current race and abandon it. Choose a Single Race in Arcade Mode again and, when you reach the Circuit Select screen, flick through the tracks to find the Grand Champion Bonus Track – in the shape of an F1 car!

Lava Mode
On the Race Qualify screen in a Single Race (as before), hold down Select and press:
□, ○, ⇧, ⇨, ⇧, ○, ✕
A message will appear to indicate that Lava Mode is activated. When you start the race, the track will now be made out of red-hot lava (well, it's coloured red anyway!), while bright orange flames stream from your rear tyres (achieved via a clever colour change for the usual smoke effect). Meanwhile, the rest of the scenery has been burnt to a cinder.
To leave Lava Mode, simply re-enter the code on the Race Qualify

screen – a message will indicate it's been deactivated.

Buggy Mode
Again, on the Race Qualify screen in a Single Race, hold down Select and press:
⇨, ⇧, △, ⇦, ⇧, □, △
A text message will indicate the mode has been activated. When the race starts, the usual cars are replaced by buggies (formed by a reduced car body and larger wheels). Although the handling and performance seems unaffected, overtaking is made slightly easier by the reduced width of the vehicles. To return to normal cars, re-enter the code on the Race Qualify screen.

Bike Mode
Choose a Single Race, then on the Race Qualify screen hold down Select and press:
⇩, ⇨, ○, △, ⇦, ⇧, □, △
A message appears to show Bike Mode's been activated. When you begin the race, the cars have been replaced by 'bikes' made out of two car wheels, one in front of the other! Again, the handling and performance is unaffected, and you can still bump into the invisible body of each car! It's a good laugh though. To return to normal cars, simply re-enter the code back on the Race Qualify screen.

Hercules
Passwords
L2 The Hero's Gauntlet:	Serpent, Medusa, Coin, Medusa
L3 Centaurs' Forest:	Centaur, Hercules Silhouette, Minotaur, Archer
L4 The Big Olive:	Centaur,

Coin, Serpent, Hercules Silhouette
L5 Hydra Canyon:	Coin, Gladiator Helmet, Coin, Soldier
L7 Cyclops Attack:	Gladiator Helmet, Pegasus, Hercules Silhouette, Archer
L8 Titan Flight:	Soldier, Coin, Coin, Lightning Bolt
L9 Passageway Of Eternal Torment:	

Gibberish Mode
On the Race Qualify screen in a Single Race, hold down Select and press:
⇦, ○, ⇧, ⇩, ⇧, ⇨, ○, □, □
This cheat totally garbles the commentary, making Murray Walker talk gibberish (so what's new?! – only kidding, Murray). Instead of describing the action, he comes out with totally unrelated random samples; eg "He's hit the tyres!" when you're still revving up on the starting grid.

German Mode
On the Qualify screen in a Single Race, hold down Select and press:
⇩, ⇧, ⇦, ⇨, ⇧, □, ○, ✕
Instead of Murray's scintillating race commentary, you get some German geezer prattling away monotonously as if it were a bowls match or something. Don't get too excited, mate!

Spanish Mode
On the Race Qualify screen in a Single Race, hold Select and press:
△, ○, ⇦, ○, △, ○, ⇨, ○
Viva España and all that…

Mode Mixing
Most of the cheat modes can be combined. For instance, you can have bikes or buggies racing in the fiery Lava Mode, as long as you enter the latter code last.

| Medusa, Soldier, Centaur, Pegasus |
| L10 Vortex Of Souls: | Soldier, Lightning Bolt, Soldier, Centaur |
| View All Movie Clips: | Pegasus, Soldier, Centaur, Soldier |

Hexen
Cheat Mode
Enter the options screen from the main

Secret Asteroids
Enter 'DUTCHMAN'. Now by pressing △, go back until you can select Options from the first menu. Select 'Credits' to play a special game of Asteroids. The controls are ✕ for fire and ○ to thrust.

Gex
Infinite Lives 1
In the first stage you can get 99 lives by going to the two secret areas over and over. First you need to run through and get all the collectables and free men. Go to the area above the camera and get the bonus area. Run through and get everything again, then go to the area that you have to crawl through and get the collectables and get the free man by running and jumping where the portal shows up. Run and jump again above the moon: there you will find another portal, but only go there after you have gone through the level at least once, then everything will be replaced.

Infinite Lives 2
In the stage 'Rock It!' in New Toonland, right after the third camera, jump onto the rocket. There is a downwards-pointing arrow made with flies. Jump down and there should be a hole there. Once down in the hole,

hit the yellow thing to the left with your tail to make it purple. Now there is an opening to the right. Inside is four extra lives and a remote control. Get them. Now jump into the spikes and die. You will start back at the camera. Jump back into the hole and repeat the above steps. Each time you die, the lives reappear so you can get as many as you want.

Pause Cheats
Hit pause, press and hold R1, then enter the following codes:

Infinite Lives: ⇧, ○, △, ⇩, ⇨, □, ⇩
Fire Balls: ✕, ⇧, ⇨, ⇧, ⇨, ⇨
Ice Balls: ○, ⇦, ⇨, ⇩, ○, ⇧, ⇨
Electricity: ⇨, ⇦, ⇨, ○, △, ⇨, ○, ⇩, ⇨
Super Jump: ✕, ○, ⇧, ⇧, ⇩, ⇨, ⇨
Invincibility: ✕, □, ⇩, ⇨, ⇧, ⇧, ⇩

FIFA '96
Secret Options
First, start the game, then pause it and select the options from the menu. Then enter one of the following codes. You should hear a 'click' if the code has been entered correctly. Exit the options menu, going back to the menu with 'Resume Game'. Press □ and you should get a secret options menu. You can then use Left/Right to adjust the settings. The ghosted options will require activating with further codes.

Invisible Walls
✕, ✕, ✕, △, □, □, □, △

Curve Ball
△, □, ✕, △, ✕, ✕

Super Power
□, ○, △, □, ○, △, □, △, △, △

Super Goalie
□, □, □, ✕, △, △, △, △

Super Offence
□, □, ○, □, □, △, ✕

Super Defence
△, △, △, △, △, ✕, △

Shoot-out
□, △, ✕, □, △, △, ✕, △

Stupid Team
□, △, ✕, □, △, ✕

Crazy Ball
✕, □, △, ✕, △, △, □, ✕

Dream Team
□, □, △, △, ✕, ✕, ○, ○

These extra codes need to be input the same way as before, but to access the options, quit the game and then go to the 'Options' menu. The new options appear at the bottom.

Federation (Data and Spock)
□, △, ✕, □, △, △, ✕, ✕

Dynamic Duo (Batman and Robin)
□, △, ✕, □, △, △, △

Default Colour Palette
□, △, ✕, □, △, △, △, ✕

Invisible Players
□, △, ✕, □, △, ✕, □

Oktoberfest
□, △, ✕, □, △, △, △

EA Custom
□, △, ✕, □, △, △, □, □

Formal Wear

Final Doom
All Weapons & Ammo
Pause game, press ✕, △, L1, ⇧, ⇩, R2, ⇦, ⇦

Invincibility
Pause game, press ⇩, L2, □, R1, ⇦, L1, ⇦, ○

Level Warp
Pause game, press ⇨, ⇦, R2, R1, ⇩, L1, ○, ✕

X-Ray Vision
Pause game, press L1, R2, L2, R1, ⇦, △, ✕, ⇨

Map All Objects
Pause game, press △, △, L2, R2, L2, R2, R1, ○

All Map Lines
Pause game, press △, △, L2, R2, L2, R2, R1, □

Level	Health	Armour	Weapons	Password	Title
2	125%	200%	All	LB173PPWPM	Virgil
3	200%	200%	All	ZSNDHQW820	Canyon
4	200%	200%	All	KS5WZH4RKH	Combine
5	150%	200%	All	J!670JKQJG	Catwalk
6	200%	200%	All	5VJTM00W64	Fistula
7	200%	200%	All	4FHDW39X35	Geryon
8	200%	200%	All	W9NRG2W820	Minos
9	200%	200%	All	C958ZKCRKH	Nessus
10	200%	200%	All	W!PQH1V71Z	Paradox
11	200%	200%	All	C!670JBQJG	Subspace
12	200%	200%	All	W7LTJOY!02	Subterra
13	200%	200%	All	K394TB8MFC	Vesperas
TNT					
14	200%	200%	All	Y8PQH1V71Z	System Control
15	200%	200%	All	F8670JBQJG	Human Barbeque
16	200%	200%	All	WXJCL68W64	Wormhole
17	200%	200%	All	CX1W3PRCPM	Crater
18	200%	200%	All	WYKBM57V53	Nukage Processing
19	200%	200%	All	CY2V4NQBNL	Deepest Reaches
20	200%	200%	All	WVGFN4!Y46	Processing Area
21	200%	200%	All	CVZY5MTFMP	Lunar Mining
22	200%	200%	All	WWHDP39X35	Quarry
23	200%	200%	All	CW0X6LSDLN	Ballistyx
24	200%	200%	All	W1DHQ!40!8	Heck
Plutonia					
25	200%	200%	All	!LQP7W26WY	Congo
26	200%	200%	All	W2FGR93Z97	Aztec
27	200%	200%	All	C2YZ8SLGSQ	Ghost Town
28	200%	200%	All	WZBKS8628!	Baron's Lair
29	100%	200%	All	HXZY5MMFMP	The Death Domain
30	100%	200%	All	0YHDP33X35	Onslaught

a-z of cheats

continued

menu and select 'Pad Config'. Hold R2 and press ⇨, ⇩, ⇨, △, ✕ at the pad configscreen. A sound will confirm correct entry. Begin playing and pause. Use the 'Cheat' selection from the menu to access God mode etc.

The Hive
Passwords
Just choose 'Load Option' from the Main Menu and when the game tells you that it can't find any files, the Passwords option will appear.

Impact Racing
Disco Fever
After completing the game, you're rewarded with a clever extra feature: the Virtual Jukebox! This lets you take out replace the game disc with any music CD and watch a load of coloured patterns on screen, reacting in time to the beat. Press Select to see the music infoand left/right to change tracks.
To go to the jukebox from the start, input 'JOURNEYS.END' on the password screen. Extra special passwords can be found by completing the game on each of the skill levels.

Level Passwords
As passwords are only given upon completing bonus levels, they're extremely precious. Here are few us get you started.

00OG4KBOMO4Q
Level 2, AR12, Double Laser

1MAT6XCE3OIL
Level 4, AR12, Missiles

0ZMAQKDS0OHG
Level 8, AR12, Quad Laser

00OG73BK26XK
Level 2, Destroyer, Double Laser

01F96MBWA79K
Level 3, Destroyer, Missiles

02MO4CCLQ84A
Level 5, Destroyer, Quad Laser

03HAV2DCMDU2
Level 7, Destroyer, Firewall

Debug Mode
Enter **RABBITBADGER** on the password screen to make 'Debug Mode' appear at the bottom of the main menu. This enables you alter the time limits, number of power-ups, enemy intelligence, and even switch the track type for each level.

Full Weapons
Enter **ALL.TOOLEDUP** on the password screen and start the game. You will have a fully supply of all the special weapons.

Bonus Levels
Enter **BONUS.LEVELS** on the password screen and start the game. Instead of playing the main tracks, you will play each bonus level in turn. This is a great way to practise them.

Invincibility
Go into the password section and enter:
I.AM.IMORTAL
When you start the game you'll be invincible.

Infinite Weapons
Enter **LOADSOFSTUFF** on the password screen for infinite ammo.

Final Level
Enter **ENDGAMELEVEL** on the password screen to play the last track.

2	IV73	3	AMQ3
4	NGH3	5	ZN03
6	WVQ3	7	HC13
8	1EZ3	9	UVM3
10	TZ93	11	U6Q3
12	2QJ3	13	KLS3
14	2XS3	15	81H3
16	8HU3	17	J5V3
18	VIH3		

Indy 500
Extra Menu Item
Press ○, ✕, △, □ three times at the title screen.

Drag Race
For one-player mode, highlight the 'Qualify' option on the Indy 500 mode screen and hold L1 + L2 + R1 + R2 + Start.
For two-player mode, hold L1 + L2 + R1 + R2 + Start at the handicap screen.

Alternate Replay Views
Hold Select and press L1, L2, R1, R2, △, □, or ✕ during the replay.

Iron & Blood
Play As Avatar
On the character select screen, hold ⇦ and press □. Release, then press ⇨ + ○. The cursor will finish up in the bottom-left corner and you'll now play as the baldie Avatar.

King Of Fighters
Extra Characters
When you are in the character selection screen, select Team Edit and enter this code: ⇧, □, ⇨, ○, ⇦, ⇩, ✕. Omega Rugal and Saisyu Kusanagi should appear

Boss Code
Choose Team Edit "Yes". Hold Start while pressing: ⇧ + ○, ⇨ + □, ⇦ + ✕, ⇩ + △. If it doesn't work, try again

Win Demo Code
This code lets you turn off the end-of-battle Victory Picture. Go to Options and then to Configuration screen. Press L1 + L2 + R1 + R2 simultaneously. You should hear a beep (sounds like entering the options) and the Win Demo Menu will pop up.

Escape Code
This enables you to exit the game at any time (except during loading) to the main

The Incredible Hulk
Level Passwords

World	Easy	Medium	Hard
Castle	70000F630A	60080FFB85	80100F8401
Ice	A0000A352F	90080ACDAA	B0100A5626
UFOs	C000010759	B008019FD4	D010012850
Maestro	300006D8BD	F01005616D	101005F9E8

Int. Track & Field
Change Swimsuits
On the Game Select screen, highlight 100m Freestyle, then press ⇧, ⇩, ⇩, ⇩, ⇩, ⇦, ⇦, ⇦, ✕, ○. When you start the swimming, the swimsuits will be changed to bikinis!

Hide Gauges
1. Go to the title screen.
2. Choose Start.
3. Enter any event and pause the game.
4. Press and hold L1, L2, R1, R2, □, ✕, △, ○
5. While still holding them, press ⇧ or ⇩ repeatedly to get the gauges to move off the screen.

Guest Appearances
Here's how you can see everything from Space Shuttles to dinosaurs:

Pole Vault – Space Shuttle
1. Clear the qualifying height (4.5 metres).
2. On the second attempt, set the pole

menu. During play, hold ○ + □ + ✕ + △, and hit Select. The menu will appear.

King Of Fighters '96
Fight As Bosses
Hold Start and press ⇧ + ○, ⇨ + □, ⇦ + ✕, ⇩ + △ at the character selection screen in any mode. Chizuru Kagura will be selectable to the right of Clark, and Goenitz will be to the left of Athena. Kick seven shades of **** out of the b*******!

Independence Day
After entering a password, enter the game selection screen and quickly press: ⇦, ⇨, □, ○, △, △, ⇩.

Plane Select
Enter MR_HAPPY as a player name (where '_' indicates a space).

City Select
Enter FOX_ROX as a player name.

Invincibility Option
Enter LIVE_FREE as a player name.

Fast Reload, Damage Bonus, & Weapons Options
Enter GO_POSTAL as a player name.

Kill Civilians & Wingman Options
Enter GODZILLA as a player name.

Extra Options
Enter TOURIST as a player name.

Cheat Mode
Enter DAB_DAB as a player name.

Passwords

Mission	Easy	Medium	Hard
Washington	DBKHN	DBKMO	DBKQO
New York	GBKHW	GBKMX	GBKQX
Paris	LLSHW	LLSMX	LLSQX
Moscow	NL9HW	NL9MX	NL9QX
Tokyo	R39JD	R39NF	R39RF
Oahu	T59HW	T59MX	T59QX
Las Vegas	Z99HY	Z99MZ	Z99QZ
Mothership	399HG	399MH	399QH

In the Hunt
Extra Continues
When your last ship has been destroyed, press & hold △ + Select. While still holding the buttons, press Start for an extra five continues.

Sneaky Trick

to 5.0 metres and clear it.
3. On the next pole setting, a Space Shuttle will fly by.

Shot Put – T-Rex
1. Get a distance that is composed of all the same digits (eg '55.55').
2. A huge T-Rex will visit the stadium.

Javelin – UFO
1. Tap a Run button once and you'll begin jogging towards the foul line.
2. As soon as you see the angle meter appear, press and hold the Angle button (get it above 73 degrees).
3. As soon as the meter rises, begin pressing the Run button rapidly.
4. Make sure you're at a high speed and let go before the foul line.
5. If you did it right, you'll hear some noises and a UFO will fall… with your javelin protruding from it!

Discus – Birds
Get a distance that matches metres and centimetres (eg '23.23').

Jet Rider
All Tracks Cheat
To enable all ten tracks straight away, rather than slugging away season after season, simply follow these instructions and all those wonderful tracks will appear as if by magic.
1. Go to the Options screen and change the Difficulty setting to Amateur. Then set the Trophy Presenter to male. Now return to the Main Title Screen by pressing Start, then enter the following on the player 1 pad: ⇧, ⇩, ⇩, ⇩, ⇨, ⇨, ⇩, ⇩, ⇩.
2. Now return to the Options screen by pressing ⊹ once, then press ✕ to enter Options. Change the Difficulty setting to Professional. Set the Trophy Presenter back to Rider's Choice.
3. Now return to the Main Title Screen by pressing Start and enter the following on the player 1 pad: ⇧, ⇦, ⇩, ⇨, ⇧, ⇩, ⇨, ⇩, ⇩.
If you've entered the code correctly, you should hear the usual 'Ker-ching' sound to confirm. Voila! All ten tracks are accessible to you, whether it be via single race, custom, or full season.

Special Codes
You gain access to these only after you've won a Full Season at Professional level on all ten tracks. Once you accomplish this, a bubble will appear on the title screen that says 'Codes Enabled'. Now each time

If you still can't finish the game with the above cheat in one-player mode, press Start on controller 2 before you die. You'll have a lot more lives to finish the game with.

International Superstar
Soccer Deluxe
Doggy Cheat!
Enter the following code on the title screen: ⇧, ⇧, ⇩, ⇩, ⇦, ⇨, ⇦, ⇨, ✕ + ○. If the cheat has worked, you should hear a bark. Now when you start a match, the ref and linesman will have turned into dogs! Don't expect any favours from man's best friends though – you'll still get booked for fouling on the pitch. It's a wonder the fans don't chant "The referee's a spaniel!"

Iron Man
X-O Manowar In Heavy Metal
Passwords
These will let you have full armour, boost, weapons, and 99 lives! On the password screen, enter one of these codes:

One Player End Level
C04A77077777777777777777

you beat the game with a different team, you'll be given a code by that team. Each team has two codes, and there is a final code presented by the crew from Singletrac themselves. Fortunately you only need to complete the game once, as you can enter any and all codes after the first time you complete the game.

Super Agility
⇧, ●, ⇦, L1, ⇦, ⇨, ⇦, ⇩

Zero Resistance
■, L1, △, ⇨, L1, ⇩, R2, △

Double Stunt Points
⇨, ⇧, ●, L2, ▲, ●, R1, R2

Show-Off Camera Enabled
▲, ✕, ■, ▲, L1, L1, R1, R1

Air Brakes
R1, R2, ⇦, L2, ⇧, ●, ⇧, ●

Rocket Racer
▲, ⇦, ⇧, L2, L2, ⇧, ⇧, ⇧

Unlimited Turbos
▲, ●, ⇦, R2, ⇧, ■, ⇩, ▲

Ice Racing
⇧, R2, R1, ⇦, L1, ■, ⇦, ⇦

Two-Player Computer AI Code
●, ■, R2, ●, ▲, L2, ⇦, ⇩

Two Player End Level
C02A77X77777777777777777

Lost Vikings 2
Infinite Energy
Input this code on the password screen (select 'Load Game'): CH3T
You can now start a new game or enter a level password to play with infinite energy.

Level Codes

1	NTR0	2	1STS
3	2NDS	4	TRSH
5	SW1M	6	W0LF
7	BR4T	8	K4RN
9	B0MB	10	WZRD
11	BLKS	12	TLPT
13	GYSR	14	B3SV
15	R3T0	16	DRNK
17	Y0VR	18	0V4L
19	T1N3	20	D4RK
21	H4RD	22	HRDR
23	L0ST	24	0B0Y
25	H0M3	26	SHCK
27	TNNL	28	H3LL
29	4RGH	30	B4DD
31	D4DY		

Johnny Bazookatone
Level Select
On the password screen, enter 'KRISTIAN'.

God Mode
On the password screen, enter 'PILCHARD'.

Bonus Level
At the beginning of the first level you start at the wall. Go to the right side of the wall (where it stops) and then jump up while holding the pad to the left. You will jump onto a secret walkway. Walk to the left and jump up again. You will enter the bonus level. Losing a life in the bonus level does not affect your lives in the game so just collect as much as you can get. When you have 1,000 music notes collected, you will get a extra life.

Jumping Flash
Start On Any World
On the title screen, press the following buttons to enter any world/stage:
⇧, ⇧, ⇩, ⇩, ✕, ✕, ⇦, ⇨, ⇦, ⇨, ✕, △, ✕, △
If you've done it correctly, the screen should turn red. Now press the Start button and use Left and Right to select a level.

Loaded

Cheat Codes
Go to the in-game options screen and hold down L1 and L2 for about ten seconds. Keep holding them and press the following key sequences. New menu options will appear for the various power-ups.
Health – ⇨, ⇦, ⇦, ⇨, ⇦, ▲, ●
Ammo – ⇧, ⇧, ⇨, ●, ⇦, ⇨, ●
Power – ⇨, ⇧, ⇨, ●
Lives – ⇦, ⇩, ⇨, ▲, ■, ✕, ●
Smart – R1, R2, ✕, ▲, ■, R1, R2, ●, ●, ■
Skip Level – ✕, R1, ▲, R1, ■, ●, R2, R2, ✕, ▲, ✕
Level Select – ⇧, ⇦, ⇩, ⇨, ▲, ●, ✕, ■, ✕, ▲, ■, ●

Secret Characters
All you've got to do is enter one of these two codes at the main menu to access the special characters. If you can get it to work, write in and tell us how, you might be in for a reward!

Nightstalker: ✕, ●, ✕, ●, L2, R1, ✕, ●
Cannonball: Select, ●, ✕, ●, ✕, R1, R2, ●, ✕

Kileak The Blood

Cheat
To start off the game with everything, follow these instructions. At the title screen, where the little 'sperms' are congregating, press ○ six times then rotate the D-pad three times, clockwise from Right. Then hit △, □, □, △, ✕, Start.

Invincibility
When the intro screen comes up, push this combo three times in less than five seconds: △, △, ⇦, ⇨, □, □, Select, L1, L2, R1, R2. The background will turn blue.

Lifeforce Tenka

All Weapons
Pause the game, hold L1 and press: △, R1, △, □, R1, ○, □, □. Then release L1.

Level Warp
Pause the game, hold L2 and press ○, ○, □, △, R1, □, △, ○. Then release L2.

Lone Soldier

To activate, pause the game and enter the following codes…
God Mode
⇧, ⇦, ○, △, ⇧, ⇦
Skip Any Level
⇩, ⇨, ○, △, ⇩, ⇨
All Weapons And Ammunition
⇨, ⇩, ○, △, ⇨, ⇩

The Lost World

Passwords
Standard
Hunter ☐☐△○✕○△○↑✕△
Velociraptor ☐☐△○☐△○✕☐△
T Rex △△☐☐☐○✕✕△△
Sarah ✕✕○○○△△○☐○

99 Lives, All DNA (beforehand)
Compy ✕✕○△☐✕✕○△□
Hunter ☐△○✕☐☐✕☐△□
Velociraptor ✕✕○△☐✕☐△○
T Rex ✕✕○△☐☐△✕△○
Sarah ☐☐△○✕✕☐△○△

Level Select
Enter the following password three times (the first two it will be deemed invalid):
☐✕○△△☐△○✕☐
You'll hear a chime and a level menu will appear. Press ⇦ and ⇨ to switch between the characters. You can also view the movies.

Machine Hunter

Enter on the password screen…
Unlimited Continues
URANUS
One Hit Kills
GRIMREAPER
Demo Droids
DEMODROIDS
Super Cheat

1. Go to the password screen.
2. Enter ???HOST??? as a password.
3. Go the Options screen and highlight 'Cheat'.

Macross: Digital Mission VF-X

View VFs At Different Angles
Go to the load/save screen after you have all your VFs and save your game (if needed). Highlight the blank box under the loading box and press ○. Choose one of the VFs from the displayed list. Press L1 or L2 to zoom and pan over the selected VF. To transform to Gerwalk, press Select, □. To transform to Battletroid, press Select, △. To activate special moves, press Select, hold R1, and press appropriate button.

Camera Controls
Use the following actions on controller 2 to adjust the camera while viewing the exterior of a VF:
⇦ : Rotate camera left
⇨ : Rotate camera right
⇧ : Rotate camera up
⇩ : Rotate camera down
△ : Pan up
✕ : Pan down
□ : Pan left
○ : Ran right
L1 : Zoom in
L2 : Zoom out
R1 : Zoom out
R2 : Zoom in
Start : Reset camera

Blue VF-1X-Plus Valkyrie
Exceed 500 kills by the last mission, then select the VF-1X-Plus Valkyrie as your fighter. Maxmillian Jenius's Blue VF-1X-Plus Valkyrie will be under your control. This fighter can only be used for the last mission.

Recover Missiles
Use controller 1 to pause the game. Then on controller 2, hold Select and press ○, ○, ○, ○, ○, ○, ○, △, □, ✕, and release Select .

Recover Special Attack
Use controller 1 to pause the game. Then on controller 2, hold Select and press □, □, □, □, □, □, □, △, ○, ✕, and release Select .

Debug Mode
Complete the game and save your status. Highlight the 'Continue' option and hold Select + ○ for ten seconds. The screen will turn black. Release ○, but keep Select held, and press ○, ✕, □, △, ○, ✕, □, △.

In-Game Reset
Press L1 + R1 + Select + Start during play.

Magic Carpet

Cheat Mode
On the options screen, enter △, △, ○,
□, △, ○, △, □. You can now select any level. Also, pause the game and press:
↵ □ for more mana
○ to restore world
△ for all spells

MK Trilogy

Access the ? Screen
Go to the options screen and highlight any of the four boxes. Hold L1 + L2 + R1 + R2 and then hold ⇧. If you've done it correctly you will here a 'boom'. You can now access the '?' in the options screen. Here are your selections:
1 Button Fatalities ON/OFF (See below for details)
Instant Aggressor ON/OFF
Normal Boss Damage ON/OFF
Health Recovery ON/OFF
Low Damage

One-Button Fatalities
To execute these, stand right next to your opponent and press any of the following buttons for the desired effect.
HP: Brutality
HK: Fatality 1
LK: Fatality 2
R2: Animality
R1: Friendship
LP: Stage Fatality
L2: Babality

Choose Your Background
In the character select screen, highlight Sonya and hold the Start button, then press Up on the control pad. If done right, you'll hear a low exploding sound. After you choose your character, you'll also get to choose your background. If two players happen to be playing, whoever enters the code is the one who gets to choose the background.

Shao Kahn's Treasure Chest
After you beat Shao Kahn, you can choose a symbol.
Box 1: Character Endings
Box 2: Fight Chameleon
Box 3: MK1 Classic Endurance Kombat
Box 4: MK2 Classic Endurance Kombat
Box 5: Random Prize
Box 6: Fatality Demo 1
Box 7: Fatality Demo 2
Box 8: Fatality Demo 3
Box 9: Super Endurance Kombat (All Females & Robot Ninjas)
Box 10: Battle With Shokan Champions (Bosses)
Box 11: Mega Endurance Kombat (All Ninjas & Chameleon)
Box 12: Supreme Fatality

Quick Exit
You can exit a game in the middle of any match by pressing the Start button and then Select. You'll then be asked if you want to continue with the fight or quit.

Play As Chameleon
To reveal the hidden character Chameleon, pick either Human Smoke, Ermac, Classic Sub-Zero, Scorpion, Noob Saibot, Rain, or Reptile. Before the round starts, hold ⇦ + HP + HK + RU + BL. Chameleon now has the abilities of the same colour ninja that he morphs into.

Classic Characters

Mortal Kombat 3

Play As Smoke
During the opening demo, wait until the Rayden screen appears, then rotate the joypad 360° clockwise until the 'Ultimate Kombat Kode' prompt appears. Quickly enter the kode Dragon – MK – Dragon – Goro – Skull – Goro by pressing: R1, △ x 6, ✕ x 6, ○ x 9. You'll hear Shao Kahn say "Outstanding!" and a message will appear to confirm the kode. Now the hidden robo-ninja Smoke is a selectable character in the one- and two-player modes.

Secret Cheat Mode
During the opening demo, quickly press ✕, ○, △, R1, R1, R2, R2, R1, R1. You'll hear Shao Kahn say, "You'll never win!" Now press Start. When the stone block appears with the word 'Kombat' in red, press Up to access a secret cheat menu.
'Free Play' gives you infinite credits in the one-player mode.
Turn **'Smoke'** on to activate him as a playable character without using the Ultimate Kombat Kode.
Turn **'Fatality Time'** off to give yourself infinite time to perform fatalities.
Turn **'Level Select'** on and you'll be able to choose any stage – including the Hidden Portal – from a menu at the bottom of the screen after you choose your fighter.

Super Run Jumps
Joypad 1: Tap □ x 3, △ x 2, ○ x 1
Joypad 2: Tap □ x 7, △ x 8, ○ 9

Combos Disabled
Joypad 1: Tap □ x 7, △ x 2, ○ x 2
Joypad 2: Tap □ x 7, △ x 2, ○ x 2

Special Moves Disabled
Joypad 1: Tap □ x 5, △ x 5, ○ x 5
Joypad 2: Tap □ x 5, △ x 5, ○ x 6

Fast Uppercut Recovery
Joypad 1: Tap □ x 6, △ x 8, ○ x 8
Joypad 2: Tap □ x 4, △ x 3, ○ x 3

Super Endurance Mode
Joypad 1: Tap △ x 2, ○ x 4
Joypad 2: Tap □ x 6, △ x 8, ○ x 9

Player 1 Inflicts Half Damage
Joypad 1: Tap □ x 3, ○ x 9

Player 2 Inflicts Half Damage
Joypad 2: Tap □ x 3, △ x 9

Both Players Inflict Half Damage
Joypad 1: Tap □ x 3, △ x 9
Joypad 2: Tap □ x 3, △ x 9

Power Bars Slowly Regenerate
Joypad 1: Tap □ x 9, △ x 7, ○ x 5
Joypad 2: Tap □ x 3, △ x 1

Real Kombat
Joypad 1: Tap △ x 4
Joypad 2: Tap △ x 4

Throwing Disabled
Joypad 1: Tap □ x 1
Joypad 2: Tap □ x 1

Quasi-Randper Kombat
Joypad 1: Tap □ x 4, ○ x 6

Blocking Disabled
Joypad 1: Tap □ x 3, △ x 2
Joypad 2: Tap △ x 2

Player 1: Quarter Energy
Joypad 1: Tap □ x 7, ○ x 7

Player 2: Quarter Energy
Joypad 2: Tap □ x 7, ○ x 7

Player 1: Half Energy
Joypad 1: Tap △ x 3, ○ x 3

Player 2: Half Energy
Joypad 2: Tap △ x 3, ○ x 3

No Life Bars
Joypad 1: Tap □ x 9, △ x 8, ○ x 7
Joypad 2: Tap □ x 1, △ x 2, ○ x 3

No Fear
Joypad 1: Tap □ x 2, △ x 8, ○ x 2
Joypad 2: Tap □ x 2, △ x 8, ○ x 2
Gives hints for Midway pinball game

Theatre Of Magic
Joypad 1: Tap □ x 9, △ x 8, ○ x 7
Joypad 2: Tap □ x 6, △ x 6, ○ x 6
Gives hints for Midway pinball game

No Knowledge
Joypad 1: Tap □ x 1, △ x 2, ○ x 3
Joypad 2: Tap □ x 9, △ x 2, ○ x 6
Displays text message only

Unlimited Run
Joypad 1: Tap □ x 4, △ x 6, ○ x 6
Joypad 2: Tap □ x 4, △ x 6, ○ x 6
Run bars stay at maximum for both rounds

Quasi-Randper Kombat
Joypad 2: Tap □ x 4, ○ x 6
Fighters randomly morph into other characters

Dark Kombat
Joypad 1: Tap □ x 6, △ x 8, ○ x 8
Joypad 2: Tap □ x 4, △ x 2, ○ x 2
Screen is dark and flashes on briefly when a hit is registered

Psycho Kombat
Joypad 1: Tap □ x 9, △ x 8, ○ x 5
Joypad 2: Tap □ x 1, △ x 2, ○ x 5
Combination of both Dark Kombat and Quasi-Randper Kombat

Play Galaga
Joypad 1: Tap □ x 6, △ x 4, ○ x 2
Joypad 2: Tap □ x 2, △ x 6, ○ x 4
Play a brief game of Galaga. Three lives, any button fires

Fight Smoke
Joypad 1: Tap □ x 2, ○ x 5
Joypad 2: Tap □ x 2, ○ x 5
Winner of first round fights Smoke

Fight Noob Saibot
Joypad 1: Tap □ x 7, △ x 6, ○ x 9
Joypad 2: Tap □ x 3, △ x 4, ○ x 4
Winner of first round fights Noob Saibot

Fight Motaro
Joypad 1: Tap □ x 9, △ x 6, ○ x 9
Joypad 2: Tap □ x 1, △ x 4, ○ x 1
Winner of first round fights Motaro

Fight Shao Kahn
Joypad 1: Tap □ x 3, ○ x 3
Joypad 2: Tap □ x 5, △ x 6, ○ x 4
Winner of first round fights Shao Kahn

With **'One Round Match'** on, fights will just last one round.
With **'One Hit Death'** on, the first player to strike will automatically win the match.

Alternative Cheat Mode
If you're having trouble accessing the secret cheat mode, here's a simpler version. During the opening demo, press ✕, L1, L2. You'll hear a whooshing sound. Now you can access a shorter version of the cheat menu without the 'One Round Match' or 'One Hit Match' options.

Random Select
Bored with the same old characters? To choose your fighter at random, either player must hold Up and Start at the same time. Ensure that Player 1's selection square is on Shang Tsung and Player 2's is on Liu Kang.

Kombat Kodes
When the Vs Screen appears, there are six boxes located at the bottom of the screen that are your doorway to a multitude of hidden secrets. By quickly pressing the High Punch, High Kick and Low Kick buttons a certain number of times, players will activate extra features during a match that range from fighting in the dark to battling undiscovered characters.

a-z of cheats

continued

Micro Machines v3

Copy Prize Cars
Go to Keepsies mode (via Party Play) and load up another character, then your main one (with lots of cars) – the order is important!. For example, load Spider and Dwayne. Select a good car for Dwayne (eg the Beamer) and any for Spider, then choose any track and make Spider win. Choose 'No More Races' and when the 'Update Characters?' option appears, say yes and let it update Spider, but when it comes to Dwayne take out the card and press Cancel. Now go to Test Drive and load up Spider.

Big Bounce
During race, press:
■, ⇦, ⇨, ⇩, ■, ⇦, ⇩.
A beep will indicate bouncy mode is enabled. To return to normal, re-enter the same code.

Double Speed
During race, press:
■, ✕, ●, ■, ▲, ✕, ✕, ✕, ✕
A beep will indicate it's worked. To return to normal speed, re-enter the code.

Debug Mode

During the race, press:
■, ⇧, ⇧, ⇩, ■, ●, ●, ▲, ✕
A beep will indicate it's worked. You can now do several things…
Select + ✕ – Quit the race and automatically win it.
Select + ⇧ ⇩ ⇦ ⇨ – Change camera angle
Select + L2/R2 – Zoom camera in/out
Select + ■ – Turn players car into CPU drone
✕ + ▲ + ● + ■ – Blow up all cars

Tanks On All Tracks
Enter the following as a character name: TANKS4ME. A noise will indicate the cheat's worked and you can now re-enter the player's proper name. **Note:** if you try to use the tanks on the water they'll keep exploding!

Change Car To Object
During race, press pause and enter:
⇩, ⇦, ⇧, ⇨, ⇩, ⇦, ⇨
Re-enter the code to change the object.

Slow Down CPU Vehicles
During race, press pause and enter:
●, ▲, ■, ✕, ●, ▲, ■, ✕
This makes winning much easier.

Behind Car Camera
During race pause and enter:
⇦, ⇨, ■, ●, ⇦, ⇨, ■, ●

Nine Lives In Single Player Mode
Enter 'CATLIVES' as a player name. A sound will confirm correct code entry.

All Tracks In Multiplayer Mode
Enter 'GIMMEALL' as a player name. A sound will confirm correct code entry.

Floating Objects
Pause during race and press:
■, ▲, ■, ■, ▲, ■, ■, ▲, ✕.

Turbo Start
Begin to accelerate just before the second beep. If timed correctly, you will begin the race with a turbo start. The phrase 'turbo start' will appear to confirm it's worked.

Racing Shadow
Go to the game options, select 1 Player Mode, pick any character, and enter his/her name as 'TANKS4ME'. Then press 'OK' twice and choose Time Trial Challenge. When it's loaded, press Start and enter the Big Bounce cheat (■, ⇦, ⇨, ⇩, ⇧, ⇧, ⇩, ⇩). Quit the game and it will ask if you want to play another challenge. Say yes. Below your picture it will say 'cheat mode active'. When the race begins and the countdown is over, your shadow will drive away on its own! What a thrill!

There are two MK1 and MK2 characters to find. To reveal all four of them, simply press Select on the appropriate character to reveal their previous incarnation. The characters in question are: MK1 Kano, MK1 Rayden, MK2 Kung Lao and MK2 Jax.

Random Select
For this to work, press ⇧ + Start at the select screen whilst the default players are highlighted.

Crispy!!!
If you hold both run buttons after you do the stage fatality on Scorpion's Lair, you can hear Shao Kahn say "Crispy". If you hold both punch buttons, Dan Forden will pop out and say "Crispy". You can hold both run buttons and both punch buttons to hear both Shao Kahn and Dan Forden say "Crispy".

Frosty!!!
Sometimes Dan Forden doesn't say "Toasty", he says "Frosty". To do this,

freeze opponent while he is in danger.

Pit Fatalities
Here is a list of pits and what to do for those spectacular fatalities.
Pit 1: Uppercut
Pit 2: Perform the Stage Fatality
Pit 3: Perform the Stage Fatality
Dead Pool: Hold LK + LP + ⇩ then tap HP
Kombat Tomb: Perform Stage Fatality
Shao Kahn Tower: Perform the Stage Fatality
Subway: Perform the Stage Fatality

Moto Racer

Cheats
All of the following cheats should be entered on the title screen (start/options) on controller 1.

Pocket Bike Mode: ⇧, ⇩, R2, L2, ⇩, ⇧, L1, ✕
Reverse Mode: ⇦, ⇨, ⇦, ⇨, □, ○, R1, L1, △, ✕
Enable All Ten Tracks: ⇧, ⇧, ⇦, ⇨,

⇩, ⇩, □, R2, △, ✕
Enable All Ten Tracks (reversed): ⇩, ⇩, ⇨, ⇦, ⇧, ⇧, ○, L2, △, ✕
Night Races: ⇧, ○, L1, ⇩, △, L2, □, ⇦, R1, ✕
All Opponents Race At 50 km/h: ⇩, ⇩, ○, L1, □, L2, ⇩, ⇧, ✕
Ultra-boosted Bike: ⇧, ⇧, ⇧, △, R1, △, R2, ⇧, ⇧, ✕

Victory Movie: □, △, ○, △, □, △, L1, ⇧, R2, ✕
Credits Movie: ○, △, □, ○, △, □, ⇧, ⇨, ⇦, ✕,

Motor Toon Grand Prix

Turbo Start
If you want to give yourself a bit of extra speed in this wild and crazy driving game, then first of all try holding down the accelerator button (✕) when the yellow light comes on.

Screaming Speed
To accelerate to top speed with any of the racers in just one second, and stay

at top speed, simply hold down the reverse button while accelerating.

MechWarrior 2

Password Cheats
Enter the following codes at the

password screen for various effects. When the code is entered correctly you'll hear the female voice that you get on the Mech selection screen.

Cruise Control Throttle

NBA Jam TE

Cheats
Select a team and, when 'Tonight's Matchup' appears, enter the code before 'Loading Game' appears.

Big Head Mode
For heads just a little bigger than normal.
[■, ✕, ○, △] x2

Mammoth Head Mode
Er… for incredibly big-headed people.
[■, △, ○, ✕] x5

Huge Mode
To turn the players into giants.
[△, ✕] x7

Baby Mode
Just to make them feel small.
[■, ○] x3

Great Balls Of Fire
Turns your balls into er… great balls of fire as you dunk.
⇩, ⇨, ⇨, ○, △, ⇦

Max Power
Enhances the ability of your men.
⇨, ⇨, ⇨, ⇨, ✕, ✕, ⇨

Power Up Defence
To boost your defending ability.
⇨, ⇧, ⇨, ⇧, ⇨, ⇨

Full Court Jams
⇦, ⇨, ✕, ○, ○, ✕

High Shots
⇧, ⇧, ⇧, ⇩, ⇩, ⇨, ○ x4, ⇩

Power-Up 3-Pointers
⇧, ⇧, ⇦, ⇨, ⇩, ⇩, ⇧, ⇧

Power-Up Offence
□, ○, ■, □, ○, ⇧, ⇨

Push One Opponent and Both Fall
⇧, ⇧, ⇧, ⇦, ⇦, ⇦, ⇦, ○, ○

Push One Opponent and Only Teammate Falls
⇧, ⇧, ⇧, ⇧, ⇦, ⇦, ⇦, ⇦, ○, △

Quick Hands
⇦, ⇨, ⇦, ⇨, ⇦

Shot Percentage Display
⇧, ⇦, ⇩, ⇨, △

Speed Up
⇧, ⇧, ⇧, ⇩, ⇦, ⇦, ⇦, ✕, △

Tele-Pass
⇧, ⇨, ⇨, ⇦, ○, ⇩, ⇦, ○, □

Hidden Characters
To play as these hidden characters, go to the name input screen and hold down the L1 and R1 buttons as you enter initials and dates.

Catling	CAT	JAN 2
Weasel	DAN	JAN 2
Goskie	GOS	JAN 6
Frank Thomas	FNK	JAN 8
Heavy D	HEA	JAN 9
Fumungus	GUN	JAN 11
Liptak	LIP	JAN 14
Blaze	BLZ	JAN 14
Larry Bird	LAR	JAN 15
Air Dog	AIR	JAN 21
Turmell	TUR	JAN 31
F Prince	FRS	FEB 2
Renaldo	REN	FEB 4
Higgins	TOM	FEB 19
Gray	ROB	FEB 23
Jax	JAX	MAR 1
Crunch	WOL	MAR 7
Carlton	CAL	MAR 25
Suns Mascot	APE	APR 2
Adrock	ADR	APR 6
Hill	ZIG	APR 7
Hutchinson	BAR	APR 9
MCA	MCA	APR 9
Sequoia	SAW	APR 10
Kabuki	KUB	APR 14
Prince Charles	CHA	MAY 4
Chow Chow	CHD	MAY 5
Tunnicliff	SAT	MAY 7
Bill Clinton	BIL	JUN 3
Shelley	SHY	JUN 8
Moore	MOE	JUN 8
Pistol	WAN	JUN 10
Hugo the Hornet	HOR	JUN 12
Snake	SNK	JUN 15
Divita	DIV	JUL 3
Mike D	M_D	JUL 1
Gordon	GOR	JUL 3
Rivett	REV	JUL 6
McHugh	BAA	JUL 8
Brutah	GOW	JUL 17
D Falcus	DAZ	AUG 6
Max	LIZ	AUG 7
J Moon	JAY	AUG 24
Benny	BEN	SEP 20
Jazzy Jeff	JAZ	OCT 9
Facime	DEL	OCT 19
Boo-Boo	THI	NOV 1
H Clinton	HIL	NOV 6
J Falcus	JAS	NOV 16
Magic Hair	STH	DEC 8
Kirby	CHR	DEC 18
Mad Mike	MUS	DEC 24
Hodgeson	HOG	DEC 31

NBA Jam Extreme

All Special Teams
On the Keep Records screen, answer 'Yes', then use the initials JBP and May 17. Note that your opponent must also enter the code to be able to access the special teams.

Hidden Characters
Start the game, then answer 'Yes' for 'Keep Records?'. Now enter the following records for the desired player and a whole league of special hidden characters:

Junior Seau – JR Jun 1
John Elway – WAY Sep 30
Marv Albert – MRV Dec 31
Frank Thomas – BIG Dec 6
Newt Gingrich – NEW Aug 12
Pirate Bill – SAL Feb 2
Mr Happy – MJT Mar 22
Dufus the Clown – GRR Jun 19
Three Feet Under – TOD Apr 17
Mr Unhappy – GEM Nov 3
Ooooh – JLH Jan 26
Who – WHO Jan 1
Brained – BCS Jan 7

Monkey Boy – PJP Nov 2
Howie – BCE Jul 10
Jim Jung – JKJ Dec 13
Huh – CBR Jun 25
Cheryl Swoopes – SWO Jan 1
Rebecca Lobo – LOB Jul 4
Carol Blazejowski – BLZ Mar 1
Bob Lanier – LAN Sep 10
Air Nick – ARN May 18
George Cervin – ICE Apr 7
XX Stinger – MSS Oct 26
XX Shamrock – JHG Aug 26
Diamond Dave – DJP Jun 29
Chris Slate – JCS Dec 8
Sausage Boy – TVC Oct 3
Richard Szeto – RTS Feb 25
Dwain Skinner – DAS Feb 21
Dave Ross – DJR Jun 8
Jeff Peters – JBP May 17
Daren Smith – DRS Apr 10
Mike Callahan – MWC May 1
The Tinman – TIM Jan 24
Mark Canus – MMG Sep 16
Roy Wilkins – RNW Sep 15
Rob Daurel – RAD Mar 19

Big Feet Mode
Hold ⇦ or ⇨ when leaving 'Big Head' select.

Head-er-oids Mini Game
You need a Multitap for this one. Hold ⇧ + Extreme on all four pads when leaving Team Select.

Marshmallow Treats
Hold ⇧ at the end of the title sequence before the screen dims.

Random Team Select
On Team Select press ⇧ + Turbo.

Random Player Select
After random team press ⇧ + Turbo again.

Team Select Codes
The following are entered by holding the relevant buttons on the Team Select screen until the Vs screen appears, then pressing the directions listed. You'll know it's worked if a programmer's head pops onto the screen.

Small Players, Big Heads
On the 'Big Head' option, press ⇧, ⇧, ⇦, ⇨, ⇩, ⇧, then select 'Yes'.

Shot % Display
Hold Extreme + Shoot and release on the Vs screen.

Infinite Turbos
Hold Turbo, then press ⇧, ⇩, ⇧, ⇩ and release Turbo.

No Turbo Meters
Hold Turbo + Extreme, then press ⇧, ⇩, ⇧, ⇩ and release buttons.

Remove Crowd
Hold Extreme + Pass + ⇧ and release on the Vs screen.

Tip-Off Codes
The following codes should be done at the tip-off, while the ref is walking out to throw the ball. They must be entered quickly without pressing any buttons too many times.

Computer Assistance Off
Extreme, Turbo, Pass x2

Beach Ball Mode
Pass x2, Turbo, Extreme, Turbo,

Pass x2
It still goes in the net!

Quick Hands Mode
Pass x3, Turbo x3, Extreme x3, Pass x3

Max 3pt Mode
Pass x8, Extreme, Pass x7

Legal Goaltending
Extreme x8, Pass, Extreme x9

Dead-Eye Dick
Turbo x5, Pass, Extreme, Turbo x6

Super Rainbow Shot
Turbo x5, Pass x2, Turbo x6

Power Push
Turbo x2, Pass x2, Turbo x2, Pass x2, Turbo x2, Pass x2, Turbo x2

Max Speed
Extreme x10, Pass x3

Keep Record Cheats
These should be entered on the Keep Record screen as your name, by selecting the first two letters, then backspacing twice,

putting in the next two letters and repeating until the complete code is entered.

Start At Playoffs
PL AY OF FS

Start At Finals
FI NA LS

2 Playoff Games Won
CH EE SY

3 Playoff Games Won
NO VI CE

45 Second Shootout
SH OO TO UT

Sound Test
KA ZO O

Programmer Players
Go to create a player and type in one of the names from the credits in the instruction booklet. Go to the free agent pool and sign him to a team. When you score a basket with this new player, the announcer will say his name.

NBA Live '97

Secret Characters
Type the name of the producers and programmers names in the 'Create A Player' option. Make sure you push Start at the last letter of each name otherwise it won't work. It will put them on the free agency list. It won't count as a created player, so you can have all the producers and still make 40 new players.

Amory Wong
Allan Johanson
Brian Krause
Dom Humphrey
Daniel Ng
Robert White
Dan Scott
David Bollo
Sebastiaan Reinarz

Sheila Allan
Michael Vanaselja
Casey O'Brien
Daryl Anselmo
Giovanni Sasso
Kim Gill
Mark Soderwall
Greg Allen
Cindy Green
David Laviolette
Adam MacKay-Smith
Traz Damji
Steve Royea
Crispin Hands
Jeff Mair
Sam Nelson
Ed Fletcher
Stan Chow
Tarrnie Williams
Michael Klassen
Marcus Lindblom
Dave Warfield
Ivan Allen
Brian Wideen
Brent Nielson

Aaron Grant
Renata Antonic
Zoe Quinn
Sean O'Brien
Novell Thomas
Al Murdoch
Ernie Johnson

Secret Codes
This cheat is dead tricky to activate but worth it. After the game has started and you are at the Game Setup menu, press: L1, X, X, L1, X, □, R1, X, □, R1, ○ (which should take you to the Credits screen). Then hold (for a second or two) ◊ + △ + □ to activate the secret codes.
Now start the game as normal and, as soon as it starts loading, hold L1 + R1 + ◊ + △ + X + □ + ◊ for as long as it takes for the

secret code menu to appear. (Top tip: use a CD case to hold down the four fire buttons.)
1. On the secret code screen, L1 and L2 alter player height up/down. The number is in inches (min = 1.5 feet; max = 12 feet!).
Note: Any height greater than 7'10" cannot slam the ball.
To change all the players on the cheat list, you must use a PlayStation Multitap with all controllers plugged in.
2. D-pad ⇧ and ⇩ control Chameleon mode (flashing colours).
3. Start and Select on controller 1 set the outdoor court on/off.
To exit the cheat area and go to the game, press △ + X on controller 1.

NCAA Gamebreaker

Secret Passwords
Press L1, R1, L2, R2 to get to the Easter Egg screen and then enter the

following passwords:
Tight Cover
Big Ref
Slow CPU
Tiny GB

Cannon
Lights Out
Angry CPU
Cruel CPU
Thunder Foot
Little Foot
Fast Clock
Slow Clock

Loose Cover
Swim Down
Blocking Down
Big Foot
Amazons
Jack T
Hammer

#AXO/A4YYA
You no longer need to hold the throttle button down.

Invincibility
##XO/X><UZ
You never need die again.

Unlock All Missions
T<XO/AXA<=
This unlocks every mission in the entire game!

Extra Mech: Elemental
T/XO/AZ<#*
The Elemental is a very small Mech, more like a suit of armour.

Extra Mech: Tarantula
#/XO/A4<LY
This leggy lovely will you give you the creeps.

Extra Chassis Variants
T#XO/AX<<<
The next time you visit the Change Mech screen you'll see extra chassis variants, each equipped with slightly different weapons.

Overweight Mechs Allowed
#OXO/A>>O/
Throw away that Slimfast: you can now carry as much weight as you like!

Unlimited Ammo
TOXO/AX>TU
Fire away to your heart's content.

Heat Tracking Off
#XXO/A4>Y+
Now the heat generated by your weapons will build much more slowly, enabling you to fire quicker without overheating.

Unlimited Jet Juice
TXXO/AZ>+X
More fuel than BP.

Jumpjets On All Mechs
#YXO/A>YOL
Even Orville could fly with these.

Monster Trucks
Cheats
Enter these on the main menu. The cheats need to be re-entered every time you race.
Tall Trucks
L1, R2, L2, R1, ⇧
Stretches the trucks vertically.
No Damage
⇦, ⇦, ⇦, ⇧, ⇩, L1, R2
Your damage meter stays full.
Super Grip
⇦, L1, R2, R1, ⇦, R2, R2, R2
The truck sticks to the road like glue.
Checkpoint Lift

L1, L1, R1, R1, L2, L2, R2, R2
Only works for Endurance races: press △ and a helicopter will come and winch you to the next checkpoint.

Extra Strength
L2, ⇦, ⇨, ⇧, ⇩, R2
Improves the durability of all the trucks.

Namco Museum
Vol 1 & 2
Galaga – Non-Shooting Enemies
On the first stage, don't shoot any of the ships as they go into their formation. Once they're all in formation, isolate the two leftmost blue bees. Kill all the other ships except these two. Once you have, let the two bees fly and shoot at you for the next 10 to 20 minutes (don't fire a shot during this time). You can hide in the right corner for most of the time, only moving out to avoid the odd shot. After a while you'll notice that the bees stop shooting at you. Once you notice this, let them do a few more passes to make sure, then kill them. Now no ships will shoot at you!

Grobda Level Select
1. At the Grobda title screen, hold L1 + L2 + R1 + R2, hen press Start.
3. Choose a level from the Battle Selection screen that appears.

Dragon Buster – Life Refill
On the Dragon Buster title screen, press Select ten times or more followed by Start to begin your game. Now, whenever your vitality drops below 32, press L1 and R1 together and it will shoot back up to 128.

Namco Museum Vol. 4
Alternative Intro
After you switch the game on, press and hold L1 and R1 as the 'Namco' logo flashes across the screen. If the cheat has worked, the usual jolly Pac-Man intro will be replaced by the sinister and incredibly spooky FMV intro to *Genji and Heiki Clan*.

Extra Continues
For any of the games on Namco Museum Vol. 4, you can increase the number of credits by pressing Select. This can be done as many times as you want.

Hidden Return Of Ishtar
Enter the Museum and go to the Return Of Ishtar room. Quickly press ⇨, ⇦, ⇧, ⇩, ○. A special version of the Return Of Ishtar game will begin.

NASCAR Racing
Secret Game
Pressing X on controller 2 during the start of the title sequence brings up a *Tron*-style light-cycle game. How's that for a bonus!

NanoTek Warrior
Random Curving
Pause the game during play and press ○, Select, ⇦, □, □, ⇩, ⇧, X.

Cockpit View
Pause during play and press △, ○, □, □, △, △, Select, Start.

Rotate Enemy & Obstacle Positions
Pause during play and press R1, R1, ⇧, ○, □, △, L2, X.

Camera Lock
Pause during play and press ○, □, △, △, ○, □, △, Start.

Destructible Obstacles
Pause during play and press □, ○, R2, R2, ⇦, ⇧, ⇩, X.

Lock-On Lightning Bolt Special Weapon
Enter X, □, △, ○, □, ○, X, △, X as a password.

Black NanoTek Ship
Enter: X, □, X, □, □, ○, X, △, X as a password.

Full Story
Insert the game disc into a PC compatible CD-ROM drive. View the STORY.TXT file for the complete version of the NanoTek Warrior story.

Screen Shots
Insert the game disc into a PC compatible CD-ROM drive. Load the JPG files with a graphics program to display screen shots from the game.

Passwords
NORMAL

2	□, △, X, △, □, X, □, △, X
3	△, □, X, □, □, X, □, □, X
Bonus 1	□, ○, X, △, □, ○, △, ○, X
4	X, △, □, X, □, X, □, □, ○
5	○, △, □, X, ○, X, ○, □, □
6	△, □, O, X, □, △, X, ○, X
Bonus 2	□, □, □, X, □, □, △, △, X
7	X, △, X, ○, □, X, △, △, □
8	□, △, X, O, X, □, △, □, X

HARD

2	□, X, △, X, □, △, X, □, ○
3	X, □, △, X, □, ○, X, □, △
Bonus 1	□, ○, △, X, □, △, ○, □, X
4	X, △, □, X, □, △, ○, □, △
5	□, △, ○, X, □, X, △, ○, X
6	△, □, □, △, X, ○, □, X, ○
Bonus 2	△, X, △, □, X, △, X, □, △
8	□, X, △, ○, X, □, △, □, X

The Need For Speed
Lost Vegas Track
1. Go to the Tournament password screen.
2. Enter TSYBNS as your password.
3. Now go back to the Head-To-Head game.
4. Cycle through the tracks and Lost Vegas will be selectable.

Oasis Springs Track
1. The TSYBNS code must be entered first.
2. In Head-To-Head mode, go to the Rusty Springs track.
3. Hold down L1 and R2 together to make it change to Oasis Springs.
4. While holding these buttons press Start to play.

Warrior Car
1. The TSYBNS code must be entered.
2. In Head-To-Head Mode, go to the car selection screen and hold down L1 and R1.
3. You should now be able to select the Warrior.

Rally Mode
1. After the TSYBNS code has been input, enter Head-To-Head mode.
2. Cycle through to your favourite track.
3. Now hold down L1 and R1 to see the title change to RALLY MODE.
4. Now press Start to enter a muddy course.

No Mercy Mode
1. Yes, the TSYBNS code triggers this one too.
2. Go to the Head-To-Head screen.
3. Hold down L1 and R1.
4. The option should change to NO MERCY.
5. This turns off the slower car catch-up, giving a fairer race.

Passwords

Track 1	WRDRTY
Track 2	ZDPBWN
Track 3	MTQRZP
Track 4	JVPZLL
Track 5	ZYMNLH
Track 6	WMRPGZ
Lost Vegas	YXGSJJ
Track 8	KJPQND
Track 9	SDQWCG
Track 10	SLZXDH
Track 11	SPZDFX
Track 12	ZVGRGX
Track 13	XJHVCK

Lunar Springs
This newly discovered circuit is another variation on the Rusty Springs course, this time with a lunar landscape!
1. Access Tournament mode and enter the password: SPKSHC.
2. Go back and choose another mode and highlight Rusty Springs on the track select screen.
3. Press and hold △, then add L1 + R1 and select Rusty Springs with X.

Machine Gun Code
Choose Head To Head mode. Immediately after selecting your opponent's car, push and hold L1, ○, □, and ⇘, until loading is complete. Now instead having a horn, every time you push up you'll fire an invisible machine gun that clears the way of any cars. This code can be used with one or two players.

Extra Weight
First go to Tournament mode and enter the password TSYBNS. After this you can continue Tournament mode or quit it. At the car selection screen, select Car Showcase, then Mechanical. From here, select Next Slide. You can now add extra weight to the car you are viewing, shown by a number of red triangles at either end. Press L1 to add weight to the front of the car, and R1 for the rear. This makes your car turn sharper.

---

to access the corresponding player.

Name	PIN	Hidden Player
AMRICH	2020	Dan Amrich
DANR	0000	Dan Roan
DIVITA	0201	Sal Divita
MUNDAY	5432	Larry Munday
PIPPEN	0000	Scottie Pippen
ROOT	6000	John Root
SNO	0103	S Snow
TURMEL	0322	Mark Turmell

NBA in the Zone 2
Michael Jordan
At the demonstration enter:
○, ⇨, □, ⇦, L1, L2, R2
Do this ten times fast, then all the hidden players become available, including Mr Jordan himself.

All-Star Team
With the cursor on 'Start', press and hold L1 + R2 + Select + Start until the screen fades out. You will then be able to select the All-Star Team in exhibition mode only.

Play With Jordan, O'Neal, Barkley etc
To play with Michael Jordan you must change the number and the name of the player called 'M Guard' in the Chicago team (using 'edit player' in the custom menu). Then trade this player to Chicago and put him in the

starting line up. When you play, you'll see that this guy really is Michael Jordan (same face, statistics, and pieces of black cloth on his arm and leg). Do the same to have Charles Barkley with Houston and Shaquille O'Neal with Los Angeles. Apparently this also works with some other missing players.

NBA Shoot Out 97
Super All-Star Difficulty
When highlighting Difficulty in Game Options, press L1, R1, L2, R2. If it worked you'll immediately see a new skill level: Super All-Star Difficulty. Warning: this mode is for real experts, as you'll soon find out.

Need For Speed 2
Extra Car
Enter LILZIP as the password to win the tournament and get the Ford Indigo.

Extra Track
Enter SHOTME as the password to unlock the extra track, Monolithic Studios.

Faster Car
Enter POWRUP as the password to get a Pioneer engine. This gives your car improved acceleration in Arcade mode, and better acceleration and top speed in

NBA Hangtime
Hidden Players
Enter the following name codes at the 'Enter Name' prompt, and PIN numbers

a-z of cheats

continued

NFL '97

Enter the following codes on the Team Select screen of Pre-Season mode.

1. L1, L1, L1, △, L1, L1
Let you play the NFC or AFC Pro Bowl teams against any team in a pre-season match-up.

2. L1, L1, L1, R1, L1, L1
Puts land mines all over the field! Watch your step or you'll be shot into the air and land on your back.

3. L1, L1, L1, L2, L1, L1
Just try and hold onto the ball! Every play of the game, the ball will be fumbled twice.

4. L1, L1, L1, R2, L1, R1
Just try and drop the ball! No fumbles are allowed no matter how bad the player in possession is.

5. L1, L1, L2, △, L1, △
Just tap the speed-burst button and your player will run at top speed for the rest of the play.

6. L1, L1, △, R2, L1, △
Whatever team you choose to play with will have the skills of a high-school side.

7. L1, L1, R1, △, L1, △
All the players get a boost in size: they're huge!

8. L1, L1, R1, R1, L1, R1
Every player is shrunk down to size.

9. L1, L1, R1, R2, L1, R1
Now's the time to go deep: any QB can throw the ball 100 yards on any Bomb Zone play!

10. L1, L1, L2, R1, L1, L2
Puts the game into super slow mode.

Simulation.

More Camera Views

At the main menu, start the race and hold:

L1 + L2 + R1 + R2 + X + △ + □ + ○.
Release the buttons when the race starts and you should have nine camera angles to choose from instead of the usual four.
Note: If you restart the race, the extra views disappear.

NFL Game Day

Secret Options

As soon as the NFL Game Day logo appears press: R1, R1, L2, L1, △, ●, ■, L1, L1, L2, R1, R2, L1, ▲, ▲. This will give you an options screen where you can select several cool things – including turning all players into John Madden, enabling Touchdown Fatalities, and changing opponents into furry rabbits.

Extra Teams

At the opening screen, press the following keys in order:
●, ●, R1, R2, L1, L2, ●, ■, ▲. Then hold down L1 and R1 simultaneously for about five seconds until the new teams appear.

Victory Screens

At the beginning when the PlayStation logo disappears, hold Down R1, R2, L1, L2 till you want to stop the graphics. This code takes you through all the win/lose screens in the game. Experience winning the Super Bowl.

Codes

At the password prompt, enter the following (all in uppercase) for various special effects:

Extra Vehicles

Enter any of the following passwords. Note that the chosen vehicle won't appear in the selection menu – just start the race and you'll be driving it. Note: These work for player 1. For player 2, simply change the 'ME' in each code to 'U' (eg 'LOGME' becomes 'LOGU').

ARMYME	Army Truck
BUGME	VW Beetle
BUSME	Bus
CITME	Citroen 2CV
CRATME	Crate
LIMOME	Limo
LOGME	Log
MAZME	Mazda Miata
OUTHME	Outhouse
QUATME	Audi Quattro
SEMIME	Truck Cab
SNOWME	Snow Truck
TREXME	T Rex
VANME	Camper Van
WAGOME	Wagon
YJME	Jeep
BEETME	Trabant?
BMRME	BMW
BNZME	Mercedes Benz
JEPME	Comanche pick-up truck
LCME	Toyota LandCruiser
VOVME	Volvo estate
TRAMME	Tram
STDAME	Stand A
STDBME	Stand B
STDCME	Stand C

New Japan Wrestling

Play As Sparrow

At the title screen press ○, ⇨, △, ⇧, □, ⇦, X, ⇩, X, ⇩, ⇦, △, ⇧, ○, ⇨, Select. At the wrestler select screen, highlight Commandant and press Select.

Play As Gorgon (the announcer)

At the title screen press L1, L1, L2, R2, R2, R1, △, X, ⇧, Select. At the wrestler select screen, highlight Agent Orange and press Select.

Play As Sallie (the referee)

At the title screen press ⇧, ⇧, ⇦, ⇨, △, X, □, ○, L1, R1, L2, R2, Select. At the wrestler select screen, highlight El Temblor and press Select.

NFL Game Day '98

Bonus Teams

Press ⇧ at the team selection screen to access Super Bowl teams for player 1. Press ⇩ at this screen for player 2. Press ⇧ again at the player selection screen to access All-Star teams for player 1 – use L1 and L2 to view more selections. Press ⇩ at this screen for

SKELETON		Two skeleton teams playing in the Bone Bowl
SNAKE		Two teams of snake with arms!
JUICE		Ten-yard speed bursts
BIG.BOYS		Large players (actual size)
OFFENSE		Better offence
DEFENSE		Better defence
STICKUM		Receivers catch almost all the passes
CANNON.ARM		Quarterback has good throwing arm
PICK.CITY		Easy interceptions
CRUNCH.TIME		Hard hits and more injuries
URNOTREDE		Computer is very hard to beat
BLITZ		Commercial break
STEROIDS		Super stiff-arm
MAYHEM		Defenders injured after hits
GOOD		Unknown effect

Porsche Challenge

Sneaky Short Cuts

USA – Drain
After the first left corner, look out for a car park on the right. Occasionally there is a white truck there which means the Drain short cut is open. When about level with the truck, take a sharp left through the gate in the wire fence – try to avoid the water as it will slow you down. The exit is by the railway station.

Japan – Temple
Hit the first basket on the left side of the course (look closely, there should be an IO logo on it). Just past the starting grid, the Temple Gate short cut will now be open.

Alpine – Village
On the first lap, the gates are closed. When you reach the base of the track on the second lap, you will see a snowplough. The snowdrift to the left is blocked by some cones: knock these down and the plough will clear the drift, opening the doors for the next lap.

Cheats

All of these cheats must be entered on the main menu screen (1-Player, Options).

All Cars Jump
Now all the other cars on the track will start jumping.
⇧ + □, ⇧ + ○, ⇧ + □, ⇧ + ○, ⇧ + □, ⇧ + ○, ⇧ + □

End Of The Game
If, like some of us, you really cannot be bothered to wait to see the end credits,

player 2 – use R1 and R2 to view more selections.

Cheat Codes

Press L1 + L2 + R1+ R2 at the main menu. Then enter each of the following passwords for various amusing effects (if you know what any of the 'unknown' ones do, please write in and tell us):

BETTIS	Stronger CPU runs
BIG_FOOT	Stronger kicker legs
BLIND_REF	Less penalties
BUSY_REF	More penalties
CPU_DEFENSE	Unknown
CPU_OFFENSE	Unknown
CREDITS	View credits
CRUNCHY	Unknown
DEEP_GRAY	Unknown
EQUAL_TEAMS	Identical teams
FIRE_DRILL	Move Quickly
FLEA_CIRCUS	Small players
GD_CHALLENGE	Increased difficulty
GLOVES	Better catches
HATCHET	Unknown
HORSEMAN	No Heads
HUMONGOUS	Large Players
JACK_HAMMER	Better stiff arm
JUICE	Very fast players
LEECH	Better DB coverage
LOOK_MA	No Hands
LOUD_MOUTH	Unknown
MCMAHON	All-McMahon team
NYSE	Unknown
PSYCHIC	Unknown
QUIET_CROWD	Unknown
REJECTION	Unknown
SHO_OFF	Unknown
STRETCH	Unknown
THIN_AIR	High Kicks
TOAST	Easier to burn a DB
VIRTUAL_POLYGONS	Unknown
WATERY_AI	Stupid CPU

NHL '97

Enter these codes during the face-off, before the puck drops on the ice. The word 'Entered' will confirm correct code entry.

Super Home Team

Press L2, L2, L1 + R2, R1, ○.

activate this cheat and you'll be whisked away to view them instantly. And look... there's even some lovely FMV of classic Porsches – how nice!
□, ○, ⇦ + Select, ⇨ + Select

Fish-Eye Lens

This is surely meant to alter the view, but we couldn't see any difference when we tried it. A bit fishy, if you ask me.
□ + △ + ○, L1, L2, R2, R1

High Voices

For that prepubescent-quality sound, just activate this cheat and those helium high notes are just round the corner.
⇧, △, ⇧, △

Hyper Car

Knight Rider eat your heart out. When this baby is activated, hold on tight!
Select + □, Select + ○, Select + □ + ○

Interactive Tracks

This lets you race on all the 'interactive' versions of the tracks, with the junctions constantly switching to alter the road as you race around. These are normally only available once you reach them in Championship mode.
⇩ + Start, ⇧ + Start, Select , Start

Invisible Car

Surely the best new design in anti-theft security. They can't steal what they can't see.
(Note: this crashes on some tracks)
□ + ○, L2 + R2, □ + ○, L1 + R1, □ + ○

Quick Game

Press L2, L2, L1 + R2, R1, R2. Stop the current game and restart to enable 20-second periods.

No Collisions

Press L2, L2, L1 + R2, R1, X.

Faster Gameplay

Press L1, L2, L1, R1, X.

More Penalties

Press L1, L2, L1, R1, L1.

More Penalty Shots

Press L1, L2, L1, R1, R1.

More Accurate Shots

Press L1, L2, L1, R1, L2.

Easier Goals

Press L1, L2, L1, R1, R2.

More Instant Replay Views

Press L1, L2, L1, R1, □

Overhead Cameo

Enable any code that starts with pressing L1. Then stop the game, select any team, and begin a new game.

Players Appear As Nets

Enter NETHOCKEY as a name.

NHL Face-Off

Seven-Game Series

To get a seven-game series, start a seven-game playoff before the end of the season. You should now have an option to continue playoff. When your season ends, it will automatically overwrite the old playoff, but keep the seven-game format in.

Alternate Team Appearance

Hold X + ○ + L2 when the 'Just a Minute' sign appears. Keep the buttons held until several seconds after the sound of a puck is played.

NHL Open Ice Challenge

Super Speed

When the game is loading, hold △ + □

Long Tracks

Everybody likes a bit of extra length, just ask the girls! But seriously, this brings up the longer versions of the tracks. These normally only become available once you reach them in Championship mode.
Select + ⇧, Select + ⇩, Start, Select

Mad Race

It's Mad Max, only this time he's driving a Porsche. Your opponents will swerve all over the track.
⇧, ⇦, ⇨ + Select

Mirror Mode

Well, humm! What could this possibly mean, I wonder? Mirror Mode perhaps.
⇨ + ○, ⇩ + △, ⇨ + □

Test Driver

The black prototype Porsche is yours to drive at any point during the game.
⇨ + □, ⇨ + ○ + Select

Tune Test Driver

How do you like your car? Well you can choose your own parameters with this handy option.
⇨ + ○, ⇨ + □ + Select

Unlimited Retries

Now you never have to worry about losing, so long as you've got unlimited retries.
L1 + L2, R1 + R2 + □

User Car Jumps

In true Dukes Of Hazard style, you too can jump, fly, zoom through the air.
□, ○, □

+ Start + Select.

Big Heads

Press ⇧ + Pass + Turbo at the 'Tonight's Game' screen.

Big Head Goalie

Press Pass, Pass, Turbo, Shoot, Pass at the 'Tonight's Game' screen.

Baby Heads

Press Turbo, Turbo, ⇧, Shoot, Shoot, ⇧ at the 'Tonight's Game' screen.

Large Puck

Press ⇧, ⇧, ⇩, ⇩, Turbo at the 'Tonight's Game' screen.

Hidden Players

Enter the following information at the User Records screen:

NHL Face-Off '97

Super Player

Choose Roster, then Create Player. Now, input any name from the following list:

Raja Altenhoff
Tom Braski
Craig Broadbooks
Josh Hassin
Tawn Kramer
Alan Scales
Kelly Ryan
Jody Kelsey
Chris Whaley
Peter Dille
Craig Ostrander

Don't fiddle with his number, position, hand or weight as it could muck up the cheat. Now press △ to exit – if you select 'Create Player' again, your man will appear with 99 ratings across the board. Go to 'Sign Free Agent' from the Roster menu. Sign the super player to your team. Then select 'Edit Lines' and insert him into one of the Scoring lines for your team. By releasing players from your team (not goalies), you can sign a teamful of super players.

Pandemonium

Cheat Modes
Enter each of the following passwords to access secret game modes:

Rock 'n' Roll
Password: TWISTEYE
Hold L1 and L2 and move the D-pad ⇦ or ⇨ to rotate the screen. Press ⇩ to centre it again.

Mutant Mania
Password: THETHING
Hold L2 and press ○, to cycle through odd shapes of your body L2 + X swaps back to normal.

U Can't Touch This
Password: HARDBODY
Makes you invincible.

Gender Switch
Password: BODYSWAP
Press △ to swap characters in mid game.

Permanent Weapon
Password: OTTOFIRE
As it says. New weapon changes as it's picked.

Extra Lives
Password: VITAMINS
31 lives are all yours.

Hearts Galore
Password: CORONARY
Loads of extra hearts.

Freedom
Password: BORNFREE
Go to any world you like.

Pinball Mania
Password: TOMMYBOY
Finish a level and you get the option to play this Pinball screen.

Speed Greed
Password: CASHDASH
Bonus screen after level is finished.

Immortal Enemies
Password: EVILDEAD
Those enemies just won't die.

Just Visiting
Password: INANDOUT
Quitting during play will return you to the map.

Passwords
These passwords will take you to any level, but with no goodies:

Level	Password
1	ADEAMIIE
2	EPIJAKCA
3	FBIJAKCI
4	KOCCCIEE
5	NGIAIBJJ
6	NIIAJBCB
7	KGCACICI
8	AHICBAJE
9	AIICFAJG
10	AIICBAJI
11	FBIIAKCK
12	FDIIAKDC
13	FFIIAKDK
14	KACACIBA
15	ADMCFAID
16	EMIIEKBE
17	OEIBIBMJ
18	FAAIAKCE

Initials	Month	Day	Player
GH	Mar	31	Gordie Howe
MJ	Jan	25	Michael Jordan

Novastorm

Level Select
Enter 'TWIRLY_' (where '_' represents 'space') in the high score list. This should enable a Level Select option to appear on the main menu.

Off World Interceptor

Loads Of Money
Go to the option screen, hit the □, X and ○ buttons in that order six times., then hit the L1 button. You can also get this cheat if you have beaten the game.

Level Passwords
lp5vk?pzqg41417p
nrqv!tb9mbjgkb8!
cqd?dc5kpl5kw741

Parodius Deluxe Pack

Hidden Stage
Shoot down the ships in the first wave of Stage 2. Then, when the second wave flies on screen, shoot the first ship and avoid all the others. After you have done this, the enemies will explode and you will be warped into a tough hidden section.

Invincibility
Pause the game and press △, △, X, X, ○ □, ○, □, ⇩, ⇦. If this is done correctly, you will hear a sound. Repeating the code turns it off.

Maximum Power-Ups
Pause the game and press ⇧, ⇧, ⇩, ⇩, ⇦, ⇨, ⇦, ⇨, X, ○. If this is done correctly you will hear a sound. This code can be repeated at any time.

Level Select
At the title screen press □ x5, △ x7, ○ x3.

Peak Performance

Special Class
Press L1 + ○ at the car selection screen under class A, B, or C. The special class will now be selectable.

Hidden Vehicles:
Note: Each of the hidden vehicles may be saved for easier selection after they are found the first time. All vehicles may also be tuned up.

Nissan 240 ZX & Bus
Drive a car and complete the Bay Area track with a time less than three minutes.

Diablo
Select a car and finish the Uptown Driveway track in first place under all three difficulty levels in one-player mode. Finish in first place in the next level. Next, race the Uptown Driveway track in time trial mode and find the parked Diablo.

Porsche
Select a car and finish the Seven Tight Corners track in first place under all three difficulty levels in one-player mode. Race the same track in time trial mode and find Porsche at the hotel.

McLaren & Truck
Select a car and Finish the Pikes Peak Hill Climb track with a time less than 2:30. Note: These vehicles may only be driven in time trial mode.

Scooter
Select a car and race the Northern Country track in time trial mode in an anticlockwise direction. Go through the gate that is near the river on the second lap to find the scooter.

Perfect Weapon

Level Codes
Ice Moon – X, □, X, □, □, ○, □, ○
Garden Mn. – ○, X, X, △, ○, ○, X, △
Forrest Mn. – ○, △, □, ○, □, □, △, △
Desert Mn. – ○, X, X, X, △, ○, △, △
Morgone – X, X, □, X, □, □, △, ○
Toran – △, △, X, □, △, △, X, ○
Shiro – ○, ○, X, □, X, X, ○, △
Renza-Fi – △, ○, X, X, △, □, △, △
Sacra-Ja – ○, X, ○, ○, □, ○, X, □
Morgone O. – X, △, ○, X, △, ○, ○, △
Lizard Guard – ○, □, □, X, ○, X, X, ○
Final Level – □, △, ○, X, □, △, ○, X

Invulnerability
Pause the game and enter:
○, □, ⇨, ⇦, R1, R2

All Moves
Pause the game and enter:
L2, R2, R1, L1

PO'ed

Stage Select
On the main menu screen, simultaneously press L1, L2, R1, R2, and ⇧. Release them, then press ○ to start a new game. On the difficulty screen, simultaneously press L1, L2, R1, R2, and ⇩. Pick a difficulty and the stage select appears.

Full Inventory
1. Go to the Map Screen (press □ + Select).
2. Press Left until the arrow (that represents you) is pointing at you.
3. Press Start to return to Standard View.
4. While the camera rotates, press L1 + □ + X + ○.
5. Press △ and you should have all the weapons.

Invincibility
1. Make sure that you have the drill before you do this (if you don't, use the Full Inventory cheat to get it).
2. Go to somewhere safe.
3. Bring up the Weapon Select menu.
4. Select Frying Pan with L1 or R1.
5. Return to the game.
6. Return to Weapon Select.
7. Press ○ + R1 to cycle through the weapons until you get a flashing 999 on your health counter.
8. To turn it off press ○ + R1 again.

Ammo Refill
1. Enter Foot Mode.
2. Do a backflip (□ + L2).
3. While flipping press ⇨ + X + ○.

Health Refill
1. Enter Foot Mode.
2. Do a backflip (□ + L2).
3. While flipping press ⇩ + X + R2.

Farting Arses
(Maximum fun mode)
1. Select Load Game from the main menu.
2. Press L1 + L2 + R1 + R2.
3. Now the walking arses will make a farting sound when firing!

See The Final Sequence
1. Select Load Game from the Main Menu.
2. Press ⇨ and hold it.
3. While holding ⇨, press ○.
4. Press △ to cancel.
5. Press □ + ⇦ and release them.
6. Press △ button to see the end.

Turn Off Collision Detection
1. You must be in jet pack mode.
2. Locate a dead body of any kind.
3. Stand on a dead body.
4. Press △ to bring up weapons.
5. Press L1+ ⇨ + ⇩.
6. You'll start falling through the floor, so use jetpack to get around.

Turn Collision Detection Back On
1. Press △ to bring up weapons selection.
2. Press L1 + ⇨ + ⇩.

Pitball

View FMV Sequences
Highlight the 'FMV Test' selection on the options menu and press ⇦, ⇨, □, ○.

Mini-Game
Highlight any ending on the 'FMV Test' screen and press □ + ○. The team ending that was highlighted determines what type of ship will appear. Pressing □ + ○ without a highlighted ending will result in a first-person view

Pop 'n' Twin Bee

Stage Select
Gain a high score of 573,000. Wait until you're at the demo screen with Princess Merora, then hold R1, L1 and use the D-pad to choose any stage. If you score 1,000,000 or higher, you can repeat this trick twice.

Dark Play
In Arcade Mode, any time during the game, pause it and press: ⇧, ⇧, ⇩, ⇩, ⇦, ⇨, ⇦, ⇨, X, ○.

Power Instinct 2

Secret Character
Start the game in Team Battle Mode and at the character screen, press: ⇦, ⇨, ⇩, ⇧, ⇩, ⇦, ⇨, ⇦, and ⇧.

Raging Skies

Extra Time
Hold L1 + L2 + R1 + R2 + X + ○ + △ + □ + ⇦ as the game loads.

Raiden Project

Full Credits
Go to the option screen where you can set your credit number, then press △ + ○+ □ + X at the same time and you'll get FREEPLAY.

Mission Select
Go to the Settings menu and choose Difficulty. Hold down R1, R2, L1, L2 and press Start.

Extra Options
During the game, hold the top four buttons (L1 + L2 + R1 + R2) together to bring up a screen which allows you to adjust the resolution and move the screen around to your liking.

Power-Up Pixie
Watch out for trees that are slightly off-

Rayman

All Levels & Abilities
Simply go to the password screen and enter: FJSJ!C620P

99 Lives
During the game, pause at any time and then press and hold the following buttons in sequence: L2, R1, L1, R2. Then release them in the following sequence: L2, L2, R2, R1. Then press △ and press and hold ⇨, ○, □, X and then release in the following sequence: ⇨, X, □, ○. You will now have 99 lives to play with.

Extra Continues
If you have 0, 1, or 2 continues left, when you are at the continue screen, press and release successively on the left controller the following directions slowly (one per second) while Rayman is staggering around: ⇧, ⇩, ⇨, ⇦. You should get ten continues. However, this doesn't work all the time, so your best bet is to save the game with one continue left, die three times, try the cheat and repeat until it works.

Picture In Picture
Pause the game whilst holding down R2, hit ○, ○, ⇦, ○, ○.

No 'Paused' Text
While paused, holding down R1 and R2 makes the 'game paused, press Start to continue' graphic disappear! Excellent for grabbing screens.

Large Rayman Demo
After the Ubi Soft logo, press and hold L1, L2, R1, R2. Then at the animation of rock wall, press and hold Start. Keep holding down everything, but release when screen goes black.

Codes
Start
38W8Z92W9M
Pink Plant Woods
L8W8Z9LW9M
Anguish Lagoon
L0W8ZH2W9M
Swamps of Forgetfulness
L04JPHLW9M
Mosquitos Nest
L044Z9LNHM
Bongo Hills
B0D4?HL29X
Allegro Presto

B0D4?1L29X
Gong Heights
B04DG13L9K
Mr Sax's Hullabaloo
B0D4?R33HP
Twilight Gulch
BH4N?1!3NP
Hard Rocks
T9DN?R33NF
Mr Stone's Peaks
49DN?1!!WF
Eraser Plains
DW44?1!CN7
Pencil Pentathlon
4NBN?1!5NF
Space Mamma's Crater
DCT4G13CDF
Crystal Palace
DCTW81!CD7
Eat at Joe's
NWTDDR!346
Mr Skop's Stalactites
NW?WD15!4Q

Rage Racer

Toggle Mirror on/off
Whilst racing in internal view mode, pause the game at any time and then press and hold △ and then tap L1 to make the rear-view mirror disappear. Press R1 to bring it back.

Mirror Mode
Providing extra course variety, the Mirror Mode reverses all the tracks so that all the corners and writing are backwards. To access it, select 'Race Start' from the main options and then hold L1, R1, Select and Start until the race begins. If the cheat has worked you will instantly notice the difference.

Advanced Colour Palettes
To access a greater range of colours to use on your team logo, perform the following:
Select 'Customise' from the main options, then select 'Design' and choose any logo or create your own. Then select 'Paint' and then press any direction until the cursor is off of the painting area. Now press a button to move onto the colour palette and then press L1, L2, R1, R2 and Select. If done correctly, additional boxes will appear on the right labelled R, G, and B. These letters represent the amount of red, green and blue hue for the specific palette that the cursor is highlighting. Pressing ⇧ and ⇩ will change which hue you alter and then pressing R1 + ⇧ or ⇩ will alter the numeric figure in the hue box.
Now move the cursor onto the painting area and press L1, L2, R1, R2, and Select. You should now see a targeting cross-hair appear in the smaller picture area (for greater accuracy we presume).
Finally, keeping the cursor inside the painting area, press L1 + R1 in conjunction with any direction to rotate your design around.

Infinite Money
Follow the steps below for infinite money:
1. You must complete the Normal GP (all the classes). Wait for the credits roll until the end.
2. Save the whole game into a brand new block in Save/Load screen.
3. Go back to play the Normal GP at class 5 and you should be able to choose only one car (GNADE).
4. Choose that car and press Race Start.
5. During the count-down (3, 2, 1, Go), press Start and choose Retire. This should let you quit the race without losing a chance.
6. Finally, enter the Normal GP again, then choose Class 1. You should now have infinite money. You can buy and upgrade any car you wish.
Note: If you repeat all the steps at Extra GP, you'll get the same cheat.

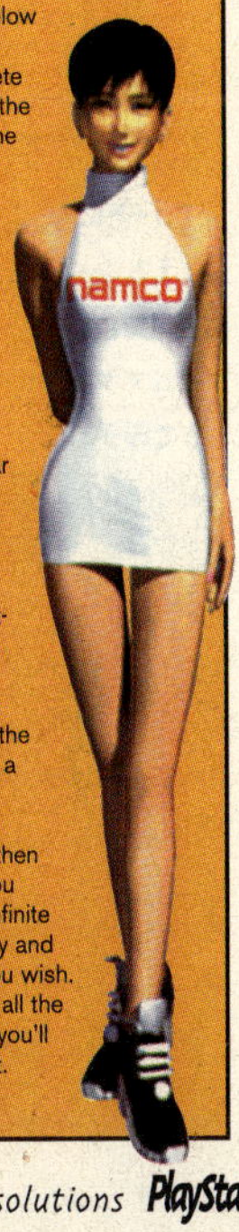

a-z of cheats

Rally Cross

Special Passwords
To be entered as either the Lap/Course Record name or New Season name.

Win Rookie Season – vet_me (_ = space)
This is equivalent to winning the Rookie season, giving you four extra cars and access to the Alpine track.

Win Veteran Season – im_a_pro
Equivalent to winning the Veteran season, this gives you four more cars and the Gardens and Stadium tracks.

Win All Pro Seasons – weeoo
This is equivalent to winning the normal, head-on, and mixed Pro seasons. You can now select the three pick-up trucks.

Heavy Cars – stone
Makes the cars stick to the road more, hardly jumping into the air.

Lighter Cars – feather
Makes the cars lighter so they bounce around more.

Low Gravity – float
Upon bouncing up, the cars float through the air longer. This completely confuses the CPU opponents.

Sharp Turning – spinner
Lets you turn quicker thanks to more sensitive steering. Keep turning to spin right round on the spot.

Fat Tyres – fat_tires
Increases the width of your tyres, although this doesn't seem to alter their grip.

No Wheels – no_wheels
Removes the wheels, so the cars float around the track!

Just Wheels – wheels
Removes the car body, so just the four wheels remain!

No Collisions – banzai
Lets you drive straight through other cars as if they weren't there.

No Slowdown noviscous
You can now keep accelerating through mud/water etc without being slowed down.

Normal Gravity radbrad
This cheat seems to be pretty useless; unless you've just activated the float cheat. All this does is return gravity to normal.

colour, generally on the right side of the screen, and which also stop your fire. Once found, get close to them and unload into them. An explosion should release a flying pixie. Capture it, and when you die, the pixie will release some power-ups.

Rapid Racer

Cheats
Input the following cheats on the name selection screen in one-player mode before they become available in the other game modes.

Extra Boats
BOA (= space)
Makes all the hidden boats selectable.

Duck Mode
_QAK
This turns all the boats into giant plastic ducks with engines!

Hurricane
HURR
Gives you control of The Hurricane, a high-speed vessel that corners like it's on rails. It's got a horrible yellow paint job, though.

Unlock Day Tracks
_DAY

Unlock Night Tracks
_NIT

Unlock Mirrored Tracks
RRIM

Random Track Generator
FRAC

Win Race
WINR
Quit the race you are playing to be awarded first place.

Day Track Select
D_#
Where # equals the number of the track you want.

Night Track Select
N_#
Where # equals the number of the track you want.

Mirrored Track Select
M_#
Where # equals the number of the track you want.

Porsche Mode
BXTR
This enables the Porsche cheat, but it only works if you load in a *Rapid Racer* saved game from a memory card that also contains a *Porsche Challenge* saved game.

Rapid Reload

Passwords
To use these passwords, wait until the title screen comes up, then press and hold L1, L2, R1 and R2 on controller 1. Then press Select and 'Push Start' should change to 'Secret Code' with two letters alongside. The left-hand letter is changed by pressing ⇧ or ⇩, and the right by using the △ and ✕ buttons, to enter the level codes:

Stage 2	MA	Stage 3 UT
Stage 4	RH	Stage 5 MK

Resident Evil

Rocket Launcher
To start the game with the rocket launcher plus infinite ammo, you must first complete the game in under three hours. Simple. When, or rather, if you achieve this, you'll be able to save the rocket launcher to your inventory and start the game more or less invincible.

Changing Clothes
It's true, by completing *Resident Evil* with a good ending (whereby you rescue BOTH team members), you'll be awarded the Special Key which will be added to your inventory and saved in preparation for the next game. This key will allow you to enter the previously locked door in the wardrobe and enter the hidden wardrobe closet. In here you'll be able to access an alternative set of togs for your chosen character. Pointless but fun.

Sun Crest
Go to the Armour room on the second floor and then push the two statues over the air vents in the floor. Now press the button on the ground and the display cabinet at the far end will open, revealing the crest.

Wind Crest
Push the statue off of the balcony on the 2F Dining Room and collect the Blue Gem from the shattered remains below. Take this gem to the Tiger Statue Room on the first floor and insert it into the statue's eye socket. This will cause the statue to pivot, revealing the crest.

Star Crest
Go to the Large Gallery on the first floor and you'll be confronted by a series of paintings. Visit each painting in sequence starting from the youngest to oldest and press the buttons. The correct sequence is as follows: New-born, Infant, Lively Boy, Young Man,

Middle-aged Man and Old Man. Finally, once you've pressed each button, go to the painting at the end and press the final button to obtain the crest.

Moon Crest
This is by far the hardest crest to obtain and it is found in the Attic. When you get there, you'll be confronted by an extremely large snake. You can either take evasive action and run around it to grab the crest from its nesting ground, or alternatively you can blast it to kingdom come and then grab the crest.

Doom Books & Medals
Take the Doom Books to the fountain which you'll come to after the underground passage, then go to you inventory, go to 'Check Item' and rotate each book around so that the pages are facing outwards. Now press ✕ and the book will open, revealing the medals needed to drain the fountain and access the lab.

Logging Onto The Computer
The log-in name is JOHN. The first password is ADA. The final password is MOLE.

Disks & Terminals
Disk 1 – Inside the hidden room in Library B.
Disk 2 – Behind the huge rock in Crank Passage.
Disk 3 – On the desk at the Stairs in the laboratory.
Terminal 1 – Inside Private Room A.
Terminal 2 – Inside the Mortuary.
Terminal 3 – Inside Power Maze B

Powering The Elevator
To activate the power to the elevator that will take you down to the final battle with Tyrant, you'll need to visit the power panel in the first room of the Power Maze. Simply go to the southwest corner of the room

and restore the power to the darkened areas. Go into the last room of the Power Maze and then use the terminal at the east end of the room – the elevator will now be active.

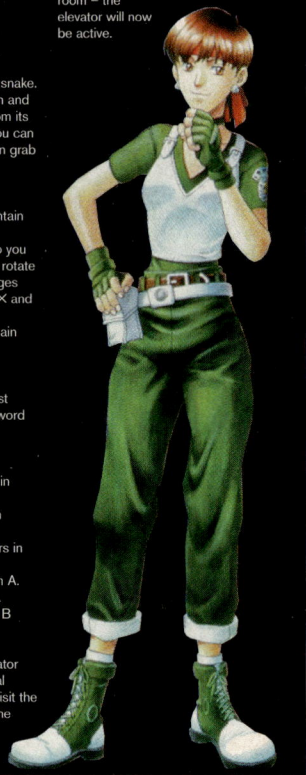

Re-Loaded

Play As Fwank – Sort of!
This cheat is bugged and doesn't really work properly, but if you want to try it anyway then read on. Whilst on the Character Select screen, press the following sequence on controller one: L1, ○, R1, ⇩, ⇩, R1, ○, ⇦, ⇦. If the cheat has worked, you should hear a sinister laugh and a red balloon will appear on the right-hand side of the screen. This will float over to the left and position itself over Sister Magpie. Now when you move the cursor over her, Fwank will be selected. However, when you start the actual game, you'll still play as Sister Magpie.

Cheat Codes
To enter the following cheats, pause

the game and then hold the L1 and L2 buttons for about ten seconds (or until the selection bar stops moving). Then input the relevant code. **Note:** You may have to enter each of the codes below in order (start with Health, then Ammo, Power, Level Skip).

Infinite Health
⇩, ⇦, ⇦, △, ⇦, ⇩
A new option called 'Health' will appear at the bottom of the menu. Now every time you get close to death, pause the game and click on 'Health' option to replenish your bar.

Infinite Ammo
△, ⇦, ⇦, ⇦, ○, △, ⇩.
A new option called 'Ammo' will appear at the bottom of the menu. Pause and

click on this when you need ammo.

Full Power
⇦, ⇧, ✕, ○
A new option will appear at the bottom of the menu called 'Power'. Pause and click on this option whenever your weapon needs powering up.

Level Skip
⇦, △, ✕, ⇦, ○, △, △
If the cheat has worked, a new option called 'Skip Level' will appear at the bottom of the menu. Pause and click on this new option to skip.

Coordinates Display
⇩, ✕, ⇧, ✕, ⇩, ✕
Unpause and your map coordinates will be shown on-screen.

Stage 6 HT

Special Codes
Small character - **CM**
Huge character - **QB**
Smaller windows - **MV**
Start with nine bombs - **YI**
Axel and Ruka turn into one-hit wonders - **TY**
Weapon power-up time starts with 999 - **SS**

Debug Mode
Set the code to MA, press Select, then change code to SV and press Start. The following commands must be entered using controller 2:
⇧ - Boosts weapon power to max (10-second duration)
⇩ - Voice mode on/off
⇔ - Gunlock type change
⇨ - Skips area (disengages invincibility)
△ - Invincibility on/off (falling will still

cause damage)
○ - Increases number of bombs
□ - Switches selected weapon type from Axel to Ruka
✕ - Increases weapon power-up time in 30-second increments

Ray Storm

Extra Credits
To receive an extra few credits, repeatedly tap Select at the title screen to set the total credits to nine.

Rebel Assault

Cheats
Go to the options screen and choose 'Enter Passcode'.

Invulnerability
△, ○, ○, △, ✕

Level Skip
△, △, ○, △, □, □

Movie Mode
△, □, ○, △, ○, ○

Access All Levels:
Easy Level
✕, ○, ✕, ○, ✕, △

Medium Level
✕, △, △, □, ✕, △ (PAL version)
✕, □, △, △, ✕, △ (NTSC version)

Hard Level
△, □, □, □, ✕, △ (PAL version)
✕, ○, □, △, ✕, △ (NTSC version)

Return Fire

Level Codes
One-Player Mode
2: Umbrella, Bird, Butterfly, Flower
3: Smiley, Cup, Rabbit, Umbrella
4: Rabbit, Umbrella, Bird, Bird
5: Flower, Umbrella, Rabbit, Cup

6: Bird, Cup, Butterfly, Bear
7: Bear, Bear, Shamrock, Bird
8: Rabbit, Cup, Umbrella, Heart
9: Shamrock, Butterfly, Bird, Heart
10: Heart, Butterfly, Cup, Heart
11: Umbrella, Umbrella, Bird, Flower
12: Flower, Cup, Shamrock, Butterfly
13: Heart, Umbrella, Shamrock, Heart
14: Rabbit, Smiley, Flower, Shamrock
15: Rabbit, Smiley, Bear, Bird
16: Flower, Umbrella, Bird, Rabbit
17: Flower, Bear, Heart, Umbrella

Two-Player Mode
2: Butterfly, Umbrella, Bear, Heart
3: Bear, Rabbit, Flower, Shamrock
4: Umbrella, Heart, Shamrock, Flower
5: Umbrella, Bear, Rabbit, Heart
6: Cup, Bird, Butterfly, Flower
7: Heart, Flower, Shamrock, Rabbit
8: Heart, Bear, Rabbit, Heart
9: Bear, Rabbit, Shamrock, Flower
10: Butterfly, Smiley, Umbrella, Shamrock
11: Bear, Flower, Smiley, Flower
12: Cup, Bear, Flower, Umbrella
13: Heart, Bird, Flower, Shamrock
14: Smiley, Bird, Shamrock, Cup
15: Cup, Bird, Shamrock, Bear
16: Umbrella, Cup, Bird, Flower
17: Smiley, Bear, Rabbit, Flower
18: Shamrock X 4

Ridge Racer

Extra Cars
Obtain all 12 standard racing cars by scoring a 'Perfect' by blasting every single alien in the Galaga game.

Mirror Mode
Start a race and drive up to the end of the slip-road, then turn around and race back to the starting line. As you approach the barrier at the back, it will disappear and you'll now finding yourself racing in reverse on a mirrored track.

Move Flag
To move the Ridge Racer flag around on the title screen, hold L1 and R1 and press the other buttons to move the flag. You can also speed up the rotation of the cars and tracks on their respective select screen by using this same technique.

Devil Car
When you place first on all three standard tracks, go to the Time Trial mode and you'll be racing against two other cars as opposed to just one. The third is the 13th Racing Devil Car. To beat it, you must overtake it whilst it is stationary on the second lap and then maintain a perfect racing line throughout the remaining duration of the race. Achieve this and the Devil Car will appear to the left of the first car on the select screen.

Ridge Racer Revolution

Extra Cars
You can boost the car quota up to a staggering 12 motors by getting a perfect result in the Galaga loading game, shooting all 40 enemy craft.

Secret Options
Don't shoot any of the ships in Galaga '88. After all the ships have gone by, there will be a small firework burst. Go to the 'Other' screen and you can now set the racing time from Normal, Morning, Evening and Night.

Spotlight Control
Hold down L1 and R1 at the main screen (with Game Start and Options commands).

Buggy Mode
To turn all the cars into small buggy-type vehicles, complete the Galaga loading game scoring a 100% hit ratio. To make this much easier, when you switch on your PlayStation on, press and hold L1 + R1 + Select + ⇩ + △. Now when you play Galaga, your ship will fire a laser beam that can wipe out enemies with ease. Start the game as normal and you'll have all the cars at your disposal, all squashed!

Toggle Mirror On/Off
Getting fed up of having a rear-view mirror on the screen? Well just pause the game by pressing Start, hold down △ and press L1 to make the mirror vanish. You can press R1 to make it reappear again too!

Zoom Car In/Out
Drive using the external view mode and pause the game. Now hold down △ and press L1 and R1 to zoom in and out on your motor.

Spinning Mode
Select a Time Trial race and when the Start command is highlighted, press and hold the accelerator and brake until the action switches to the track.

You begin the race as normal, but will see the message 'Spinning Point' appear as you reach the first bend.

Take your finger off the accelerator and quickly press it again to send your car into a spin.

You can perform 360°s, 540°s and even 720°s with a bit of practice. You'll get marked on technique and there are three spinning points in each track!

Mirror Mode
You can play the tracks backwards with corners bending the opposite way and the writing reversed by following these simple instructions…

Start the game as normal, drive a little way down the track and turn the car around. You will see a barrier ahead meant to stop you racing the wrong way. Line your car up and attack it! If you hit the barrier at exactly 100kph you will go straight through and be able to race the track backwards!

Play Link-Up With One Disc
You normally need two copies of the game to play a two-player link-up, but this special technique lets you do it with one.

Hold down the door sensor on PlayStation #1 (under lid at the back right – use Blu-Tac and a matchstick) and load the RRR CD. When you see the RRR title screen, remove the disc and replace it with a music CD. Don't release the door sensor – you must grab the disc while it is spinning! (Note: This is entirely at your own risk. PowerStation takes no responsibility for any damage caused to your machine or game.)

Then hold down the door sensor on PlayStation #2 and load up the game. It should now display the 2P-Link Option on the RRR title screen. Leave the RRR disc in PlayStation #2.

If you don't see the '2P-Link Option', press Start once on one or both of the machines, then exit back out to the title screen and you'll see it.

Due to the fact the game loads the first track into memory anyway, you can now have a linked game on the first track, Novice. If you want a different track, do the following. Select another track and press Start on both machines, then when the 'loading' screen appears, wait for the RRR CD to spin to half speed (track has loaded at this point) then quickly swap with the music CD on the other PlayStation. If your timing is right, the track will now load on the other machine and the game will start.

Slamscape

Cheat Passwords

Hidden Movie
□, □, X, □, □, △, ○, □

Unused Art Level
△, ○, X, △, X, X, △, ○

Uraniumania
X, X, X, △, ○, X, □, △

Repsychler
□, ○, □, □, △, ○, △, △

Endless Bummer
□, ○, □, X, △, △, □, X

Viva Los Vagrantes
○, △, X, △, X, □, □, △

Credits
○, ○, ○, □, ○, X, X, △

Game Over/Win
○, ○, ○, △, X, X, △, ○

Invincibility
Hold Select, press: □, □, ○, ○, □, □, △

Full Weapons Power-Up
Hold Select, press: ⇦, □, ⇨, ○, ⇧, △
(Repeat to power-up weapons again.)

Kill Danger Ranger, Queen Snagger
Hold Select, L1, R1, press ⇦, □, ⇦, □, ⇦, □

Level Passwords
Uraniumania
△XX□○△X△

Repsychler
X○○△□□○X

Endless Bummer
X△X○△□○X

Viva Los Vagrantes
○△X△X□□△

Special Cars
There are three special cars to discover and drive in RRR. To get them you have to win Novice, Advanced and Expert in Time Trial after you have completed them in normal race mode. You get the Devil #13 in Novice mode, Kid Car #13 in Advanced, and the superb White Angel #0 in Expert.

Rise 2: Resurrection

Boss Codes
Input the following codes on the character-select screen :
Vitrol – ⇨⇨⇨⇧⇧⇩⇦⇦⇩⇩
Assault – ⇨⇧⇧⇨⇩⇨⇧⇧
Mayhem – ⇦⇨⇩⇦⇧⇦⇩⇦⇩
Anil 8 – ⇧⇨⇩⇨⇨⇧⇦⇧
Supervisor – ⇩⇨⇩⇧⇨⇩⇦⇩⇧⇨⇧

Robotron X

Power-Up Codes
Enter the following cheat codes during play for various power-ups.
Flame Thrower: ⇩, ⇨, ⇩, ⇨, ○
4-Way Gun: ⇩, ⇩, ⇧, ○
3-Way Gun: ⇨, ⇨, □, X
2-Way Gun: ⇧, △, ⇧, △
Pulse Wave: ⇧, ○, ⇩, ⇨, □
Shield: ⇩, ⇦, □, ○
Speed Up: ⇦, ⇦, ⇨, ⇨, △

Rockman X3

Final Stage
Enter the stage select screen and highlight the 'X' logo. Quickly press ⇩ + □ + X. The cursor will move to the bottom of the screen to confirm correct code entry.

Zero's Light Sabre
Enter 7357, 7533, 6462, 7835 as a password to start a game with that weapon.

All Enhancements
Enter 6414, 4155, 6872, 3356 as a password to start a game with the special capsules (Double Air Dash, Hyper Charger, Super Armour, I Tracer) already obtained.

Passwords

Introduction	3721, 1281, 3751, 4456
Gravity Beetle	5623, 4888, 5851, 4221
Blast Hornet	1745, 5231, 5441, 2486
Neon Tiger	3621, 4867, 5851, 2227
Tunnel Rhino	5728, 1263, 5754, 2458
Blizzard Buffalo	7671, 2857, 2144, 1247
Volt Catfish	1778, 5253, 2444, 3488
Crush Crawfish	5718, 1266, 2727, 7458
Doppler's Lab	5718, 1263, 2627, 7458

Rosco McQueen

Passwords

Laundry 2	FLUFFY
Laundry 3	SWEATY
Auto 1	HOTROD
Auto 2	GREASE
Auto 3	BIGEND
Harold's 1	SMELLY
Harold's 2	WIDETV
Harold's 3	PILLOW
Leisure 1	TRICEP
Leisure 2	MOTION
Leisure 3	HIPHOP
Residential 1	KENNEL
Residential 2	BARREL
Runaround	SPLASH

Runabout

Hidden Cars
SIR/NSR – Beat easy mode.
GTR/BUS – Beat medium mode.
DAM/LIM – Beat hard mode.
GTS – Beat easy mode with total amount over $1,000,000.
ELS – Beat medium mode with total amount over $2,500,000.
360 – Beat hard mode with total amount over $2,500,000.
FD7 – Beat easy mode within 4 mins.
GT1 – Beat medium mode in 4 mins.
TAC – Beat hard mode within 4 mins.
TRD – Trash truck. On the freeway section of the Seaside course, break the speed limit by at least 60–75 mph.
19A – Indy car. Complete Downtown with no accumulated money.
PLC – Police cruiser. Complete Seaside with no accumulated money.
TNK – Tank. Complete Metro city with no accumulated money (no damage).

Running High

Bonus Character And Track
Complete the game and press ⇩, ⇩, ⇧, ⇧, ⇦, ⇨, ⇦, ⇨ at the mode selection screen.

Star Gladiator

Invisible Walls
If you beat the game on any skill level, go to the options screen and a new option will have appeared that allows you to turn the invisible walls on or off. This means that there'll be no more Ring Outs.

Fighting In The Dark
Select your character as per normal and then press ⇩ + L2 + R2 and hold them until the fight starts. You'll now notice a distinct lack of light as you commence the fight.

Fight As Bilstein
This cheat can only be accessed in one-player mode, but once it has worked you'll be able to access the character in two-player mode. On the character select screen, go to Hayato and press and hold Select. Now move to Gore and press X, ○, X, ○, □, □, □, △, △, △, X + ○. Bilstein will now appear to the right of Gore.

Fight As Kappah
Once again this cheat can only be accessed in one-player mode, but once the cheat has worked, you'll be able to access the character in two-player mode. You must perform the Bilstein cheat before you can get this to work. On the character select screen, go to Bilstein and press and hold Select. Now move to Hayato and press ○, □, △, □, X, □, △, □, ○, □, X + △. Kappah will now appear to the left of Hayato.

Play As Blood
Once you've got the Bilstein and Kappah codes to work, go to the character select screen once again and then move your cursor to Bilstein. Now press and hold Select whilst entering the following code: X, □, X, □, X, □. Now move to Kappah without highlighting any other characters in the process and press: ○, △, ○, △, ○, △. Finish off by pressing L1 + R1, and if the cheat has worked you should hear the suction noise that rang out after the previous two cheats. Now cycle through the characters and Blood will be available.

Big Head Mode
After choosing your character, press and hold ⇨, Start, ○ and □. Continue to hold them down until the round starts. To get the shrunken head mode, use the above cheat but press ⇦ instead of ⇨.

Super Bilstein
Set all the options to the default settings and then complete the game in six minutes or under to compete against the Super Bilstein character. You'll find he is slightly bigger than the normal Bilstein and his stage is dramatically different as well.

Half-Gravity Mode
You must first complete the game on any skill level for this to work. During the stage load, simply hold ⇧. The Invisible Walls option is on automatically, so you don't have to worry about ringouts. Every time you smack the opponent hard, they'll go flying miles and bounce off the walls!

Soviet Strike

Mission Passwords
1: WORSTCASE
2: GRANDTHEFT
3: GROZNEY
4: CHERNOBYL
5: CIVILWAR
If you wish to start Campaign #4 with five lives, simply input the password: **NOSFERATU.**

Password Cheats
Enter the following passwords after inputting the desired level code. They can all be used at once.

ELVISLIVES Infinite choppers

DAVEDITHER More powerful weapons

IAMWOMAN Unlimited armour

MOUNTANDEW Unlimited fuel

MIDNIGHOIL Infinite ammo, fuel and invincibility

FUGAZI Infinite ammo, fuel and lives

THEBIGBOYS Infinite ammo, fuel and double damage

VULTURE Double mileage (slow fuel depletion)

ANGRYLOCAL Soldiers and hostages crowd round chopper

QUAKER Enemies don't fire at you

STRANGELUV Unlimited ammo

EARTHFIRST Unlimited Fuel

GHANDI Helicopter is viewed as friendly

Sangoku Musou

Fight As Zhuge Liang
Finish the game with Guan Yu, Zhang Fei, and Zhao Yun.

Fight As Cao Cao
Finish game with all characters except Guan Yu, Zhang Fei, and Zhao Yun.

Fight As Lu Bu
Finish the game with Zhuge Liang and Cao Cao.

Fight As An Ancient Japanese Warlord
Enable Zhuge Liang, Cao Cao, and Lu Bu (see above). Now quickly press □, ⇧, △, ⇩, X at the title screen. The sound of a bell will confirm correct code entry. You can now choose the warlord by pressing L1 or R1 at the character select screen.

Fight As Sun Seung Heung
Quickly press ⇦, ⇦, ⇧, ⇩, △, □, L1, R1 on the one-player battle screen. The sound of a bell will confirm correct code entry. Choose this character (a girl) by pressing L1 or L2 on the character select screen.

Samurai Shodown 3

Play As Zankuro
1. Choose Vs Mode and go to the character select screen.
2. Hold down the Start button and highlight the following characters in order: Haohmuru, Ganjuro, Basara, Kyoshiro, Ukyo, Rimruru, Haohmaru, Shizmaru, Nakoruru, Hanzo, Amakusa, Gaira, Galford, and Shizmaru.
3. Now hold Start and press X + ○. Zankuro will appear as a character.

Sexy Parodius

(Japanese)

Power-Up
To fully power-up your craft with every available weapon, pause the game at any time and press: ⇧, ⇧, ⇩, ⇩, L1,

▶

a-z of cheats

continued

R1, L1, R1, X, O.

Power-Down
To lose all of your weapon power-ups, pause the game and press: ⬆, ⬆, ⬇, ⬇, ⬅, ➡, ⬅, ➡, X, O.

Shockwave Assault

Cheat Codes
To activate the codes, pause the game, type the password and then quit (Select button). Do this separately for each one. O, □, X Allows you to enter the following codes:

O, O, X, O, △, □ Special laser
O, X, □ Refuels you
□, X, △ Invincibility
□, X, O Smart Bomb
□, X, □, O Mission Success

Everything Unlocked
Pause the game while you have lasers on screen, then press:
□, X, □, O, △, O, △
Press Select to activate it.

Sim City 2000

Free Credit
On the budget screen, hold △, then press L1, L2, L1, L2, R2, R1, R2, R1. You can now have bonds at 0% interest.

One Million Bucks
1. Load or Start a city. Once you're in the game, access City Info/Budget. At the Budget Screen…

Street Fighter Alpha 2

White Dhalsim & Vega
Select Training Mode, choose Dhalsim or Vega, then start playing. Do the teleport move: at the instant the fighter disappears, press Start, go to the menu, highlight normal mode. Start again and your fighter will appear in white. To revert to normal colour, teleport again.

Old-Style Chun-Li
Hold down the Select button for five seconds before pressing one of the other buttons to select her.

Fighting Turbo Akuma
To meet the Super Turbo Akuma character in arcade mode, simply battle through the game on any level setting and try to get at least eight Super Combo finishes before you reach the final match against your respective boss. Now, instead of fighting them straight away, the 'Here comes a new challenger' message will appear and Akuma will warp down onto that stage.

Play As Turbo Akuma
Highlight Akuma on the character-select screen and hold Select for a few moments. Now press the following sequence on the D-pad: ⬇, ➡, ➡, ⬇, ⬅, ⬇, ⬇, ⬅, ➡, ➡, and – if you have followed this correctly your cursor

should start and finish on Akuma. Now hold Select again and then push another button to select.

Super Combos Moves (these also work in Street Fighter Alpha):

Ken
Super Dragon Punch – ⬇ ⬊ ➡ ⬇ ⬊ ➡ + P
Vacuum Dragon Punch – ⬇ ⬊ ➡ ⬇ ⬊ ➡ + K

Ryu
Super Fireball – ⬇ ⬊ ➡ ⬇ ⬊ ➡ + P
Vacuum Hurricane Kick – ⬇ ⬋ ⬅ ⬇ ⬋ ⬅ + K

Sagat
Tiger Cannon – ⬇ ⬊ ➡ ⬇ ⬊ ➡ + P
Tiger Raid – ⬇ ⬋ ⬅ ⬇ ⬋ ⬅ + K

Sakura
Super Fireball – ⬇ ⬊ ➡ ⬇ ⬊ ➡ + P
Rising Dragon Wave – ⬇ ⬊ ➡ ⬇ ⬊ ➡ + K
Kick Devastation – ⬇ ⬋ ⬅ ⬇ ⬋ ⬅ + K

Sodom
Super Jitte Slice – ⬇ ⬊ ➡ ⬇ ⬊ ➡ + P
Super Power Bomb – rotate 720° + P

Zangief
Final Atomic Buster – Rotate 720° + P
Aerial Russian Slam – ⬇ ⬊ ➡ ⬇ ⬊ ➡ + P

Charlie
Sonic Break – Charge, ⬅➡ ⬅➡ + P
Somersault Justice – Charge, ⬋⬊ ⬋⬊ + K
Crossfire Blitz – Charge, ⬅➡ ⬅➡ + K

Chun-Li
Super Fireball – ⬇ ⬊ ➡ ⬇ ⬊ ➡ + P
Thousand Burst Kick – Charge, ⬅➡ ⬅➡ + K
Rising Heaven Kick – Charge, ⬋⬊ ⬋⬊ + K

Dan
Super Fireball – ⬇ ⬊ ➡ ⬇ ⬊ ➡ + P
Super Dragon Punch – ⬇ ⬊ ➡ ⬇ ⬊ ➡ + K
Desperation Combo – ⬇ ⬋ ⬊ ⬇ ⬋ ⬊ + K
Super Taunt – ⬇ ⬊ ➡ ⬇ ⬊ ➡ + Select

Dhalsim
Yoga Inferno – ⬇ ⬊ ➡ ⬇ ⬊ ➡ + P
Yoga Strike – ⬇ ⬋ ⬅ ⬇ ⬋ ⬅ + K

Gen
Mantis Style:
Terror Shadow – ⬇ ⬋ ⬅ ⬇ ⬋ ⬅ + P
Death Curse – ⬇ ⬋⬊ ⬋⬊ ⬅ + P
Crane Style:
Snake Bite – ⬇ ⬊ ➡ ⬇ ⬊ ➡ + P
Mad Tooth – ⬇ ⬋ ⬅ ⬇ ⬋ ⬅ + K

Guy
Bushin Thunder Kick – ⬇ ⬊ ➡ +

K
Bushin Air Punch – ⬇ ⬋ ⬅ ⬇ ⬋ ⬅ + P

M Bison
Knee Press Nightmare – Charge, ⬅➡ ⬅➡ + K
Psycho Crusher – Charge, ⬅➡ ⬅➡ + P

Rolento
Mine Sweeper – ⬇ ⬋⬊ ⬇ ⬋⬊ + P
No Mercy – ⬇ ⬋ ⬅ ⬇ ⬋ ⬅ + K

Rose
Aura Soul Spark – ⬇ ⬊ ➡ ⬇ ⬊ ➡ + P
Aura Soul Throw – ⬇ ⬊ ➡ ⬇ ⬊ ➡ + P
Soul Illusion – ⬇ ⬋ ⬅ ⬇ ⬋ ⬅ + K

Birdie
Super Head-Butt Rush – Charge, ⬅➡ ⬅➡ + P
Super Chain Slam – ⬇ ⬊ ➡ ⬇ ⬊ ➡ + P or K

Adon
Jaguar Assault – ⬇ ⬊ ➡ ⬇ ⬊ ➡ + P
Jaguar Revolver – ⬇ ⬋ ⬅ ⬇ ⬋ ⬅ + K

Akuma
Super Fireball – ➡ ⬇ ⬊ ➡ ⬇ ⬊ ➡ + P
Super Dragon Punch – ⬇ ⬊ ➡ ⬇ ⬊ ➡ + P
Super Air Fireball – ⬇ ⬊ ➡ ⬇ ⬊ ➡ + P
Instant Hell Murder (AKA Raging Demon) – Jab, Jab, ➡, Short + Fierce

Spider

Recharge Weapons & Energy
Pause the game and enter the following code: △, X, X, X, O, X, □, △, X, △, O.

Shrink
Pause the game and press: △, □, O, △.

Passwords
Laboratory
Lab Floor 1
FMLC939GPR8F3BF7KT1
Sinks
CHMLC939GPR8F3LWGTS3
Lab Top

86MLC939GPR8F3VFQ5S4
Seventies Room
FW1MC939GPR8F3BF7KT1

Factory
Boxes
W1MC939GPR8F36DTTS3
Conveyors
BSRMC939GPR8F3VTKKT1
Machine Room
WDRQC939GPR8F3LM8S95
Tubes
8WV5L939GPR8F36DTTS3
Mechanical Arm Boss
8WV5L939GPR8F3G1QJB4

City
Down The Street
9WV5L939GPR8F3LRT6S4
Side Of Building
6SXXS939GPR8F3LRT6S4
Park
W9PNT839GPR8F3B9LVS3
Under The Street
N7KB3Y19GPR8F3V95HR5
Along The Street
N7KB3Y19GPR8F3GGK4T3

Museum
Display Cases
P7KB3Y19GPR8F3BPFGC3

Volcano
G7KB3Y11GPR8F3BPFGC3
Dinosaur Bones
H7KB3Y1QFPR8F3QXSDS4
Model City
J7KB3Y1GWPR8F31766D1
Temple
K7KB3Y1B15S8F3QXSDS4
Museum Boss
K7KB3Y1B15S8F3BTQBB4

Sewer
Wells
V7KB3Y1B15S8F3QS7QC1
Along The Sewer

W7KB3Y1VBVP8F3LC1M95
Food Carton
X7KB3Y1VLN7BF31CH1C3
Up The Well
Y7KB3Y1VV16QF3QS7QC1
Ryan's World
Q7KB3Y1LDRTQD3VKCDT1

Evil Lab
Circuit Boards
Q7KB3Y1LDRTQD3LCQSR3
Lab Top
R7KB3Y118H56T1WTY4R4
Hard Drives
S7KB3Y118H56T1TCQSR3

Brian's Folly
T7KB3Y118H56T1FNY4R4
On The Ceiling
T7KB3Y118H56T1TC4LD1
Kip's Bonus
68KB3Y118H56T151P6C4
Brain Boss
68KB3Y118H56T1TMVM35

Soul Blade

Play As Soul Edge
Method 1 – Simply complete the game with every character. Do this and the title screen will change from the plain blue design into a montage of all the characters. Now go to the character select screen and a new skull face representing Soul Edge will have appeared.

Method 2 – We couldn't actually be bothered to try this one, but apparently if you play the game for 20 hours without switching the machine off, Soul Edge will appear in much the same way.

Play As Sophitia!
Simply complete the Edge Master Mode with Sophitia (not too difficult), get the eighth weapon and then the next time you return to arcade mode, she'll be there for the taking (please note that you have to go to the left of Hwang on the character select screen to see her appear).

Play As Siegfried!
Complete the Edge Master Mode with Siegfried and obtain his eighth weapon. Then the next time you enter the arcade mode, Siegfried! will appear.

Play As Sophitia!!
Getting this other variation on Sophitia is slightly harder than the first. You basically have to complete Edge Master Mode, getting all 80 weapons. Good luck!

Play As Han Myong
To obtain this secret character, you must first complete the game with Hwang and Seung Mi Na and view their default endings. Then you must complete the game again and obtain their second endings. Please note that you must complete it each time with Hwang first. Do this

and Han Myong will be yours.

Changing Voice (Jap version only)
When the main title screen is displayed and you hear a gruff voice say "Soul Edge", it is possible to change the voice by holding L1 and L2 and pushing a direction on the joypad. Here are some examples:
L1 + L2 + ⬇ – A husky voice will say "Soul Edge" very slowly.
L1 + L2 + ⬅ (or ⬆) – Seung Mi Na will say "Soul Edge" very quickly.

Snazzy Outfits
If there is anyone out there who still can't find each and every costume for each character, here's how you do it:
Costume #1 – □   Costume #2 – X + □
Costume #3 – O   Costume #4 – △
Costume #5 – X + △

Alter Endings
When each Game Over sequence begins, there will be a point where the screen goes from being letter-boxed (ie squashed, with a black border) to full-screen. As soon as the picture becomes full-screen, frantically bash the joypad buttons and rotate the D-pad. If all goes according to plan, it will alter the ending sequence.
   The only instance where this doesn't apply is during Mitsurugi's ending where you have to fight Tanegashima in a first-person perspective. To kill him, simply use ⬅ or ➡ to dodge his arrows, then keep pushing forward whenever you get the opportunity. Finally, finish him off by using a slash button. And also, to get Voldo's second ending you must rotate the D-pad when he starts caressing the sword ('ere, don't blame us, we don't write these games).

Change The Camera View
To do this, you'll need a Sony Multitap and a second controller. Plug the Multitap into any port on the PlayStation, and then plug the second controller into port two of the Multitap. Now battle away using the first controller, and then at any time during the fights, press R1 or R2 on the second controller and the camera perspective will be dramatically altered – there is even a first-person view for both characters! With some of the camera angles, you can use the directional pad to rotate the action; and by pressing □ or X you can even zoom in and out.

Random Stage Select
To fight on random stages during the two-player versus mode, simply press and hold Select until each bout begins.

Coliseum Stage
If you go to the Game Option screen and set the ring size to 20M, you will be able to fight in the secret Coliseum stage in two-player mode.

Seung's Voice
Totally pointless, but did you

know that when you boot-up the game, one out of seven times the voice that says "Namco" at the start will be Seung Mi Na's instead of the usual deep-voiced bloke?

Super Puzzle Fighter II

Hidden Characters
All these can be discovered on the character-select screen.
Note: They are selectable in all modes except Street Puzzle Mode.

Play As Akuma (Gouki)
For Player 1: Move the cursor onto Morrigan, then hold Select and enter ⇩, ⇩, ⇩, ⇦, ⇦, ⇦, ○.
For Player 2: Move the cursor onto Felicia, then hold Select and enter ⇩, ⇩, ⇩, ⇨, ⇨, ⇨, ○.

Play As Devilot
For Player 1: Move the cursor onto Morrigan, then hold Select and enter, ⇦, ⇦, ⇦, ⇩, ⇩, ⇩, and when the timer reaches ten seconds exactly, press ○.
For Player 2: Move the cursor onto Felicia, then hold Select and enter ⇨, ⇨, ⇨, ⇩, ⇩, ⇩, and when the timer reaches ten seconds exactly press ○.

Play As Dan
For Player 1: Move the cursor onto Morrigan, then hold Select and enter ⇦, ⇦, ⇦, ⇩, ⇩, ⇩, ○.
For Player 2: Move the cursor onto Felicia, then hold Select and press ⇨, ⇨, ⇨, ⇩, ⇩, ⇩, ○.

Play As Hsien-Ko's (Lei-Lei's) Sister
For Player 1: Move the cursor onto Morrigan, then hold Select, move the cursor one square to the right and press ○.
For Player 2: Move the cursor onto Felicia, then hold Select, move the cursor two squares to the left and press ○.

Play As Amanda
For Player 1: Move the cursor onto Morrigan, then hold Select, move the cursor two squares to the right and press ○.
For Player 2: Move the cursor onto Felicia, then hold Select, move the cursor one square to the left and press ○.

Play Against CPU Devilot
Before you reach Stage 7, you must do all of the following, without continuing:
1. Defeat an opponent within one minute in one round.
2. Have at least one Super Combo.
3. Have a maximum chain of four or more.
4. You must have a maximum Power Gem of at least 20 units.

Play Against CPU Dan
Before you reach Stage 6, you must do all of the following, without continuing:
1. Defeat an opponent within one minute in one round.
2. Have at least one Super Combo.
3. Have a maximum chain of four or more.
4. You must have maximum Power Gem of at least 20 units.

Stage Select
After selecting your character, hold L2, R2 and Select, and choose your handicap. Then, whilst still holding L2, R2, and Select, press one of the following:

Ryu: ⇦	Chun-Li: ⇩
Ken: ⇨	Sakura: △
Akuma: L1	Dan: No Button
Morrigan: ⇧	Donovan: ○
Felicia: □	Hsien-Ko: ✕
Devilot: R1	

2. Hold R1 and press ✕, ○, △, □, release R1.
3. Hold L1 and press ✕, ○, △, □, release L1.
4. Hold R2 and press ✕, ○, △, □, release R2.
5. Hold down L2, Press ✕, □, △, ○, release L2.
6. You should hear a cheer and your cash will increase to $1 million.

Skeleton Warriors

Invincibility
Pause during play and press: ⇩, ○, □, □, ⇧, ✕. Unpause and you'll be translucent and invincible.

Space Griffon VF-9

Max Energy & Ammo
Pause and press △, □, ✕, L1, L2, R1, R2 during a normal game.

Space Jam

Unlimited Power
At the 'Space Jam' title enter:
□, △, ○, ⇦, ⇨, L1

Extra Menu
At the options screen, hold L1 + L2 + R1 + R2 and press ✕. This should bring you to a new screen.

Infinite Turbo
Get a flawless opponent on Speedy's Space Race.

100% Shooting Percentage
Get a flawless opponent in Sam's Shootout.

Free Goaltending
Hit only the top targets in Lola Bunny's Hall Of Hijinx

Alternate Ships In Space Race
Win the Intergalactic tournament on the Hard difficulty level with any Tune Squad member, then play another game. Go to Space Race at intermission to see ships.

Speedster

Cheats
Enter the following codes on the Speedster screen with the message 'PRESS A KEY'.

✕, ⇧, △, ⇩, R1, L1	Hidden Track
⇦, △, R1, ○, L1, ⇩	Reverse Tracks
⇨, □, ⇦, ○, ⇧, ✕	Super Cham/ship
L1, R1, L1, □, R1, ⇧	Heavy Metal Cars
⇧, ⇦, ⇨, ✕, ○, □	Performance Cars

Spot Goes To Hollywood

Cool Menu
On the title screen press: △, ⇧, ⇨, ⇩, ⇦, △, ⇦, ⇩, ⇨, ⇧, △.
A new 'Cool' option will appear on the menu. Select it and you can choose Open All Options, which lets you start from any level.

50 Lives
Enter the Cool Menu code, pause the game, and press □.

View All FMV
Enter the Cool Menu code and go to the Level Select screen. Hold □ and press Start.

Starblade Alpha

Rapid Fire
On the title screen, press ⇧, ⇧, ⇩, ⇩, ○, △, □

Infinite Continues
On the title screen, press ⇧, ⇨, ⇩, ⇦, ✕, ✕,✕

Steel Harbinger

Full Health
Pause during play and press L2, L2, R2, R2 ⇧, L1, ⇧, R1. A beep will confirm correct code entry. This code may only be enabled five times during the game.

All Weapons
Pause during play and press ✕, △, R2, △, ✕, L2, R2, ⇩, L2, □, ⇨. A beep will confirm correct code entry. Note: This code may only be enabled three times during the entire game.

M-16 Full Ammunition
Pause during play and press ⇩, □, □, □, ○, ○, ⇧, ⇨. A beep will confirm correct code entry. The M-16 will now have 999 rounds of ammunition.

Rocket Full Ammunition
Pause during play and press ⇦, ⇦, L1, R2, □, R1, ⇨, ⇨. A beep will confirm correct code entry. Note: This code may only be enabled five times.

Shield
Pause during play and press △, ✕, △, ✕, △, ✕ □, ○, □, ○, ⇧, R1. A beep will confirm correct code entry. **Note:** This code may only be enabled three times during the entire game.

Arctic Card
Pause during play and press ⇧, ⇨, △, ○, ⇩, ⇦, ✕, □. A beep will confirm correct code entry. Note: This code may only be enabled once per level.

Net Node Card

SF EX Plus Alpha

Revealing Hidden Characters
Expert mode is the place to be, and completing the missions is the task at hand. For every time you complete a mission, you'll be given a certain number of points. As your points build, so does the characters available to you. The following is the points required, with the instructions telling you how to retrieve them:

Character	Points Needed
Evil Ryu	100
Evil Hokuto	200
Cycloid Gamma	300
Cycloid Beta	400
New Vega (M Bison)	600
New Garuda	800
New Gouki (Akuma)	1000

To select the 'New' Vega, Gouki or Garuda, move onto the appropriate character and hold Start (in Arcade Mode, the green gauge will vanish, and in the other modes the selection box will turn from white to yellow), then press any button. Now, these are the CPU counterparts that you have fought against before. Although similar to their 'Normal' counterpart versions, these guys inflict more, and take less damage.
When you have managed to get all seven characters, a barrel will appear; this keeps track of the missions completed. When you've performed 220 missions, the Options Plus menu will appear; in the options menu funningly enough! At first, there is only one option available, but as you complete the game in various ways, more options are revealed.

Vs CPU Gouki (Akuma)
The Options Plus menu must be enabled for this to work. Set the 'Enemy' option to 'Plus'. You'll now able to fight against CPU Gouki and Garuda; although you'll be unable to fight Dhalsim or Sakura.
Select a game on Arcade with any difficulty and settings. Now comes the tricky part: for eight missions straight you must NOT lose a round. During the tenth round, Gouki will appear and take out Vega with his Blink Hell Murder Super Combo. You now fight Gouki, and even if you were to lose, you'll be able to continue, or even pick another character.
Unlike in previous Street Fighter epics, you can still reach Gouki with Gouki or CPU Gouki. Plus you can finish any which way you like. Whether it be a normal, super or time out.
When the ever tough CPU Gouki is no more, the following options become selectable in the 'Option Plus' menu. They only apply to the Training mode:
Training Partner
Fix (normal) or move (2-player against you). Only works when 2-player joypad plugged in port 2.
Super Combo Gauge
Three (normal) or infinite (gauge never changes).
Super Cancel Limit
On (normal) or off (cancel similar super combos)

Otedana
Off (normal) or on (opponent moves slower through air).

Fight CPU Gouki Bug!
Following the steps above, when you come to the match against Gouki, join the match on the second player side. Now, with the second player's fighter beat the crap out of player one. Then, before the 2-players vs CPU match commences, continue, pick a character and beat the second player. When the CPU battle finally begins, it will have reset to Battle 1. The match will still be against Gouki, but in Thailand! The next ten battles are against Gouki in other locations.

Fight CPU Garuda
With any character, you must get two perfects and four super finishes before battle 10. On top of that, you must perform a level 3 super combo finish. If your character has a level 3 super (Gouki, Evil Ryu & Zangief), then that can be utilised.
Now, each character below must perform a combo at least once during the game that does the following number of hits:

Allen Snider & Darun Mister – 6 Hit Combo
Blair Dame, Cracker Jack, Ken, Pullum Purna, Ryu & Zangief – 7 Hit Combo
Guile, Hokuto, Kairi & Skullomania – 8 Hit Combo
Gouki & CPU Gouki – 9 Hit Combo
Doctrine Dark – 11 Hit Combo
Chun-Li – 12 Hit Combo
Garuda, CPU Garuda, Vega, CPU Vega, Evil Ryu & Evil Hokuto – 13+ Hit Combo

Hidden Barrel Game
Highlight the Practice option on the mode selection screen and press Start. Then press ⇧, ⇧, ⇨, ⇧, ⇨, ⇧, Start. A message will appear to confirm correct code entry. Select the Bonus option under Practice mode to play the bonus barrel game from *Street Fighter 2.*

CPU-Controlled Team Battle Round
Select Team Battle mode. Hold L2 + Select at the 'Vs Loading' screen until the match begins. The CPU will control your fighter for this round.
Note: This code may only be enabled once per team battle.

View Hits In Survival Mode
Press Select at the Survival result screen to display the number of hits completed.

Hiding Your Fighters
This little extra can often prove useful; because if you don't want your opponent to see what you're selecting, simply hold L2 down, then select your characters. When you release L2 they'll be replaced by question marks.

Gouki's (Akuma's) Beads
Simply finish Gouki off with a Super Combo, and his necklace will break off. Probably a Christmas cracker job!

Street Fighter Alpha

Computer-Controlled Dan
Getting to fight a computer-controlled Dan is easy… and beating him is even easier. All you've got to do is win the fifth, sixth, or seventh match and hold Up + L2 + R2. Keep these buttons held down until the winning quote is displayed and then release. If this has worked, you'll go to the next fight in the sequence and just before the blows start flowing, the immortal line 'Here Comes A New Challenger' will flash up on screen before you're whisked away to Dan's hidden location.

Computer-Controlled Akuma
The twisted master can be accessed via two different methods. Firstly, you can try beating the game without losing a single round and also achieving a minimum of ten super combo finishes (that's ten victories with the 'S★' symbol displayed). Do this on any level higher than four and Akuma will stroll on and humiliate you after the final boss. Alternatively, try positioning your cursor over the character you wish to fight as on the character select screen and hold L2 + R2, then press and hold ✕. Hold the three buttons down until Akuma has pulverised your opponent, then fight.

Selecting Dan
Go to the random select box on the character screen and hold L2. Now press the following code in sequence: △, □, ✕, ○, △. If the code has worked, Dan will appear as your selection. To get Dan in his other strip, simply input the code backwards so it reads: △, ○, ✕, □, △.

Selecting Akuma
During the character select screen, go to the random box and hold L2. Now press the following code in sequence: ⇦, ⇦, ⇦, ⇩, ⇩, ⇩, □, △ (⇦ = towards outside of character box). Akuma will appear as your character selection if the cheat has worked. To play as Akuma in his other strip, finish the code with ○, ✕, instead of □, △.

Selecting M Bison
Go to the random box on the character select screen and hold L2. Now press the following code in sequence: ⇦, ⇦, ⇩, ⇩, ⇦, ⇩, ⇩, □, △ (⇦ = towards outside of character box). Alternatively, finish the sequence with ○, ✕ (instead of □, △) to get the Bison in alternate colours.

Dramatic Battle
If you reckon you're the business at *Street Fighter Alpha*, this hidden game will test your might to breaking point. If you complete the game on any skill level higher than four, a new option called 'Dramatic Battle' will appear in the options menu. Plug in two controllers and have an able-bodied friend at the ready and you'll both take on Bison with Ken and Ryu. Fast, frantic and over nearly as soon as it begins, this battle sure is tough – especially seeing as both players share the same energy bar. Once you've obtained the Dramatic Battle option, save it to your memory card for evermore.

a-z of cheats

Time Crisis

Easy Arcade Mode
Select the arcade mission from the main selection screen and then, on the next screen that allows you to choose between Time Attack mode or the Story mode, shoot outside of the screen. If the cheat has worked, you'll see the word 'Easy' appear over the Story mode option. Now select it and start playing and you'll now have five lives and a lot more time.

Alternate Reload
Plug a standard control pad into port 2 of the PlayStation and then during the game you'll be able to press □, X, ○, or △ to duck down and reload instead of the gun button. You can even place it on the floor and use your foot!

Cheat Mode
At the main screen, where you choose the three boxes, shoot one bullet into the middle of the loop of the 'R' in 'CRISIS', then two into the centre of the cross-hairs (next to 'TIME'). If you get it right you'll be taken to a cheat menu where you can choose nine lives, no reload, and infinite continues.

Pause during play and press ⇦, △, ⇨, R1, ○, R1, ⇩. A beep will confirm correct code entry. Note: This code may only be enabled three times during the entire game.

Teleport Credit
Pause during play and press L1, R1, R1, L2, R2, L2, ○, △. A beep will confirm correct code entry. Note: This code may only be enabled 100 times per level.

View Credits
Press □, □, □, □, ○, ○, ○, □, □ at the main menu.
View FMV Sequences

Press L2, L2, R2, R2, L1, R1, □, ○, ⇩ at the main menu.

Play Single Level
Enter one of the following button sequences at the main menu to play the corresponding level:
Los Angeles
○, ○, R2, R2, ⇦, ⇨, ⇩, L2, L2, △.
LA7
○, ○, L2, L2, ⇦, ⇨, ⇩, R2, R2, △.
Las Vegas
□, □, L2, L1, ⇧, ⇩, R1, R2, ⇦, ⇨.
Las Vegas 7
□, □, L2, L1, ⇧, ⇩, R1, R2, ⇨, ⇦.
San Francisco
○, □, L2, R1, △, L1, R2, ⇩, ⇧, ⇨.
Houston
L2, L1, R1, R2, ○, ⇦, ⇨, △, ⇨, ⇩.
Washington
○, ○, L1, R1, L2, R2, ⇦, ⇨, △, □.
Florida
L1, R1, □, ○, R2, L2, ⇧, △, ⇩, ⇩.
Nebraska
□, □, ⇦, ⇨, □, ○, ○, ⇧, ⇧, □.
Moonbase
R1, R1, L2, R1, □, △, ⇦, ⇨, R2.

SF: The Movie

Choose Akuma
Highlight Guile and press ⇧, R1, ⇩, L2, ⇨, L1, ⇦, R2. If done correctly, Guile's face should turn into a blur and you will now be Akuma.

Secret Configuration
Pause the game while fighting. Press Select, a menu will appear to configure your buttons.

Street Racer

Level Codes
Silver **TRAFIK** Platinum **DOUGAL**
Gold **NEJATI** Super **TURGAY**

Secret Car
By entering the 'Dougal' password, you'll have access to a brand-new hidden Rabbit car which has three new personalised tracks.

Secret Options
By entering the 'Turgay' password, you'll have access to a secret options screen which allows you to change the side of your car, turn the weapons on or off, remove the other cars, plus much more besides!

Striker '96

Special Teams
Yes it's true, not only can you compete against the special Warner and Rage teams, but Trekkies can also enjoy thrashing a whole team of characters from the various Star Trek generations. All you have to do is win the World Cup to enter a bonus Special Cup tournament featuring all of the above teams. Reckon you can take on the intergalactic celebs?

Super Buster Bros Collec.

Level Select
Hold ⇩ and select tour mode.

Expert Mode
Press X on controllers 1 and 2 while selecting tour mode.

Tempest X

Level Skip
In any game, press and hold the following buttons: L1, R1, ⇳, △, ○, Start and Select. If done correctly, you will hear a loud grinding noise. Let go of the buttons and immediately press and hold the following buttons: L2, R1, X, △, and ⇩. You should hear a word spoken if done correctly. Now any time you wish to advance a level, simply press L1 + L2 + R1 + R2. You will skip to the next level as soon as there are no enemies on the web. The easiest way to do this is at the very beginning of the level before an enemy appears, or press the top four buttons and then use a Superzapper.

Ten Pin Alley

Taunts
During Team Play mode, one team can

taunt the other during their approach by pressing L1 + L2 + R1 + R2.
Then:
△ – "Choke!"
□ – "Loser!"
○ – "Miss!"
X– "You Suck!"

300 Game Tournament
Enter 'Vllooma' as a name in the sixth saved game slot to play in a 300-game bowl-off tournament.

Loading A Previously Saved Player
The instructions in the game manual are incorrect. Here's how to load a saved player... Highlight 'Player 1' and delete. This will display a load option. Highlight 'Load' and press X. This will display previously saved characters. Now highlight the character to be loaded and press X.

Test Drive: Offroad

Cheat Codes
Type these special codes in as the player's name for various effects:
friendly	Dirt track
alltrack	All tracks available
fifty	Hot rod
lowrider	Stock car
beefy	Monster truck
sprinter	4X4 buggy

Tetris Plus

Stage Select
1. Choose Puzzle Mode and select Password.
2. As soon as the Password screen appears press: ⇩, ⇩, ⇨, ⇧, ⇧, ⇨, ⇧, ⇧, ⇩, ⇨.
3. Repeat Step 2
4. Press X
5. When the game starts, a Stage Select will be available.

Theme Park

Instant Millions
Enter your nickname as **BOVINE**, then during play hold down ○, □ and X for ten seconds to receive ten million dollars.

Tigershark

Invincibility
Enter KURSK as a password.

Infinite Ammunition
Enter KIROV as a password.

Weapons Upgrade
Enter RUBLE as a password.

Low Gravity
Enter SOYUZ as a password.

Sea Hunter Mini-Game
Enter SNEEG as a password.

View FMV Sequences
Enter KIEV as a password.

Preview Game (Bug Rider)
Enter BUGGY as a password.

Passwords
2	AKULA	3	PASHA
4	MIRAS	5	NAKAT
6	REZKY	7	TUCHA
8	ZARYA	9	VOSTA

Tokyo Highway Battle

Cheats
After winning your first race in Scenario mode, try entering these codes on controller 2 during your next race:
⇧ + Select – Displays best lap time
⇨ + Select – Displays best time
⇩ + Select – Displays program number (pointless!)
L1 + Select – Changes the colour of the speedometer to white

Change Car Colour
Once you have won at least one race in Scenario mode, go to the Car Select screen and then press R2 on controller one to change the colour of the motors.

Maximum Points
When the 'Jaleco' logo appears as the game starts up, press and hold L1 + L2 + R1 + ⇩ + Start on controller 2. Now when the FMV intro begins, press Start on controller 1 (make sure that the

---

Tekken

Extra characters
By completing the game with each of the eight standard characters, you'll earn yourself the opportunity to play the game as the respective character's sub-boss. Although some aren't great variations on the original character, it's still good for a laugh!

Heihachi Mishima
The final boss bloke is slightly harder to obtain. You must complete the game in under five minutes, 30 seconds without continuing.

Devil Kazuya
To access Devil Kazuya in Arcade mode, you must complete the Galaga loading game with a 'Perfect'. To do this, you have to blast all eighth levels of the game without missing a single craft. To assist you, try blasting the first wave in less than 18.5 seconds to receive a duel-craft for double the firepower. You can also practice each wave by pressing Select after it has finished to repeat the stage again – however, by doing this, you wont be able to obtain the Devil.

Duel Galaga craft
To obtain two Galaga crafts, press and hold ⇧ L1 △ X on the second control pad as you switch on your PlayStation. You wont be able to use this cheat for the Devil.

Tekken 2

Choose A Pose
You can determine which of the two victory poses your character performs. After you've won a bout, press and hold □ or X (right through the replay) to get the first ; ○ or △ to get the second.

First-Person Perspective
1. First of all you must obtain all the hidden characters in the game.
2. Go to the character-select screen.
3. Hold down the L1 and L2 buttons and select

your character in the normal manner.
4. Now your fighter will appear as a wire-frame model.
5. When the fight starts, the view will change to a first-person perspective.

Big-Head Mode
1. Acquire all the hidden characters in the game.
2. Start again but hold down the Select button when you select your fighter.
3. Keep it held down until the round begins.
4. You should now see that your fighter's head has been blown up!

Sky Mode
If, having obtained all of the secret characters, you press ⇧ + Select when choosing a character, lo and behold you will enable SKY MODE! You must hold down this button combination until the fight actually starts, at which point you will hear a 'punch' sample to confirm that the cheat has been activated. Basically it allows you to fight à la Mortal Kombat, with certain uppercut-type moves resulting in your opponent flying high up into the sky. For some reason it works with sweeps as well.
Note: This particular cheat also enables Big Head Mode 1.

Easier Roger/Alex
There's an easier way to get Roger/Alex. First get all the players selectable. That is including Kazuya and Devil/Angel. Now all you have to do is go to practice mode and do one 10-hit combo with any character. Make sure that you turn off the tool bar at the bottom of the screen and do the buttons to press, otherwise it won't work. When it's activated, you should hear the word 'great'.

Bigger-Head Mode
1. First perform the Big-Head Mode cheat.
2. If you're playing in arcade mode, hold down Select when you reach the continue screen.

3. Your head and arms will now be bigger than ever before!
4. If playing in Vs Mode, go back to the character select screen and hold Select again whilst choosing a fighter for the same effect.

Purple Kazuya
1. All the secret characters must be accumulated first.
2. Start a new game and highlight Kazuya.
3. Now hold down Start while selecting him.
4. He'll now fight in his third, purple costume.

Thought Bubbles
1. Play in practice mode.
2. Leave your character alone for a while.
3. You'll now see thought bubble appear above his or her head!

Obtaining Kazuya Mishima
1. Acquire all the sub-bosses by completing the game using the ten original fighters.
2. Play through using a sub-boss.
3. Once completed, Kazuya will be added.

Devil & Angel
To obtain this duel character, Complete the game with Kazuya.

Fight Roger/Alex
1. Get to the Devil or

Angel...
2. Start a new game with any character and when you reach the third fight, defeat your opponent on the last round with only a particle of energy left.
3. If you do it right you will hear the word "Great" and the next fight will be against Roger or Alex.

Theatre Mode
View the Tekken 2 endings at your leisure!
1. Unplug the second controller.
2. You must have all the available characters stored in your memory card.
3. Load up the game. When the words 'Namco Presents' appear, press ⇧, ⇨, ○, X, and Select – holding the last four down when you press them. It's tricky as you need to enter this sequence quickly before the words disappear.
4. If unsuccessful, the game will load the normal opening intro. Try again.
5. If successful, you'll be taken to the Tekken 2 Theatre. Here, you can scroll down the list of FMV endings (and openings!) and play any one of them.
Note: After about 10 seconds or so of inaction, this mode will exit automatically, so keep moving around if you plan to stay.

Yet More Poses
Six of the fighters have a third finishing pose after winning a fight: Law, Paul, Michell, Jack 2, P Jack, Kunimitsu, and Kuma. Simply hold both kick buttons down, from the moment you win the fight, right through the replay to the end.

Time Commando

Secret Level
There is a special hidden level in this time-travelling beat-'em-up adventure. At the password screen enter: **COMMANDO**. This puts you inside a boxing ring where you get to fight several different enemies.

Level Passwords
Roman Empire: TUHOUEFY
Japanese: ADSAZGLY
European Middle Ages: ZJFKYGLZ
Conquistadors: EBELPWNF
Western: EVXGPWNN
Modern Wars: ENQOEQHJ
Future: NDWMHGEC
Beyond Time: XEMJBDFS

Special Passwords
All weapons: HUIBON
Max health: VONLUX

Cheats
Pause the game, highlight 'Sound FX',

then enter the desired code. A sound will confirm it.

X, △, △, ●, △, △, ●, □, X
Restores health (can be repeated when needed)

X, □, X, △, ●, □, X, ●, X, △
Go to the next stage

●, X, △, ●, □, ●, X, □, △, ●
Go to the next world

■, ●, △, X, ●, □, △, ●, X, △
Maximum size for energy bar

△, X, ●, □, X, □, ●, △, X, ●
All weapons

△, ●, △, X, □, X, ●, □, △, X
Infinite ammo

■, X, ●, △, ●, X, □, △, ●, △, ■
Automatic recharge for certain weapons

buttons on controller 2 are still being held). Now when the title screen is displayed, select Scenario mode and go to the Speed Shop. Upon entering, you'll immediately notice that you have 9,999,999 points to spend on any car modifications you want.

Maximum Money
On the second controller, press and hold L1 + L2 + R1 + Start + ⇩, immediately after the opening demo (when the checkered flag title appears) until the title flashes and letters finish flying in.

Extra Cars & Colours
When you defeat Drift King, three more cars (Supra, NSX, and GT-R) become available. Use one of those cars and defeat him again to activate a colour select. Go to car selection screen and push R2 to change colour.

Tokyo Highway Battle R
Maximum Funds
At the title screen, press the following on controller 2:
⇧, △, ⇧, X, ⇨, □, ⇦, ●, Select, Start

All Parts
At the title screen, press the following on controller 2:
⇨, ⇨, ⇧, ⇩, ⇧, ⇦, ⇩, ⇦, ●, △

Bonus Parts
At the title screen, press the following on controller 2:
⇧, ⇩, ⇧, ⇩, ⇦, ⇨, ⇦, ⇨

Total NBA '96
All-Star Games
This allows you to play either the '94/'95 (Phoenix) or '95/'96 (San Antonio) All-Star Game. It has the All-Star Weekend court, and the team names are from the Eastern/Western conferences...
At the Exhibition Game screen, press R1, L1, R1, L1, R2, L2, R2, L2 – '94/'95 or
R1, R1, R2, R2, L2, L1, L2, L1 – '95/'96

Top Gun
New Level Codes
Miramar
1   82813
2   81723 or 99764
3   20582 or 20873 or 47924
4   79613 or 81835 or 82372
5   79523 or 81772 or 82282
6   07631 or 20213 or 22172 or 40773 or 81454

Cuba
1   20123 or 22082
2   15940 or 20423 or 20624 or 57131 or 81664 or 82732
3   38332
4   32880 or 82072 or 82123
5   55272 or 89332
6   20906 or 79442
7   21854

Korea
1   44673 or 82432
2   27914 or 79754 or 81424
3   79103 or 79344 or 82852
4   20693
5   76252
6   21701
7   81712 or 82222
8   06604 or 79944
9   20162
10   21170

Libya
2   21551 or 79535
3   20804 or 81844
4   76734 or 79451
5   38902
6   20411 or 21860 or 21911 or 51493
7   81484
8   45726 or 76760 or 79885 or 82285

Power-Up!
There's a handy cheat in the game to give yourself 10 continues, 10 planes and 10 plasma shots. Just start a game and then pause it and click on the options in the screen that contains 'Play Game'. Now press △, □, L1, L1, □, △, L1, L1, R1. Now if you press the picture to the right you should come up with a skull. Now press △, □, L1, L1, □, △ and the game will restart with all your lovely goodies installed!

Toukon Retsuden 2
Trick
At the title screen press: L1, Select, L2, Select, R1, Select, R2, Select, △, Select, ●, Select, X, Select, □, Select.
Note: After each press of the Select button, 'Press Start' will flash on screen. Wait until it's finished flashing before entering the next part.

Triple Play '97
Monster Homers
Enter and hold: L1, L2, R1, R2. Now enter (without holding): ⇧, ⇧, △, △, ⇧, ⇧, X, X
You should hear a chime: now simply hit the ball for an automatic home run.
Note: You must enter this for each new batter.

Mystery Stadium

When choosing the stadium press L1, R1, L1, R1 (hold the last R1), then press Start. This brings up a new stadium to play ball in.

Super Runner
Enter 'Dennis Hirsch' at custom players for a superfast runner.

Triple Play '98
Bonus Fields
Press L1, R1, L1, R1, □ on the stadium selection screen. The Field Of Dreams cornfield, Ebbets Field, and The Polo Grounds are now available to select.
Note: The latter two stadiums will appear in monochrome.

Players In Underwear
Enable the 'Bonus Fields' code (L1, R1, L1, R1, □ on stadium selection screen). Highlight the cornfield and press L1, R1, L1, R1, □. Enable the 'EA Sports Dream Team' code (L2, R2, L2, R2, ● on team selection screen) and select them as the home team. The team will be in their underwear when play begins.

Always Hit Home Runs
Hold L1 + L2 + R1+ R2, then press ⇧, △, ⇦, ⇨, □, ●, ⇩, X while in the batter's box.

Always Strike Out The Batter
Throw one pitch for a strike. Before selecting the next pitch, hold L1 + L2 + R1 + R2, then press X, ⇩, ●, □, ⇨, ⇦, △, ⇧. The batter will strike out after missing the next pitch.

Crowd And Stadium Comments
Hold L1 + L2 + R1+ R2, then press □, ●, □.

Weather Comments
Hold L1 + L2 + R1+ R2, then press ●, X, ●. The announcers will make a comment about the weather.

Sponsor Comments
Hold L1 + L2 + R1+ R2, then press △, ●, △. The announcers will make a comment about a sponsor.

Crowd Cheers
Hold L1 + L2 + R1+ R2, then press the following

button: ⇩, X, ⇩, X, △.

Crowd Boos
Hold L1 + L2 + R1+ R2, then press ⇩, X, ⇩, X, X.

EA Sports Dream Team
Press L2, R2, L2, R2, ● at the team selection screen, then select the 33rd overall team.

Super Pitch
Press X to throw a fastball, then immediately press □ + ⇩.

Twisted Metal
Level Codes
You can skip straight to some of the levels in the game by using these passwords.
Freeway level
X, □, □, ●, △
River park level
X, △, □, ●, □
Cyburbia
X, □, △, △, △
Warehouse level
●, △, □, ●, X
Rooftop final stage
□, △, X, ●, X

Multi-Cars
If you want to have a real fight for your life, try out this password. It results in five cars all chasing you at once!
□, △, ●, □, □

Helicopter View
To have a view from high up, use this password, then press Start + ⇩ on either the Arena or Rooftop stage.
●, ●, △, X, Space

Invincibility
There's no easier way to succeed in a game than by using this code.
□, △, X, Space (press ⇨),
●

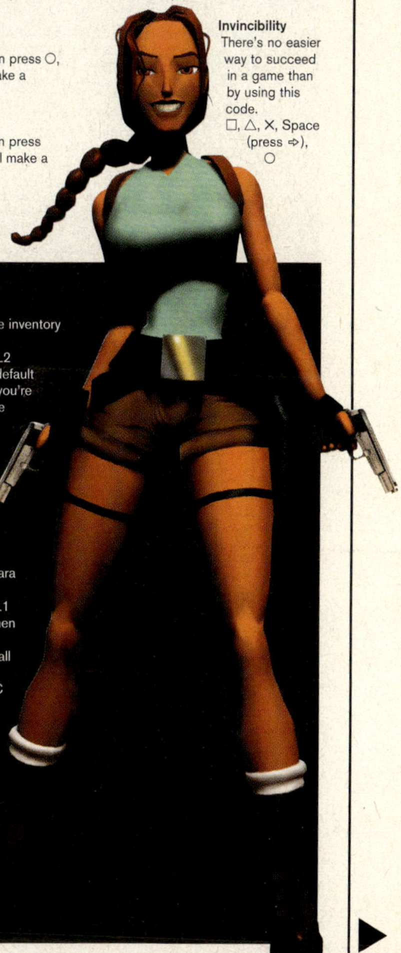

Tomb Raider
Level Skip
Enter this code once on the inventory screen:
L2, R2, △, L1, L1, ●, R2, L2
Note: This works with the default control system (Type 1). If you're using one of the others, use the relevant alternative sequence...
Type 2: L2, R2, ●, △, △, L1, R2, L2
Type 3: L2, R2, R1, △, △, L1, R2, L2

Maximum Weapons
Enter this sequence in the inventory screen to make Lara sigh.
L1, △, L2, R2, R2, L2, ● L1
Now return to the action, then when you return to the inventory screen you'll see all those lovely weapons.
Note: If you have the NTSC version of the game, press R2 for L2 and vice versa. This code works with the default control system (Type 1). If you're using one of the others, use the relevant alternative sequence...
Type 2: △, ●, L2, R2, R2, L2, L1, △
Type 3: △, R1, L2, R2, R2, L2, L1, △

Tobal 2
Big Players/Little Players
When selecting your character, hold L2, R2 and push the △ button. Now during the bouts, you can increase and decrease the size of your character by pressing L2 (shrink) or R2 (grow). This works on all modes except for Quest.

Alternative Costumes
Press ⇧ + △ when you select your character and they will enter the battle arena in a different set of clobber.

Hidden Characters
There are loads of secret characters in Tobal 2. Here's how you

get to play as them:
Mufu – beat the game on easy mode.
Nork – beat the game on normal mode.
Udan – beat the game on hard mode.
Trix (Toriyama Robot) – beat the game on easy mode using a monster.
D Purple – beat the game on normal mode using a monster.
Red Zeppel – beat the game on hard mode using a monster.
Black Attacker – beat the game on easy mode without using continues.
Mono Eye – beat the game on normal mode without using continues.
Dark Elf – beat the game on hard mode without using continues.

Tri Horn – becomes playable after a certain number of replays have been saved.
Chocobo – beat Practice (1st) Dungeon.
Mark – beat Egyptian Ruins (2nd) Dungeon.
Dog – beat the Desert Spaceship (3rd) Dungeon.
Mark2 – beat the Castle (6th) Dungeon.
Totem 1st – see all ten endings on easy mode.
Totem 2nd – see all ten endings on normal mode.
Totem 3rd – see all ten endings on hard mode.

then enter the desired code.

Total NBA '97
Super Difficulty
On the game options screen, press L2 + R1 and a new 'Super' difficulty level will be available.

Maximum Skills
On the Create Player screen, hold Select + ⇦ + □ + ● to make your player's skill bars shoot up to maximum.

Total Eclipse
Mission Codes
2nd Mission
X, ●, △, □, X, X, X, □

3rd Mission
△, △, ●, X, △, △, X, □

Polaris 5
●, ●, ●, △, X, △, □, □

Level Select
Instead of messing around with those level codes (unless you want to do things in order) you can try out this handy cheat to give a level select. All you've got to do is highlight the password option but don't press anything. Instead hold down the Select button and tap the following sequence: □, △, L1. Now release Select and press: □, △, L1, □, △, L1. The screen should then say 'STAGE – 1' and you can select any stage.

An All-Star menu option appears, allowing you to turn various cheats on.

Remove Stats
Press L1, L2, R1 & R2 during a break or at half-time

Crazy Ball!
1. Use Shawn Bradley or George Mureasan.
2. Goaltend, rebound the ball with either one, and shoot a three-pointer.
3. The ball will fly into the air, do some loops, and you will score a point and then have the ball back.

a-z of cheats

continued

Infinite Weapons
Arm yourself to the hilt.
△, Space, □, ○, ○

Final Level Cheat
On the final level of the game, just after beating all three cars on the rooftop, quickly drive your car off the edge of the roof. While you're falling you should get the announcement of the fight with Minion and you'll be put back up onto the roof with full energy and all the weapons you started with!

Play As Minion
To drive around the game as Minion, just choose the tank and enter this code on the password screen:
□, △, △, Space, □

UFO: Enemy Unknown

Save Money
One to two hours before the end of the month, transfer all of your scientists and engineers to another base. Since they are in transit they don't get paid.

Easy Money
This is an easy way to get millions of dollars. First go and investigate a crash site, then when you finish it, research Alien Alloys. Once it's researched, manufacture a lot and sell it all for a nice profit – it costs $3,000 to make, but sells for $6,400. Also, sell all but one alien corpse. After you research it, sell it and get $20,000 for each one.

Never Die
You need a memory card for this one. When you start the mission, save the game. Then, after you end your turn, if none of your guys die, save after the aliens' turn is over. Continue until someone dies, in which case Abort Mission and Load Game. Then do something different from last time. Continue until the mission is over and none of your guys will die.

V-Force

Secret Options
Once you've reached level 16, return to the main menu screen. Two more options have been added to the previous three. Now select the bottom option to display a secret option screen. The options allow you to view the FMV sequences, play the background music, view the character biographies, and reveal the storyline.

V-Rally

Cheats
To activate the cheat mode, load the game and wait for the Infogrames logo to appear. Then quickly press:
⇧, ⇩, △, ○, ⇧, ⇩, △ + ○ (press the last two buttons together)
The phrase 'Lock Off' will appear to confirm correct code entry (and unlock all the Arcade tracks). Before the screen changes, press one of the following controller actions to activate the corresponding cheat function…

Unlimited Time
Press and hold ⇦ + L1 to get infinite time on Arcade mode.

Narrow Tracks
Press and hold ⇦ + L2. The Arcade tracks are now narrower – as confirmed by the 'Narrow Tracks Loading' message before a race.

Jeep
Press and hold ⇦ + R1. A small Jeep will replace the Peugeot 106 Maxi. This cheat also activates the secret Rollercoaster track.

Restart Race
Press and hold ⇦ + R2 to allow an Arcade mode race to be restarted.

Debug Mode
Press ⇦ then ⇨. Game debug information will be displayed. Press Start to access a 'Memory' option that displays more information.
All Cheats
If you want the first four cheats active at the same time, simultaneously press and hold ⇦ + L1 + L2 + R1 + R2 when the 'Lock Off' message appears.

Secret Rollercoaster Track
Activate the cheat for the Jeep, then select the 'Sweden 1' Championship track in Time Trial mode. The screen should say it's loading the '????' stages to indicate you've accessed the secret circuit.

V Tennis

Secret Characters
Mr Tonkin: When playing in normal mode, move the cursor over any player, then press L2, L2, R1, R1, R1, ⇩, △ x 4, ○.
Mrs Tonkin: Hold L1, R2, ⇧, □, then press ○.

Victory Boxing

Extra Heads
Whilst competing in the main event, once you have fought and beaten Takeshi Hangman, The Champ and Alan Kidd, return back to the 'create you own boxer' mode (whilst keeping with the same gym you used to beat them), and the highlight the 'head' option. Now scroll off of the list available by either going left or right, and then the heads of the three boxers we just mentioned will be available for you to select.

Secret Fighters
If you beat The Champ and then successfully defend your title five consecutive times in each different fighting style, you'll reveal six new characters. They are as follows:
Peek-a-boo
Kiki & Mimi, Edward King
Detroit
Roboxer Beta 1, Carrie the Bunny
Open
Jack-in-the-Box, Snake

Viewpoint

Passwords
Here are the passwords for every level, except 5-3 which many players are unsure whether or not it exists:

Level 1-1	**CGG**	**Level 1-2**	**CLL**
Level 1-2	**CLL**	**Level 1-3**	**CRR**
Level 2-1	**FGD**	**Level 2-2**	**FLJ**
Level 2-3	**FRN**	**Level 3-1**	**HGD**
Level 3-2	**HLG**	**Level 3-3**	**HRL**
Level 4-1	**KGG**	**Level 4-2**	**KLD**
Level 4-3	**KRJ**	**Level 5-1**	**MGJ**
Level 5-2	**MLD**	**Level 6-1**	**PGL**
Level 6-2	**PLG**	**Level 6-3**	**PRD**

Skip To The Movies
To go straight to the end-of-level movies, and enter: □, ○, △, ⇨, ⇦, ⇩, R1, L2, R2, R1

Invincibility
Becoming invincible is always useful when playing a shoot-'em-up, but this game might be a bit unstable if you use this: □, □, ○, ○, △, X, □, ⇧, ⇧, ⇩, ⇩, L1, R1, Select

VR Baseball '97

Field Of Dreams Stadium
Highlight the credits option and press: □, ○, □, ○, △.

Twisted Metal 2

Advanced Attacks
⇦, ⇨, ⇧ – Freeze Blast (Blue ball, slightly homing)
⇨, ⇦, ⇧ – Napalm (Just like the normal pick-up weapon)
⇧, ⇧, ⇦ – Jump (Well, you jump!)
⇧, ⇧, ⇨ – Shield (The green dome of protection; lasts 3 seconds)
⇦, ⇨, ⇩ – Rear Attack (Fires the currently selected weapon behind your vehicle)
⇨, ⇦, ⇩ – Mine Attack (Drops one huge mine)
⇨, ⇩, ⇦, ⇧ – Cloaking Device (Renders your vehicle invisible for 3 seconds)

Extra Character Codes
To get two extra characters just execute these codes at the car selection screen for a one-player tournament game. Once done, you can select the extra cars in any other mode. Also, these codes need to be re-entered each time you load the game.
⇧, L1, △, ⇨ – Adds Sweet Tooth to the character selection screen
L1, ⇧, ⇩, ⇦ – Adds Minion to your character selection screen

Extra Level Codes
You'll need to execute these codes at the track selection screen for a two-player challenge match. If done properly you should hear a loud noise and the game will advance to the character selection screen. Like the Extra Character Codes, you'll need to re-enter these each time you load the game:
⇩, ⇦, R1, ⇩ – Rooftops Level (From the first *Twisted Metal*)
⇧, ⇩, ⇨, R1 – Jet Rider Level (Based on the game, *Jet Rider*)
⇩, ⇧, L1, R1 – Cyburbia Level (From the first game)

Homing Napalm
1. You must be holding three napalms (no more, no less).
2. Now fire one of them and keep the button held down.
3. While holding the fire button, enter this code: ⇧ ⇩ ⇩ ⇦ ⇦ ⇦ ⇨ ⇨ (keep the fire button held and try again if it doesn't work straight away).
4. You will receive about a dozen extra napalms which will now home in on enemies.

Level Codes For Vehicles
Axel
Los Angeles – N/A
Moscow – X△XX_
Paris – ○△□_△_
Amazonia – △△□○○_
New York – _△□□X_
Antarctica – XX△□△○
Holland – ○X○△○○
Hong Kong – △X○XX○
Dark Tooth – △□△□_□

Grasshopper
Los Angeles – N/A
Moscow – △X○___
Paris – X△○□□○
Amazonia – _X○○△○
New York – ○△X○_□
Antarctica – X□□○_△
Holland – △△X□○△
Hong Kong – ○□□□△X
Dark Tooth – X_X□□_

Hammerhead
Los Angeles – N/A
Moscow – _△XXX_
Paris – _X△□X△
Amazonia – △__X○
New York – △△X△XX
Antarctica – △X△○X□
Holland – △□□X□_
Hong Kong – ○△○□□△
Dark Tooth – ○○○_△X

Mr Grimm
Los Angeles – N/A
Moscow – △△XX○_
Paris – ○X△○△X
Amazonia – X□□△△△
New York – △__○X○
Antarctica – ○△X△X_
Holland – XX△_○X
Hong Kong – _X○△□□
Dark Tooth – _□△○○△

Mr Slam
Los Angeles – N/A
Moscow – XX△□X_
Paris – X__○X□
Amazonia – ○△□_□X
New York – △X○□_○
Antarctica – △_△○△△
Holland – _○__○_
Hong Kong – □__△_△
Dark Tooth – □_□△○X

Outlaw 2
Los Angeles – N/A
Moscow – _X○_△_
Paris – △△X○△_
Amazonia – △□□□△_
New York – ○X△△△_
Antarctica – X△○□△_
Holland – X□□_△_
Hong Kong – _△X□XX
Dark Tooth – _○X_△_

Roadkill
Los Angeles – N/A
Moscow – ○X△□□
Paris – △_△__○
Amazonia – XX△○□△
New York – ○__X_X
Antarctica – _△□X○_
Holland – X__△_□
Hong Kong – △△□△○△
Dark Tooth – △○X△□X

Shadow
Los Angeles – N/A
Moscow – □__△△_
Paris – XX○_△X
Amazonia – X△X□○△
New York – X__X○□
Antarctica – ○X○○X○
Holland – ○△□△□_
Hong Kong – ○_△_□X
Dark Tooth – ○△_△○_

Spectre
Los Angeles – N/A
Moscow – ○△XX△_
Paris – _△□○○X
Amazonia – ○X△□△X
New York – _X○XX△
Antarctica – X__○△
Holland – △__□X□
Hong Kong – X△X△○□
Dark Tooth – X○○○_△

Thumper
Los Angeles – N/A
Moscow – ○__△X_
Paris – X□□○○△
Amazonia – △X○_□_
New York – XX△△X△
Antarctica – △△□___
Holland – X△X_□△
Hong Kong – △__□△_
Dark Tooth – △_□□X○

Twister
Los Angeles – N/A
Moscow – X__△○_
Paris – △X○○X△
Amazonia – _△□X□○
New York – X△XOX_
Antarctica – ○__X□△
Holland – _XX__○
Hong Kong – XX△X□_
Dark Tooth – X□_□△○

Warthog
Los Angeles – N/A
Moscow – △__△□_
Paris – △□□□X□
Amazonia – ○□□○XX
New York – X□□_X○
Antarctica – _X○△_□
Holland – △X△□_X
Hong Kong – ○X△○_○
Dark Tooth – ○□_○○□

Life For Murder
Simply run over ten citizens to recharge your health fully!

Train Bonus
After destroying a train in the subway at Hong Kong, your next weapon will be twice as powerful.

Sell Your Soul
To exchange all your weapons for increased health, during play press: ⇩, ⇧, ⇨, ⇦, ⇧, ⇧, ⇩, ⇩
'Sell Your Soul' will appear at the top of the screen. The more weapons you give up, the more health you'll gain.

Backwards Freeze
When without ammo, press: ⇦, ⇨, ⇩, ⇦, ⇨, ⇧

Minion's Special
This can be done with any character, but you must have full advanced-attack power. Just hold R2 (machine gun) and press ⇧, ⇩, ⇧, ⇧

WarCraft II

Passwords

Tides Of Darkness – Human
1 – Hillsbrad **HLLBRD**
2 – Ambush At Tarren Mill **MBSHTM**
3 – Southshore **HSTHSH**
4 – Attack On Zul'Dare **TTCKNZ**
5 – Tol Barad HTLBRD
6 – Dun Algaz **DNLGZ**
7 – Grim Batol **GRMBTL**
8 – Tyr's Hand **TYRHND**
9 – The Battle At Darrowmere **BTTLTD**
10 – The Prisoners **PRSNRS**
11 – Betrayal And The Destruction Of Alterac **BTRYLN**
12 – The Battle At Crestfall **BTTLTC**
13 – Assault On Blackrock Spire **SSLTNB**
14 – The Great Portal **GRTPRT**

Tides Of Darkness – Orc
1 – Zul'Dare **ZLDR**
2 – Raid At Hillsbrad **RDTHLL**
3 – Southshore **RCSTHS**
4 – Assault On Hillsbrad **SSLTNH**
5 – Tol Barad **RCTLBR**
6 – The Badlands **BDLNDS**
7 – The Fall Of Stromgarde **FLLFST**
8 – The Runestone At Caer Darrow **RNSTNT**
9 – The Razing Of Tyr's Hand **RZNGFT**
10 – The Destruction Of Stratholme **DSTRCT**
11 – The Dead Rise As Quel'Thalas Falls **DDRSSQ**
12 – The Tomb Of Sargeras **TMBFSR**
13 – The Siege Of Dalaran **SGFDLR**
14 – The Fall Of Lordaeron **FLLFLR**

Beyond The Dark Portal – Human
1 – Alleria's Journey **LLRSJR**
2 – Battle For Nethergarde **BTTLFR**
3 – Once More Into The Breach **NCMRNT**
4 – Beyond The Dark Portal **BYNDTH**
5 – The Shadows Seas **SHDWSS**
6 – The Fall Of Auchindoun **FLLFCH**
7 – Deathwing **DTHWNG**
8 – Coast Of Bones **CSTFBN**
9 – Heart Of Evil **HRTFVL**
10 – The Battle Of Hellfire **BTTLFH**
11 – Dance Of Laughing Skull **DNCFTH**
12 – Bitter Taste Of Victory **BTTRTS**

Beyond The Dark Portal – Orc
1 – Slayer Of The Shadowmoon **SLYRFT**
2 – The Skull Of Gul'dan **SKLLFG**
3 – Thunderlord And Bonechewer **THNDRL**
4 – The Rift Awakened **RFTWKN**
5 – Dragons Of Blackrock Spire **DRGNSF**
6 – New Stormwind **NWSTRM**
7 – The Seas Of Azeroth **SSFZRT**
8 – Assault On Kul Tiras **SSLTNK**
9 – The Tomb Of Sargeras **DPTMBF**
10 – Alterac **LTRC**
11 – The Eye Of Dalaran **YFDLRN**
12 – The Dark Portal **DPDRKP**

Cheat Codes
Simply pause the game and enter them on the password screen.

Win Level
NTTSCLNS
Automatically completes the current mission (after a few seconds).

Lose Level
YPTFLWRM
Though why you'd want to do this is a mystery!

Invincible Forces
TSGDDYTD
Your units cannot be harmed in battle.

More Gold, Oil & Timber
GLTTRNG
Gives you lots more resources to play with.

Build More Things
DCKMT
Lets you build more stuff from the start.

Fast Building
MKTS
Buildings and units are created in mere seconds.

Map Cheat
NSCRN
See the entire level map from the start.

Wipeout

Access Rapier Class
If you are unable to succeed at the Venom class and experience the extra thrill of Rapier, then do the following to get straight to the speedier action. Hold tight!
1. Highlight One Player on the startup screen.
2. Hold down all of the following buttons: L2, R2, ⇦, Start and Select.
3. Keep holding them and press the × button.
This should take you to the class screen. Now you can get down to some serious racing!

Hidden Track
This is a top cheat to allow you to get another track called Firestar. You would only normally get it by completing all the tracks in the Rapier class. Well now you don't need to. It's fast, bendy and pretty darn fun!
1. Highlight One Player on the startup screen.
2. Hold down all of the following buttons: L1, R1, ⇨, Start, □ and ○.
3. While still holding the above, press ×.

Turbo Start
Is achieved by having the red rev bar on the second line from the end when the announcer says "go". The best way is to press accelerate as the orange light comes on or in the middle of the announcer saying "one".

Repeat Lap
In a race if you hit one of the air brakes hard and steer that way to do a 180° turn whilst crossing the line, the game will ignore that lap and let you do another one, enabling you to catch up with the leaders.

Wipeout 2097

Cheats
The following three cheats are accessed on the opening options menu (the one from where you select the mode, team, and track) by keeping L1, R1 and Select held down. The rest are accessed whilst in a race.

Piranha Ship
Keeping the aforementioned buttons held down, press: ×, ×, ×, ×, ○, △, and □. Now go to the team select and you'll instantly be rewarded with the inclusion of the Piranha ship – a state-of-the-art craft that is perfect in every respect.

Phantom Class
Hold down L1, R1 and Select and press △, △, △, ○, ○, and ○. Now go to the track select and you'll notice that the extra-hard Phantom class is now available to race on.

Track Cheat
Keep L1, R1 and Select held down and press □, ○, △, ○, and □. This cheat allows you to race on each and every track in the easy Vector class – giving you every opportunity to practise and perfect the multitude of circuits at a speed that is altogether easier to handle.

Machine Gun
Pause the game at any time during a race and hold L1, R1, and Select. Then press □, ○, ×, □, ○, ×, and △. When you unpause the game again, you'll see a blinding green flash to indicate that the cheat has worked. Now by pressing the fire button, you'll activate a newly installed machine gun on your craft.

Infinite Energy
You'll never have to slip into the restoration lane again by activating this essential trick. Simply pause the game at any time during a race and then hold L1, R1 and Select. Now with those buttons held, press △, ×, □, ○, △, ×, □, and ○. Unpause and you'll be instantly invincible.

Infinite Time
Pause the game at any time during a race and hold L1, R1 and Select. With those buttons held, press △, □, ○, ×, △, □, ○, and ×. Then unpause to activate the cheat.

Infinite Weapons
During a normal race, pause the game and hold L1 + R1 + Select. Then whilst they are held, press ×, ×, □, □, ○, ○, △. Unpause the game and you should see a green flash. Now whenever you use a weapon, you should have it replaced straight away. You can also toggle through the various weapons by pressing the 'drop weapon' button.

Farmyard Animal Mode
Switch on the PlayStation with the disc inside and hold L1, R2, Select + Start until the title screen is displayed that says 'Start'. Then take your finger off Start and press it again to go through to the main options screen with team and craft selection on it. The craft sprites will have changed into various farmyard animals!

Passwords
Challenge I: □,○,□,△,○,△,△,○,□,□,□,△,×,□.
Challenge II: □,○,□,△,○,△,×,□,×,△,△,×,○,○.

WCW Vs The World

Hidden Fighters
By beating the eight bosses in the game, they're added to the list of playable fighters and can be used in any mode except the league challenge.

First, do a league challenge and fight with a JR class wrestler. Win all six divisions with the same guy and you will fight a boss. In WCW it's Jeff Jarret. There are others such as Major Tom, Steel Talon, and Grizz Lee.

If you win all six divisions there will be a new division called Super JR. Win in that and the penultimate hidden fighter is Jaguar.

Then go on and do the same thing with a heavyweight class. You will fight the same bosses through the six divisions. Winning them all reveals a new Super Heavy division whose boss is The Giant – the final hidden fighter.

Old 'Uns
To fight as the old Hogan or the old Sting (doo doo doo?), press Start (instead of ×) to select them. Do the same for Masahiro Chino and he'll fight with an NWO shirt on.

War Gods

Cheat	On Code	Off Code	Action
Enable Fatals	7453	3547	Enables fatalities (off by default)
Free Play	0705	5070	Free play in options screen
Player One Invincible	2358	8532	Makes player 1 invincible
Player Two Invincible	1224	4221	Makes player 2 invincible
Player One Extra Damage	7879	9787	Player 1 cause more damage
Player Two Extra Damage	3961	1693	Player 2 cause more damage
Quick Finish Game	4258	8524	Finish game after killing one CPU player
Easy Fatalities	0322	2230	Pressing □ + ○ triggers a fatality
Grox	6969	9696	Enables player 1 to play as Grox
Exor	2791	1972	Enables player 1 to play as Exor
Level One Select	5550	5556	Allows you to play on level 1
Level Two Select	5551	5556	Allows you to play on level 2
Level Three Select	5552	5556	Allows you to play on level 3
Level Four Select	5553	5556	Allows you to play on level 4
Level Five Select	5554	5556	Allows you to play on level 5
Level Six Select	5555	5556	Allows you to play on level 6
Level Seven Select	5557	5556	Allows you to play on level 7

Warhawk

UK Codes
('_' = space)
●▲●_×●■▲
Preview the epilogues
●×■_××●× Check the special upgrades
▲■▲■_●●●
Warhawk A-La-Mode
××●■▲■××
Infinite weapons
●▲▲×▲●×●
Thor mode
×■●××■■▲
Kali mode
▲●_●●×■●
Preview the movies
■●●■▲▲●▲
Face-to-face with Kreel
■●×■▲×■●
Kreel's door is open
■●●×▲▲▲■
Above 3rd force field
■●●▲■▲■×
Above 2nd force field
■●▲●▲■●×
Above 1st force field
■●▲■●××▲
Stormland
■××■●■■●
In with the gatekeeper
■×●●▲■▲×
West gauntlet boss
■×▲■×●×●
East gauntlet boss
■××●■●▲×
Gauntlet level
●▲●■■×●▲
Volcano boss is active
●■■●●×▲●
Volcano level
××■×▲■■×
Airship rear hangar is open
×●■▲×▲▲×
Post-transformation airship
×▲▲××●●■
Airship level
■■×●■×■●
Approaching Uma
■■●■●■▲×
In the canyon with Crystal
■▲■▲■●●■
In the canyon with Belle
■▲●▲●●●▲
In the canyon with Amber
■■●×▲×●▲
Canyon level
▲■×■●×▲●
Desert is all but done
▲●×●■●×▲
Pyramid has risen
▲●▲×●■×▲
Desert level

Wild Arms

Secret Aliens
Go to the three islands located in the Southern region of the map. After fighting eight to ten battles, you'll then battle a secret alien race known as the Hayokonton. On top of all the experience and gella you'll receive from them, they sometimes give you duplicators.

Williams Arcade Greatest Hits

Debug Mode
Hold L1 + L2 + R1 + R2 and push Select. Do this twice. This code takes you to the operator's option screen. It can be used on all the Greatest Hits games.

Mortal Kombat 3 Sounds
Turn on the PlayStation without a CD inside and access the audio CD player from the menu. Now insert the game CD and you'll see two tracks. Move to track two and press a button to play it. You'll now hear over five minutes of *MKIII* sounds.

Wing Commander IV

Scene Select
When you get to the game copyright screen, enter the following code: ⇧, ⇩, ⇩, ⇧, R2. You can now select any scene in the game by pressing R1 or R2.

Cheat Kill
With the Scene Select cheat activated, you can kill any ship with just one shot by pressing L1 + L2 + □.

Worms

Sheep And Banana Bombs
When at the weapon select screen, simply press □ and × eight to 10 times and you should then gain access to both the big banana bombs and exploding sheep. Woohoo, what a fruity/lamby combination!

Exploding Sheep
Go to the Worms Option screen, then go onto the Weapons Option Screen. Move the cursor away from the Exit logo and press these buttons:
×, □, □, ×, □, □, ×, □, □.
Lamb chops aplenty!

WWF In Your House

No Damage
Pause the game and press L1, R2, L1, R2, L2, R1 and you will have no human damage.

Fatality Moves
To do these, simply pin your opponent for the final time and tap in the following combinations:

Brett Hart: ⇩ ⇧ △ ⇩ ⇧ △.
Vader: ⇩ ⇧ ×××
Owen Hart: ⇩ ⇧ □□××
British Bulldog: ⇩ ⇧ □□△×
Undertaker: ⇩ ⇧ ○○△△
Golddust: ⇩ ⇧ ○ ⇩ ⇧ ○
Shawn Michaels: ⇩ ⇧ □○○□
HHH: ⇩ ⇧ △△△△
Ahmed Johnson: ⇩ ⇧ □△○×

Cheat Codes
Pause the game at any point during a bout and enter any of the following codes for the desired effect:
Computer players off – ⇦, ⇦, ⇧, ⇩, R2
Big damage on – ⇧, ⇧, L1, L2, ⇩
Combos on – R1, L2, R2, L2, ⇨
Small human damage – ⇩, ⇧, L2, ⇨, ⇦
Auto super pin – ⇩, ⇩, ⇩, ⇩, L.

Xevious 3D/G+

Play As Tekken Characters

Heihachi
At the Game Select screen (highlighting 'Xevious 3D/G'), hold × + ○ + ⇦ + Start on controller 1. Keep holding them until the Xevious 3D/G title screen appears, then release Start (nothing else) and hold it again to start the game. Keep the buttons held down until your ship starts the level, upon which it magically transforms into Heihachi, with built-in spray fire.

Paul
At the Game Select screen (highlighting 'Xevious 3D/G'), hold × + ○ + ⇨ + Start on controller 2. Keep holding them until the Xevious 3D/G title screen appears, then release Start (nothing else) and press it again to start the game. Keep the buttons held down until your ship starts the level, upon which it magically transforms into Paul, who speeds around the screen.

Infinite Continues
On the Game Select screen (highlighting 'Xevious 3D/G'), hold L1 + L2 + R1 + R2 and press ○ rapidly as many times as you can while the game loads. If you've done it right, when you start the game, where the credits were it'll display 'FREE PLAY'. You can now continue as many times as you need.

Debug Mode
Select the original Xevious game. At the Xevious title screen, press □ + × + Start. The Debug Mode will appear and the game will start.

Black Ship
Highlight the 'Reset' option on the title screen and hold L1 + L2 + R1 + R2 + Start. The 'Game Start' option should now be highlighted, so (still holding the shoulder buttons) press Start again. Continue to hold all the buttons until your ship changes.

Fat Ship
First, you have to get the Black Ship. Then go back to the Xevious title screen, select Configuration Mode and highlight 'Exit'. Now, as before, highlight 'Reset' and hold L1 + L2 + R1 + R2 + Start. The 'Game Start' option should now be highlighted, so (still holding the shoulder buttons) press Start again. Continue to hold all the buttons until your ship changes.

Twisting Ship
If you have a NeGcon controller, you can use it to twist your ship.

X2

Cheats
To enter these cheats, go to Options and select Password:

267776	8 Credits
220969	Start with 9 ships
713948	Start Level 2
900277	Start Level 3
213490	Start Level 4
866141	Start Level 5
321904	Start Level 6
196861	Start Level 7
040186	Start Level 8
841003	Start Level 9
216409	Start Criticus
180771	Invulnerable ship
300167	End sequence

Zero Divide

Hidden Comics
1. After beating the game in Easy mode without continuing or losing a round, go to the title screen and highlight the option icon.
2. On controller 2 hold L1, L2, R1, R2, Start and Select to view the comic strip featuring Neco.

Hidden Game
1. Switch on the PlayStation and hold Start + Select until a new loading sign appears.
2. Keep the buttons held down and a new game will eventually appear, called Tiny Phalanx. It's an old-style side-scrolling shoot-'em-up – ahh, I remember the days when…

end

Other superb titles in the
Secrets, Strategies, Solutions series

PlayStation
Secret, Strategies, Solutions
Volume 1
RRP £14.95 • ISBN 1 873650 05 1

Over 200 pages in full colour containing cheats and codes for over 100 PlayStation games. Includes full solutions to Alien Trilogy, Crash Bandicoot, Doom, Formula 1, Mortal Kombat, Resident Evil, Street Fighter Alpha 2, Tekken 2 and more.

Lylat Wars
Secrets, Strategies, Solutions
RRP £9.95 • ISBN 1 873650 14 0

A complete guide to the world's best Nintendo 64 shoot-'em-up, Lylat Wars (also known as Star Fox 64). Hidden cheats and characters exposed. Multiplayer mode tactics. Star system map with every secret warp revealed. Over 200 pages.

PlayStation
Secret, Strategies, Solutions
Volume 2
RRP £14.95 • ISBN 1 873650 06 X

Massive playing guides to all the top PlayStation games, including Command & Conquer, Mortal Kombat Trilogy, Pandemonium, Soul Blade, Tobal No 1, Tomb Raider and many more. More than 200 full colour pages; cheats and codes for 150 games .

Goldeneye
Secrets, Strategies, Solutions
RRP £9.95 • ISBN 1 873650 11 6

All the maps, all the cheats and all the characters for Goldeneye contained in over 200 pages of raw adrenaline. Discover how to play as Jaws, Odd-Job and every other Bond character. Uncover the two secret levels. Find out all the codes and challenges.

Tomb Raider II
Secrets, Strategies, Solutions
RRP £9.95 • ISBN 1 873650 13 2

The complete mapped solution to Tomb Raider II featuring all the hidden cheats, items and levels. Indispensable walkthrough covers the entire game; every secret unlocked. Includes bonus solution to the original Tomb Raider game.

Super Mario 64
Secrets, Strategies, Solutions
RRP £9.95 • ISBN 1 873650 07 8

A complete walkthrough to the world's best video game, Super Mario 64 plus tactics for every villain. In over 200 pages you'll discover 15 worlds explored in unrivalled detail, locations of all 120 stars, secret rooms and bonus levels plus a superb boss guide.

Final Fantasy VII
Secrets, Strategies, Solutions
RRP £9.95 • ISBN 1 873650 12 4

Essential walkthrough spanning 200-plus pages to one of the biggest PlayStation games ever. Profiles of all nine characters (including hidden ones), cheats and codes, materia combinations, enemy guides – every secrets and strategy fully exposed.

Nintendo 64
Secrets, Strategies, Solutions
RRP £14.95 • ISBN 1 873650 08 6

Lavish full-colour, 200-page book featuring complete solutions for Lylat Wars, Mario Kart 64, Super Mario 64, Wave Race 64, International Superstars Soccer, Shadows of the Empire, Pilot Wings, Turok, Blast Corps, Killer Instinct Gold, Mortal Kombat Trilogy and many more.

PlayStation secrets • strategies • solutions